Sectarian Mobilisation and the Role of Caste Associations in Karnataka

About the Author

K.G. Gayathridevi is currently working as an Associate Professor of Sociology in the Centre for Ecological Economics and Natural Resources in the Institute for Social and Economic Change, Bangalore. She started her career in 1973 as a Lecturer in Sociology in the PG Department of Research and Studies in Sociology and pursued her Ph.D at the Institute of Development Studies, both at the University of Mysore and obtained her Ph.D. in 1989. She also taught Sociology in a few First Grade Colleges of the Bangalore University before joining ISEC in 1989. This book is the revised version of her doctoral thesis.

Her research interests include policy studies on social mobility among marginalised communities, Decentralisation and Governance, Gender Issues in Environment and Development and Child Labour, which she has carried out for State and Central Governments as well as for external funding agencies like The Ford Foundation, World Bank, International Labour Organisation and the International Food Policy Research Institute, Washington DC.

Gayathridevi has co-authored four books and published a few research papers in edited books and journals besides presenting papers in national and international seminars on gender, decentralization and development. She has also organised as well as participated in a number of capacity-building programmes at ISEC and outside.

Sectarian Mobilisation and the Role of Caste Associations in Karnataka

KG Gayathridevi

CONCEPT PUBLISHING COMPANY PVT. LTD.
NEW DELHI-110059

ISBN-13 : 978-81-8069-967-2

First Published 2013

Published and Printed by

Concept
Since 1974

Concept Publishing Company Pvt. Ltd.
A/15-16, Commercial Block, Mohan Garden
New Delhi-110059 (India)
T: 25351460, 25351794, *F*: 091-11-25357109
E: publishing@conceptpub.com, W: www.conceptpub.com
Editorial Office: H-13, Bali Nagar, New Delhi-110 015, India.

Cataloging in Publication Data--Courtesy: D.K. Agencies (P) Ltd. <docinfo@dkagencies.com>

Gayathridevi, K. G.
Sectarian mobilisation and the role of caste associations in Karnataka / KG Gayathridevi.
p. cm.
Includes bibliographical references (p.) and index.
ISBN 9788180699672

1. Dalits—India—Karnataka. 2. Caste—India—Karnataka—Societies, etc. 3. Social mobility—India—Karnataka. 4. Political participation—India—Karnataka. 5. Social change—India—Karnataka. 6. Reverse discrimination—India—Karnataka. I. Title.

DDC 305.56880954 23

FOREWORD

The present work is essentially the result of a work prepared as a doctoral thesis in the University of Mysore. Since Dr.Gayathri Devi was my doctoral pupil, I can claim to have a certain inside knowledge of the work virtually from the time she conceptualized it to seeing it through to its finished form. Soon after the thesis was awarded, the doctoral degree with warm commendations from her examiners, we both felt that the thesis, especially certain pats of it, merited publication and also sooner the better. However, for a variety of reasons, wholly unconnected with the object of the study, Dr.Gayathri found it impossible to attend to its publication. And with the passage of time, updating of the data became imperative which further delayed the publication. I am pleased that this work is now set to reach the public domain.

There is no dearth of studies on the issue of reservations and mobilization based upon considerations such as caste, a genre that Gayathri picturesquely characterizes as sectarian. The problem has attracted the attention of scholars over several decades and many have made stellar contributions to the inquiry. But there are dimensions to the present work which set it apart from the general run of the literature in this area of study. A major facet that this study presents is the study of caste associations which have emerged as an important form of parallel organizations. To my knowledge, Gayathri was one of the first to collate data relating to these parallel bodies in meticulous form. In fact, a significant landmark work in this field by a noted authority, G.Thimmaiah, cited the data compiled by Gayathri in the discussion of caste associations. But I should hasten to add that it is not merely the detailed data on caste associations that are a special feature of her work. She relates this data to the larger issue of mobilization and demonstrates how this exercises an impact on the entire development dialogue. The central thrust of this study is on unraveling the way in which a process such as development is influenced by, and in turn, influences other processes and activities in society including political formations. The significance of this consists in the fact that in spite of all the expected effects of modernization and globalization, primordial loyalties like caste continue to exercise influence over social, economic and political developments. This is what must have led the doyen of such studies in India, Professor M.N.Srinivas, to speak of the 'twentieth century avatar' of caste. Far from disappearing from the scene as many hoped in the early years of state-initiated economic development, it has found new avenues and in some ways, appears not to have exhausted its appetite for spreading its tentacles. Other prominent sociologists like A. M. Shah have been pointing to numerous examples of caste displaying signs of mobility giving the lie to its so-called static and monolithic character.

Even at the quantitative and descriptive level, Gayathri's is perhaps the only work where a researcher can easily locate a source of data on over 220 main caste groups. This is important since many in our society lack an intimate awareness of the richness of our social groups as well as the attendant complexity. To this, I should add that Gayathri patiently sought out and interviewed a number of tall figures in the non-Brahmin movement in princely Mysore (many of them are no longer with us). While she is not the first to analyse the internal cleavages within the broad spectrum of the composite non-Brahmin movement she has supplemented secondary material with interview-based primary data and I have pleasure in recording that she is a researcher who possesses very impressive credentials in this sphere.

In this context, one illustration would not be out of place. After the last parliamentary elections, the print media in Karnataka published lists of the elected members from the state classified by caste. Some years ago, while there used to be references to the representation of 'forward' and 'backward' castes in the electoral fray, discussions generally took place in muted fashion. The language was generally suggestive, rarely outright. Of late, on the contrary, the issue is debated openly with the result that a fairly sensitive dimension such as the representation of the 'left' and the 'right' among the Scheduled Castes is explicitly discussed in the media. The same is found in relation to the forward castes such as the Lingayats. There are criticisms that this or that section in the caste has not been treated fairly. All in all, recent developments serve only to vindicate what Dr.Gayathri pioneered decades ago.

Another dimension of the book requires specific mention. This is the changing relations between different groups such as 'forward' and 'backward' especially in the early days after the publication of the Havanur report. Gayathri has shown how certain alliances which were attempted at that juncture did not prove to be enduring. I refer to the attempt to forge alliances among all those not listed as backward by the Havanur Commission and more important the Government Order that followed. This same sensitivity to empirical evidence, more broadly to the altering scenarios of social reality, is seen throughout her expert handling of caste equations in Karnataka. Gayathri analyses the social conflicts that have emerged as a result of the implementation of policies aimed at positive discrimination. I should also draw attention to the skill with which she has situated the nexus between what she very rightly terms sectarian mobilization and the problematique of development. The politics of positive discrimination is a field rich in material that requires keen analysis which Gayathri has provided in her work.

Another important aspect of her work relates to the role of caste associations in education. It is interesting that while the forward and the dominant intermediate castes have been active in 'professional/technical' education for fairly long, the entry of the Scheduled Castes and the numerically smaller groups is a recent development. Obviously this has its own implications for inter-caste relationships as also for the larger question of socio-political mobilization vis a vis education. This is another facet of caste mobilization via the formation of associations and through utilising education as an instrument that Gayathri has opened up for imaginative inquiry.

I am pleased to write this foreword to a book which I am sure will prove a valuable addition to the literature in this area of inquiry.

V.K.Natraj
Former Director,
Madras Institute of Development Studies,
Chennai & Institute of Development Studies,
Mysore

ACKNOWLEDGEMENTS

The Foreword to this book makes a reference that this publication is based on my Ph.D thesis submitted to the University of Mysore several years ago. The topic was chosen at the instance of Professor V. K. Natraj, former director of the Institute of Development Studies, Mysore University, Manasagangotri, Mysore and of the Madras Institute of Development Studies, Chennai. I am grateful to him for suggesting this topic, since its importance has only been growing over the decades acquiring newer dimensions. He was also kind enough to guide me in this research endeavour by being my research supervisor. He has been a constant source of support and encouragement for all my academic accomplishments, both as a teacher and researcher. I owe a deep sense of gratitude to him for the same and feel considerably guilty to have delayed this publication beyond a reasonable time.

The study, on which this work is based, has benefited from several institutions and persons, during its course of completion. The list includes the best known academicians and luminaries of Karnataka. Most prominently, late Professor M. N. Srinivas had evinced a lot of interest in the findings of this research study and was constantly urging me for its publication. Professor G. Thimmiah, former Director, ISEC, had not only referred to this thesis when he wrote his classic book on the Backward Classes and Reservation Policy in the late nineties, but also persuaded me to publish this work as soon as possible. This research work was also fortunate to catch the attention of Justice O. Chinnappa Reddy during his tenure as the Chairman of the

Backward Classes Commission in Karnataka during the late eighties.

There are a large number of important personalities of the state who were consulted during the course of this study. It has richly benefited out of discussions held with several of them, such as the then Chief Minister late Sri Devraj Urs (hailed as the champion of backward classes), late Sri L. G. Havanur (the Chairman of the most famous BCC nicknamed after him as the 'Havanur Commission'), late Sri Masti Venkatesha Iyengar, Jnana Peetha awardee and littérateur of Karnataka, a number of the then leaders of Backward Classes Movements in the state such as, Sri Kalle Shivothama Rao, Sri V. T. Rajashekara Setty, late Sri H. Guruv Reddy (the father-in-law of the first Chief Minister of Karnataka), late Sri E. R. Ethirajulu Naidu, leaders of the contemporary dalit liberation movement such as late Sri R. Krishnappa of the DSS, late Sri Devayya Harave, faculty member at the Institute of Kannada Studies, University of Mysore, and a dalit activist, Sri Dyavanura Mahadeva, a well known Kannada writer, president of more than 40 caste associations, upcoming and old private educational trusts, Religious heads of mutts in the State, leaders of political parties, the then Vice-Chancellor of Mysore University late Sri D. V. Urs, Professor Gopal Rao, the then Director of the Institute of Development Studies (IDS), University of Mysore, Mysore, Dr. Lalitha Natraj, Political Scientist and faculty member and Dr. Shashikala Sitaram, fellow researcher at IDS and many others. I am beholden to all of them for their kindness in providing the required information and insights in understanding the complex issue of caste-based mobilization in Karnataka.

My grateful thanks are also due to Professor John Whitworth. From Simon Fraser University, British Columbia and late Prof. M. Rajashekaraiah, former Professor of Political

Science and Chair in Dr. Baba Saheb Ambedkar Studies, Dharwar, who were the two examiners of my thesis, for their very useful suggestions and observations in improving the thesis for publication. I will be failing in my duty if I do not remember the help by Sri Suryanarayana of Mysore who typed the thesis so neatly. I owe my grateful thanks also to the editorial help offered by Sri V. S. Parthasarathy, retired faculty of Sociology unit at ISEC. I am thankful to Smt. B. Akhila, senior stenographer at ISEC for her help in obtaining a computerized draft and to the Concept Publishing Company Pvt. Ltd. for accepting this work for publication.

All along, my family has been consistently protecting and encouraging my academic interests and look forward to the publication of this work. I am grateful to my husband, father, brother, cousin and my daughter for their very meaningful support in this endeavour. But most of the pressure and encouragement to bring the thesis out to the light of the day came from my husband. It is too late now to personally thank him. At best, I can only rest content by dedicating this book to his memory.

PREFACE

Development aims at inclusive growth by enabling improvement of the social and economic conditions of the poor and other weaker sections of a society. In India, the constitution, as also several programmes of the state, have only reinforced this emphasis upon assisting the underprivileged sections of the population. As a consequence of the Constitutional mandate by way of affirmative action or reservation of seats in both educational institutions and employment, the central and the state governments have followed up with a number of measures for the upliftment of the weaker sections. Thus, one of the chief instruments of achieving social and economic equality in India has been the policy of protective discrimination or reservation or affirmative action.

At the same time, we find that in societies such as ours, where glaring inequalities – social and economic – exist, the fight for sharing of gains assumes added urgency and sharpness. It, therefore, invariably happens that groups are mobilised under a common banner like caste, language, ethnicity etc., to press for their claims. Mobilization is explained as a process where the existing economic, social and psychological patterns of socialization and behaviour of individuals are disrupted and new patterns emerge.

Further, such an importance given to socio-economic development has led to increasing participation by different sections of the population to fight for greater share in the gains of development. Although caste and its role in such mobilization processes has been long recognized, there seem to be divergent views about its present status. The first view considers caste as only a façade for class conflicts. There is a second view that does not recognize class or at best is indifferent to it. There is a third opinion, which clearly delineates caste class relationships and analyses their significance for development and change. It is at least probable that processes of mobilisation revolve around class interests holding, however, caste as the base. Appeals through caste and loyalty to caste may be only a front behind which economic interests loom large. Nevertheless, caste cannot be ignored as one of the factors which merit a thorough examination.

The above point becomes clear when we look at the modern attempts at mobilisation which appear to move on sectarian lines. A close observation of these movements and their goals indicates that class interests cut across caste cleavages. The impact of modernization through industrialization, education, urbanization, globalization and other such interventions has, contrary to expectations, not led to any decrease in the emphasis on caste in economic matters and also its use in day-to-day life. Caste-class disparities are not clearly discernible at all levels of the social ladder but seem to become conspicuous as we move up the ladder. Thus, there is observed, an in-built network within the broader caste structure.

Besides all this, we find that the state of equilibrium in any society gets disturbed when new elements enter into it. This leads to the outbreak of conflicts and socio-economic tensions. The problem then become centred around the resolution of conflicts and, in particular, the question that arises is whether conflicts can be contained and resolved within the system or large systemic changes are required. Thus, social tensions, conflicts and disturbances are almost endemic to modern societies. However, these are especially found in societies like ours where planned development through state intervention is being followed. In other words, the issue of protective discrimination has often led to a series of clashes and tensions across different caste groups.

It is generally accepted that long-drawn and wide spread conflicts and tensions hinder or obstruct social progress. The question that arises here in the light of the above observations is that if caste is being used as an issue for mobilization, then what is its net impact upon the total development of the society? Are the movements for mobilization by caste groups successful? If so, do they appeal to the whole group as such? Do the attempts at dismantling the caste structure end only with its modification to suit economic and political interests?

The Theme of the Book

In an attempt to find answers to the above questions, the present study investigates into the whole spectrum of caste and class issues in the light of the processes of mobilization in Karnataka and its effect upon politico-economic development. The caste-class nexus and the associated conflicts are studied against the background of the backward classes movements in the State.

The universe of the study is the state of Karnataka where the processes of mobilization on sectarian lines have acquired much importance. This is because of the fact that the schemes for economic and educational development concerning SCs, STs and OBCs are being launched here through a number of comprehensive programmes. The policy of reservations has a long history in Karnataka dating as far back as 1874. The process got accelerated after independence resulting in the setting up of many Commissions of enquiry on the backward classes' issue. Among them the appointment of the Karnataka Backward Classes Commission (or the Havanur Commission) in 1972 is perhaps the most important in the present context.

It was in the same year that Karnataka's political history showed signs of transformation when the state came to be ruled by a government comprising an impressive number of members from hitherto unrepresented, backward and minority communities. This government and its measures for the amelioration of the weaker sections of society could be viewed as a far-reaching development in general.

These circumstances are understood to have placed Karnataka at a crucial phase of social change in the recent decades. Although the system of reservation and other socio-economic measures for the welfare of the weaker sections are common to all the states of India, Karnataka appears to have achieved for itself a coveted place in this respect. This is chiefly due to the interplay of certain socio-political factors operative in the state.

It was, therefore, intended to trace historically the origin and growth of the process of mobilization in Karnataka and analyse its effect upon the process of development.

Methodology and Contents of the Book

Of all the techniques of mobilization generally sought by the caste (even ethnic and religious) groups in India, the formation of associations is found to be important and popular. Acting as political interest groups, these 'Para-Communities' (Rudolphs 1967) viz., caste associations, characterize one of the chief instruments of mobilization. They act as links between the respective caste groups and the Government in projecting the needs and demands of the former.

Further, an analysis of mobilisational attempts by caste groups in India points out that one of their fundamental aspirations is to seek the educational development of their members. While the various Backward Classes Commissions in both Princely Mysore and modern Karnataka made provisions for the above demand of the non-Brahmins, in the form of reservation of seats in educational institutions, a few castes – the dominant ones—even attempted to establish their own private schools and colleges as early as during the second decade of the present century. What started as a practice confined to one of the two dominant castes of the state (the Lingayats) resulted in emulation by a number of other castes, some successfully and others attempting hard to succeed, not excluding even the then 'forward' Brahmins.

These two processes, the formation of caste associations and the establishment of private educational institutions – are treated in the present book as constituting the chief strategies of caste-based mobilization process in the state. Hence, a detailed analysis of the rise and growth of these two institutions is made.

It is well known that any process of mobilization depends, for its success or failure to a large extent, upon the nature and composition of its leadership. Similarly, the caste-class nexus, which we were presently attempting to investigate, would be clearer, if the leadership pattern amongst these groups – whether backward or forward – is explored.

The book consists of eight chapters. Chapter one constitutes an introductory note that presents the main theme of the problem and methodology of the study. A detailed analysis of the subject matter, the relevance of the state of Karnataka as the universe of our study and the chapter-wise presentation of the data are made in the introductory chapter.

In the second chapter, an evaluative and critical appraisal of the existing literary material on the subject under presentation in the book is made. It begins with a conceptual note on mobilization and development and their implications for the sectarian channel. Since studies of the present kind are not new, it is attempted to explore any new dimensions of mobilization in India as well as in Karnataka, that have to be dealt with by the existing works on social change, mobility and mobilization.

In chapter three, a revision of historical data concerning backward class movements in India and Karnataka is made. This intends to facilitate an understanding of the important factors influencing caste mobilization in the state. It also helps understand better, the socio-political constraints operative in the genesis, growth and spread of the movement from the beginning of this century till the present times. The history of the backward class movements also facilitates an understanding of the disputes on sectarian lines and the important aspects of intra-group competition that have been in vogue since the 1930s and the 1940s.

A detailed historical and evaluative study of the various caste associations of Karnataka is presented in the fourth chapter. This includes a descriptive analysis of the social, economic and political factors responsible for the success or failure of these interest groups in projecting the demands of the respective castes they represent. The study also projects the growing importance of caste associations as an effective medium for mobilization. It further portrays the interrelation between the government's policy of reservation and caste mobilization. This is evident from the manner in which caste associations have increased in their number and activities with the appointment of successive backward class commissions in the state. A detailed questionnaire covering the aspects of origin, growth and functions of the various castes and tribal associations in the state was prepared and administered to a number of such associations in the places of their main activity. Care has been taken to include all the active caste associations for which data could be elicited.

The analysis of caste associations is followed by another crucial aspect of caste mobilization in the state, viz., the practice of establishing private educational trusts by various caste and religious groups. The interrelation between the two is evident from the fact that quite a few private educational trusts in the state are managed under the auspices of the respective caste associations. The fifth chapter traces the history and growth of the private educational trusts in Karnataka and their role in caste mobilization. Although the emphasis is on caste-sponsored trusts, a few non-Hindu trusts have also been covered wherever they were active.

An analysis of the politics of reservations is made in the sixth chapter with a view to understanding the interplay of political factors in social mobilization. Certain groups in society have made a demand upon the state for protective discrimination. In turn, the state has formulated and implemented welfare measures partly out of a commitment to egalitarianism and partly to retain power. This last consideration is particularly true of cases where the demand for protective discrimination has come from economically and politically strong sections. Further, it is obvious that the benefits of protective discrimination policies do not always percolate to those who need them most. It is here that the class character of the demand and the class bias of the policy both become apparent.

Against this background, chapter six examines the thorny question of the politics of reservations in Karnataka. Since the state of Karnataka has a long history of such policies, the analysis is set in a historical perspective. It examines the entire question from the days of Princely rule to the present times. Of particular relevance are the policies followed by Sri Devraj Urs (1972-80) and the controversy surrounding the issue of capitation fees.

As discussed earlier, conflict constitutes an essential component of any process of mobilization. The keen tussle for the gains of development has led to a series of tensions and feuds between the different caste groups classified as forward and backward in the state. Such caste conflict is further noted to be not only inter-caste but also intra-caste in character. At least six layers of inter and intra-group tensions have been identified as prevailing currently in the state and each has been analysed in the seventh chapter. Such a probe into the negative aspects of reservation has brought out the after effects of the incidents of social tensions on the society at large.

The concluding chapter summarises the main findings of the study. Since the impact of mobilization on development cannot be quantified, the attempt is to bring together in perspective the socio-economic and political variables, which have influenced and continued to influence the process of sectarian mobilization in Karnataka. Following this, the implications of this process for development and change have to be further delineated by planners, policy-makers, academia and others.

CONTENTS

1 The Context

Ever since the realisation came about in the 1950s and the 1960s that the growth-oriented approach showed only minimal concern towards human dimension of development, there has been a dramatic transformation in the world thinking on development interventions and policies (Tinker and Bramsen : 1976). Development and change have thus become striking characteristics of almost all-modern societies, but the accent on these processes is naturally more pronounced in the developing countries. The latter have, by and large, sought to orient towards development, defined in a holistic perspective, through need-based planning and state interventions. In recent years, even this is modified against the backdrop of a decentralized and people-centred or participatory development effort (Aziz and Arnold : 1996).

The degree to which the state, and in recent times, the decentralised bodies, have made a conscious effort at development and the extent of success achieved, varies from society to society. The processes of 'development' and 'change' or 'change through development' is not unique to modern societies, but even the traditional societies experienced them in varying degrees. However, their importance has been heightened in the former. The process of development came to be regarded as a concomitant of modernisation and globalisation, but, again, it should be remarked that the term modernisation itself came to be used in a relative sense.[1] With all this, the concept of development, as also that of change, have acquired, and indeed continued to acquire, wider meanings.

Secondly, development today has become somewhat an omnibus term, used under a variety of circumstances. Although a single, universally acceptable and rigid definition of development is as elusive as an universally acceptable theory of development, the term is nonetheless capable of being defined, with reference to vital parameters. It has come to be accepted, that, in the first place, development stands distinguished from growth, in the sense that the former represents something more than quantitative increase in the national and per capita incomes. Development connotes, in its broadest sense, the affording of an opportunity by every person in a society to realise her or his fullest potential. In course of time, the term came to imply, in essence, a process aimed at creating a socio-economic order in which the basic needs of everyone were satisfied, and where a constant progress towards equity was made (Todaro : 1977). It hardly needs to be stressed that the development process did not always work effectively in this direction, and that it was quite frequently subjected to distortions of various kinds.

A logical consequence of treating development as a comprehensive concept was that the study of the development process had become interdisciplinary. Besides its long-recognised economic dimensions, its social and political dimensions are now regarded as occupying a place of centrality in development studies. The very fact of development being a process, and not an entity, which can be temporarily arrested, compels us to recognize the interplay of social, economic and political forces in shaping this process.

Another important component of development through change, or change through development, is the process of Mobilisation. It was generally described as referring to "a significant rise in the degree of popular involvement in the process of societal transformation" (Hettne and Tamm : 1974). Mobilisation is considered as an attempt towards change, when the existing mode of social control is challenged by certain social movements (Oberschall : 1973).

While most of the definitions of mobilisation have pointed towards the social aspects, a distinction came to be made between social mobilisation and political mobilisation (Rudebeck:1970). In its political implications, the process was recognized to be leading to, among other things, the sudden growth of politically relevant groups. Further, we find Apter's (1965) attempts to construct a typology of political system from the point of view of 'Economic Development and Modernisation'. He distinguished between "the reconciliation system and the mobilisation system," and dealt with mobilisation as a system rather than as a process. Similarly, Nettl (1967) defined mobilisation as "the process by which people in any society are made aware of what they have in common and in what ways they are different from others." As a process, mobilisation was (1) Attitudinal – a commitment to action, and (2) a means of translating this commitment into action. In the opinion of Etzioni (1968), mobilisation is a 'process in which a social unit gains relatively rapidly in control of resources it previously did not control'. The resources might be economic or military, but also political or psychological. This apart, amongst the various approaches to mobilisation is the "structural approach, stressing the pre-conditions for mobilisation, and the processual ones, stressing its dynamics."

What all approaches have in common is that mobilisation is referred to as a "significant rise in popular involvement in processes of change" (Hettne & Tamm :1974).

The last statement referring to the involvement and active participation of the people in bringing about changes in society needs to be elaborated to understand the significance of mobilisation. When, in the course of development, new opportunities are created, there naturally emerge a fight for appropriation of the gains of development; and as a consequence of this, both individuals and groups begin to organise themselves in order to participate in such competition. Under such circumstances, it invariably happens that groups are mobilised under a common banner like caste, language, ethnicity, and so on, to press their claims. Mobilisation acquires a sectarian character when it is associated with some segments of society such as, caste/sub-caste groups or religious or ethnic/racial groups. This is especially so (as an inevitable process) in less developed countries, which have to rest content with the limited nature of available resources, due to their large and increasing demands.

All these have necessarily led, among other things, to sectarian organisations. These 'Para Communities', known as caste associations (Rudolph and Rudolph : 1967), have acted as pressure groups to bring about development and change in the social unit which they claim to represent. In India, one of the important channels of sectarian mobilisation is the caste associations or organisations of caste and sub caste groups (Shah : 1977).

Caste in India continues to constitute an important component of its social stratification (Srinivas 1993). This is, however, not the place to dwell, in detail, upon the definition and characteristics of this unique social institution. There is also lack of consensus among sociologists and social anthropologists as to the debates regarding the genesis of the institution of caste in India. While the traditional theory of caste considers different caste groups to have been born out of divine origin, the occupational theory rests itself upon the theory of division of labour (Ghurye : 1932). Caste is characterised by the concepts of purity and pollution that ascribe statuses of superiority and inferiority to individuals.

Despite the controversies that surround it, caste has continued to constitute an integral part of the social, economic and political milieu in India. It has also undergone tremendous changes in its structure and functions. An important aspect of the structural change that caste has undergone refers to the process of fission by which castes are divided and subdivided into smaller sub and sub sub castes. This breaking up of castes into numerous units, each being endogamous and hierarchically arranged, within the larger group that constitutes it, has gained such momentum, that, in recent decades, Srinivas found the *Chaturvarnya*[2] philosophy inadequate to explain and examine castes in modern India. In the place of 'Varna', he considered the 'Jati' model more appropriate, as each caste is made up of many, many sub castes and sub sub castes (Srinivas : 1979).

There is a nexus between caste and inequality. While inequality is an ubiquitous phenomenon in all societies, it is especially pervasive in the developing countries. Inequality results from a number of factors, of which the unequal distribution of wealth is perhaps the most important. The caste system with its scheme of stratification has rendered the inequality problem more intractable. However, caution is required in analyzing the relationship between caste and inequality. There is a danger that all forms of inequality is wrongly attributed to the caste system – wrongly because, while caste is one source of inequality, it is by no means the only one, and also, there are noticeable differences within caste and sub caste groups (Srinivas :1979). Caste groups contain in themselves class divisions and cannot be treated as being homogeneous. This is a point of importance because it has significant implications for the functioning of organisations, which are formed to further the interests of specific caste groups. What is required is an approach that uses, judiciously, both caste and class, in order to analyse the nature of inequality and the effects of this in terms of mobilisation.

One has to consider, in this context, the approach used by Beteille to the question of inequality, and the efforts to achieve equality by the developing societies. He has distinguished between 'simple equality', which is commonly found in all societies "as a general principle of distribution of certain values, and 'proportional equality' which tries to maintain a just proportion while taking into account the differences among people" (Beteille : 1981). While doing so, the latter considered the differences among people, based on merit or need, leading to the "Meritarian" and "Compensatory" principles (Beteille : 1981).

In India, the compensatory principle or the policy of protective discrimination, has acquired saliency. Apart from the legal abolition of untouchability, through Art.17 of the Constitution, a number of schemes and programmes were also launched to bring about improvement in the life of the ex-untouchables and other weaker sections of the society. The Constitution and several programmes of the state have long since been embarked on the objective of assisting the underprivileged sections of the population. Under such circumstances, the question that is repeatedly posed is the dilemma of choosing between the need of the group, *vis-à-vis* the need of the individual (Beteille :1981).

The compensatory principle is not without its negative aspects. It has, in course of recent decades, sparked considerable tensions and debates (Srinivas :1993). The introduction of new elements of change into any society is bound to disturb its state of equilibrium. This equilibrium is, however, never constant and is always subject to transformation. A wholly stable equilibrium would indicate stagnation. But the disturbance of an existing equilibrium means the emergence of conflicts and tensions. The problem then centres on resolution of conflict. The question that arises is whether conflict can be contained and resolved within the system, or, whether large systemic changes are required. Nevertheless, social tensions are an important manifestation of society's resistance to change.

The principle of compensatory discrimination is one such change that has led to tensions and conflicts. The Constitutional provisions enabling the state to make reservation in education and employment have rested upon 'caste' as the basis of such consideration. Although the constitutional provisions have made reservations possible [Articles 15(4)) and 16(4)], the tendency has been to equate classes with caste. Backwardness of communities deserving constitutional support is identified in terms of their caste identity alone. This has led to certain categories of these so-called forward and backward groups juxtaposed in a conflicting position. The policy of reservation has led to increased attempts by the same groups to obtain (in the case of the former) and to retain (in the case of the latter) Constitutional protection earmarked in their favour. Such mobilisation by caste groups has manifested itself in the emergence of channels like the caste associations (and other means like starting of private educational trusts) in the case of Karnataka more than elsewhere. Beteille has cautioned "against a policy of protective discrimination which sets out to decrease inequalities between castes and communities, but ends by increasing inequalities among individual members of each caste and community" (Beteille : 1981).

It can be inferred from the above that the social structure in India (made up of a complex system of castes and sub-castes), and the recent changes inherent in it, are marked not only by the phenomenon of 'caste', but also of 'class'. Although the two units of stratification were no doubt recognised by social scientists in their works much earlier, there are persistent divergent views on this subject. Some of them are as follows :

- the first view is one that considers caste as only a façade for class interests;
- there is a second view that does not recognise class, or at best is indifferent to it;

- thirdly, it is sometimes argued that Indian society may be represented in terms of either caste or class structure; and
- there is, however, another opinion that clearly delineates the existence of caste/class relationships.

It is clear now, that the process of mobilisation in India has tended to revolve around class interests, holding, however, caste as a 'front'. Appeals through caste and loyalty to caste, are used increasingly as the mask, behind which economic interests loom large.

The last statement does not imply that class is substituting the institution of caste. Instead, it tries to argue that caste continues to wield considerable influence, combining with class-based interests. This becomes clear when we look at the modern attempts at mobilisation, which appear to be channeled through sectarian lines. A close observation of these movements and their goals sheds light on the fact that class interests may be cutting across caste cleavages. The impact of modernisation through industrialisation, urbanisation and secular education is, perhaps, leading to a decreasing emphasis of caste in economic matters and also its use in day-to-day life. The caste-class disparities are not clearly discernible at the lower levels of the social ladder. Thus, one, is an in-built class network within the broader caste structure. Any emphasis on one, to the total exclusion of the other, is likely to give an incomplete picture.

If caste is used as an issue for mobilisation, then what is its net impact upon the total development on the country? Are these movements successful? And if so, do they represent the whole caste as such, which they represent? Do the attempts at eradicating caste end only with its modifications to suit economic and political gains?

An attempt has been made in the following chapters to find

answers to the above questions by tracing the nature and dimensions of the process of sectarian mobilisation in Indian society. It sets out with an analysis of the whole issue of caste and class in the light of the above process, to discover its effects upon politico-economic development and change in the Indian society.

The Theme of the Book

The state of Karnataka with its long history of policy of reservations is an interesting case in this regard, with its on-going and diverse process of caste-based mobilisation. The process has, in fact, accelerated after independence, due to keen competition among the various caste groups, seeking recognition as backward groups. This resulted in the setting up of many commissions of inquiry on the issue of backward classes. It was the Karnataka Backward Classes Commission, set up under the chairmanship of late Sri L. G. Havanur that had, for the first time, placed certain prominent caste groups in the non-backward category. The Commission had classified the Brahmins, the Bunts, the Vaisyas and the Lingayats as non-backward, and this had triggered off a series of mobilisation processes, characterised by conflicts and tensions in the state.

An important aspect of the above process of mobilisation, whether in Karnataka, or elsewhere, is the awareness about their continued backwardness now permeating among such marginalised communities, like the Scheduled Castes, the Scheduled Tribes, the Other Backward Classes (the OBCs) and non-Hindus, particularly the Muslims and Christians, as minority religious groups. It is in this context that the formation of caste associations is found to be a significant development. Acting as political interest groups, these 'Para Communities', viz., caste associations, characterise one of the chief instruments of mobilisation in the state of Karnataka. They act as links between the respective caste groups and the government, in projecting the needs and demands of the former (Shah : 1977).

Apart from the formation of associations, another important aspiration of the caste groups, as seen in the recent decades, is the establishment of educational institutions by caste-based private organisations. There is a keen competition to start caste-based private educational trusts and formation of caste sponsored educational institutions in the state. In this context, Karnataka stands out in the whole of India in the number of private professional (management, engineering and medical) colleges started in recent decades. These have led to a process of emulation of the strategy of caste-based mobilisation by even those caste groups traditionally placed in a disadvantageous position (at the lower levels of the social ladder), economically and socially.

Objectives of the Book

An attempt has been made in the present work to look into the whole gamut of the issue of caste and class, in the light of sectarian mobilisation in Karnataka, with a view to understanding its impact upon development in Karnataka. The caste-class nexus in its diversity, and also the conflicts that are prevalent, have been discussed against the backdrop of the on-going caste-based social processes in the state. It intends to locate or map the role of caste in the present-day socio-economic and political development and to find out how caste is continued to be used as a basis for mobilisation. It also analyses the nature of social change occurring in contemporary Indian society, as a result of the policies relating to protective discrimination. Based on these, the study highlights the following issues:

1. The extent to which the sectarian movements revolving around caste and class portray attempts at bringing about the development of the concerned groups, which they claim to be representing.

2. The degree to which caste is used as a front or facade for protecting class interests.
3. The possibility of caste-sponsored institutions of higher education being able to help the socially and economically weaker sections of their own communities, and
4. The net impact of such a process of mobilisation on development in Karnataka.

Methodology

The book is based on the work carried out for a doctoral dissertation. Data have been subsequently updated to include all the later developments. Available literary material from books, periodicals, and documents has been an important source of secondary information. However, considering that studies of this kind are not numerous, additional information on the subject has been extensively derived out of primary sources. These included, in the main, interviews with a cross-section of respondents ranging from leaders of caste associations, heads of religious mutts, political parties and people of eminence. A detailed questionnaire covering aspects of the origin, growth and functions of the various caste/tribal associations was canvassed. Available information was updated with fresh information collected from the same organisations and individuals.

The book has been presented in eight chapters. The first chapter introduces the theme of the book, the aims and objectives, methodology and the scheme of presentation.

In chapter two an attempt has been made to provide a conceptual framework to the study, along with a review of literature on the subject.

The third chapter peeps into the history (both past and current history) of the backward classes' movement in Karnataka, against the backdrop of similar movement at the all-India level. This has been done to gain insights into the whole issue of caste mobilisation in the state, an exercise that has facilitated an understanding of the factors influencing it. It has also helped in understanding better, the social and political constraints operative in the genesis, growth and spread of the movement, i.e., from the beginning of the 20th century, till date. It enables us to obtain a view that the process of sectarian mobilisation is not a characteristic of only the present times, but has been in vogue for several decades.

Chapter four dwells at length upon the various caste associations of Karnataka. This includes a description of the social, economic and political factors responsible for the success or failure of these interest groups in projecting the demands of the castes they represent and as effective medium for mobilisation. It has portrayed the interrelationships between the governments' policy of reservation and caste mobilisation. This is evident from the manner in which caste associations have increased in their number and activities, with the appointment of successive Backward Classes Commissions in Karnataka.

The fifth chapter traces the history and growth of private educational trusts in the state and their role in caste mobilisation. Although the emphasis is on caste-sponsored trusts, a few non-Hindu private educational trusts have also been covered, wherever they were operating (and competing with the former).

Chapter six discusses the political aspects of mobilisation by taking into account the politics of reservation policy. It captures the demand made by various castes, tribal and religious groups for increased protective discrimination. In turn, the state has formulated and implemented certain welfare measures partly out of a commitment to egalitarianism and partly to retain power. This last consideration is particularly true of cases where the demand for protective discrimination has come from economically and politically strong sections. It is also obvious that the benefits of reservation did not always percolate to those who needed it most. It is here that the class character of the demands, and the class bias of the policy, both become apparent. Against this background the thorny question of the politics of reservation is analysed in this chapter. Since the state of Karnataka has a long history of such policies, the analysis is seen in a historical perspective, wherein the question has been examined from the days of Princely Rule in the erstwhile State of Mysore, till the present times.

As discussed earlier, any process of mobilisation is bound to lead to tensions and conflicts since it questions the base of social inequality in any society. The policy of protective discrimination has led to tensions between the different castes, for claiming a status of being 'backward' and 'more backward'. They are not only inter-caste, but also intra-caste or intra-group tensions. Some of them, as they have figured in the realm of mobilisation, have been discussed in the seventh chapter.

The last chapter presents the conclusions of the study. Since the impact of such caste-based mobilisation on development cannot be always quantified, the attempt here is to bring together, in perspective, all the socio-economic and political variables, which have influenced and continue to influence the process of sectarian mobilisation in Karnataka. Following from this, the implications of this process for development and change have been delineated.

Notes

1. The terms modernity and tradition have been attributed a relative meaning not entirely in contradictory terms but as complementary to each other. See, Rudolphs 1967; 3-14 for an excellent, critical exposition of these terms.
2. The Varna model refers to the four-fold division of society, viz. Brahmin, Kshatriya, Vaisya and Sudra.

2 Review of Literature

Any examination of the process of development in India leads one to the establishment of a nexus between the system of social stratification based on caste and mobilisation. Mobilisation is the active participation by a group of people to achieve certain common goals. It generally assumes the form of a social movement against discrimination but as experience has shown, fails to protect itself from similar forces and gets influenced even in its effort to counter discrimination. Caste/religion/language or region act as the bases upon which individuals and groups organise themselves. Thus, mobilisation assumes a sectarian character under circumstances, where the movement revolves around caste and religious, ethnic or linguistic differences. Associations based on sectarian lines emerge and function as corollaries of the mobilisation process. The competition between different sections of the population for the gain of development often leads to conflicts and tensions, ultimately resulting in disequilibrium and disruption of the existing social set up.

Apparently, social stratification, inequality, social conflict and mobilisation are interrelated. The study of any one of these concepts necessarily demands a reference to the others, as they are complementary to each other and not contradictory. The level of development attained by a society also determines the extent of mobilisation and its success as these have implications for the ways in which different groups compete for a share in the gains of development.

This chapter attempts to critically look at the various lines of thinking on sectarian mobilisation and development and their implications for documenting social transformation and change in Indian society.

We have noted in the introductory chapter that there is no single theory of development, which is universally acceptable. Moreover, as the term development has become more comprehensive in meaning, and its ambit covers diverse social and political dimensions, defining it with a single definition has become quite a difficult and complex process. It is true that traditional development theory was largely the concern of economists from Adam Smith onwards.[1] But very soon it was "recognized that an interdisciplinary perspective is required in order to understand why development is slow, or lagging in some societies". Since one of the principal concerns of development now is the need to reduce both absolute and relative levels of poverty and to reduce inequalities, it is natural that the arena in which development effort takes place, that is the social framework, is subjected to close scrutiny. Attention is to be inevitably drawn towards seminal works such as Myrdal's "Economic Theory and Underdeveloped Regions" (1957), "Asian Drama" (1968), Griffin and Enos' Planning Development" (1973), Sweezy's "Theory of Capitalist Development" (1972), Paul Baron's "The Political Economy and Growth" (1957) and the contributions from Gunder Frank and the Dependency School. To these must necessarily be added the important contribution made in widening the scope of development by Streeton 1972, Seers 1972 and Leys 1977. The interrelated nature of social and economic factors in any process of development is highlighted in such studies as for example, Smelser's "Economy and Society". Hoselitz and Moore's "Sociological Aspects of Economic Growth" (1975), is another contribution of importance in this regard. Economists have also contributed their share to the study of inequality, but in the main, they concentrated attention upon income inequality.

There are works, which deal with the problem at a philosophical level such as R. H. Tawney's "Equality" (1929). Among others, we may note the contributions of Adelman and Morris (1967), Chenery (1975), Titmus (1962) and Anand (1973). All of them no doubt make an attempt to place the whole question of income inequality against the backdrop of the socio-political order although that is obviously not their main concern.

The process of development in a society is invariably associated with change. The strategies of development – like education, secularisation, politicisation and industrial and agricultural production – generally affect the entire fabric of a social system resulting in large-scale transformations. In other words, development necessitates a corresponding growth or progress in the social structure. Thus, an inevitable consequence of development is a collaborative process of change. Such a relation between development and change has been emphasised in a vast amount of early social science research in India (see, Smelser and Lipsett : 1966; Moore : 1962; Srinivas : 1966; and Myrdal : 1968).

The process of development tends to get impaired or disturbed by the existence of inequalities in society. Inequality is a common feature of all societies, but exhibits itself in different forms in different societies. It is an outcome of the system of stratification. Distinction between persons in socio-cultural spheres like occupation, education, ethnicity, language, prestige, authority and so on ascribes to the members of society certain positions and roles which constitute layers of social differentiation (Buckley : 1959). When social differences are graded or evaluated as high and low, it leads to a situation of social inequality.

Inequality, not only as a feature, but also as a problem of social systems, has acquired added significance in the developing countries. A number of theories on the pervasive question of inequality have been advanced by social scientists. These were labelled by Beteille, as the "European" and the "American" approaches. The former holds the issue of class and inequality as based along "philosophical speculations of the moral basis of equality" (Beteille :1969b). The American approach, on the other hand, concentrates on specific and limited areas of "social stratification". He maintains that while the former tends to be more pre-occupied with the problem of class in the narrow Marxian sense of the term, their American counterparts deal more generally with the broader problem of social stratification.

Ever since systematic attention came to be paid to the problem of inequality, the two traditions have co-existed. The earliest approaches have defined inequality as a human condition; they attempted to account for it in its origins, correlates and consequences in terms of one or several aspects of social organisations and structures. Different types of inequality have also been delineated. Rousseau (1754) in France and Adam Smith and John Miller (1971) in Scotland gave the earliest analyses of inequality. They considered equality as a natural state of society and the introduction of the concept of private property as having led to a situation of social inequality. Rousseau distinguishes between inequalities of "natural capability" and of "social position".

The most important contribution to the study of inequality was made by Karl Marx, which analyses it in terms of property relations. According to him, division of labour existing in society between owners of production and owners of labour led to the genesis of social groups and social classes. Conflict and change, Marx argued, are the necessary outcome of inequality (1883).

Like Marx, even Max Weber viewed ownership and non-ownership of property as central axes of social inequality. He further differentiated between three types of inequality based on class, status and power. Unlike Marx, Weber considered even non-economic factors as leading to inequality (Gerth and Mills 1947).

A number of follow-up studies on the lines of Weberian ideology have stressed the importance of the study of inequality as it is a "pervasive and persistent feature of human society involving the evaluation of various qualities and actions of individuals" (Runciman : 1969).

The existence of a wide range of explanations and conceptual postulates concerning inequality has led to a theoretical divergence among scholars. The post-Marxian/Weberian explanations are termed "functionalist and conflict theories", the two categories grouped together for analytical purposes. The conflict theories of social inequality as advanced by Dahrendorf (1959) view inequality as based upon the struggle among individuals and sub-groups within a society for goods, privileges and rewards. In such groups, there is a stress on "power and authority", as explained by Weber.

In recent years, increasing theoretical sophistication of stratification data and the new arenas of such studies in the industrialised, advanced and globalising countries have led to attempts by both American and Continental social scientists to see a synthesis of both the approaches (Buckley : 1959, Parsons : 1940 and 1953, Stinchcombe : 1963, Tumin : 1953, 1955, 1963 and 1967). There is also a marked tendency to shift the focus from the formulation of master theories to the analysis of social stratification with the help of a limited set of conceptual categories such as "status", "wealth" and "power".

However, the significance of conflict theories is high in the Third World, although any cursory glance at them would tell us that the functionalist approach comes mainly from America and the conflict theories from the continental sociologists. These differences set by social history were not recognised in modern writings for a long time.

The study of social stratification in any society depends upon or draws its subject matter from certain structural units, constituting the essence of the system. Generally, three terms are used as units of stratification. They are caste, estate and class. Bottomore adds another division to these three known as "slavery" (1966).

Caste continues to constitute an essential and unique unit of stratification in India. It is unique in the sense that it exhibits certain traits peculiar to India. Although caste-like entities exist in other societies, they do not constitute castes since they exhibit only certain features of caste. There is no doubt that caste occupies an important position in any analysis of Indian society, as it constitutes its integral part.

Systematic studies on caste date back to the beginning of twentieth century (Nesfield : 1885; Dubois : 1906; O'Malley : 1932; Kroeber : 1930; Weber : 1952; and Bougle : 1958). They defined caste as a hierarchically ranked hereditary group, characterised by endogamy and the concepts of purity and pollution (Srinivas : 1961; and Dumont : 1966). The studies also made a distinction between the structural and cultural properties of caste (Singh : 1977). The tradition of holding caste as a hierarchical and endogamous unit of stratification in India is, in fact, a cultural view as is best reflected in the early literature on it. Later on, thinkers like Davis and Moore (1951), and Myrdal (1968) also emphasised upon this. In its essence, the cultural view of caste holds that the caste divisions are only a part of the general principle of stratification operative all-over the world as also in India. As Kroeber says, "Castes are a special form of social classes which in tendency at least are present in every society. Castes differ from social classes. However, in that they have emerged into social consciousness to the point that custom and law attempt their rigid and permanent separation from one another. Social classes are the generic soil from which caste system has at various times and places independently grown up" (1930, 254a-57a).

Like Kroeber, Weber also believed that caste represents an extreme case of stratification. He maintained that when a status group was separated from others through contact, it became caste. Further, Weber introduced the concept of ethnicity into the genesis of caste. Thus, castes are closed communities (*Gemeinschaften*), endogamous and claim descent from a common ancestor. Caste, thus, in Weberian terms, is a product of conjunction between status group and ethnic community.

Substituting this with the cultural view of caste is the explanation that caste is an ideal type of stratified system and as such it would exist forever. To the structural-particularistic view belong sociologists like E. R. Leach, who considered caste as only a particular case of social stratification. Treating caste as to its actual nature (Leach : 1960), he provided the example of Weber's analysis of the 'Protestant Ethic and the Spirit of Capitalism' as one example of such ambiguity.

Contrary to the structural theory is the 'Cultural-Particularistic' view expounded by Louis Dumont when he explained caste as a cultural phenomenon peculiar to India. Despite these various arguments, the structural-particularistic treatment of caste is considered the most dominant line of thinking in studies of stratification in India (Singh : 1977). In most of these writings, caste has been defined as a hierarchically ranked hereditary group, with institutionalised patterns of behaviour in the sphere of occupation, marriage, and economic division of labour. It is characterised by the enforcement of certain cultural norms and values and performance of certain rituals based on the principles of purity and pollution.

Thus, traditional India was a 'Prototype of hierarchical system'. Here, hierarchy has not been a part of social structure, but is considered even proper and desirable, normatively

(Beteille : 1977). Along with hierarchy, mutual expulsion is also considered a fundamental cultural norm underlying caste, while its other attributes are mentioned as hereditary specialisation and hierarchy (Bougle :1958). All these factors have combined in giving an institutionalised form of social inequality in India. Indeed, these institutionalised systems of cultural norms and their economic and social characteristics assign a unique position to caste in Indian stratification.

Being peculiar to India, the phenomenon of caste has found a predominant place in any analytical work on the structure of Indian society, popularly described as the five-fold division of Hindu society and referred to as the 'Varna scheme'. The word 'Varna', understood in its literal connotation as meaning colour, led some thinkers to put forth the racial theory of caste. But the social meaning of 'Varna' excels its general meaning as only a category of persons and implies a 'social order'. In this sense, any explanation of caste only in terms of the Varna model appears unscientific and a gross over-simplification of facts, as it misinterprets the structure and functions of caste as a four-fold division of society (Srinivas : 1962 : 63-69). It is therefore, replaced by what is known as the Jati model, "as Jatis constitute the real unit of social stratification in India". The caste groups existing at present can be best termed as *Jatis* as they constitute the divisions amongst broader caste groups, a modern development as a result of a process of fission in the system (Ghurye : 1932). This has left the Varna scheme as helpful only in so far as it brings systematisation into the Jati-fold and also as a line between different Jatis. Every Jati has developed into an endogamous group following a traditional occupation and endeavour with a certain amount of cultural, ritual and juridical autonomy.

The distinction between caste and Varna also substantiates the fact that a process of fission has gained momentum and

Jatis are innumerable.[3] This methodological stand also shows that any analysis of caste in India requires to be made in association with the multiple changes that the institution has been exposed to.

Monographic literature on the changing dimensions of caste has appeared extensively during the past three decades.[4] Simultaneously, with the growing awareness about caste and its predicaments, an expanding intrusion of it in all spheres of political activity has been found. It has made inroads into the educational, political and economic aspects of life engulfing every activity of the life of Indians (Srinivas : 1966). Just as any foreign observer would be surprised to see the omnipotent nature of caste in India (Ghurye : 1961), one would be equally shocked to observe its sustenance through the ages, despite many changes.

Social change or mobility in India is generally analyzed in terms of the functional diversities in caste system, though the changes in its institutional properties have come to be recognised of late. An important consequence of changes in the caste system has been the existence of conflict – both intra-caste and inter-caste. Social conflict is treated in socio-legal writings as a natural process (Weber : 1962). It is also held as aiming not only at a gain in the desired values, but also an attempt to neutralise, destroy or eliminate rivals (Coser :1957: 232).

In a socially unequal society, it is only natural that the gains of development are monopolised by an affluent dominant, minority, rich class to the discomfiture and disadvantage of the large section of lower classes. The influx of modern ideas and values acting as elements of change often leads to imbalances in the existing social order, resulting in a conflict of old beliefs and new values. In other words, disturbance of an existing equilibrium means the emergence of conflicts and socio-economic tensions. Social tensions are an important manifestation of conflict. While conflicts, tensions and disturbances are considered as almost endemic (Deutsch : 1961) to modern societies, they generally result in changes in the existing social order. Conflict and change are intimately linked. Long-drawn conditions of tensions and conflicts often result in the genesis of social movements (Oberschall : 1973). When social movements by organised groups seek to reform and revolutionise the existing institutions or, on the contrary, defend the social order under attack, it is termed as mobilisation towards change (Moore : 1965). Mobilisation thus refers to the process of forming crowds, groups, associations and organisations for the pursuit of collective goals. During periods of mobilisation a social unit gains relatively in control over resources it previously did not control (Etzioni : 1968 : 243).

Social change is a process of shift from one set of ideas, both qualitatively and quantitatively, resulting from the interplay of various forces – economic, social, cultural and political (Moore : 1965). Inherent in every dimension of change in India is an element of caste mobilisation, a factor emerging out of the omnipresent nature of caste. The extent of caste mobility depends upon a number of variables like the socio-political factors active in the region and such others.

Any analysis of social change in India is bound to consider the role and impact of the British as an important starting point. Alien rule, especially the British, is very favourably held by many writers on caste as initiating or heralding a new era of social change in the subcontinent. British rule is held as having changed the social order from static to dynamic state by throwing open many avenues of modern living through such channels as education and employment. The developments, on the material side, like the setting up of industries and the consequent growth of urban areas, advancement made in the fields of science and technology, transportation, communication, education and a thorough process of politicisation—have all combined in pushing caste to the forefront (Srinivas : 1962 and 1969). These forces have acted as levers of social change, as a result of which caste groups are undergoing transformation in their behaviour patterns and lifestyles. These modifications in their socio-cultural life were explained by Srinivas as the process of 'Sanskritisation' and 'Westernisation' (Srinivas : 1966).

Even Marx held the view that caste would be weakened as a result of British impact. He, with his profound insight, saw what impact British rule would have on Indian society. However, his expectations that the caste system would weaken due to the combined thrust of urbanisation, industrialisation and Western influence have not been wholly fulfilled. While British rule has made an important influence on Indian society through the introduction of Western education, industrial growth and improvement in transport and communication, it has not led to the atrophy of the caste system. It resulted rather in a substantial modification of the role of caste (Marx : 1853).

The process of mobilisation in Indian society with reference to its caste structure can be analysed in two contexts, viz., pre-independence and post-independence periods. Changes in the structural base of caste began to occur as early as in the last quarter of the nineteenth century. Some of the salient features of this process have been generally recognised as follows:

(a) An increasing stress came to be laid upon the process of upward mobility by the lower castes in the hierarchy through such channels as occupational and spatial mobility.
(b) The occurrence of a process of fission wherein each caste group divides itself into many sub castes and sub sub castes leading to complexity in the system.
(c) A counter process of fusion by which attempts were made to bring about horizontal solidarity within the

group, adopting such political variables as caste association, interest groups and the like (Rudolphs : 1967; Hardgrave : 1969; Irschick : 1969; Rao : 1958 and 1970).

Although the above developments were initiated and even attained a considerable significant stage, functioning as the forces of social change in Indian society during the years before independence itself, they are noticed to have been carried further in tune with the changes in the social, economic and political profile of the country in the post-independence era also. To this situation were added legislative measures to bring about transformation and development in the form of the policy of protective discrimination to the backward classes, minorities and other weaker sections of the country. Since caste groups have been the central point around which mobilisation efforts took place and since the demand for seats in the offices under the state was mainly articulated by them, the Constitution, not unnaturally, evolved a scheme for providing the disadvantaged groups with positive help in the form of reservations. Whether the Constitutional scheme sanctified caste is in itself a matter for much debate (Beteille :1981, KBCC Report : 1975).

Caste in India thus presents a picture of continuous dynamism today. While being affected by the existing social forces, caste itself is a social force. All the above mentioned processes merging with the new challenges posed by the passage of time have together been responsible for bringing about substantial and effective changes in the relations between caste and the economic and political frontiers. These changes in the structure of Hindu society, especially in its lower rungs, have been brought out by a number of significant works (Srinivas : 1968, Ghurye : 1932; Bailey : 1957; Dube : 1958; and Rao : 1970).

These analytical studies are useful in that they constituted the first ever-descriptive works of caste and social change in India. A majority of them have based their analyses using caste as either an economic or a political variable. Others have concentrated their prime attention on the legal sanctions behind mobility among the downtrodden. In all of them, caste constitutes a crucial unit of mobilisation. These studies, though substantial in giving a vivid picture of caste mobility, tended to emphasise the role of only caste. Though caste plays a crucial role in the socio-political milieu of the country, there is the need to stress the role of other factors too. But ever since systematic studies on Indian society have been made, there is a tendency to consider caste as the sole criterion.

Class, along with caste, appears to be quite meaningful in the context of Hindu social structure. It also has an important place in the study of Indian society. Thus, it is recognized as another aspect of social stratification in India in recent years. But in most of these works, class appears along with caste almost as an afterthought. There is also a lack of consensus as to the conceptual framework within which class is defined or identified (Singh : 1977). It is also alleged that the existing studies on class in Indian society are oriented towards urban areas to the clear exclusion of rural areas (Rosen : 1966).

An integrated and suitable definition of class is to be found in the words of Lenin, who considered classes as "groups of people holding distinctive positions in the historical system of social production and their role in the social organisation and of labour and consequently by the dimensions and methods of acquiring the share of social wealth that they obtain" (Lenin n.d.).

The increasing need for an integrated approach to the study of social phenomena in India is being raised by few social scientists in recent years. That any deep analysis of the present day social processes highlighting the existence and role of both caste and class interests is proved in various social contexts and processes. For example, while there is evidence regarding the occurrence of mobility in caste, a further probe would point out that the process is more pronounced amongst the dominant and upper strata within the backward class category. Some castes are more able to mobilise themselves than others because of the interplay of certain socio-political factors. This has resulted in a situation where the upper caste/class groups access benefits of developmental programmes more regularly.

Can we argue that in modern India, caste groups almost stand out as distinctive classes? That they assume class-like features under various situations. This is clear when we look at the phenomenon of caste conflicts. Sharp cleavages do exist amongst the backward classes characterised by competition for a greater share of politico-economic gains. Interaction between castes is also class-oriented. Alliances are sought on class and elitist lines.

The alternative is that an integrated approach to the study of Indian society, involving both caste and class elements, is evolving in the recent times. While most of the early studies upheld the omni-present nature of caste, the recognition of an element of class is a welcome sign. However, this integrated approach has resulted in certain complex theoretical postulates. Caste and class are either considered as identical processes (Rajashekar : 1979), or as aspects of the same phenomenon. There is also the tendency to view them as distinctive-wholes. There is the third proposition that Indian society can be studied "either on caste or class lines" (Beteille : 1981 : 107).

Against this background, it is argued that the process of mobilisation in Indian society deserves a multidimensional and macro-sociological approach. Based mostly on sectarian channels, the process is found to be drawing its ingredients from both caste and class factors. Their role is no doubt being recognised in social science research. Nevertheless, these studies seem to operate at national levels. One limitation they pose refers to their inadequacy to generate general or even middle range hypotheses or propositions regarding social stratification. One therefore stresses here studies with an interdisciplinary approach using caste, class and other categories.

Apart from/along with these, studies on social conflicts, especially those stemming from the interplay of caste, class and other related factors should form an integral part of any study of social stratification. The role of social conflict cannot be underestimated since, if not resolved in time, conflict would endanger the proper functioning of the society leading to systemic imbalances (Dahrendorf : 1959, Beteille : 1969, 1971 and 1978; Wesolowski : 1969 and 1979 and Berreman 1965).

The above situation is specific to societies that have embarked upon planned development through state interventions. Development being a lever of social change and social progress, it encounters and stimulates inevitable conflicting reactions in all its stages. Identification and effective treatment of conflict, whether inter or intra-caste, is a necessary ingredient of any programme of development.

It should be made clear at this juncture that the process of mobilisation is central to the analysis of the processes of development, change and social inequality. While mobilisation is generally referred to as being social in nature (Apter : 1965; Rudebeck : 1970; Nettl : 1967; and Etzioni : 1968), a distinction is made between social mobilisation and political mobilisation (Hettne and Tamm : 1974). There is also the structural approach to the study of mobilisation that "stresses the pre-conditions for mobilisation, and the processual one, which stresses its dynamics" (Hettne and Tamm : 1974; 10).

The above and other lines of thinking on the subject of

mobilisation commonly emphasise its role in leading to a "significant rise in popular involvement in the processes of change". Social mobilisation is a "process in which major clusters of old social, economic and psychological commitments are eroded or broken and people become available for new patterns of socialisation and behaviour (Deutsch : 1961; 29). "Mobilisation refers to the process by which a discontented group assembles and invests resources for the pursuit of group-goals" (Oberschall : 1973; 28). Such discontentment arises when people, who are mobilising, "become aware of the contradictions between their own aspirations and the existing structural and institutional arrangements of the society they live in (Rudebeck : 1970). The participation by people in a large number in mobilisation processes leads to the emergence of a social movement. Thus, mobilisation attempts to bring about changes, to result in the genesis of social movements, which challenge the existing mode of social control (*ibid.*).

In India, the attempts by various caste and religious groups to mobilise for achieving higher socio-political power and status have led to the emergence of social movements. A wide range of literary work exists on the subject of social movements in India. In most of them, the interrelationships between protest and reform have been stressed. When a social movement is characterised by the active involvement of people, it invariably happens that groups are mobilised under such common banner, like caste, ethnicity, religion, language and regionalism – to press their claims. Thus, the movement acquires a sectarian character with such segments of society participating in it.

The sectarian character of social movements has been highlighted in a number of studies by sociologists and social scientists. Studies by Aiyappan (1965), Alexander (1968), Harper (1968), Parvathamma (1971), Patwardhan (1973), Rao (1957; 1978). Zelliot (1972) and others deal with the interplay of politico-economic factors in fundamentally religious movements. Similarly, monographic literature by Abraham (1968), Aurora (1968), Azaraiah (1932), Bobb (1970), Bailey (1957), Baker (1975), Beteille (1971a), Bose (1948), Desai (1966), Dube (1958), Gough (1952), Hardgrave (1969), Harper (1968), Ishwaran (1966), Lynch (1969), Mahar (1972), Marriott (1955), Mayer (1960), Mazumdar (1958), Shrikant (1968), Srinivas (1956b), Trivedi (1977) and Zelliot (1966), and several others have concentrated, directly or indirectly, on movements for upward mobility by specific caste groups, particularly those at the middle and lower levels of the hierarchy.

The above studies on sectarian social movements present a picture of social change in the pre-independence and early post-independence periods. Other studies by Bhatt (1945), Brass (1965), Epstein (1962), Kothari (1970) etc., have also dealt, though indirectly, with social change in the caste system using socio-political variables.

However, the introduction of certain legislative or Constitutional measures in the pre-independence days, through the Covernment of India Act of 1953 (but with a greater emphasis after independence through the Constitution in the year 1950) has added a momentum to the already existing processes of mobilisation and change. The problem of untouchability came to be tackled in the writings of Ambedkar and Gandhi. Studies by Omvedt (1976), Parvathamma (1971), Patwardhan (1973), Rajagopalachari (1946), Rudolphs (1967), Zelliot (1972) and a few others have discussed aspects of leadership of Gandhi and Ambedkar and the extent of its effect on the depressed classes of India.

Further, the problem of untouchability has also been discussed widely in sociological literature. Agarwal (1934), Aiyappan (1944), Alexander (1968), Beteille (1969), Bhatt (1975), Burman (1970), Chauhan (1969), Chitnis (1981), Cohn (1955), Dushkin (1974), Ghurye (1957), Issacs (1964),

Lynch (1969), Mahar (1972), Patwardhan (1973), Reddi (1950), Srinivas (1966), Trivedi (1977) and others have portrayed the nature, dimensions and the effects of social change among ex-untouchables and tribals in the country.

An essential part of any social movement in India is the middle castes of the hierarchy. They are more specifically the dominant castes of the area in consideration. The non-Brahmins constituting another chief dimension of social movements in India led movements opposing Brahmin supremacy in matters of education and government service and claiming equality with them. Popularly known as the Backward Class Movements (BCMs), they were chiefly led by the dominant castes of the region in the pre-independence era (Srinivas : 1966). A reference to these movements (and many-a-times a detailed analysis also) constitutes an important element in most of the studies of social change in the country. The BCMs themselves have been vividly studied, as occurring in the different states of India, by Dushkin (1974), Hettne (1978), Irschick (1969), Manor (1972), Omvedt (1976) and Washbrook (1975) in their works.

Studies by Irschick and Washbrook, among others, have dwelt upon the backward classes movement and the politico-social development relating to it, in the state of Tamil Nadu (erstwhile Madras Presidency). Similarly, Omvedt has analysed the movement as it occurred in Western India in relation to its caste and class network. Concerning Karnataka, Dushkin has made a direct study of the movement by the backward classes in Princely Mysore, while the work of Manor and Hettne have looked at the subject from political and administrative angles.

Studies of this kind in the post-independence period are, however, not numerous. The process of mobilisation with particular reference to the caste dimension in Karnataka is not being subjected to scrutiny, although there are divergent approaches.

What appears lacking in all attempts is a look at sectarian mobilisation in a holistic perspective in which both caste and class elements are synthesised. The major attempts are those of Dushkin (1974), Hettne (1978), Manor (1972), Natraj (1979), Srinivas (1993) and a few others who have concentrated especially on the thorny question of reservations.

The policy of protective discrimination has become a highly controversial subject over the past few years. It has been viewed from both the legal (Singh : 1981, Stanton : 1979), and socio-legal [Havanur (1963), Natraj (1979), Galanter (1984)] perspectives. Comparative studies of the policy in India and elsewhere (America) have also been attempted [Stanton (1979), Beteille (1981), Paramanand Singh (1982) and Galanter (1984)]. Both the policy as well as its effects on the total society has drawn considerable attention from social scientists (Srinivas : 1979, 1980 and Srinivas and Panini : 1984). Most crucial has been the dilemma between 'merit' and 'efficiency' and 'caste' as the determinant of socio-economic backwardness (Beteille : 1981 and 1983).

It is possible to say without much fear of controversy that one welcome feature of the recent trend in the awareness among scholars of different schools of thought, reviewed so far, is that it would not be profitable to look at sectarian mobilisation and protective discrimination from either a rigid caste-centred approach or an inflexible class-centred one. It appears that what will produce the most interesting and useful results are the emergence of approaches, which, while having a strong theoretical foundation, also take into account the empirical realities. The general studies (Namboodiripad, 1979, Roy : 1979) mentioned above are important in this respect. These and the seminal works of Dushkin (1974), Manor (1972), Hettne and Tamm (1978), etc., should be pursued further in the light of changing circumstances, to arrive at a theory of sectarian mobilisation which explains the emerging situation in Karnataka. One field in which there is an upsurge of interest is the realm of politics, here connoting the process of governance and decentralisation. The volume 'Shift in Indian Politics' (Mathew : 1984), as also some papers have attempted an analysis of the role of caste in politics. However, studies with this perspective of caste associations, private educational institutions etc., are still scanty. The present work is a modest attempt in this direction.

Notes

1. The traditional theory of classical and non-classical types concerned only with growth; hence, not applicable to the developing countries. See, 'Does Development Studies Have a Core?' (Toye 1980) for a survey of divergent views on this.
2. Class constitutes an important aspect of stratification in the works of Ossowski : 1963, Bottomore : 1966, Lenski . 1966, Parkin : 1971, Schumpeter : 1951, Mandel : 1968, Banks : 1970.
3. Weber thinks that individual castes develop some measure of distinct cults and gods (Weber : 1952).
4. Ghurye had counted as many as 2,000 Jatis in each linguistic area in 1932 itself (Ghurye : 1932).

3 Historical Analysis of Sectarian Mobilisation in India

Introduction

In the study of any society, its history constitutes an important part or component, as it not only provides clues to understand the present, but also acts as a guide to speculate the future. This chapter attempts to provide, a brief sketch of the history of mobilisation and reform in Indian society. It has special reference to the nature and dimensions of social inequality and the attempts made to reform Hindu society through certain socio-political measures.

1. Social Stratification in India and Caste

Hindu social structure follows a rigid and distinctive pattern of stratification, with castes and sub castes constituting its social divisions. "Caste", as a unique feature of Hindu society, is traditionally defined as a social group characterised by hereditary occupations, endogamous marriages and bound by the concepts of purity and pollution (Srinivas : 1964). Each major caste group is further divided and sub-divided into many sub castes and sub sub castes, leading to a highly complex system of social stratification. Though in its earlier stages, caste, as envisaged by Manu, was only a four-fold division of the Hindu society into Brahmin, Kshatriya, Vaisya and Sudra groups (Kane : 1974. Also, see, Karve, I : 1958), it has undergone a thorough process of diffusion in the recent decades. These changes are those that followed certain social, political and economic changes in the country, leading to considerable heterogeneity in the system. Caste has engulfed every aspect of the life of Indians that it has come to be regarded as an important key to the understanding of the Indian social structure itself. Interestingly enough, caste has also affected some non-Hindu groups like Muslims and Christians among whom many aspects of caste are observed (Ghurye : 1957). This is more so in the case of converts to other religions from the low caste groups who have continued to follow their earlier life-style even after conversion. Besides this vertical division of the society, there is also found a horizontal line of stratification, further dividing the caste groups into social classes. Though social classes are a common feature of all systems of stratification, in India, class divisions cut across the traditional caste differences, and have come to occupy an important place in, and tend to influence every aspect of, the life of Indians.

The genesis and growth of the institution of caste has been the subject of sociological debate since long. Explanations on the issue of the origin of caste system have concentrated upon such factors as occupation (Ghurye : 1924, 1957 & 1961; Karve : 1968; Risley : 1915) and division of labour and so on. There is also a marked tendency to correlate caste with Aryan invasion.

Further, "the traditional hierarchization of the Hindu society along caste lines, more or less corresponded with the political and economic ones" (GoI : 1980: 141). In other words, the pattern of social organisation generally resembled what Dahl (1961) called 'Cumulative Inequality'. It was also comparatively a stable order and in terms of Galtung's (1972) conceptualisation, it did not have rank disequilibrium (Galtung : 1976).

It is evident from historical records that both during the pre-Vedic and the Vedic periods, caste was comparatively less rigid and complex. But, in course of time, rituals and sacrifices began to occupy a dominant place in social life, giving rise to the power of the priestly class. Considerations of artificial purity tended to make the existing caste groups rigid and an increasing stress was laid on the performance of rituals and sacrifices. As pointed out by Kothari (1970), the social order was flexible and even in pre-British India, the lower and tribal groups were able to gain entry into the middle caste order.

In course of time, these factors came to have a lasting impact on the nature of hierarchy in India. Inter-caste relations were marked by a feeling of severe segmentation and discrimination, which reached its zenith in the case of the lowest strata known as the exterior castes or the ex-untouchables. The notions of inferiority and superiority coupled with notions of purity and pollution have led to untold misery and hardships to the ex-untouchable population of India.

2. Protest and Reform in Hindu Society

Pre-British Phase

Such exclusiveness of caste and its disadvantages have been protested and rejected from time to time by social reformers resulting in the formation of dissenting "Sects". Both Buddhism and Jainism carried out battles against tradition and "sought to provide a rational scheme for the ritual-stricken, caste-ridden man to discover himself" (Radhakrishnan : 1948).

In the 12th century, Basava developed the same thesis through his teachings and his was a social revolution carried out by the side of a religious revolution (Rice : 1897). Some saints like Sant Dyaneshwar and Tukaram in Maharashtra worked towards modifying the rigidity of caste, its endogamous nature and exclusiveness through reformation on religious grounds. They sought to raise the Sudra classes to a position of spiritual power and social importance almost equal to that of the Brahmins.

Reformist measures like the above were oriented towards developing humanism and to emphasise "the doctrine of mutual toleration". They, no doubt, appealed to the people as their leaders spoke in the language spoken and understood by the masses. But these movements were "particularistic" in nature and hence could not succeed in healing the sufferings of the people. They failed in evoking mass sympathy and concern towards the problems of the ex-untouchables. They also seldom concerned themselves with the reform of the social institutions, but provided only spiritual consolation to the people than bringing any solace to their day-to-day problems (Natarajan : 1959).

It was against this background that the British invaded India and British rule came to be held as providing a boon to the age-old problems of the Hindu society. Any study of social reform movements in India should take into consideration the impact of British rule over Hindu social institutions. The society in India on the eve of British conquest was characterised by chaos and anarchy due to the interplay of a number of socio-political factors. The atmosphere was marked by conflict of faith and ideals. Colonial rule over the subcontinent initiated a process of secular social change with a radical and lasting impact on its society and culture. It brought under its influence the various aspects of Hindu social organisation and became responsible for many structural and functional changes in the system. Such a transformation is attributed to the introduction of two processes, viz., secular education and technology (Srinivas : 1966). Along with these, British rule is also regarded as having introduced into the country some measure of unity, protection against external aggression and the rule of law. Alongwith these, British rule also introduced a system of modern education and secular employment—all of which helped in popularising the doctrines of equality and development.

Thus, India came under the influence of this new process of change, and educated Indians began to examine the problems confronting the traditional Hindu society. They attempted to liberate the society from the clutches of tradition and superstition and to reform it in order to bring about socio-economic changes. All these efforts are considered as manifestations of the inner changes taking place in them as a result of western education and training (Tarachand : 1967).

These changes were invariably revolving around the nucleus of caste, but could affect only those castes, which were relatively better placed in the social hierarchy. In other words, new opportunities like diversification of occupational structure and the introduction of secular education could influence the upper, middle, and to some extent lower-middle caste groups while the ex-untouchables remained far away from any such impact due to their extreme backwardness and inferior status imposed on them.

3. Reform and Change in Hindu Society during British Rule

Nevertheless, the liberal system of administration introduced by the British stirred up a process of socio-religious movements, falling into three categories. The first set of reforms held that gradual changes should occur without altering the old pattern. In other words, they wanted the old society to remodel itself on certain new lines. Secondly, there were a group of radical reformers who opted for complete transformation of Indian society, irrespective of caste, creed or language. There was also a third group which represented the revivalist attitude. They preferred the glorification of Hindu religion and society in the current form.

These three lines of social reform culminated in the development of two different ideologies. The national leaders differed on the issues of social reform Vs political reform, leading to the division into 'Moderates' and 'Extremists'. A close observation of the history of 19th century India makes it clear that the ideas of social reform led in course of time to the urge for independence. The nationalists' urge gained momentum so much so that towards the end of the 19th century, there arose a controversy as to whether political freedom should take precedence over social reform, or *vice versa* (Srinivas : 1966).

Ultimately, political freedom was given preference when the Indian National Congress in its 1906 Calcutta Session declared its goal as "the obtaining of the system of self-government in the self-governing British colonies". Thus, the emphasis was shifted from social reform to political struggle keeping freedom of the country as the goal. As was common before and in other areas of mobilisation, the political reform movement came to be led by a group of upper caste/class people whose active supporters were drawn from the 'caste-Hindu' sections, with the depressed classes being at best on the periphery.

4. The Rise of Sectarian Mobilisation in India

British rule is stated to have brought in certain changes that proved to be the beacon light for the oppressed and depressed classes of India and created certain amount of social awareness amongst them, further inculcating in them a spirit of reason and revolt. A number of caste groups from the middle and lower levels of caste hierarchy were able to mobilise themselves towards greater economic emancipation and political participation (Bailey :1957; Hardgrove :1969; Aiyappan :1944; Rao : 1957, 1970 and 1978; Marriot : 1955; Kothari : 1970; see, Rudolphs : 1964; and Beteille : 1965, 1967). Such a change was generally succeeded by a high degree of 'Sanskritisation' of lifestyle culminating in acquiring a high socio-ritual status to the caste groups. Examples are the Teli or Oilmen caste of eastern India,

Noniyas or salt makers of Uttar Pradesh, the Kolis of Gujarat and so on (Srinivas : 1966). Genteel social reform movements aiming at eliminating caste disabilities, emancipation of the untouchables, abolition of evil practices like Sati, child marriages and encouraging women's education, widow remarriage, etc., characterised the major attempts in this direction. Though simple and non-violent in the beginning, these movements gathered momentum in course of time and assumed the form of militant, aggressive reform movements. They sought to abolish Brahminical culture and dominance, as in the case of the non-Brahmin movement led by E.V.Ramaswamy Naicker (Periyar, as he was popularly known) in Madras[1], or of Jotiba Phule in Maharashtra, and more recently, of Shri Narayana Dharma Paripalana Yogam Movement of the Ezhavas of Kerala (which was also militant and more inward-looking) (Rao : 1978). But the urge for equality found a most powerful expression in the process of Sankritisation (Srinivas : 1958).

(a) The Role of Census Operations

It would be appropriate to mention here the role played by the Census undertaken by British. Among other things they evolved widespread mobility among the backward classes. The years 1867-1871 marked the first ever nation-wide census in India, on which occasion, few caste groups attempted to claim a higher status to themselves in the caste hierarchy. Such claims became more prevalent by the census of 1901 because of the decision of the Census Commissioner to provide an accurate record of the ranking of Jatis in the census. There was a very quick and wide response by many ambitious caste groups to this opportunity, which combined all their efforts in this process of mobilisation. Introduction of modern communication and a wide network of transportation facilities by the British enabled the increase in horizontal solidarity and integrated participation in the process of mobilisation by the backward classes.

The process of caste mobilisation through census accelerated in course of years and people in increasing numbers came to be aware of this 'new and government sponsored channel of caste mobility' (Srinivas : 1966, 92). But it also had the negative effect of stimulating inter-caste rivalry and competition. The tendency of caste enumeration in the census continued over the years till 1941, when the British Census Commission had to eliminate the column about caste from the list, due to increasing pressure from different caste groups competing for higher status. Thus, the census operations, especially from 1901 onwards, while initiating a process of horizontal mobility, also created many problems of intra and inter-caste conflicts, which dominated the backward classes' movement of the following decades.

(b) Formation of Caste Associations

The introduction of Census operations was followed by another important channel of social mobility, viz., the emergence of caste associations. A number of them sprang up in different parts of the country during the first decade of the 20th century, whose aim was to secure a high socio-economic status to their members. Newspapers and journals started by these associations enabled spreading the ideas of caste mobility over a wider area. Caste conferences were held and funds collected for purposes of building hostels and providing scholarship to students. Reformative measures in the direction of Sanskritising their socio- ritual habits were an important part of the aims of such conferences.

On the whole, the processes of education and Sankritisation created in the minds of the non-Brahmins an urge for upward mobility and freedom from the clutches of orthodox Hinduism. There existed a keen fight to catch up with the higher castes – the Brahmins. Dominance of Brahmins in education and modern occupations provided reasons for the subsequent reformers and radical thinkers to protest against them. This attitude finally resulted in the emergence of a mass movement popularly known as the 'Backward Classes Movement' (hereafter BCM). It marked the revolt of all low castes against Brahminical supremacy and it is only natural that the movement was rampant in South India, where the Brahmins enjoyed maximum supremacy in matters of education and government service. By the dawn of the 20th century, the forces against Brahminical dominance were quite pronounced and the stage was all set for the emergence of the Backward Classes Movement.

5. The Backward Classes Movement

This movement, which could be considered an integral part of India's political, economic and cultural history, was strongest in Tamil Nadu (then called the Madras Presidency) in South India. There is, however, evidence of a similar movement in the other parts of India. In eastern India, Bengal, where the feeling of caste distinctions was not high, is described as the initiator of the BCM in India. During early 20th century, in Bengal, the Yogis and the Namasudras expressed strong desire for mobility (Bose : 1967). Arya Samaj attracted many low castes in Northern India to change their occupations and religious practices. The census of 1871 also records the attempts by a few low castes in some districts of Uttar Pradesh and Punjab to move up in the caste hierarchy. The Shuddhi Movement founded by the Samaj prevented many ex-untouchables from seeking conversion to other religions. Even in Orissa, the Samaj attracted many so-called 'inferior' communities such as the Kurmis, and the Musatras to its fold. In Gujarat, the landed caste of Patidars had shown remarkable changes in its lifestyle and occupation for the past 250 years, particularly towards the end of the 19th century.

The BCM was more intense in Tamil Nadu, though Maharashtra also joined the race soon. The term 'backward' in Tamil Nadu, Hyderabad and parts of Travancore-Cochin was taken to mean all castes except the Brahmins. Anti-Brahminic tendencies provided the common ideological base in all these areas of which Madras and Bombay became important due to their political prominence. Strangely enough, the feeling came to be shared by the Muslims. the Christians and the Parsis. Apart from the above main centers, the movement percolated through other sub-centres like Madurai, Kallakurichi, Chidambaram, Bangalore, Kolhapur and Poona.

But the cultural and intellectual predominance of Madras and Bombay, coupled with their political power structure, raised the status of these provinces in the views of educated Indians of South India who sought for leadership in them.

In Maharashtra, a region dominated by Marathi speaking population of Western India, "a movement of cultural revolt rose" during the beginning of the 19th century, "against a background of the increasing poverty of the lower classes under British rule and the domination of the largely Brahmin native elite". This non-Brahmin movement originated in 1873 "when a leader of middle caste status, Jotirao Phule, founded the 'Satyashodhak Samaj' as a rationalistic and egalitarian socio-religious reform organization". The Maharaja of Kolhapur subsequently provided support to it. The movement was initially opposed to the Brahmin dominated national movement. Suspecting the replacement of British rule by Brahmin rule, the non-Brahmins organised a "separate and loyalist political party". In course of time, as the movement stabilised, its young leaders attacked not only Brahmins' social dominance, but also their "ineffective leadership of the national movement". By the 1920s, the movement was led by mostly educated rural youth who followed not "traditionalistic authority patterns", but possessed the ability to portray the economic and cultural demands of lower class non-Brahmins. But it was during this decade that the leadership came into "contact and conflict" with the national movement led by Gandhi and with the emerging Communist organization among the Bombay working class. But the impact of the former was greater than others that the movement was gradually absorbed into it (Omvedt : 1979: 1-2).

Anti-Brahminic tendencies, though common all over the South, were especially so in Madras. The feeling was more intense here, predominantly caused by the lead taken by the Brahmins over other communities in matters relating to education, which was held responsible for their distinctive representation in Government service (Irschick :1969). Studies reveal that between 1892 and 1918, the Brahmins outnumbered others in, and in some cases even monopolised, the field of government service. The non-Brahmins, such as the Vellalas, the Naidus, the Thakurs and the Chettis, being the dominant castes controlled the agricultural and industrial sectors of Madras Presidency, lacking only in representation in government service. The nationalistic and cultural awakening developed first in the Province of Bengal and Bombay, with Madras coming under its influence much later. Simultaneously, there developed in Madras Presidency a minority intelligentsia who tried to link Madras with Bengal and Bombay. This group constituted the educated Brahmins who, by virtue of their education and enlightenment, could bring Madras on the map of the nationalistic movements (Irsthick : 1969).

Thus, by 1913, economic, political and educational cleavages between the Brahmins and the non-Brahmins were quite pronounced and the conflict that emerged later was only an articulation of this traditional rivalry. Accordingly, a movement broke out during 1916-1929, between the 'nationalistic politicians' (Brahmins) and a group of non-Brahmins who opted for political representation, administrative position and economic security. The movement was strengthened by the wide publicity given to it through such mass media like newspapers and journals in English and other South Indian languages. Above all, a political party was subsequently organised to serve the interests of the non-Brahmins at the Madras Legislative Council. The non-Brahmin leaders founded the Madras Presidency Association (MPA) through which they sought communal representation to safeguard their interests.

The MPA and several other such organisations founded by prominent non-Brahmins established hostels for their community students. The ideological base upon which the movement survived and its demands given public announcement, were provided by the 'non-Brahmin Manifesto' released in the year 1916.

It was under such a socio-political climate that the Minto-Marley Reforms were announced in 1909. The report held that separate electorates were detrimental to the safety of the government, "as it would stereotype existing relations" and held "as posing a very serious hindrance to the development of the self-governing principle" (Irschick : 1969: 92). But the fact that despite its recognition of the evils of communal representation, the report provided such benefits to Muslims and Christians, led to frustration among the backward classes. They felt that their case was more deserving than Muslims or Sikhs, who in their view enjoyed a better status in society.

In the wake of such political awakening came Montagu's announcement on August 20, 1917, of "increasing association of Indians in every branch of administration and the general development of self-governing institutions, with a view to the progressive realisation of responsible government in India" (Irschick : 1969: 53). He had also expressed his wish to lead a mission to India to study the political scene and learn about the interests of different groups, with a view to formulating plans for Constitutional Reforms.

In Madras, these political activities led to a division among the non-Brahmins. Two groups of non-Brahmins evolved in the Congress party, as opposed to those in the Justice Party, which was founded in the year 1916. The British supported the latter. Each section strove to show its strength in representing the cause of the poor masses of the Province. Intensive programmes and representations were planned to uphold this cause. Of importance is the fact that the non-Brahmins, in their eagerness to impress upon the Secretary of State of their popularity, even contended that the Justice Party represented the ex-untouchables greatly. To prove this, several meetings of the so-called outcastes were organized by these leaders during 1917 in Madras, in a bid to orient towards winning the support of the ex-untouchables, who constituted nearly one-fifth of the total population of the provinces. But, the non-Brahmins' offer of advice and help was promptly refused by the so-called outcastes, whose leader, the President of the Pariah Mahajana Sabha, is reported to have stated that the "Panchamas would get crushed irrespective of who achieves power, whether the Brahmins or non-Brahmins" (Irschick : 1969: 71).

However, the political events in the city and the country had stirred up considerable political awakening and created an urge for participation among the depressed classes – the term originally used to denote the ex-untouchable and tribal communities of India. Many depressed classes' organisations presented memoranda to Montagu, expressing their grievances. Among those associations representing the ex-untouchables were the Panchama Kavli Abhivarthi-Abhiman Sangha and the Madras Adi Dravida Jana Sangha, representing 60,00,000 aborigines. A few depressed class organisations from Bengal and Bombay also met Montagu during his tours.

The British were aware of the growing strength of the Brahminical supremacy in administrative and political positions much before the commencement of the non-Brahmin movement in Madras. They also saw in such domination a potential threat to their rule over the sub-continent. In the following years government help to such anti-national backward classes movements increased. This was especially so in the provinces of Madras.

The first instance of distrust by the British of Brahmins was expressed in political circles during 1918-19. Whether it was their desire to experiment with some ideals of social justice or their intention to keep the nation divided and weak – in the wake of Mrs. Beasant's 'Home Rule' activities – the British rendered their support to the BCM in Madras. Such an act of the British could only be understood as 'natural' in as much as any government trying to control the dominance of elite over public life would do the same.

Such rationalistic overtones of a BCM in Madras were typical of all the other such movements in different parts of India. A feature common to these movements was that they used the legislative councils to assure a definite position to themselves in government service. As Irschick says, in the process of mobilisation, these communities have come to develop "a myth of antiquity and cultural superiority", along with an organisation to voice their demands and a political party to represent their woes (Irschick : 1969).

The Justice Party took up the task of securing communal representation to the non-Brahmins in Madras. It represented them at the Joint Select Committee's hearings in June 1919, along with the Muslim League, the Congress, and the Home Rule League, the Madras Presidency Association, the Moderates and the others. After a detailed analysis of the facts, the Committee intended to consider the implementation of the

Montagu-Chelmsford Reforms through the Government of India Bill. Amidst much opposition, the Justice Party was able to secure communal representation to the non-Brahmins. In the elections of 1919 held under the Government of India Bill, the Justice Party secured success and the non-Brahmins achieved power as ministers. This further facilitated the working of the reforms. It is suggested that the success of Justicites was made easy with the Congress boycotting the elections. The party remained in power till 1926. Although, even later when power went to the Swaraj Party, it did not lessen the influence of the Justice Party on local politics.

The above picture of the BCM in Madras and the mobilisation of certain caste groups for purposes of socio-political gains was the beginning of a long process of social reform through legislative means. Throughout the process, it is evident that a few economically and culturally articulate groups took the lead, with the conspicuous absence of any depressed classes in it. It is to be seen here that though the term 'non-Brahmin' was used as a synonym for all those who were not Brahmins, it came in course of its operation, to be applied to only those groups who fall in the non-Brahmin, non-untouchable category.

The Justice Party, while involving itself with the cause of the non-Brahmins, never considered that of the ex-untouchables, despite that they also came under the banner of the non-Brahmins. Its attempted association with the outcastes ended as soon as it assumed power. Soon it turned out to be an entirely caste-Hindu party. The leaders of the ex-untouchable communitics were all well aware of this attitude of the non-Brahmin leaders, which is expressed in the statements made by the former. M.C. Rajah, a chief representative of the ex-untouchables at the Legislative Council stated that the feeling of traditional animosity towards the untouchables was prevalent amongst the Justicites since the beginning. A few incidents of clashes between the Harijans and the caste-Hindus (like the Puliyanthope[2] incident of 1921 in Madras) were manifestations of such feelings (Irschick : 1969 : 189 & 191).

This position of inferiority and helplessness of the depressed classes was not without valid reasons. The ex-untouchables were nowhere near the other non-Brahmins, who were economically well advanced and politically more cohesive. Leadership potential was completely lacking among them as the community's extreme poverty and the prevailing socio-cultural barriers never permitted it to seek education or employment outside the prescribed ones.

On the political side, the Congress, of course, passed a resolution in the year 1917 to the effect that all disabilities imposed by custom upon the depressed classes must be removed. The Act of 1919 recognised, for the first time, the existence of the depressed classes as a "political entity" to be given due recognition in any of the future reforms.

But, the depressed classes' fight for separate electorate, though indicative of their political awakening could not make much headway due to a number of socio-political conditions then prevalent in the country. The Southborough Committee of 1918-19, which was to advise on measures to secure representation of "minorities, of special interest or of backward classes" considered that "in no case do we find it possible to provide an electorate on any satisfactory system of franchise" (Report of the Southborough Committee). It, therefore, recommended nomination of depressed classes representatives for each Provincial Council. The Committee also considered a system where the number of Brahmins selected to the Legislative Councils would be limited and also where the non-Brahmins are given reserved seats in plural member constituencies.

It was under these circumstances that the depressed classes or the outcastes of India saw a ray of hope in the leadership of

Dr. B.R. Ambedkar, who is described as the champion of the ex-untouchables in India. Mahatma Jotirao Phule largely influenced him, among others, about his concern for the so-called outcastes of India. Being himself a Sudra, belonging to the Mahar caste group of Maharashtra, Ambedkar had undergone oppression that was part of the life of an 'untouchable' and described practice of 'untouchability' as "the cancer in the body politic of India" (Ambedkar : 1946). Among other measures towards its mitigation, he founded the Bahiskrat Hitakarni Sabha (B H Sabha) on July 20, 1924, the aims and objectives of which were to promote the educational, economic and cultural standards among the depressed classes. Through this Sabha, he presented a memorandum to the Simon Commission demanding joint electorates with reservation of seats for the depressed classes. The Sabha demanded 22 out of 140 seats in the Bombay Council and insisted upon the extending of the principle of election to them, as opposed to the principle of nomination. The Madras Central Adi-Dravida Mahajana Sabha and the Bombay Provincial Non-Brahmin Party supported the stand taken by the Sabha. The memorandum contended that political education was necessary and demanded a place in the cabinet for the depressed classes.

The Commission suggested 10 reserved seats for the depressed classes with joint electorates and 33 per cent of elected seats out of the 140 seats to Muslims with separate electorates for Bombay. Dr. B.R. Ambedkar reacted to this in his report by saying, "the safety of the depressed classes lay in being independent of the Government and the Congress. But political power cannot be a panacea for the ills of the depressed classes (Ambedkar : 1925).

Further, the Indian Statutory Commission, 1930, also favoured nominations, as separate electorates would lead to difficulties in defining the boundary. It held that such a demarcation would not only amount to stigmatising each individual voter but would further perpetuate it. Moreover, any attempt to segregate these sections would be against the very principle of helping them to rise up in the socio-economic scale.

Thus, the depressed classes were not considered for the allocation of seats on the basis of their full proportion. The fact that they suffered from many handicaps like poverty and lack of education stood as hindrances in securing substantial increase in political participation. The above Commissions, though they did not help in solving the problems of the depressed classes, at least marked the beginning of a new awakening among them. There was consensus of opinion among the members of the Indian Central Committee, 1929, and other such Commissions for the representation of the depressed classes in the legislature. But their only point of difference was on the issue of joint electorate vis-à-vis separate electorates. It was this controversy that later led to the battle of ideas between Gandhi and Ambedkar. Earlier to the Round Table Conference, the Indian Franchise Committee, 1932, went round the country and a number of Depressed Classes' Organisations submitted memoranda to the Committee, demanding political representation. This shows not only the growing political awareness among the ex-untouchables, but also their pitiable condition. The notes of dissent presented by the members recounted their degraded living conditions. Furthermore, the Provincial Franchise Committee also acted as a unifying force among the depressed classes, preparing them for political action.

At the Round Table Conference, Ambedkar submitted a scheme to the Minorities Sub-committee earmarking certain fundamental political safeguards towards the cultural, religious and economic rights of the depressed classes in the future Constitution of India. Among other things, it included conferring equal rights of citizenship, abolition of untouchability and discrimination in any form. It demanded adequate representation in the legislature and the right to elect their own men as their representatives by separate electorates and adequate representation of depressed classes in services. The controversy between Gandhi and Ambedkar started at this time during the second session of the Round Table Conference, which met in order to re-examine and amplify the reports prepared by a corresponding Committee. To Mahatma Gandhi, freedom and self-government in India was the basic issue, while Ambedkar held that the "emancipation of scheduled castes was first and freedom of the country next". Dr. Ambedkar placed the basic issue of depressed classes before the Committee. To quote him, "If we understand perfectly well before we start that the Committee will not merely concern itself with the question of Hindus and Mohammedans, of Hindus and Sikhs, but will also take upon itself the responsibility of considering the depressed classes, the Anglo-Indians and the Christians, I am perfectly willing to allow this adjournment resolution to be passed without any protest" (Ambedkar : 1925).

The Communal Award, which was announced on 17th August 1932, enabled the Mohammedan, the Anglo-Indian and the Sikh voters to have separate electorates. Referring to the depressed classes, it said that they would vote in a general constituency. But in view of the fact that there were not adequate numbers of members of depressed classes in the legislature, special seats were to be assigned to them. These seats had to be filled by elections from special constituencies in which members of only depressed classes would vote, apart from voting in a general constituency.

Mahatma Gandhi, to whom the Award was a shock, resolved to go on a fast unto death demanding abolition of separate electorates. Finally, a compromise was brought between the two leaders (Gandhi and Ambedkar) on 24th September, 1932, which is termed as the Poona Pact. The moderations of the depressed status accorded to the classes under a "reserved seats system" brought about a return to normal. The fact that Gandhi solely represented the Congress at the Conference and Ambedkar the depressed classes could be termed as the strategic points upon which such a compromise was reached. Both Ambedkar and the Congress leaders were, perhaps, concerned about the life of Gandhi.

While Gandhi's ceaseless activity for the welfare of the ex-untouchables was going on, many prominent caste-Hindu leaders were having second thoughts about the Poona Pact. The protests registered against its terms frankly admitted saying Gandhi as the cause for the Poona Pact. In course of time, numerous bills granting entry into temples were affected by legislative measures against them. Further, the elections of 1934 proved to be disastrous to the legislative measures for temple entry. Even after the elections, social reform measures were not taken up and a few years were spent in the discussion on Constitutional reforms. Assuming of office followed this by Provincial Congress Ministries in 1937, which was concerned about economic than social reforms.

In the years that followed, the nationalist leaders laid emphasis on political reforms while the country's social problems were accorded less importance and were considered as being only a reflection of the continued political subjugation of the country. With the attainment of freedom also came many problems like the issue of Indian Muslims along with a number of economic disabilities, which rocked the country.

The Constituent Assembly which met between 1946-50 directed much of its discussion on the question of defining the term 'Backward Classes', as the term 'Scheduled Castes" was already debated and was almost settled before independence (Galanter : 1978). It would be pertinent to note here that the term "Backward Classes" was in vogue since 1874[3] and it referred to all castes and communities and even to the Muslims. For example, the Miller Committee appointed by the Mysore Government continued with the definition of the term backward classes in the census of 1911, which considered all those communities having less than 5 per cent literacy in English as backward. The Other Backward Classes (OBCs) were also included in the list of the backward classes, along with the SCs and the STs in Art. 10 (3), which came to be later referred to as Art. 16 (4). In his speech, Dr. Ambedkar however stated that "the authority for determining backwardness rests with the respective state governments". "A backward community is a community which is backward in the opinion of the Government" stated Dr. Ambedkar (Constituent Assembly Debates 1948, November 30, Vol. VII, p. 702). But the later developments indicate that the matter was not as clear as the phrase suggested. As T.T.Krishnamachari remarked, it came to be "a paradise for lawyers" (Constituent Assembly Debates 1948, November 30, Vol. VII, p. 699).

What is to be stressed here is that even before the Constitution came into effect, the term Backward Classes was in vogue in many states. Several states had employed such categories and they further expanded the list after obtaining constitutional sanctions.

The Constitution came into effect from 1950 and provided several concessions to the SCs, the STs and the OBCs. In the post-Constitution era, two problems emerged concerning the policy of reservations. The first controversy revolved around the backward classes, while the second problem was centred on the desirability of providing educational preferences to them.[4]

According to Article 29(2), "no discrimination should be made on grounds of religion, race, caste, language or any of them in the matter of admission of students to educational institutions maintained or aided by the state". Similarly, Article 15(1) and 15(2) prohibit discrimination "on grounds of religion, race, caste, sex, and place of birth or any of them". The same article through Clause (4) confers powers on the state to make "special provisions for the SCs and the STs". In fact, Clause (4) of Article 15 was introduced as a result of the Supreme Court judgment in *State of Madras* Vs *Champakam Dorairajan* case.

It is interesting to note here that while the Constituent Assembly provided for reservation of seats in Government service for the backward classes, no such provision was made with reference to their educational benefits in Article 29. The Constitutional Order, 1950 was challenged in the Madras High Court with respect to reservation in educational institutions in the Champakam Dorairajan case and was struck down.

When the matter was taken to the Supreme Court, it was again struck down on grounds that there was no Clause in Article 29 and Article 15, like Clause 4 of Article 16, reserving seats in educational institutions for the backward classes. The Supreme Court shook the foundation of reservation system prevailing in South India when it struck down the Order of 1950 upholding the decision of the Madras High Court and barred all preferential treatment outside the area of government employment. This and the decision of the Supreme Court in *Venkataramana* Vs. *the State of Madras* necessitated the amendment of the Constitution in the year 1951 when Clause 4 was added to Article 15. Speaking of this, Dr. Ambedkar declared that the word "class meant a group of castes and the backward classes were nothing but a collection of certain castes" (KBCC Report : 1975: 109). The Supreme Court in 1951 held that the concept of "Backward Classes" included, in its purview, the Harijans (SCs) and Backward Hindu Communities (KBCC Report : 1975). Many members expressed concern about the possible misuse or misinterpretation of the policy of Protective

Discrimination. The Prime Minister, Nehru, reacting to the demand for inclusion of the term "economically" in the Article, stated that the special treatment given through Constitutional Reforms should be directed towards solving social inequalities of certain castes and communities, as they seemed to "unduly compound the differences" (Constituent Assembly Debates : 1948, Vol. XII-XIII, Part II).

In the analysis of the history of reservation policy in India, it is to be noted that the fifties marked the beginning of a new approach to the problem of backwardness at both central and state levels. The Government of India appointed the Backward Classes Commission under the Chairmanship of Kaka Saheb Kalelkar, in order to suggest the criteria for categorising the communities other than the SCs and STs, to be determined as socially and educationally backward.[5] The Commission gave its recommendations in the year 1955 and listed 2,399 castes as backward keeping caste as the criterion. These communities were declared eligible to avail the benefits on par with the SCs and the STs. But, five years later, in 1961, the government disapproved of the Commission's recommendations and the state governments were asked to adopt the criterion of income than caste.

Since the fifties, many state governments have set up Backward Classes Commissions under Article 340 (1) to identify the areas of backwardness and prepare lists of eligible communities and caste groups in their respective provinces.[6] These Commissions have considered caste as the criterion of backwardness. The reorganisation and formation of linguistic states on November 1, 1956 presented a set of new socio-cultural problems concerning the nature and composition of caste groups. These developments on the social plane coupled with certain drastic economic problems and political drawbacks have led to a different form of social hierarchisation in India. In other words, caste has undergone considerable structural and functional modifications in modern India. While the pre-independence era marked the increasing and enthusiastic process of mobilisation by different caste groups at the lower levels of the hierarchy, it appears, this process has very much continued in the present times, with a shift in its emphasis.

HISTORY OF RESERVATIONS IN KARNATAKA

Any study of the process of mobilisation in Karnataka should take into consideration the social, religious and political factors, which constitute the important stages in its historical development. South India, of which Karnataka is a part, exhibits many features that are markedly different from that of North India. This is generally attributed to the impact of foreign invasion and the consequent clash of cultures, beginning with the "first significant process of interaction (that) took place between the northern Aryan and southern Dravidian cultures" (Hettne : 1978: 27). This has resulted in a more complex social organisation in the south than in the north.[7] Apart from its orthodox nature, South India is also characterised by a very rigid social structure where traditionally Brahmins enjoy a high social and ritual status. Historians contend that this 'closed' nature of Hindu Society with its rigid hierarchical organisation was further intensified by the invasion of Muslims. On the eve of British rule, India, especially South India, was characterised by a highly ritualistic social order where the Brahmins were at the apex of the hierarchy and the Hindu kings upheld the institution with their political power.

The evils of such a system were many. Supremacy of Brahmins was, however, the common ground, which, in a way, contributed for a number of protest movements from time to time by individuals and groups. This was an all-India phenomenon, and in the south such expression of protest and reform developed in the form of the "Bhakti Movement", which further diversified into the Vaishnava and the Shaiva Movements culminating finally in the emergence of certain sects. In the 12th century, Basava preached his social and moral philosophies upholding social equality and the importance of duty, the Veerashaiva or the Lingayat cult being an offshoot of this movement (Parvathamma : 1972).

The Veerashaiva or "Lingayat philosophy" is considered to be the first social movement, which was able to develop a "counterculture" to "Orthodox Brahminical Hinduism" (Hettne and Tamm : 1979). But the movement resulted in the creation of a caste group, the Lingayats, who were able, in course of time, to establish themselves as a dominant caste in the northern parts of the state. Dushkin considers this movement as the first and a major landmark in the history of social movements in Karnataka (Dushkin : 1974).

The advantages of British rule, mainly education and representation in government employment were being increasingly availed of by the Brahmin community all-over India, a fact which could be attributed to their socio-cultural position in the hierarchy. The process was more conspicuous in the south where the Brahmins "as the priestly caste, was more elevated" (Subramaniam : 1969). While Brahmin dominance was a common feature in the South, it was more striking in the Madras Presidency, where they were distinguished as a remarkable group owing to their scholarship in the field of education (Irschick : 1969).

The British are held responsible not only for initiating a process of "Westernization" but also a corresponding process of "Sanskritization" through which the castes in the lower rungs of the hierarchy aspired to move up the ladder by adopting the upper caste lifestyle (Srinivas : 1966). In other words, the introduction of modern education and secular jobs stirred up a process of caste mobility. But this mobility was confined to only a few classes. While the lower caste groups like ex-untouchables were unable to follow up the process on account of their utmost poverty and social backwardness, the twin processes of Westernisation and Sanskritisation attracted the intermediate groups, those immediately below the Brahmins, but above the ex-untouchables. In most areas, these groups, which called themselves non-Brahmins, enjoyed considerable economic and political power in rural areas, constituting the landed gentry. Despite this, the process of Westernisation had created a wide cultural, social and economic disparity between the Brahmins and the non-Brahmins. Thus, the non-Brahmins discovered that to catch up with the Brahmins, mere Sanskritisation was not enough. In their claim for higher status, both political and economic, they became more determined to obtain Western education and thereby become eligible for the benefits it would provide.[8]

As could be concluded from the above, the predominance of Brahmins in higher education and government professions as also the existence of a wide gulf between them and the non-Brahmins — all contributed towards the development of a backward classes movement in the state. The cultural and intellectual position of Madras in South India placed it at a superior level compared to other areas. Consequently, educated and politically keen interest groups looked for leadership to emerge from Madras. Thus, Madras became the centre for the BCM as Bombay represented Western India (Omvedt : 1976). In other words, the BCMs in different parts of the country were not completely autonomous and the leadership pattern, though constituted by different caste representatives (generally from the dominant communities of the region), was similar in its class characteristics. The leaders were, generally, in contact with one another making the movement possess certain common traits in its origin, growth and effect. This process of integration was due to the "composite character" of Madras Presidency, which trained young, educated non-Brahmin leaders who migrated to other regions like Karnataka and Andhra to sow the seeds of the new ideology in these places. Although the center for the movement was Madras, there were many sub-centres like Madurai, Chidambaram, Bangalore, Tothapur and Poona (Srinivas : 1966).

The non-Brahmin movement in Mysore[9] made its beginning around the latter half of the 19th century after the Princely Government was restored in 1881 (Hettne and Tamm : 1974: 45-65). Prior to this, many upheavals and tensions marked the political scene in Mysore. From 11th century onwards, when large parts of north India were increasingly dominated by Muslim rulers, the Vijayanagar Empire in the South stood as a great hindrance to the conquests of Muslims to expand their kingdom. Karnataka came under this protection given by the Vijayanagar kings who acted as protectors of Hinduism. Its administrative decentralisation process facilitated the emergence of a number of petty kingdoms all along its borders. The Princely State of Mysore was one such "little kingdom". After the disintegration of Vijayanagar Empire during the 17th century, Mysore came to be ruled by the "Wodeyars" as an autonomous unit.

Although Muslim rule was again established in Mysore in 1761, due to continued external threat coupled with the lack of internal administrative stability, its four-decade long rule was put to an end in the Mysore War of 1779, when the deposed royal family devised a treaty with the company officials. Though this marked the end of Muslim rule, it resulted in the beginning of a long rule by British over Mysore. Restoration of political power to the Wodeyars was not without problems. British help and approval were very much needed to protect themselves against the powerful local enemies (Manor : 1977). This fact could be clearly understood by analysing the nature of caste network in Mysore during this period.

Unlike other Princely governments, the Wodeyars lacked any acquaintance with the local, powerful, dominant communities (the Lingayats and the Vokkaligas) that controlled most of the landed property. The minority position of the Arasus coupled with differences in economic and religious matters (as they followed occupations, which were different from those followed by the Lingayats and Vokkaligas) was never conducive to the development of any cordial relations between them and the locally dominant groups. In other words, in the absence of any strong kinship or caste ties with the local landlords, the Arasus encouraged an attitude of liberation towards local administrative units, in order to keep them happy and undisturbed which would, in turn, facilitate smooth administration.

Such internal insecurity resulted in keeping the imperial power as the principal source of legitimacy for the Mysore government. Further, obtaining British favour was made easy by the policies of the British Commissioner and an administrative structure based on the Bombay and Madras models.

During the last half of the 19th century, the social structure of Princely Mysore consisted of a hierarchical order, which was more or less common to other parts of India. The social hierarchy included the Brahmins, the Kshatriyas, the intermediate groups and the low castes or the ex-untouchables. The intermediate castes consisted of, predominantly, two castes, viz., the Lingayats and the Vokkaligas. Besides these, there were a number of lower-middle caste groups, generally referred to as the "service communities" or "village functionaries" (Srinivas : 1960). Apart from these, there were the two non-Hindu groups of the Muslims and the Christians, of whom the former were a numerical majority, perhaps, owing to the rule by Muslim kings for a long time in the past. They were frustrated as they had lost their political power with the fall of those kings - Hyder and Tippu, which explained their active participation in the non-Brahmin movement in its early phases.

One of the noteworthy developments that is very much a part of caste mobilisation but occurring prior to the non-Brahmin movement in Mysore, was the existence of internal factions even amongst the broader category of Brahmins. Though it is common to speak of inter-caste rivalries in a highly unequal society like India, the importance of class differences, which co-exist, cannot be underestimated. It is also difficult to identify a social movement only from a single standpoint, be it communal or any other; as such movements generally develop over a period of time and tend to be caused by a number of reasons. In other words, movements may have a dominant factor as the prime cause, but may well be made up of many other sub-factors.

The sub-divisions among the broader category of Brahmins into the Srivaishnavas (Iyengars), Smarthas and Madhvas, each with many sub and sub-castes, came to assume less importance in the wake of the non-Brahmin movement. But the factions amongst these sub castes became important when Dewan's rule was started in Princely Mysore in 1881. Many Dewans were "imported" from the State of Madras as it produced a group of highly educated and sophisticated young Brahmins who benefited from the process of Westernisation. These Brahmins (or the Madrasis) stood in contrast to the Mysore Brahmins whose position was only 'secondary' compared to their 'Madrasi' counterparts. The selection and appointment of these Brahmins as Dewans was also indicative of the latter's increased involvement in the administration of the state. Probably, the royal family of Mysore also (belonging as it did to a 'minority'[10] caste group) favoured imported Dewans. These 'imported'

Brahmins from Madras helped the British to establish a "collective elite" in Mysore also, which facilitated administration and policy-making (Hettne and Tamm : 1974: 72-73). The Hebbar Iyengars, a sub-caste of Iyengars, who had hitherto held high position in the administration, were thus relegated to the back when selection was made of Rangacharlu, a Madrasi, as the first Dewan of the Princely State of Mysore.

The rift between the two groups was particularly high during Rangacharlu's Dewanship. It went on for about 30 years. Hettne quotes Gustafson as emphasizing that the "lines of demarcation were not clear" (Hettne and Tamm : 1974: 73). A few conservative, retired European officials, who represented Sir Mark Cubbon's regime, supported it. The conflict was also affected and generated by the media of newspapers, which had just begun to make their appearance in Mysore. While the *Bangalore Spectator* represented the government, the Hebbar Iyengars controlled the *Karnataka Prakashika*. There was also another opposition paper, viz., the *Bangalore Examiner* (Hettne and Tamm : 1974:73).

The struggle between the "Madrasis" and "Mysoreans" gained added momentum when the choice for the next Dewan fell on Sir K. Sheshadri Iyer, also a Madrasi and a prodigy of Rangacharlu. But the protest was not restricted to only the Hebbar Iyengars, but was led by a new force consisting of largely, non-Iyengar Mysore Brahmins. The fact that the two groups (Iyengars and non-Iyengars) had no "grass-root support" led to the conclusion that the conflict was only "a struggle within the power-centre (Hettne and Tamm : 1974: 74). Such a tendency continued till 1910 after which year, the Brahmin non-Brahmin controversy lost interest in the conflict between "Mysoreans and Madrasis" when confronted with the more pressing problem of non-Brahmin competition.

The Lingayat and Vokkaliga communities, which took a

leading part in the non-Brahmin movement in Mysore, are termed the 'dominant' communities of the state (Srinivas : 1959). Their economic and political position in rural areas, coupled with their numerical strength, constituted an important factor in contributing to their dominance. But the large percentage of Brahmins in government service and their success in the field of education caused much jealousy and competitive spirit among these dominant groups. With the spread of "Westernization" and the gradual changes it led to in princely Mysore, a few urban-based, elitist families from these sections (who, invariably, were economically and politically well-off) could also afford to achieve political awareness on account of their high education and cultural standards. Being influenced, and to some extent led by, the advancement of the non-Brahmin movement in Madras, these men began to organise a small circle of activists challenging Brahminical dominance and demanded representation in government service.[11] They even established organisations based on caste to voice their demands. These came to be known as the "Mysore Lingayat Education Fund Association" (MLEFA) and the "Vokkaligara Sangha" established in Bangalore in the years 1905 and 1906 respectively (Dushkin : 1974 and Manor : 1977). As noted by Dr. D.V. Guṇdappa, the formation of the Vokkaligara Sangha was generously helped by the then Dewan V.P. Madhava Rao, who belonged to the group of Madrasi Brahmins (Gundappa : 1971).[12] These associations devoted much of their activities and efforts to the advancement of the educational level of their caste (people). But their work was limited to the cultural gap that generally existed between the state (urban) and the local (rural) arenas, which kept the rural masses ignorant.

Thus, the membership of the associations was limited to a few urban, educated groups among them, who more or less failed to attract the rural uneducated kinfolk. These leaders also never appear to have tried to develop any popularity among their rural, caste brethren and represented only a minority among the respective caste groups. However, they became politically more mobile by virtue of which they came to occupy the special Assembly seats granted to communal associations in 1913. This platform was further used by them to mobilise themselves at a greater pace. The leaders of these two associations claimed themselves to be the representatives of the total Lingayat and Vokkaliga populations and pleaded for reservations in government service and such other concessions to the said groups. Their efforts at caste mobilisation could be termed as more oriented towards earning status and power for themselves, than the general welfare of the groups they claimed to protect (Manor : 1977).[13]

This feeling of resentment towards the dominance of Brahmins in government service was prevalent by late 19th century, not only among the two dominant groups but the feeling was also shared by the British. This prompted them to encourage any protest against Brahminical supremacy and any demand for change in the existing system. The British were actuated more by the desire to keep the people divided than by the desire to help the Lingayats and the Vokkaligas. Apart from the Brahmins, such a development is reported to have been propagated by the brother and uncle of the Maharaja, ruling at that time (Gundappa : 1971).

It was under such circumstances that a real beginning was made of the non-Brahmin movement in Karnataka through Dr. C.R. Reddy, a non-Brahmin leader from Madras who came to Mysore in 1909 as a Professor in a city college. His high position, insight and dynamism acted as connecting factors between him and the royal household (which had been hitherto inaccessible to the Mysore non-Brahmins) as well as the Vokkaliga and the Lingayat leaders. All shared a common sentiment of anti-Brahminism, which resulted in the genesis of Mysore's first formal political association, "The Praja Mithra Mandali.[14]

The Praja Mithra Mandali held many conferences during 1917 and led a campaign to secure special provisions for the non-Brahmins. In the following year a delegation comprising important Lingayat and Vokkaliga leaders met the Maharaja and presented a memorandum to him. In response to it, the Maharaja appointed a Committee in August 1918, to inquire into the problem of communal representation with the British Chief Justice of the Chief Court of Mysore, Sir Leslie F. Miller, as its Chairman. The official name of the Committee was "Committee Appointed to Consider Steps Necessary for the Adequate Representation of Backward Communities in the Public Services (Report of the Miller Committee : 1919).

The "Miller Committee", as it came to be known, presented its report in 1919, which consisted of reservations for non-Brahmins in educational institutions and government service. It recommended that, within seven years, the non-Brahmins should hold at least 50 per cent of higher appointments and two-thirds of lower jobs.[15] It "significantly" fixed literacy in English education as the criterion of backwardness (Dushkin : 1974). But the report did not attempt to distinguish between the different backward communities. The Order was modified subsequently after two years in 1921 and the Government Order of 1921 implemented the modified version of the Committee's recommendations.

Both the setting up of the Miller Committee and its Report came to face a very strong reaction from the Brahmin administrators in the government. The protest was so strong that the Report could not be released for nearly two years after its submission to the government. The contention of the Brahmins was that they were not against the policy of reservations, which could help in improving the general living condition of the non-Brahmins, and their only point of argument was that there should be efficiency in Government service.

The Government Order on the Miller Committee Report was no doubt passed in May 1921, with a delay of two years. But again due to severe opposition to it by the Brahmin members of the Representative Assembly, to the extent of even organised boycott, the subject could not be discussed in its June session. However, in the October meeting, the issue was discussed and debated "extensively". The Brahmin members vehemently criticised the move on the part of the government in instituting such a Commission. K. T. Seshaiya, R. Gopalaswami Iyer and K. Venkataswamaiya argued that nowhere in history was "Government service held to be a representative institution to be recruited on a communal basis". They also argued that there was "demand" and the Brahmins "furnished" the supply. They believed that "professions must be distributed among people", and that "if all classes of people take up the same avocation, the country will not prosper". The opposition to the reservation policy reached its climax with the resignation of Sir M.Visvesvaraya from the office of Dewanship (Gundappa : 1971, Rao : 1973, Hettne : 1978, Manor : 1977 and Dushkin : 1974).[15]

What was the reaction of the non-Brahmins to the Miller Committee Report? They were all tremendously happy and welcomed it with considerable applause and gratitude. But this rejoicing was not without certain resentment too. Since the different non-Brahmin groups were treated by the Committee as a single unitary group (as non-Brahmins), the reaction of the non-Brahmins to it was on different lines. While the caste Hindus were happy at the outset, the Lingayats aired their displeasure in a subtle way at having been grouped along with the Shudras, but sought to mobilise themselves through seeking entry into institutions of Sanskritic learning (Archives of the MLEFA, Bangalore).

The Muslims never treated their inclusion in the non-Brahmin category as gainful and pleaded for separate identity "to maintain good relations with all communities and to secure proper share as before" (Address by the Anjuman-E-Mahadavia Dairat-Ul-Islam, a Muslim association).[16]

The Christians asserted their strong faith and dependence upon the government for their development - educationally and otherwise. They also hoped for further improvements in the Government Order (Address by the Indian Christian Association).[17]

The depressed classes (or the Harijans[18]) who included the Harijans and other lower castes felt that the Government Order lacked any special provisions for them and feared that the other backward classes might grab all the opportunities (Address by the Adi-Dravida Mahajana Sangham).[19] This statement by the depressed classes, who came very much under the banner "non-Brahmins" (in their ideology) is noteworthy for its socio-political implications.

The non-Brahmin movement of the post-Miller Committee days is remarkably different from that of its predecessor in the late 19th and early 20th centuries. Many changes at the political level of both the states and the nation during the 1920s gave a new turn to the Government in Mysore. The resignation of Sir M.Visvesvaraya was followed by the appointment of Sardar M.Kantharaje Urs (the uncle of the then Maharaja) as the Dewan, under whom the non-Brahmins felt more secure to obtain the benefits that the Miller Committee provided them (Gundappa : 1971).

When Urs resigned after a short term, owing to bad health, a Bengali-Brahmin, Sir Albion Banerjee was appointed in his place "in an effort to keep aloof from the Brahmin-non-Brahmin controversy" (Hettne and Tamm : 1974:71). The selection of Banerjee was made with strong political interests. Incidentally, it is rumoured that Banerjee opposed some of the policies of Sir M.Visvesvaraya, during the latter's Dewanship (Gundappa : 1971: 214).

Throughout these years, after the Committee's recommendations were implemented, those who benefited from the concession most were the more articulate sections among the urban-based Lingayats and the Vokkaligas, who constituted the kin of the leaders, and the leaders themselves. As could be expected, there were already signs of frustration and disunity amongst the non-Brahmins, notably among the two dominant communities. Such internal cleavages could be attributed to the very nature of the structuring of these groups (categories) which were heterogeneous in their composition.

Disintegration and internal factions amongst the non-Brahmins increased with the departure of their leader, Dr. C.R. Reddy, who was, to a large extent, able to maintain the cohesiveness of the group.

To the existing cleavages between the dominant groups of the Lingayats and the Vokkaligas was added another new conflict - that which developed between the non-Brahmin Hindus and the Muslims. In the year 1926, Sir Mirza Ismail became the Dewan of Mysore. Mirza also happened to be a close friend of Sir Abbas Khan, a Muslim leader of Bangalore. The latter was the "informal leader" of the Praja Mithra Mandali.[20] The non-Brahmin Hindus feared that the Muslims were getting more organised under Ismail's regime. The reluctance with which the latter welcomed the Miller Committee Report and also the subsequent inclusion of the Muslims in the backward category in 1927 further strengthened their fears. The Hindu-Muslim cleavages gained momentum especially after the Bangalore communal riots in 1928.[21] While it acted as a threat to the government being generated by the Brahmins to express their frustration towards the appointment of a few non-Brahmin and Muslim Dewans, the incident also shook the Muslim dominance of the movement.[22]

The Brahmins made no attempt to distinguish between the different backward communities. The Order was modified subsequently after two years in 1929 and the Government Order of 1929 implemented the modified version of the Committee's recommendations.

Whether the communal riots were spread by the Brahmins or not, they, nevertheless succeeded in creating a split in the non-Brahmin movement, which was already filled with internal cleavages. By 1928, the non-Brahmins had also felt disappointed by the rate of improvement caused by the Miller Committee Report, as the Brahmins still continued to dominate government service.

The tardy progress made by the depressed classes and even by the upper caste groups coming under the non-Brahmin category despite reservation may be attributed to one important lacuna in the reforms themselves. There seems to have been little emphasis on "educational reservations" in the Miller Committee Report. While the eagerness of the non-Brahmin leaders in stressing for job reservations is understandable owing to its immediate benefits (like socio-economic status) how an important area like education was not considered equally important causes concern.

Corresponding to all these new developments and the resultant changes in the non-Brahmin movement, there developed a team of new, young non-Brahmin leaders, who were mostly educated at Madras and thereby had gained acquaintance with the movement there. Instead of the ascriptive, traditional caste associations, these new leaders sought to gain administrative control through the electoral system. Being drawn from rural areas (unlike their predecessors who represented only major urban centres), these leaders were inspired by Gandhian ideals. Their familiarity with the rural areas facilitated them to gain popularity there. "The Assembly provided a framework within which these men could gather on a regular basis for the airing of grievances to the government." Its importance in the political history of Mysore lay in that it acted as a place where leaders from the scattered districts and taluk level political arenas could begin to establish a sense of participation in the state-wide arena of politics." These networks of connections provided ultimately "the basis for the challenge which was to bring down the princely government in 1947" (Manor :1977: 67).

A non-Brahmin conference (the first ever) was organised by the leaders in Bangalore in 1929. The following year a new non-Brahmin political party came to be established and was called the Praja Paksha. What interests us is the declaration by the new party that its membership was open to all communities including the Brahmins. While this new spirit was entirely for public consumption", "it indicates a clear departure from the older generation's, narrowly parochial style of politics" (Manor 1977: 67).

An important dimension of the activities of the new batch of non-Brahmin leaders was to draw themselves close to the rural masses. The opening of District Boards to which they became elected representatives was a novel move in this direction.

In course of time, the movement became less anti-Brahminic due to its greater identity with the national movement, especially after Mahatma Gandhi appeared on the scene of national leadership. The non-Brahmin political party the "Praja Paksha" had, by the mid-thirties, assumed a different outlook in the form of its emphasis on "greater democratization." "Distrust over the Government's intention towards popular representatives was crystallized in 1930 when... Sir Mirza Ismail publicly dismissed proposals for greater democratization" (Manor : 1977:71).

In an effort to "adopt a more active opposition role", the leaders of the Praja Paksha, under the leadership of Dr. K.C. Reddy (who was the first non-Brahmin leader of village origins), founded in January 1935 a new political party known as the People's Federation. Both the Praja Mitra Mandali and the Praja Paksha merged into the People's Federation, the new party.

However, the non-Brahmin leaders soon realised the need of the hour, which indicated a growing nationalist spirit. This also gave the Congress a strong base. More articulate among them, like Dr. K.C. Reddy and others, understood the significance of the Congress, i.e., the national movement, compared to the regional movement. The "Brahmins" (like Sri K.T. Bhashyam) also perceived it. These circumstances finally led to a merger between the People's Federation and the Congress in 1937.

It is to be remembered here that all through these years, the Harijans or the depressed classes had remained aloof from the process of mobilisation, owing to their socio-economic backwardness. The Christian and the Muslims were, however, reluctant to follow the non-Brahmin Hindus. The mass mobilisation process after 1930s and 40s, under the Congress, was a political force mainly including the Brahmins, the Lingayats, the Vokkaligas, along with the Kurubas and a few sections of the students and labour groups.

The internal cleavages of Princely Mysore intensified during the second phase of the non-Brahmin movement. One of the important reasons for this could be the preponderance of Vokkaliga leaders in the movement, some of whom represented the rural areas. The spirit of nationalism dominated over all other forces and the non-Brahmin movement lost its pace and almost degenerated. Its leaders became leaders in the national movement in Princely Mysore. However, this period witnessed the rise of a number of Vokkaliga leaders, who were to hold important positions in independent India. Concurrently, post-independence rule in Mysore started with a Vokkaliga as the first Chief Minister[23], who had been an active Congressman in the pre-independence days.

The Post-Independence Period

The process of caste mobilisation and the policy of reservations have continued in the post-independence era, being initiated in the year before 1947. The discussion so far made has highlighted the important stages and phases of these two developments in the pre-independence period.

The Constitution of India came into effect in January 1950, which declared equality and justice to all citizens, irrespective of the socio-cultural differences amongst them. It also guaranteed a number of facilities and concessions in the sphere of education, employment, political participation and economic security to the weaker sections.

Thus, history had created a divide. While earlier it was a fight to guarantee benefits, after 1950, it was a struggle to obtain them.

What follows is a brief analysis of the developments, in the socio-legal spheres, concerning mobilisation of caste/class lines in Karnataka which have emerged after the Constitution was promulgated.

The process of forming organisations and holding conferences, by the various caste groups, to secure the benefits of reservation had continued with greater vigour and enthusiasm after 1950. Apart from the keen fight to gain the fruits of reservation, the question of granting of Constitutional guarantees has led to a legal battle, ever since they were implemented. In 1950, the year the Constitution came into effect, the Government Order allotting seats in educational institutions was challenged in the Madras High Court, under Article 226, in the *Champakam Dorairajan Case.*

In Karnataka, as elsewhere, the policy of reservation to BCs in educational institutions and government service came to be challenged ever since the Constitution came into effect. Inspired by the Supreme Court's decision in the *Venkataramana Case* (AIR 1951, SC 229), which holds the communal Government Order void and illegal, the communal G. O. was challenged in the Mysore High Court in 1956 in the *Keshava Iyengar Case* (AIR 1956, Mysore). The petition held that several posts out of ten were given to the members of BCs. The court held that Clause (4) of Art.16 was an exception to Art.16 (2) and that reservation of posts to the Backward Classes could only be a small portion out of 10 seats. Further, the court justified the allotment of seats by saying that "it was only a small portion as they were given to different communities coming under the general Backward Classes category. Hence this should, in no way, be inconvenient to the members of these communities, who are well represented in services" (the KBCC Report, Vol. I, Part I, 1975, GoI).

This statement by the Mysore High Court was viewed by the only "well represented community, the Brahmins", as denying the fundamental right guaranteed to every citizen in Art.16 (1) and (2). They felt it necessary to act against such a Communal G.O. as they realised the consequences it could lead to (KBCC report, Vol. I, Part I, 1975, GoI).

It was during this time that the State Reorganisation took place in the year 1956, which brought together four parts of different states under the State of Mysore. These integrated parts (Hyderabad Karnataka, Bombay Karnataka, parts of Madras

Presidency and Coorg) represented differences in their backward classes' lists and the nature of reservation policy and categories of the backward classes.[24] Thus, it was felt necessary to bring uniform lists of backward classes, in Mysore after its (the State's) reorganisation.[25]

On account of such a heterogeneity in the nature of the backward classes' category, the Mysore Government brought out a G.O. in July 1958, which categorised all castes except the Brahmins and non-Hindu communities like the Christians and Muslims as backward classes. 57 per cent of jobs were reserved for the backward classes, in addition to the 15 per cent for the SCs and the STs. Only 25 per cent of jobs were left for open competition.

The Order was considered imperfect and was struck down when it was challenged in Writ Petitions 567, 572, 574 and 575 in the year 1959. The government again passed an order, which categorized even Baniyas and the Kayasthas along with Brahmins as non-Backward and all the others as backward classes. By another G.O. issued also in 1959, the Government divided the population of the State and made compartmental reservation in educational institutions and government employment in the form of allotting a certain percentage of seats to each one of these groups (67 per cent of seats in educational institutions and 57 per cent in services for the OBCs). But, the OBCs are a heterogenous category.

These two orders also came to be challenged in the Mysore High Court in *Ramakrishna Singh case* (AIR, 1960, Mysore). "After referring to Article 12, 338, 340, 154 and 162, the court held that the specification of backward classes by the President was not a condition precedent for the executive of a State who could specify the backward classes in the absence of Presidential specification. In regard to the mode of effecting percentage of seats to each one of the groups of backward classes, it 'abridged' the rights of the backward classes" (the KBCC Report, Vol I, Part I, 1975, GoI, p. 125).

Upon the decision of the Mysore High Court to strike down the two Government Orders of 1959, the Government appointed a committee known as "the Mysore Backward Classes Committee" in January 1960, under the Chairmanship of Dr. R. Nagan Gowda. The terms of reference of the Committee were "to find out the criteria to be adopted for determining the backward classes in the State and also to suggest to the Government how these criteria must be applied to determine the class of persons who should secure preference in respect of admission to technical institutions and appointments to government service" (the Mysore Backward Classes Committee Report, MBCC,1960).The Committee used literacy as the criterion for social backwardness and the number of students per thousand population in the last three years of high school as the criterion of educational backwardness.

Since the High Court held in 1959[26] "that the literacy test" was "the only possible test", the Committee adopted the extent of literacy in a particular caste or community as the basis for determining its backwardness, along with representation in services as the criteria. It also inflated the population figures basing on 1940 and 1950 censuses.

The Interim Report of the Nagan Gowda Committee (as the Mysore Backward Classes Committee came to be popularly known) was submitted in 1960 pending further investigation. On the basis of the Report, the government categorised, through issuing an Order, very few castes as backward and reserved a small percentage of seats in educational institutions to them (22 per cent), with an additional 15 per cent and 3 per cent to the SCs and STs respectively (the MBCC Report, 1960). This left 60 per cent of seats for open competition.

The Interim Report of the Nagan Gowda Committee was

also challenged in the Mysore High court in the *Partha Case* (AIR 1961, Mys 220 and 230). The attacks made in this case were similar to the ones made in the *Ramakrishna Singh Case,* but with less vigour (the KBCC Report 1975). The court in this case accepted the Committee's statements that the caste categories as backward had a student strength of lower the state average of 0.76. The court also held that the criterion of literacy was "not the only test". On the question of inflating the literacy figures, it said that such a move was "more rational and inflating of population figures as not utterly unreliable" (the KBCC Report, 1975).

The Mysore Government, in 1961, on the submission of the Final Report by the Nagan Gowda Committee, passed orders treating about 90 per cent of the total population as backward, inclusive of the SCs and STs. It reserved only 30 per cent of seats to the OBCs, against the Committee's recommendations for 50 per cent.

The Final Report of the Nagan Gowda Committee raised considerable controversy. Significantly, the Committee grouped the Lingayats, who had enjoyed the privilege of backwardness all these years, from the ones given by the Committee in support of the non-inclusion of Lingayat students in the backward list was that the number of Lingayats per thousand population in the three years of higher secondary education was slightly higher than the State average of 6.0.

This resulted in considerable protest from the Lingayats, including the political leaders belonging to the community. They also succeeded in bringing pressure upon the government to include the Lingayats also in the list of backward classes. A member of the Nagan Gowda Committee[27] even wrote one dissent note against the unjust treatment meted out to the Lingayats by not including them in the list of backward classes.

The government had to finally yield to the increased pressure and confer the status of backwardness on the Lingayats by an Order in 1962. It is notable here that it fixed the quota of reservations at a much lower level than that recommended by the committee. The Government Orders of both 1960 and 1961, which were based on the recommendations of the Nagan Gowda Committee, did not follow its suggestion for compartmental reservation for the "backward classes" and the "more backward classes" (but this was, however, overruled by the Order of 1962 which increased caste quota for the OBCs to 50 per cent).

The fact that the 'Mysore government continued to support the policy of caste quotas, despite strong judicial opposition, is indicative of the role played by the two dominant castes in the state'. This was confirmed by its Order of 1962, under Art.15 (4) reserving seats in the medical and engineering colleges in the state for the backward classes and the SCs and STs (28 per cent for BCs and 18 per cent for the SCs and the STs). Thus, a total of 68 per cent was reserved leaving only 32 per cent to the merit pool.

The validity of even this G. O. of 1962 was challenged by candidates who could not secure admission only by the reason of the G.O. Along with this, even the basis adopted in 1961 to specify the educationally and socially backward classes was also challenged in the *Balaji Case* in 1963 (AIR, 1963, SC 649).

The *Balaji Case* is regarded as the *locus classicus* in the sphere of reservation facilities to the backward classes (KBCC Report, Vol I, Part I, 1975). As noted above, the Nagan Gowda Committee made recommendations to the effect that 60 per cent of seats in engineering and medical colleges were reserved for the BCs, more BCs, the SCs and the STs. This left only 32 per cent to be available to the merit pool. The G.O. based on this scheme issued by the Mysore Government was challenged by candidates who had secured more marks than those admitted under the G. O. but had failed to get admission only by reason of the G.O.

The Court ruled that in relation to Hindu society, caste was a relevant test for determining backwardness, but this test could not be exclusive and had to be used in conjunction with some neutral or non-communal criteria such as poverty, occupation, residence, etc. Caste could only be an index of social backwardness and not conclusive evidence of such backwardness. Backward classes, it was ruled, could not be equated with backward castes. An important feature of the Supreme Court judgment in the *Balaji Case*, Justice Gajendra Gadakar speaking for the Court, was the Court's observation that the caste test could not apply to the Lingayats since they purported to be non-Hindus. The Court was also highly critical of the procedure adopted by the government in lowering the educational attainment of the Lingayats and raising the State average presumably, to show that the Lingayats were below the State average (*Balaji* Vs *State of Mysore*, AIR, 1963, SC 649, KBCC Report, Vol. I, Part-I, Chapter XVI, V. K. Natraj, Unpublished paper, 1981).

On the striking down of the G.O. in the *Balaji Case*, the Mysore government, purporting to go by the decision of the Supreme Court, issued yet another order, as a temporary measure. The Order further stated that the problem of determining the socially and educationally backward classes is a very complex one. It held further that an elaborate investigation and collection of data and examination of such data, which would inevitably involve considerable length of time, may be desirable.

The new order took family as a unit for purposes of Art. 15 (4) with its economic condition and occupation as determinants (Mysore Government Order, 1963). This G.O. was also challenged in the Mysore High Court in the *Viswanatha Case* (AIR, 1964, Mysore, 132). The Court advised the Mysore

Government that it was necessary to add tests of caste and residence.

The new order reserved 30 per cent of seats to the OBCs and to the SCs and STs. It considered, instead of castes, individuals belonging to certain kinds of occupations as cultivators, artisans, petty business and certain inferior occupations based on manual labour and earning less than Rs. 1,200 per annum, as being eligible for the benefit of reservation policy.

In other words, under the revised Order, a family whose income was less than Rs. 1,200 per annum and which pursued an occupation specified in the Order was considered as backward, irrespective of caste, religion or race. The scheme was upheld in *Chitralekha* Vs. *State of Mysore* (AIR, 1964, SC 1823). In this case, the Supreme Court repudiated its earlier stand (in *Viswanatha Case*) that caste and residence are necessary to be added to the tests of backwardness and allowed that caste might be omitted entirely if backwardness could be ascertained by other relevant criteria. The revised scheme of 1962 was, as stated earlier, intended to be a temporary measure,"...in spite of the observation of the Mysore High Court that the new scheme was a very imperfect one, that caste was a relevant, nay, an important criterion and that if the State government did not soon make an appropriate classification its bona fide should be questioned, the Government did not make any investigation and did not collect the data until 1972" (KBCC Report, Vol. I, Part I, p. 138).

The above account of the judicial battle on the issue of reservations is suggestive of the problems inherent in any policy of social equality, in a highly heterogeneous society. It is also indicative of the impact of the interplay of a number of political and cultural factors, on the policy of preferential treatment. In Karnataka, the question of reservation to the OBCs, specially, has been influenced by the structure of political rule over the decades since independence. This fact is also clear from the analysis of the history of backward classes' movement in the state that the two dominant castes of the Lingayats and the Vokkaligas have had a leading role to play all through the movement cannot be disputed. The non-Brahmin movement of Princely Mysore was, invariably, controlled and led by the representatives of these communities. History repeated itself, at least during the fifties and the sixties, when the State was governed by Vokkaligas and Lingayat chief ministers. The Lingayats, who gained in number after the state's reorganisation in the year 1956, have been an important group politically and economically.

A breakthrough was made into the 'monopoly' of the dominant castes over political power when the state came to be ruled by a Ministry headed by a leader from one of the minority groups, the Arasus. The significance of this Ministry, under the Chief Ministership of late Sri D. Devraj Urs, lay in the fact that it was composed of members from a few, hitherto non-represented, backward classes like the Kurubas, Edigas, the Besthas and a few others, apart from the SCs (ex-untouchables) and Muslims.

Although the Urs Ministry did not, and could not, contain many leaders from the minority and backward groups, it is at least certain that the regime and the political transformation it resulted succeeded in creating certain different channels of caste mobilisation.

These burning issues of reservation were further intensified owing to the reformative measures undertaken by the Devraj Urs Ministry. In 1972, the Karnataka Backward Classes Commission was appointed by the State Government to probe into the problems of the backward classes, to determine the criteria for backwardness and to prepare lists of such classes (Mysore Government Order, 1972).

The commission consisted of, apart from its Chairman, late Sri L.G. Havanur, six members who themselves represented various backward and minority communities.[28] It emphatically stated that "we have ignored the principle of caste, the principle of high and low, in deciding social backwardness." Instead, the Commission applied "multiple tests such as economic condition poverty and isolation, social enforcement and reinforcement of that poverty and isolation and the development of cultural traits that are adaptive to poverty and exclusion" (Galanter : 1984: 240). Thus it determined the backwardness of people "on criteria other than caste." In support of this, the Report says that some communities despite their comparatively high ritual status (like the Arasus who are a section of the Kshatriya class and the Satanis and the Ambalavasis who are temple priests and temple managers respectively, have been classified as backward. Similarly, a few others despite their low ritual status (like the Bhunts and some sections of the Lingayats) "who being Shudras, and therefore low in the conventional sense of the term" were excluded by the Commission for being economically and educationally advanced (KBCC Report, Vol.I, Part I, pp. 307-308). Repudiating the view that backward classes should be selected on the basis of income and occupation, the KBCC followed the twin criteria of caste and economic backwardness.

The KBCC is held by scholars in the field as 'the most ambitious attempt to characterize social backwardness', under the Chairmanship of L. G. Havanur, a committed and scholarly student of the subject (Galanter : 1984: 239). The Commission considered the following factors as criteria for backwardness:

1. Residence (in rural, isolated and segregated areas).
2. Economic condition in terms of land ownership and other forms of property.
3. Occupation, in terms of being very unremunerative, unclean or inferior and therefore low.

4. Caste prejudice (its extent) entertained by people by advanced castes and communities.
5. Low status or inferiority associated with their caste placing restrictions on access to places of cultural training or to have religious and secular education.
6. Segregation from advanced communities caused by social taboos against inter-dining and inter-marriages and against similar opportunities on association.
7. Prevention from enjoying status in society due to age-old social customs.
8. (Consequent) apathy for education (KBCC Report, Vol. I, Part I, 1975).

Further the Commission held caste and class as synonymous terms. It repudiated the "Balaji-Chitralekha" approach and concluded that it was less discriminatory. It rejected "the vested interests of the so-called merited, to have their due share in all walks of life" (KBCC Report, 1975, Chairman's covering letter). It further held that "Differential treatment of backward classes alone can give equality of opportunities to all. Equality of opportunities in absolute terms for unequal castes means aggravation of inequality" (*Ibid.*, p. v).

A massive survey of castes, tribes and communal groups in Karnataka was conducted by the Havanur Commission based on which a list of castes, communities and tribal groups was prepared for purposes of reservations. The Commission took into consideration SSLC as the level of education for measuring educational backwardness. The number of students in a community passing the SSLC examination in the year 1972 was compared with the average number of students passing per thousand of the state's population. Those communities falling below the State average but with more than 50 per cent of the state average were separately categorised as Backward Castes and

Backward Tribes. The Report clarified that though "the Mysore High Court in *Viswanatha Case* (AIR 1964, Mysore,132) said that the majority population in our state was backward, we are constrained to confine the population of the OBCs to only 44.52 per cent because of the application of the educational tests suggested by the judiciary, (KBCC Report, Vol. I, part I, pp 314-316).

The Commission reserved 32 per cent of seats in Government service in favour of the listed castes and tribes in addition to what was already reserved for the SCs and STs. On the basis of the surveys and tests that it conducted, the Commission did not include the Brahmins, Bhunts, Vaisyas, Kshatriyas, Jains and Lingayats into any one of the backward classes.

Subsequently, the High Court of Karnataka ordered the deletion of the Arasu caste for purposes of both Arts. 15 (4) and 16 (4) of the Constitution from the list of backward communities. A few other communities like the Devadigas, the Ganigas, Rajputs, and Satanis were also deleted from the lists under Art. 16 (4).

Thus, the Havanur Commission may be rightly credited as having followed *Balaji* faithfully by limiting reservation to only 50 per cent. The Report felt that the Supreme Court erred in the *Chitralekha Case* by trying to interpret *Balaji* (KBCC Report, Vol.I Part I, p.144). However, the reservation of 50 per cent recommended by the Commission came to be implemented by the government only for a short period. It had to, presumably, yield to political pressure resulting in the expansion of the lists with another 8 per cent. Thus, a total of 40 per cent of seats were reserved in favour of the OBCs. In other words, the government introduced the category of the "Special Group" which consisted of those persons belonging to the self-employed, artisan and other occupational categories, having an income of not more than Rs. 4,800 per year. A criterion of Rs. 8,000 was imposed on the BCs. In the subsequent Orders, the percentage of reservation earmarked for the Special Groups was also raised. The income limit has been raised to Rs.10,000. By February 1977, the government had issued Orders providing for the following reservation:

Open Competition	42 per cent
Backward Communities	20 per cent
Backward Castes	10 per cent
Backward Tribes	5 per cent
Special Groups	5 per cent
SCs and STs	18 per cent

Furthermore, the Muslims were conferred the status of a backward community, shifting from their earlier classification under the "Special Group".

The significance of the KBCC lies in the fact that it categorised the Lingayats, for the first time, as a forward group, along with the Brahmins, the Bhunts, the Vaishyas and a few others. The conferring of backward status to the Vokkaligas, a dominant caste (and a rival of the Lingayats) has added a touch of competitive jealousy to the latter's demand for a backward tag.

The details of the Lingayats' attempts at caste mobilisation are covered under the fourth chapter as well as at various contexts in the book. The Havanur Report, although not the first report on the BCs in the State, stirred up a series of mobilisational movements by different caste, tribal and religious groups in Karnataka. It was not just a social measure towards the weaker sections but was allied with many political processes that followed. That it had turned many communities at loggerheads with each others in its wake is, no doubt, true. Apart from providing the backward classes with the benefit of reservation, the Commission has often been accused of having accelerated the process of politicisation by the castes through such interest groups as caste associations. Along with these, even the incidence of conflicts and tensions, was also noticeably high in the years following its recommendations. "The Lingayat community found itself divided on the issue of the reservation scheme based on the Havanur Commission Report. Also on this issue an alliance of the Vokkaligas with the Lingayats could not take place as the two groups found themselves in different camps" (of the backward and forward respectively) (KBCC Report, 1980, Vols. III to VII, Part II).

The Lingayats, particularly a section of the urban Lingayats, were disturbed and angered by the Havanur Report and the subsequent G.O.s based on it. Demonstrations were held in different cities of Karnataka, protesting against the Report. They were carried out under the aegis of their caste association, viz., the Akila Bharatha Veerasaiva Mahasabha. The President of the Mahasabha, late, Sri J. B. Mallaradhya, a retired IAS officer, led crusades against the Order (Mallaradhya : 1979b and Chennabasappa : 1979). The protests came to assume the form of a movement in the years that followed. A conference of all castes, adversely affected by the Report, was held at Bangalore, during July 1979. Many Lingayat legislators reportedly held meetings on the Report and the resultant G.O.s, certain individuals and institutions even questioned the Constitutional validity of the lists of the backward classes and the matter was taken to the Supreme Court in 1979.

The agitation by the Lingayats and their opposition to the Havanur Report also came to be challenged through counter agitations, meetings and discussions held in Bangalore and Mysore, among other places, highlighting the merits and the Constitutional righteousness of the Report. When an article appeared in Indian Express (March 1, 1979), by a Toronto-based Indian Social Anthropologist, criticizing the methodology of the Havanur Survey, it invited "counter-critiques by a section of scholars—social scientists and journalists."

Apart from these incidents of conflicts and tensions, another chief dimension of the implementation of the Havanur Commission Report's recommendations was the marked increase that it invoked in the sphere of mobilisation by all castes and communities alike. What is most commonly expressed in the form of demands by a number of caste-tribal and religious groups, was for 'more backward status'. Thus, the demand is for a reclassification of the backward classes leading to a revision in the list.

The above process, which was in a way "initiated during Devraj Urs' regime, found greater expression and met with notable success during Gundu Rao's Chief Ministership which succeeded Urs." Success refers to the encouragement given by this government for sectarian interests to mobilise themselves. The years between 1990s were characterised by an intense sectarian activity by a number of caste groups - upper, middle and lower alike. The number of caste-based associations and caste-sponsored educational institutions increased sharply during this period. What was constantly and repeatedly emphasized by community after community in the conferences and meetings was the need to extend and confer their present status with that of greater backwardness.

These multifarious mobilisation activities were given an added impetus when the Janata Government, that succeeded the Congress for the first time in the state, heeded to the demand for a thorough review of the Havanur Commission Report. It appointed on 8th April 1983, a new BCC, the fourth of its kind and the third Commission to be set up after the reorganisation of the state. Along with the BCC, the Ramakrishna Hegde government also appointed a Minorities Commission, headed by R. H. Goodwala, a senior advocate from Hubli.

The setting up of this new Commission was led by the incidents following the above process of demand for backwardness by almost all comunities in the state. The G.O. based on the Havanur Report was challenged in the Supreme

Court (K. C. Vasant Kumar and others in Writ Petition Nos. 1297-98 and 1407/79 and SLP (Civil) No. 6656/79 and SLP 9854/79). This petition was inspired by the Lingayats led by the late Sri J. B. Mallaradhya. However, after the case had been heard, the Counsel for the State represented that the State Government proposed to appoint a Commission to look into the whole question.

It may be noted that at this time, elections to the Karnataka Assembly were expected to be announced any time. It is at least plausible that the government wanted to offer some hope to those who were vituperating against the Havanur Report. This may be interpreted as yet another attempt made by the Gundu Rao government to woo some sections at least of the Lingayats. It is also interesting to know that the Janata Government which took office in January 1983 did not request the Supreme Court, taking into consideration the changing circumstances, to pronounce judgment on the Writ Petitions. On the contrary, the government appointed the Second Backward Classes Commission.

The Karnataka Second Backward Classes Commission (hereafter KSBCC) was headed by a retired judicial officer, Sri T. Venkataswamy. Popularly known as the Venkataswamy Commission, this new Commission was constituted under the Commission of Enquiry Act, 1952. The announcement of a move to appoint a Second BCC to "review inter alia reservation of seats in professional colleges, institutions of higher learning and representation in Government service", was made by the then Chief Minister, late Sri Ramakrishna Hegde in February 1983. He had also stated that the "Cabinet decision to set up the Commission as sequence to the commitment given by the previous government (the Gundu Rao Government)", to the Supreme Court in a case filed by the All India Veerashaiva Maha Sabha, challenging reservation for weaker sections based on the

Havanur Commission's recommendations. When the counsel for the Government expressed the Government's readiness to constitute the review Commission, the Court has stated that "it would not pass orders on the merit of the case." Further, the Court was also quoted by Hegde as providing guidelines for constituting the Commission which was sought to be set up by the government. Thus, the KSBCC was appointed following a directive to this effect from the Supreme Court in November 1982, in response to a memorandum submitted by the State. While the stipulated time of one month given by the Court was abided by the neighbouring Tamil Nadu Government, the Karnataka Government did not do so. It was further clarified by the Chief Minister that the review Commission would not come in the way of the Government in implementing the present policy of reservations which would continue pending final decision of the Supreme Court (Deccan Herald, February 6, 1984).

The Government held it improper to annul the Government Order of the Havanur Commission Report and restored the same formula of classification of BCs as it existed before the Havanur Commission. Inaugurating the State level annual conference of the All India Veerasaiva Mahasabha, held at Mysore on the 24th April, 1983, the Chief Minister refused the Mahasabha's President (the new President who had succeeded the late J.B. Mallaradhya), I.M. Magdum's plea "to annul the unjust Government Order issued in 1984 at a time when the Supreme Court could deliver judgment in respect of a petition challenging the G.O. and when the State Government had appointed a new Committee to determine backwardness" (*Deccan Herald*, April 25, 1983).

The KSBCC, on its appointment, decided to take up a socio-economic-cum-educational survey (in the form of a complete enumeration of population) to assess the socio-economic and educational conditions of different castes and communities in the State (Deccan Herald, January 7, 1984).

A household level schedule was also designed to gather data of the socio-economic and educational particulars in each household in the state. A complete enumeration of population was decided to be taken up to facilitate obtaining of caste-wise population in order to assess the socio-economic and educational conditions of different castes and communities in the state. The Commission sought government assistance in this regard. In view of this, the government extended the time limit for submission of the Commission's Report (Deccan Herald, January 1, 1984).

The appointment of the KSBCC and its methodology for the proposed socio-economic survey in Karnataka did evoke considerable response and attention from both laymen and social thinkers. It was both greeted and criticised. It was greeted by the Chairman of the previous BCC, Sri L.G. Havanur who suggested the appointment of retired Supreme Court and Karnataka High Court judges like Justice K.S. Hegde, Justice Somnath Iyer and others to the Commission (Prajavani, February 7, 1984). It was also, on the other hand, came to be criticised as "aiming at the impossible and a futile exercise" (H.M. Marulasiddaiah, Deccan Herald, February 10, 1984).

The Commission held "sittings at important cities like Bangalore and Mysore meeting delegations of individuals and institutions (like caste and religious associations) (Star of Mysore and Deccan Herald, January 1, 1984). It undertook a state-wide survey of the population of all castes, tribes and other communities to look into the issue of their backwardness.

With the derecognition of the Venkataswamy Commission's Report on the issue of determining the backward classes, the state government went ahead to appoint yet another such backward classes commission. This time it was the government headed by a different political party, viz., the Janatha Party with late Sri Ramakrishna Hegde as its chief minister. Dreaming of a 'compact commission', and directed by the five member team that had expressed dissent against the report of the Venkataswamy Commission, the government went about looking for a judge of the high court or even the supreme court to head this commission (Thimmaiah : 1993). Thus was constituted in the year 1988, yet another BCC under the Chairmanship of Sri O. Chinnappa Reddy, a judge of the Supreme Court of India to look into the issue of backwardness of various castes and communities and suggest for their categorisation. Notable was the fact that the Commission comprised this time of a single person who was its Chairman, and withou any members.

The Chinnappa Reddy Commission too realised the need to conduct a comprehensive survey of the state's population for gathering information on people's backwardness. In this context, it unleashed a stream of comments on its predecessor, the methodology and recommendations of the Venkataswamy Commission. However, it did not realise then that it was a 'one man commission' and the chairman travelled from Hyderabad (where he stayed) to Bangalore whenever there was work on the commission. This mode was totally insufficient to gather systematic information on the innumerable castes and communities that existed in the state. Though a test survey was conducted, the commission simply based its recommendations upon the conclusions drawn upon the nature of socio-economic backwardness that the communities in Karnataka posed, as derived from the data of the Venkataswamy Commission (Thimmaiah : 1993). There were a number of discrepancies in the data that was projected from 1984 to 1988. In fact, all the discrepancies of the data collected by the previous commissions (from Havanur to Venkataswamy Commission) were continued as the commission did not make effort to collect data afresh. This remains a major anomaly in the Third BCC in Karnataka.[32] As rightly concluded by Thimmaiah (1993), the OBCs are too divided today with sectarian and sectional politics to concentrate on the 'unjust reservation policy'. But instead of the policy 'loosing importance in the political agenda of Karnataka', we find a spurt of sectarian activities in the form of revival of interest in the caste associations and continued to socio-economic conflict for the benefits of development (Thimmaiah : 1993).

Conclusions

What has been attempted in this chapter on the history of mobilisation movements in Karnataka (with the All India situation in perspective), was to bring together the various stages and developments in the sphere of sectarian mobilisation in the State. The points highlighted in each context have been elaborated and analytically examined in the subsequent chapters.

Notes

1. Now renamed as Chennai. But in this book we continue to use the term Madras to denote the city of Chennai.
2. "After the words 'Puliyan' and 'tope', that is, 'the place where Puliyans (the ex-untouchables)' live."
3. "The Mysore Government, following the Madras scheme made reservation in favour of backward classes as far back as in 1874". Further, "in January 1895, (it) issued a circular reserving posts in favour of the backward classes" (Singh ; 1982: 81 and KBCC Report, Vol. I, Part I, 1975: 57-58).
4. Constitutional Assembly Debates (1947, 1948, 1949 and 1951). Also see Paramanand Singh 1982, for a detailed examination of these controversies (chapters IV and V).
5. Appointed in the year 1953 (January 29), the Commission submitted its report on March 31, 1955, with the chairman's (Kaka Sahab Kalelkar's) dissenting note.
6. Backward classes commissions were set up in the states of Andhra Pradesh, Jammu and Kashmir, Bihar, Karnataka, Kerala, Maharashtra, Tamil Nadu and Uttar Pradesh.
7. Though debated, it is generally held that the submission of the Dravidians to the Aryans resulted in not only the establishment of an Aryan Kingship

over the sub-continent, but it further led to the origin of the caste system (Ghurye, 1961). Also, see, Sharad Patil (1979 and 1982) for a critical and scholarly exposition of the institution of caste.

8. Discussed with prominent Backward Classes leaders who had participated in the movement in one way or the other, revealed that they were sympathetic to the cause of the ex-untouchables (discussion with late Sri H. R. Guruva Reddy, father-in-law of the first Chief Minister of the State of Mysore in 1947, Sri K. C. Reddy; with late Sri G. R. Ethirajulu Naidu, Advocate General of Mysore, etc.).
9. The Brahmins had come to power during Purnaiya's rule. P.N. Krishnamurthi, who later became the Dewan was the grandson of Dewan Purnaiya. Of the Iyengars (Shrivaishnavas) who "constituted the smallest and the most orthodox subcaste", the Hebbar Iyengars were the most important subdivision (Hettne and Tamm : 1974).
10. In fact, the Government Order, stating that the site is awarded to the Sangha, is being maintained by the office of the Sangha at Bangalore in its archives (Interview with the Secretary of the Sangha, Bangalore). It is also referred to in the Souvenir of the Golden Jubilee of the Sangha held in 1972.
12. A detailed and analytical study of these two associations has been made in the following chapter on caste associations.
13. These have been culled out of a narration by a group of respondents, who had either lived through these years when these developments took place, or who constituted the kith and kin of the main participants in the movement.
14. These issues indicating caste/class conflict in the pre-independence era have been discussed and critically examined in the chapter on 'social conflict'.
15. Hettne and Tamm, 1974.
16. Ibid.
17. The term Harijan was popularly used by them.
18. Ibid.
19. The leaders of the Praja Mithra Mandali were "self-appointed spokesmen for their rural community fellows, but it appears that they were particularly active in asserting the interests of town dwellers like themselves" (Dushkin : 1974: 11).
20. The details of the disturbances appear under the chapter on "Social Conflict".
21. The non-Brahmin movement during this time was led chiefly by the Muslims and the Lingayats. Their dominance in the Praja Mithra

Mandali is noted to have turned the party "extremely communal" (Hettne and Tamm : 1978 : 151). The twin protoganists of the communal party were Messers Mohammed Abbas Khan and G. Paramasivaiya. "They have converted the legislative house into a caste caucus". "It is they who set the tune to which a preponderant number of their fellow members dance." (*The Journal of the Karnataka and the Indian Review,* Reviews, November 1925 and July 1929).

22. In selecting the candidates for appointments to posts of District Munsiffs in the Madras sub-ordinate Judicial service, the Madras Public Service Commission followed the Communal G.O. of the Madras Government. According to the G.O., there was reservation of seats in favour of various castes, communities and religion (such as Harijans, Mulisms, Christians, Backward Hindus, non-Brahmin Hindus and Brahmins; Different and unequal age limit was fixed for candidates from these categories, and the list of selected candidates was published.
    One unsuccessful candidate hailing from a non-Brahmin caste (which had been allotted only 4 out of total 61 posts by the communal (G.O.) validity of the G.O. and challenged the selection made under Art. 16. The court held that Art.16(4) authorised reservation of posts only in favour of any backward class citizen of India. But reservation for other classses are not warranted by Art. 16 (4) and are in violation of Arts. 16 (1) and 16 (2). The communal G.O. was held to be void and illegal as it denied equality of opportunities to all (Subramanium : 1969).
23. As mentioned earlier, it was Sri K.C. Reddy, son-in-law of Veteran BCM leader Sri H.R. Guruva Reddy. K.C. Reddy hailed from Kyasamballi village in Bangarpet block of Kolar district, part of old Mysore State. He was the Chief Minister during 1947-52.
24. The Lingayats were more vocal in the agitation for the formation of a united Mysore state, while Vokkaliga leaders from Old Mysore state were less enthusiastic. Being predominantly distributed in the districts under the Bombay and Hyderabad Karnatak, areas, the former were unhappy with the policies of these two areas controlled administratively by the Marathas and Gujarathis.
25. After re-organisation in 1956, the caste balance of Mysore state stood at 15 per cent of Lingayats and 11 per cent of Vokkaligas.
26. In *Ramakrishna Singh Case,* AIR, 1960, Mys. 338.
27. M.S. Patil, who was a Lingayat.
28. Refer to appendix I for the details of members' profiles.

4 Caste Associations of Karnataka

Introduction

An essential consequence of development is the process of mobilisation that it generates in its wake. Mobilisation of human resources poses its own challenges, especially if the society in question happens to contain a heterogeneous population, followed by cultural diversity. It is generally accepted that the process of development assumes greater significance in societies which are characterised by structural inequality where inequality is institutionalised. Such significance refers both to the processes at work stressing the need for development, as well as in setting up or identifying strategies for development.

The society in India is characterised by structural inequality that is reflected in its functions as well. It could be argued that inequality in the Indian context is predominantly a result of the cultural system with the caste network at its core. It is an all-embracing system, the stamp of which is reflected in all activities of the people. The importance and impact of caste are so intense that it has succeeded in engulfing the lives of even non-Hindus as well (Ghurye : 1961) and has been emerging under various forms or 'avatars' (Srinivas : 1993). With all its potentiality of being an agency of social control, it has continued unabated with the passage of time despite large-scale changes in the country. It has shown excellent adaptability and elasticity to accommodate the new within the old structure.

There is no dearth of Sociological and Social-Anthropological thinking on the system of caste and its multi-faceted functions. While its origin is still being debated with several theoretical explanations (traditional Vs. occupational), its growth over the centuries in alarming proportions and with diverse subsystems has left no chance to any analyst to dispute its existence. The analysis of caste has proved to be an indispensable variable in any study of Indian society, whether in the past or at present times. This could be attributed to the fact that caste has a wider applicability and broader connotation, than being just an entity in itself. Caste enables an insight into the society where it exists and has all the characteristics of a social group, encompassing its basic divisive nature. Each caste is a micro-organisation with in the social structure; it is also a macro-institution to its members. In other words, it traditionally acts as both a divisive as well as a unificatory force. This it could achieve by successfully combining with in its functions the fundamental economic and political activities of its members thereby exercising complete control over them. It has shown excellent adaptability and elasticity to accommodate the new within the old structure.

Much has been written on these structural-functional aspects of social change in India. There is also the consolation that of late, the existence of a parallel system of class stratification has come to be recognised in sociological works, albeit being accompanied by such dubious considerations that "caste is class" (Rajashekar :1979) and *vice versa*; or that "Indian society could be studied either on caste lines or on class lines" (Beteille : 1983:117).

There is another equally significant factor which has directly as well as indirectly strengthened the importance of caste. In India, a number of welfare programmes for the poor and the needy have taken caste as the fundamental criterion for providing facilities to the deserving communities. This process of granting legal provisions to the backward and the downtrodden sections of the society in India was initiated during the British rule and encouraged by several backward classes movements and finally with the efforts of Dr. Ambedkar culminated with the granting of Constitutional Reforms. Labelled as "Protective Discrimination" under the Directive Principles of State Policy and Fundamental Rights, these legislative provisions have primarily chosen caste as the sole criterion for judging backwardness.

This new status of caste, which was also being highly disputed in contrast with the individual need concept of Beteille, gave a new dimension to the understanding of Indian society. Caste forming the basis of Constitutional Reform, while the Constitution itself was advocating equality of all citizens against any sort of discrimination (whether caste-based or otherwise), it became a highly debatable point in academics and public life.

Despite all this controversy surrounding it, caste has continued to enjoy its importance in Indian society. What is more, it gained a new kind of adaptation to the present circumstances and came to be increasingly used as the platform for asserting one's inequality as well as equality with others, besides being a key strategy for mobilisation.

Formation of Caste Associations

Mobilisation on caste grounds has gained significance in recent decades as a chief mode of social mobility in India. The census operations commissioned by the British had kindled the spirit of low castes who tried to register for a better social status through changing their existing caste names to sanskritised ones in the census records, as early as during the latter part of the 19th century. Many caste groups aspiring for a higher ritual status had placed requisitions before the census authorities to classify them as a 'superior' caste than what they actually had been at that time. This is just one phase of the whole process of caste mobilisation, as the demand was only for change in their caste names. The process of Sanskritisation (Srinivas : 1956b) and the introduction of English education created awareness among the so-called non-Brahmins regarding Brahminical dominance and supremacy over them. The process of modernisation introduced by the British through the setting up of industries and opening of educational institutions offered an open system of employment to all, irrespective of one's caste; transportation and communication network and the system of education contributed towards a new awakening among the non-Brahmins resulting in BCMs in different parts of the country. The movement marked the revolt of all so-called 'low' castes against Brahminical supremacy. It was naturally more pronounced in south India where Brahmins enjoyed maximum superiority in matters of education and government service (Irschick : 1969, Rudolphs : 1967, Srinivas : 1966 and Rao : 1979).

Census operations and the emergence of the BCM were followed by yet another channel of social mobility, viz., emergence of caste associations. "Such 'Sabhas' were not unknown previously, but the census operations of 1901 made them more popular" (Srinivas : 1966:96). The first decade of the twentieth century witnessed an upsurge of such associations, which pledged to secure a high socio-economic status to their caste-folk. The establishment of such associations came to be considered as an important aspect of the process of mobilisation by different caste and subcaste groups. Their importance lay in the fact that they cannot be categorised as just organisations with a welfare motto, but their emergence, existence and activities were all closely linked to the socio-political changes introduced in a region (Omvedt : 1976). They emerged out of strong political considerations and continued to function as Para-political entities (Rudolphs : 1967:29).

What is striking in the case of caste associations is the incongruence that exists between their stated goals and their actual activities. A historical analysis of the caste associations leads one to the conclusion that they tended to satisfy, in the long-run, the needs of only a limited section of the community they claimed to represent. Further, as each caste or subcaste tended to be a complex unit, its leadership pattern also raised many questions about universal acceptance and dominance. This was because many caste associations have been the training camps for emerging politicians in the post-1970s. They have been acting as 'interest groups', thereby enhancing the role of caste in politics furthermore (Dushkin : 1974, Rudolphs : 1967 and Manor :1977).

The nature and substance of caste associations and their role in social transformation is highlighted by a number of studies on social movements and social change (Hardgrave : 1969, Rao : 1957, 1970 & 1978, Irshick : 1969, Manor : 1977, Dushkin : 1974, Srinivas : 1964 & 1966 and others). They have discussed their role in bringing about changes in the communities that they represented. Some of the studies argue that there was a link between the forces of modernisation, urbanisation, industrialisation, etc., and the process of caste mobilisation. The forming of caste associations and publishing of a caste journal were the key steps to social change. Thus the studies have projected the image of caste association as an indispensable tool for mobilisation. The process of mobilisation is a complex one, which involves the active co-operation between the varied spheres of human activity. While changes in the food habits, occupation and aspirations of the members of a caste group constituted one aspect of the mobilisation process, the setting up of caste associations came to be the first step towards politicising the process. Such a step gained increasing popularity among the various castes providing a front to any attempt towards the progress of the castes. In other words, the caste associations were looked upon as the media for establishing links with the external society acting as spokesmen of the mobilisation attempts of the groups concerned.

Thus, it is established that social mobility in India has been characterised by an important dimension due to the emergence of such interest groups as caste associations. While it is true that the process of modernisation has led, indirectly, to an organisational effort on the part of different caste and religious groups by establishing associations, there is another important and comparatively new dimension to the whole issue of the emergence of caste associations.

While the system of granting government aid to certain caste groups was in vogue during the pre-independence era, the effort was strengthened and given a wider application with the country's independence. Under the circumstances, certain provisions were earmarked for the amelioration of the conditions of the weaker sections of the society, not only the SCs and the STs, but also "the other socially and educationally backward classes of citizens". This necessitated the states to appoint Backward Classes Commissions to assess and determine the backward groups in their respective regions.

Accordingly in Karnataka, Backward Classes Commissions have been set up from time to time. They have categorised a number of caste and tribal groups as backward and have granted facilities to them. The reliance of these commissions on "caste" as one of the chief determinants of backwardness has given an added impetus to the institution of caste which was already in the limelight owing to its structural superiority in the Indian social system. The consideration of "group need" and not "individual need" has increased the role of caste in the socio-political context (Beteille : 1981).

It is under the above circumstances that the process of caste mobilisation has gained momentum in the recent years in India, which in turn has accelerated the process of emergence of caste associations. It is observed that with caste forming the basis for reservation, there has been a growing competition among the various caste and tribal groups to secure the gains of development. Setting up of caste associations and holding of periodical caste conferences have become regular features of caste mobilisation attempts by many castes. This is certainly a common feature in recent decades.

This leaves us with the fundamental question: what are the main forces that have induced the older caste associations to become active in the recent decades? Why is there a sudden upsurge in the number of caste associations? What is the nature of leadership in them? Is a caste association representative of the whole group? More crucial would be to ask – what is the net impact of such sectarian movements upon the socio-political framework of India's development? This chapter attempts to highlight the politico-economic issues operating behind an active caste association besides providing details of their genesis and growth.

Problems of Identification

Caste associations, with their offices located in urban centres did not pose any problem for their identification. Formation of associations on caste basis has been, thus, nothing surprising or new to the state. This is a phenomenon that best explains the secular and sectarian value attached to caste as an ethnic group. Secondly, it also points towards its continued importance with adoption of caste as the basis of certain developmental programmes. All these have in a way institutionalised caste in a different form. Identifying oneself with one's caste or religion is viewed as not just one's personal identity but a matter of politico-economic necessity. The process of caste mobilisation is becoming manifest with the passage of time. Critics of reservation policy seek in it justification for their argument that caste is being perpetuated rather than being abolished in a secular society (Beteille : 1981). More than the application of the term caste to ascription of traditional roles to members, like occupation, the application of the term in recent years is to expose to the outside world, the relative backwardness of each caste group. This is done predominantly to seek government help. Further, it should not be concluded that this whole process can be analysed keeping caste in isolation from its important counterpart – the class.

It is observed that older caste associations in Karnataka have been active and new ones formed at certain selected intervals (Dushkin : 1980) i.e., in response to a political process. Establishing of a caste association is generally accompanied by placing certain demands before the state claiming to benefit the entire caste as a whole. For example, request for granting of private educational institutions was one such. The practice of starting hostels, schools and colleges is seen as a direct consequence of the non-Brahmin movement, which aimed at breaking the monopoly of Brahmins in the fields of education and government service. Interestingly, this practice, started in the first decade of the 20th century, has continued over the years. While the earlier associations concentrated their attention upon starting of schools and hostels, the recent ones are more geared up to fulfil the wider political and economic ambitions of their leaders.

It is to be noted that all castes have not been able to form associations. The non-Brahmin movement of the late 19th and early 20th centuries gave a call for the middle and low castes in the hierarchy to mobilise themselves to attain backward status. But in the final event, it was those castes that were numerically preponderant, economically strong with good social awareness which could augment their resources and participate actively. Underneath what appeared to be an essentially caste movement were strong class interests, and in the fight that followed, only those caste groups with a comparatively numerical preponderance, economic support and social awareness participated actively. The process of mobilisation appears to have a close link with caste hierarchy. Higher the position of a caste in the social ladder, greater is its potentiality for mobilisation. This privilege of ritual ranking combined with the concomitant economic gains has prompted many castes to exploit new avenues for development. The government's measure to herald equality has given new dimension to the process of caste mobility in Karnataka.

Thus, some of the upper and upper-middle caste associations have stabilised their existence with economic assets like buildings in important commercial areas, used as shops, student hostels, marriage halls (choultries) and other forms of commercial establishments. But there are a large number of new associations representing the middle-middle and the lower-middle caste groups that have come up since the 1980s which lacked such assets. Apart from the recent origin of their associations, these groups owe their disadvantageous position to the comparatively low economic and political status that they enjoy in the social hierarchy.

Locating these associations proved to be somewhat difficult, as there was no direct official source about it. Although every association is required to be registered, it was found that many of them have become either defunct or have had periods of inactivity in between. One of the officials in the Surveyor's office, Bangalore, expressed her inability to provide an accurate figure of the number of caste associations in the state, in the absence of any procedure at the government level to prepare and maintain an exclusive list of only caste associations. Sometimes, the associations are also called by names which are not caste-based, but are indicative of a region. For example, the 'Sourashtra Association" represents the "Jamkhanadavaru", a minority caste group (also known as 'Patnulkarans') engaged in weaving.

As noted already, there appears to be a direct link between the emergence of caste associations and the appointment of Backward Classes Commissions in the state. This is especially evident in the case of the KBCC, popularly known as the Havanur Commission, appointed in the year 1972, when late Sri Devraj Urs was the chief minister in Karnataka. The increase in the number of caste associations during 1972-73 bears good evidence to this phenomenon. The starting of a caste-based association, holding of caste conferences and its other activities are also being given publicity through the newspapers, a mode popularly afforded to be adopted by only the dominant castes earlier. These sources were explored in order to identify, specially, the more recent and economically less preponderant caste associations.

Another important source was the KBCC Report itself which contains some of the memoranda submitted by different caste leaders when they deposed before the Commission to place their grievances (KBCC Report : 1975). The ex-secretary of the Karnataka Backward Classes and Minorities Cell (which is a non-governmental organisation), was helpful by supplying a list of most of the caste associations – old and new – functioning at Bangalore.

The fundamental questions pertaining to the role and nature of caste associations at Bangalore were tested over a group of respondents. Based upon its results, the analysis was applied to a wider area. Verifications and cross-verifications with the respondents brought out, as a basic step, the existence of many subcaste associations representing caste groups which have emerged as a result of the process of fission in the system.

Methodology

Data were collected from these caste associations by using an nterview schedule containing both open-ended and closed-ended questions. Scope was also given to elicit any other information apart from what the interview schedule demanded. The President of the association generally constituted the respondent. Only in those cases where the President was not available – for a long duration – the Secretary or the Vice-President replaced him as the respondent. Wherever possible, both the President and the Secretary were interviewed with the hope of not only getting more information[2] but also to crosscheck the data each of them provided. Every generation of office-bearers, especially the rank of the President and the Secretary, differed from both its predecessor and successor. Such differences in their education, occupation and attitudes tended to have a definite bearing on the progress or otherwise of the caste association. In some select associations, which showed signs of either growth or decay, the past President and the Secretary (under whose regime the above signs were found) were also interviewed. This helped a great deal in learning more about the history of those caste associations (see the list of office-bearers in Appendix 4.1 and 4.2).

Analysis of Caste Associations in Karnataka

Totally about 45 caste associations were covered by the sudy and are discussed in this chapter. These consisted of caste groups belonging to all the three segments of the caste hierarchy – upper, middle and the lower.

I

Of the various caste groups, the Lingayats or the Veerasaivas were the first in the state to establish a caste association, as early as in the year 1904, at Bangalore. This was followed by the Vokkaligas (the dominant counterpart of the Lingayats) who established the "Vokkaligara Sangha" in the year 1906. The years of establishment of these two sanghas is partly an indication of their attempts at caste mobilisation, especially after the government's intervention in the form of granting Constitutional reforms (and remedy to the question of their backwardness). In other words, the caste associations of the two dominant castes – the Veerasaivas or Lingayats and the Vokkaligas - were established owing to the impact of the non-Brahmin movement in the erstwhile Madras Presidency (now the State of Tamil Nadu) and in the Bombay-Karnatak area, during the early part of the 20th century. Similarly, the differential treatment under the system of "Protective Discrimination", recommended by the various commissions set up by the government[3] seems to have made a tremendous impact upon the organising and forming of the "Akila Karnataka Brahmana Maha Sabha", the caste association of the Brahmins, in the year 1971.

1. The Akila Karnataka Brahmana Maha Sabha

The establishment of the "Akila Karnataka Brahmana Maha Sabha", as late as in 1971, owes its significance to a number of political and economic factors. The Brahmins felt comparatively 'secure' till the year 1970 when the two dominant castes enjoyed much political power by appointing their men as Chief Ministers. As is widely recognized, it was late Sri Devraj Urs who, with his political acumen, could bring in a break in the long-continued rule by the Lingayats and the Vokkaligas and pave the way for the minorities and the backward classes to represent in state politics (Natraj & Natraj 1982).

How the Brahmins activated their organisational roles after Urs came to power is a question which deserves a broader analysis. It should be remembered that the Brahmins, although they had never been in power, enjoyed a fairly comfortable position, at least in the South, till the country's independence despite the rampant non-Brahmin movement. The community had to face many dificulties, particularly after the Constitutional Reforms were granted and strictly implemented. Although they had been affected by the policy of protective discrimination under the Princely Rule and the British, the effect was far greater after independence when the policy of reservations came to be implemented with far more zeal and emphasis. While the system of reservations for the SCs/STs itself was much resented, at least privately, the addition of the OBC category thereby expanding the reservation quota, has added more fuel to the whole issue (interviews with the presidents of the Maha Sabha).[4]

In addition to the above, a few other factors may be considered while examining the delay in the formation of the Brahmana Maha Sabha. Comprising only 4 per cent of the state's population, they are a numerical minority group. This drawback, coupled with the prevalence of intra-caste rivalry within the broader category of Brahmins, came as obstacles to any effort at unifying and forming the organisation. Further, the superior status enjoyed by the Brahmins that facilitated their attainments in the spheres of education and government service instilled in them confidence characterised by self-dependence as well as trust in one's own ability to face the challenges posed by the new situation.

In the pre-independence days, the Brahmins were not only isolated from others as a forward group, but at the same time, they also faced, quite frankly, little competition from the dominant communities. Being isolated, they could not present a front against others. By the 1970s, they could make some common cause with the Lingayats. Their internal bickering may have also subsided to a certain extent. Further, they probably saw the OBC not as a homogeneous group.

One point to be added here is that the Brahmins cannot be totally construed as disinterested in mobilisation attempts, at least in the period earlier to the year 1971. Careful observation does point out that like the Lingayats and the Vokkaligas, the Brahmins have also made attempts to establish educational institutions and student hostels. While hostels started by different Brahmin sub-caste associations catered only to the boys, the colleges started by a few Brahmin leaders did not bear caste titles nor did they bring in purely communal motives in their functions. There are quite a few such institutions of higher learning like the National Institute of Engineering at Mysore and the National College of Bangalore, which owe their origin to a band of inspired, educated Brahmins. But they have not been labelled as communal institutions as much as the others founded by non-Brahmins are.

As discussed earlier, the changes in the socio-political environment in the state after 1970 appears to have prompted the Brahmin community, which till 1971 did not have a unified organisational base, to follow the other castes in the mobilisation process. This study has shown that a concerted effort was made during the beginning of the seventies by the Brahmins to assemble together all the sub-castes from all over Karnataka to a common platform to project a united front against the non-Brahmins. Reservation of seats in educational institutions and in the field of government employment had affected this so-called "forward" group, adversely, by then, as they were left out with the only weapon of "merit" to fight the "caste" factor. Distress brought the different conflicting sections of the same group under a common plank, in the same way as it had mustered the congregation of each one of these sub-castes under a separate pedestal in the pre-independence era.

It is necessary to recall here, the existence of internal factions among the three major/broad divisions of Brahmins into the Smarthas, the Madhwas and the Srivaishnavas (although these three subcastes contain many subcastes within them), which reached a climax with the starting of Dewan's rule in Princely Mysore in 1881. The policy of 'importing'

Dewans from the state of Madras due to the availability of a better educated and sophisticated Brahmin youth there enraged the Mysore Brahmins. The most affected were the Hebbar Iyengars, a subcaste among the Srivaishnavas (Iyengars) who had hitherto held high positions in the administration (Hettne and Tamm : 1974: 72-73).

Anguished and affected by this trend, the local Brahmins (Mysoreans) began to mobilise a protest movement with the aim of competing with their Madrasi counterparts in the field of administrative service. No sooner did they realise the value of education (English education), a strong urge to promote the cause of education among their younger generation was mooted. Ascription of priestly profession, accompanied by the study and preaching of the Vedas and the Puranas no doubt provided the Brahmins with a superior status. But at the same time, denial of economically productive jobs like agriculture, trade or industry, (although they were traditionally allowed to own land), reflected itself upon the life of a Brahmin. This necessitated a great deal of welfare work in the form of raising donations (money) to encourage the Brahmin boys to take up higher education by way of helping them with scholarships, freeships, hostel facilities, etc. As a result, caste associations were formed essentially to promote education among the community's children. Unlike today, when the Brahmin community is mostly urban based, it was common to find at least a few families in every village, who functioned as Village Accountants – Shanubogs as they were then known. This observation excludes quite a number of them who were landlords in many parts of the Princely State. It is keeping these rural Brahmin youth in mind, that many caste associations are claimed to have been established to cater to their needs like food, shelter, school fees, etc., and also with the hope that their migration to the city would generate a sophisticated cult among the students. Such a tendency to lay emphasis upon the educational progress of the community as a key to greater economic gains as well as security has been the basis upon which caste associations are formed, both in the past as well as in the present times.

However, education alone cannot be construed as the motivating factor behind the formation of caste associations. Although it is an important variable in development, it also constituted the starting point in a series of mobilisation processes, the other notable factor being politicisation. In other words, the different caste groups took to establishing educational institutions under the organisational protection of their caste associations. But any close observation of the phenomenon of caste association would tell us that it was more a battle between elite from the respective castes for economic gains under the disguise of group improvement.

When a community's socio-economic base is disturbed owing to any internal or external forces, in the imbalance that resulted, there occurred a keen competition for sharing the benefits. While this is purely a clash of individual interests, in a caste society where the group is superior to the 'individual', the fight tended to assume a 'group' form. This need not necessarily mean the exclusion of class interests which may cut across caste interests.

Similarly, when the different caste groups became conscious of group mobilisation, beneath such a move were categorically class intentions. This fact may be proved by the data on the constitution of caste associations, be they Brahmin, Vokkaliga or untouchable. The structure of leadership and membership, the place where these caste associations are located and a brief survey of their welfare activities are enough to throw light on this 'class' factor. The following discussion throws light on the above issue :

As we look at the activities of the caste associations, we observe that whatever occurred at the macro-level echoed at the micro-level too. Since a subcaste is nothing but an offshoot of the main caste, differing from it, only on regional, linguistic, ethnic and economic grounds, the process of mobilisation is common to all the castes and subcastes. Nevertheless, the processes of fission and fusion, occurring as they did at frequent intervals and also largely influenced by the politico-economic changes in the social structure, have added a lot of dynamism to the whole process.

As noted in the previous chapter, census operations were largely responsible for initiating a process of fission in the caste system. A number of caste and subcaste groups, in their efforts to sanskritise their lifestyles, appealed to the then Census Commissioner for change of caste name from the existing to a sanskritised one. Similarly, the policy of protective discrimination also heralded awareness about group unity, both among the beneficiaries and the non-beneficiaries. The subcastes imitated their major castes. The presence of sub-divisions among the Brahmins and also among others at the middle and lower levels of the hierarchy testify to this fact.

A look at the years of establishment of the seven or eight Brahmin subcaste associations would tell us that they were the result of a combination of the effect of the non-Brahmin movement and the policy of protective discrimination in the pre-independence era. The "Hoysala Karnataka Brahmins", a subcaste of Smartha Brahmins were the first to start an association as early as the year 1908. This was followed by the Hebbar Iyengars, who were already angered over the "Madrasi-Mysorean controversy", when they started the "Hebbar Srivaisnava Sabha" in the year 1918.

The other four associations, each representing a subcaste among the Brahmins, viz., "Badaganadu Sangha", "Bettadapurada Sankethi Sangha", "Madhwa Yuvaka Sangha" and "Babbur Kamme Seva Samithi", were started between the years 1934-45. It is interesting to note that the fillip to start these associations was given by the Dewans, administrators and other highly educated and well placed Brahmin officers belonging to these subcastes (Souvenirs of the Sanghas).

The Hoysala Karnataka Sangha

The Hoysala Karnataka Sangha represents the Hoysala Karnatakas, a subcaste among the broader Brahmin caste group. The community claims to be the inhabitants of the districts of Shimoga, Chickmagalur, Hassan, Tumkur and Mysore in Old Mysore and has spread later to other districts. The Hoysala Karnataka Sangha was established in the year 1908 at Mysore, at a time when caste associations were just beginning to be established in the state. It carries the credit for having held a caste conference at Mysore on April 19th and 20th 1908 and for "promulgating ideas of intra-caste unity at such an early period". However, owing perhaps to political changes at the state level and other reasons, it became defunct after surviving for a few years. Even during its short span of life, it had made a collection of Rs. 17,000 meant for welfare activities. But, its activities were revived in 1942 and a branch was opened at Bangalore in the year 1944. Again, after a gap of nearly three decades, it became more active when more branches were opened at Hassan (1970), Bhadravathi and Shimoga (Souvenir of the AKBMS : March 1978).

The Hoysala Karnataka Sangha is at present running hostels for the students (boys) of the community at Bangalore, Mysore, Hassan etc. It is also organising at regular intervals (once a year) caste meetings and conferences at Bangalore[5] where the progress made by the Sangha in its welfare activities and in solving the problems of the community members is discussed. It is also taking active participation in the annual conferences of the wider association, the Akila Karnataka Brahmana Maha Sabha.

The Hebbar Srivaishnava Sabha

The Hebbar Srivaishnava Sabha stands second in the list of the order of establishment of Brahmin caste associations. It appears to be comparatively more stable in its early stages of functioning than the Hoysala Karnataka Sangha. It was founded at Mysore on September 6, 1918, under the presidentship of Sri V. N. Narasimhaiengar, Palace Controller and functioning with support from a few local college students of the Maharaja's college[6], all hailing from this caste, the Sabha aimed to herald the cause of "education, culture and good citizenship......." and "to build up an adequate capital fund........." To be used for "granting educational scholarships..". and for "the establishment of schools and such other educational institutions" (Souvenir of the AKBMS : 1978).

"The Sabha grew in strength gradually and in the year 1943, it shifted its headquarters to Bangalore and celebrated its silver jubilee". By 1968, it had its own building, where the Golden Jubilee celebration of the Sangha was held during that year.[7]

Apart from Bangalore the Sabha has branches at Mysore, Mandya, Hassan and "has plans to open a few more Upasabhas" (discussions with Lalitha Parthasarathy and G. Rangaraju, Hon. Secretary of the Sabha, Bangalore).

Babbur Kamme Seva Samithi

The Babbur Kamme Seva Samithi, being next in the order, was founded in the year 1934, although the foundation for the Sangha had been laid in the year 1931 with a "magnificent" Students' Home started at Bangalore. It may also be inferred that the effort was sympathetically and encouragingly supported by Dewan Bahadur Rajakarya Praveena K. Ramaswamy, after whom the Student's Home is named.

In the year 1939, another hostel was started with only 20 students. "The students' Home has always been accommodating the poor and deserving students of not only the Babbur Kamme community, but also students of other Brahmin communities". The Samithi claims to have "served as a liaison between members of the community, with annual get together". It has separate branches for the educational, cultural and economic wings (Souvenir of the AKBMS).

Sri Madhwa Yuvaka Sangha

Compared to its two counterparts, the Madhwa Yuvaka Sangha received substantial monetary help and moral support from mutts and Swamijis both for its establishment and expansion. The idea of forming a Sangha occurred to a group of young Madhwa men holding high administrative positions in the Princely government. They could successfully materialise their dream into a reality in the year 1945 when a few Swamijis of Madhwa mutts came forward with monetary help.[8] Due to the paucity of funds, initially only a scholarship scheme was started. Money was collected later for the scholarship fund through holding of cultural programmes by a few Madhwa artists. Subsequently, donations were collected to start students' hostel at Bangalore for the benefit of the "poor" and the "needy" students of the community. Notable among the donors to the hostel fund is Dewan Pradhan Shiromani Nyapathi Madhava Rau.

The Sangha owns several hostels and other buildings in Bangalore and at a few other places in the state. Its first President was Sri Subhodh M. Rama Rao of Mysore followed by late Dr. P.H. Krishna Rao, who was also the President of the Akila Karnataka Brahmana Maha Sabha.

Badaganadu Sangha

Founded in the year 1942[9], the Badaganadu Sangha is another well-established and important Brahmin subcaste association. Passing evidently through a slow phase of growth and expansion in the fifties and the sixties, the Sangha expanded itself in the seventies. This may be related to the emergence and impact of the Akhila Karnataka Brahmin Maha Sabha in the year 1971. This is supported by the fact that the Badaganadu Sangha also functions as a wing of the Sabha's office at Bangalore. In other words, most of the official activities of the Brahmana Maha Sabha are carried out at the spacious Badaganadu hostel building which has been constructed in the year 1972 to commemorate the silver jubilee of the Sangha. Apart from a students' hostel the building also contains a marriage choultry, both constituting one part of the structure, while the remaining portions have been rented out. A book library and a lodging complex were the later additions to this property of the Sangha.[10]

Bettadapuradha Sankethi Sangha

The Sankethis constitute one of the many Brahmin subcastes (apart from the three major sub-divisions mentioned earlier). The Bettadapuradha Sankethi Sangha, the caste association of the Sankethis, though founded in the same year (1945) as the Madhwa Yuvaka Sangha, has expanded in the recent decades. Like the other Brahmin Sanghas, the Sankethi Sangha also has added few student hostels to its credit. However, caste conferences and meetings of the members of this Sangha have been regular only since 1974. In addition to its other welfare activities, "the Sangha is taking active interest in the unification of all the Brahmin communities for safeguarding Brahmins' interest in all walks of life" (Souvenir : 1978).

The Brahmana Yuvaka Sangha

The Brahmana Yuvaka Sangha, the association representing the youth of all the Brahmin subcastes, was established on November 7, 1971 along with the state level association of the community. The Yuvaka Sangha is a reflection of the process of modernisation within the sectarian set up representing, thereby, the unification of all Brahmin youth, irrespective of subcaste differences. It also points to the upsurge of the youth force in the movement of the Brahmins against their present day problems (Interview with the Secretary, Visweswara Co-operative Bank, Bangalore). It is common to find a large number of young Brahmin men and women participating in the caste conferences and in the Sabha's meetings in the recent years.

The Mysore Chathada Sri Vaisnava Association

The analysis of subcaste associations among the Brahmins throws light on a process of mobilisation for better status within the caste structure of the Brahmins an offshoot of a keen competition amongst the three Brahmin subcastes to claim superiority over each other. While one can set aside this factor as nothing new, there is noticed a fight for seeking recognition of their origin as an upper Brahmin caste by a few "border" Brahmin caste groups who also follow traditional occupation of temple worship. Although such groups claim a typical high Brahminical status they are not recognised so by the three major Brahmin castes, viz., the Smarthas, Madhwas and the Sreevaisnavas. The fact that these marginal subcastes claiming complete Brahminical status are found concentrated in a particular, usually small, geographical area, has in itself added to a feeling of insecurity (Memorandum submitted to the Mandal Commission : 1979).

The Chathada Srivaisnavas represent one such caste group, who seem to have resorted to a variety of ways to sanskritise their lifestyles in order to strengthen their claims for a higher Brahminical status. Interestingly enough, these claims are not just for a superior Brahminical status, but also, simultaneously, for a higher backward status. According to the Secretary[11] of the association at Bangalore, the Chathada Srivaisnavas existed as superior Brahmins even before Sri Ramanujacharya, the saint who "made Vaisnavism reputed in the world and who classified Vaisnavism into two classes for the purpose of temple worship, viz., Shatathadhavan and Shathinavan." Those who were in Vaishnavism even before Ramanuja and followed the path of Alwars were called the Shatadavar while those who joined Vaisnavism after Ramanuja and followed the path of Vedas were called "Shatinis". "Because of political influence and power the latter (Shatinis) are alleged by the Shathadavars as capable of being identified as Brahmins and enjoyed all the benefits of that status while the Shathadavars were listed under the Shudras. Gradually, their political and economic incapability forced the Shatadas down into social and educational backwardness" (Memorandum : 1979).

The 'Sudra' status, no doubt, fetched a backward tag to the Chathadha Sri Vaisnavas, which they claim to have enjoyed till the year 1960. It facilitated some of their members to get higher education and gain entry into government service. But they were excluded from the list of backward classes in 1960 by the Nagan Gowda Committee set up by the Mysore Government. The reasons for such exclusion, as presented by the president of the Sangha are attributed to "wrong estimation of their population by the commission" (discussions with K. N. Muthuraju, President of the Chathada Sri Vaisnava Association).[12]

The Karnataka Backward Classes Commission did not include them under the backward classes' list for the benefit of Art.16 (4). On further request to the government by the Satani caste association pleading that "the population figures of the community considered by the Commission was less than the actual figures and that the neighbouring states of Tamil Nadu and Andhra Pradesh have considered the community as most backward and backward respectively, and that more than 95 per cent of Satani population did not have the ability to own land or house due to poverty, the government were pleased to issue final orders on the commission' report including the Satanis among others as socially and educationally backward under both Art.15 (4) and 16 (4) (Memorandum :1979).

However, the problems faced by the Association in obtaining a backward status for the community did not seem to have stopped at this. The memorandum submitted by it to the Mandal Commission in the year 1979 stated that "The High Court of Karnataka, while disposing certain Writ Petitions, has held the orders of the government as arbitrary basing such decision on the sole submission of the Advocate General. The government has no other materials apart from those collected by the Commission to arrive at this decision. The Satani community was not party in the Writ Petition and hence the decision of the High Court and the subsequent government order has struck the community as a bolt from the blue" (Memorandum : 1979, p. 3).

This apart, the caste association of the Satanis though established in the year 1940 has not made much progress as far as its assets and welfare activities are concerned. Much of its activities were oriented towards making periodic claims for backward status as well as attempting to confirm its claim over greater Brahminisation. While it is not the only one of its kind in doing so, it is interesting to note that each one of these Brahmin subcastes tried to establish superiority over the other, making all others in the competition its subcastes. For example, the Satanis claimed that the Chathada Sri Vaisnavas, the Bettadapuradha Sri Vaisnavas and the Jamakhanadavaru were their subcastes (Memorandum : 1979).[13]

As mentioned earlier, the AKBMS was formed in the year 1971 signalling thereby a new phase in the caste cleavages among the Brahmins. The Sabha under the Presidentship of Dr. P. H. Krishna Rao,[14] a retired civil servant, who was also the Census Commissioner for Mysore during the year 1941, was started with great zeal and enthusiasm. It was a product of the politico-economic despair encountered by the Brahmin community, which led to coming together of all the Brahmin subcaste associations under one platform/banner.

The fundamental reason behind the formation of an All-Karnataka Association is given by its President[15] as the promotion of the educational development of the community. The Sabha's emphasis was prompted by the policy of reservations which denied higher, especially professional, education to "deserving" Brahmin students. The practice of capitation fees and the reservation of seats in educational institutions to the backward classes were described as having deprived the merited students of that caste from exercising their right to seek higher (professional) education. It is for this reason, that the Sabha advocated starting of educational institutions – especially professional ones – to cater to the benefit of community students, so that they need not depend on the government or the ones founded by dominant castes (who ran the majority of the private educational trusts in the state).[16]

Another noteworthy point is that in all the conferences of the caste association stress is laid upon intra-subcaste unity, integrity and co-operation.[17] The unification of the associations of the subcastes and the formation of the Akila Karnataka Brahmana Maha Sabha in 1971-72 was a significant move in this direction. The seventies marked the beginning of the third decade of continued reservation facilities to the backward classes. The Brahmins have been, all through these decades, the only caste to be categorised continuously as a forward group, beginning from the Miller Committee days. It is the only caste not to have experienced the benefits of reservation policy althrough these decades, both in the pre and post-independence days. This is viewed by the Mahasabha as having affected the community, particularly the Brahmin youth in regard to access to higher education and employment. Modernisation process, in the form of occupational and spatial mobility had already added its share to their misery, when the status and privileges that they enjoyed since centuries in the traditional caste structure was forfeited owing to the changes introduced by modernisation.[18]

To begin with, the Sangha restricted its activities to the capital city of Bangalore only. In the following years, branches have been opened all over the state.

The appointment of Dr. P. H. Krishna Rao[19] was mainly in recognition of his services to the community during his tenure as a civil servant. He was associated with such work both as Census Commissioner and later as the President of Sri Madhwa Yuvaka Sangha.[20] The Sangha, "under the able leadership of Dr. Krishna Rao, was able to establish, within a decade of its rejuvenation and to expand its branches in many parts of the state", like in Hassan, Shimoga, Dakshina Kannada and Uttara Kannada, Belgaum, Mysore, Tumkur and so on, wherever Brahmins were found residing in substantial numbers. A few of these federal bodies have also established schools in these areas while most of them have started student hostels (This is particularly true of the three major subcastes of the community – the Smarthas, the Madhwas and the Srivaisnavas).

The progress made by the Sabha in the recent years includes many welfare schemes and plans and programmes to expand its assets. Banks and a co-operative society are started at Bangalore "for the benefit of the community" (Vipravani, the magazine of the Sabha). Financial help for the poor members of the community for conducting marriages, death ceremonies, and other life events has been arranged. Marriage halls have been constructed in many places, rented out at concessional rates to the community members.

Membership to the Sabha has definitely increased over the years since the inception of the Sabha in 1972. But this has reportedly been made difficult by the prevalence of subcaste differences. Since each subcaste functions as a separate caste in itself, assembling them together is not an easy task. Cultural and ideological differences come to the surface under such circumstances. However, the subcaste associations have come together and attempted to unify themselves under the common banner of the Maha Sabha and not as separate associations.

One of the predominant tasks which the Brahmana Maha Sabha has set before itself is to bring about inter-caste (intra-Brahmin) equality. This process was initiated by the first president Dr.Krishna Rao, under whose leadership the community gave support to the unification move, at least during times of crisis. But after his resignation in 1982, internal bickering occasionally came to the fore, especially during the annual caste conferences. Utmost care is taken to see that all the three 'mathasthas' (subcastes) representing the three major sub-castes among the Brahmins are given their due importance to an equal extent.[21] But all this has not in any way deterred internal conflicts from occurring and should be understood in their proper perspective, i.e., as natural products of competition to share the economic and political gains.

2. The Akila Bharatha Veerasaiva Mahasabha

The Veerasaivas or the Lingayats[22] constitute one of the so-called upper castes in the social hierarchy of Karnataka, being economically, numerically and politically important in the state.

Found mostly in the State and its surrounding parts from the states of Maharashtra and Andhra Pradesh, this community has a historical background of its own (Murthy : 1973). The biggest argument is whether Veerasaivism as a Sect was founded by Basaveshwara (or Basava) or whether it existed much earlier to him (Mallappa : 1973 and Naganna n.d.). It is, nevertheless, true that Veerasaivism has developed mostly in the post-Basava period. What is more, a demarcation exists between the various Veerasaiva religious mutts on the basis of their patronage to these two explanations about the origin of the sect.

Veerasaivism, forming an important religious sect of Karnataka has had quite a distinguished politico-cultural history in the State (Parvathamma : 1972). The numerical preponderance of the Lingayats spread over nearly fourteen out of the nineteen districts of the erstwhile Mysore state (though not totally absent in the other five districts) and their economic and political dominance, strongly supported the progress made by the community and for being termed as one of the two 'dominant' castes in the state (Srinivas : 1959).

The above aspects of the history and nature of the Lingayat community deserves attention while attempting to analyse the process of mobilisation among the Lingayats. It would be also pertinent to divide such an analysis into two parts – one referring to the pre-independence era, and the other, to the post-independence periods. Its dominant status has helped the community to play a crucial role in the process of caste mobilisation in the State which goes a long way in shaping the political history of these two periods. Reference to the political history of Lingayats in Karnataka is also necessary for a study of their caste association. Studies by James Manor (1972 &1977) and, particularly, by Lelah Dushkin (1974) have richly shed light on the political and sociological aspects of this phenomenon. While Manor's study has concentrated its emphasis on the purely political strategies which led to the non-

Brahmin movement, Dushkin's analysis projects the interaction between the various social factors in the making of a BCM in Karnataka. Both have documented the process of caste mobilisation among the Veerasaivas and other non-Brahmins only during Princely rule in Mysore.

As is common to any caste group, the caste association of the Lingayats is also a product of a socio-political process which developed in the form of a non-Brahmin movement during the early part of the twentieth century. Inspired, as it was, by a similar movement in the neighbouring, erstwhile Madras State (now the State of Tamil Nadu), the non-Brahmin movement in Karnataka was championed by the two dominant castes of the region – the Lingayats and the Vokkaligas – and aimed at attacking the so-called supremacy of the Brahmins, not only ritual supremacy, but also economic and administrative.

Introduction of English education and decentralisation of the administrative system by the British opened the gates of a hitherto traditional society to let in modern ideas based on science and technology. Although the Brahmins were the first beneficiaries of this system, it gradually spread to the other groups through a thorough process of emulation. The first batch of beneficiaries were a few rich, urban-living, English educated men belonging to the dominant castes of the different Indian states, who were hitherto largely agricultural groups. Brahmin domination in government service, starting from the office of the Dewan, came to be widely resented by these young non-Brahmins who were encouraged in such action by such stalwarts of the non-Brahmin movement like late Dr. C. R. Reddy (Manor : 1977, Dushkin : 1974, Hettne and Tamm : 1974).

The main objective of the movement was to seek representation for the non-Brahmins in government service and seats in educational institutions seeking thereby to achieve the same status and power as enjoyed by the Brahmins. Since education, especially higher education, was considered the key to access government jobs, the leaders of the non-Brahmin movement gave serious attention to the starting of their own educational institutions to enable the children from their community to seek such education. This needed not only enterprise but also huge sums of money to support them. Thus, the idea of forming a caste association occurred to their minds, that was a result of the influence of a similar process of mobilisation by the non-Brahmin castes in Tamil Nadu and Maharashtra (Irschick : 1969 and Omvedt : 1976).[23]

At this point of time, as well as the Lingayats constituted a dominant community in both the Princely Mysore the Bombay-Karnataka and the Hyderabad Karnataka areas. They enjoyed numerical, economic and political dominance as the second most populous community in Princely Mysore.[24] They were also well distributed in the State (12 per cent of the state's (Princely Mysore's) population in 1931 (Manor : 1977).

Though the three regions represented considerable cultural diversity, in terms of linguistic differences, the attempts to mobilise their caste were launched on almost an equal footing by the Lingayats. However, the initiative to establish a caste association was mooted by a few educated young Lingayat men from the Bombay-Karnataka area.

Just as the way the non-Brahmins in Princely Mysore came under the influence of the non-Brahmin movement of the then Madras[25] state, the movement led by the Marathas and other landed non-Brahmin communities in Western India appears to have inspired a few Bombay-educated, rich Veerasaiva young men to protest against the so-called Brahmin domination. While the Dewans to Kings in Princely Mysore were accused of appointing Brahmins to all key positions in the administration apart from other forms of exploitation through their socio-ritual supremacy, it was the Peshwa rule in Western India that enraged non-Brahmins who constituted the major communities in the Bombay-Karnataka area (Omvedt : 1976). Education was held by a few enlightened non-Brahmin leaders as the panacea for all the ills of their communities like backwardness and economic exploitation. Along with it came the lure of government employment as a means for seeking progress. As in the Madras Presidency, representations were made by the Lingayats and the Marathas to the Bombay government requesting them to give preference to the non-Brahmins while appointing officials to higher government posts.

As stated in the previous paragraph, the movement against Peshwa rule – in terms of the Peshwas' (Brahmins) monopoly over education and government employment – in the Bombay-Karnataka areas was an offshoot of a broader movement in Maharashtra. This, no doubt, facilitated the Lingayats with a model to organise a movement, but did not help them fully. In other words, the movement did not either prove beneficial to the Lingayats or were they successful in participating in it fully. Instead, it was feared that the movement might just use them for providing numbers to it while the rewards went to the Marathas. The Lingayats had to guard themselves from two types of exploitation: one by the Brahmins and the other by their non-Brahmin counterparts – the Marathas. This was especially true in the case of those Lingayats inhabiting the northern-most districts of the state like Belgaum, Bijapur and Gulbarga. The feeling of insecurity and frustration on the part of this group emerged from the fact that they belonged to a different culture than that of the Marathas, who led the non-Brahmin movement in that part of the country.[26] The language, religious practices, food habits and other cultural habits of the Lingayats differed substantially from the Marathas who constituted a major section of the population in the region.

It is commonly observed that in any social movement, which

involves the active participation by more than one group, it is the most resourceful group that wins over the others in capturing all the gains of development. The less resourceful ones, who may even be the largest in their number in the region, may fail to compete with the former.

To counter the Maratha dominance, the Veerasaivas had to inevitably seek help from the south – the Princely Government in Mysore. But for the support which the Marathas enjoyed in the Bombay-Karnataka area, the Lingayats did not lack much of what the former possessed. Religious autonomy, numerical strength along with economic resources etc., were the advantages which the Lingayats possessed as compared to the non-Maratha population in Princely Mysore. Some zones in the Bombay-Karnataka region contained a number of rich, aristocratic landlord families among the Lingayats, who also ruled their respective provinces as petty kings or rulers.[27] In that region such rulers were addressed as Desais in the pre-independence period. These petty rulers had also developed political relations with the British and in fighting between them and the Peshwas and the Marathas. Some of these rulers (Desais) had also taken recourse to English education and were practicing as lawyers at the Bombay High Court.

Apart from these, several other factors have to be looked into while tracking the origin of the Veerasaiva caste association in Karnataka. The fundamental strengthening factor in this process was the support given by a highly developed, autonomous, culturally and economically resourceful religious base upon which Veerasaivism stood. This went a long way in putting the socio-political imprint of the community on the map of Karnataka. The Veerasaiva religious mutts headed by Swamijis (many of which are found in northern Karnataka where the social movement by Basava had its origin) gave extensive financial help and moral protection to the Lingayat leaders in their efforts to mobilise the group educationally and socially.

Due to the farsightedness, courage and competitive spirit of the Veerasaiva leaders, and above all, their aspirations for economic gains and social status, the Akila Bharatha Veerasaiva Maha Sabha (ABVMS) was formed in the year 1904. It was established at Dharwar, a "central place in northern Karnataka". The leadership was provided by Sri Kumara Swamigalu of Hanagal Mutt and a group of Veerasaiva leaders, among whom were rich landlords, legal experts, philanthropists, two rulers (or Desais), two Dewans, freedom fighters and other key persons (elite) of the community (Souvenir of the Mahasabha : 1973).[28]

The first Conference of the Sabha was held at Dharwar in 1904 under the presidentship of Sri Lingappa Jayappa Sirdesai of Sirsangi, a petty ruler from Belgaum who donated a huge sum towards the Sabha and later towards the establishment of an Educational Society. The Karnataka Lingayat Education Society (KLE Society, as it is popularly known) is the oldest and one of the leading Educational Societies in the State, running a number of schools and colleges not only in Belgaum and other northern districts but also in the south and in the capital city of Bangalore.

In the following year, Desai presided over the second conference held at Bangalore, which emphasised the growing need for facilities for education like hostels and scholarships to Veerasaiva students, particularly those coming from rural areas. As a result, Veerasaiva Educational Fund Associations were established by the Mahasabha in several places. They came to be located at places where Lingayats were living in large numbers, like in Dharwar, Bagalkot, Bellary, Davanagere and Bangalore. This is how the Vidya Vardhak Sangha of Dharwar and the Mysore Lingayat Educational Fund Association (MLEFA) of Bangalore came into existence during this period. The selection of these two urban centres spoke about their importance as key centres of mobilisation representing northern and southern Karnataka.

The Veerasaiva Mahasabha was thus established as an offshoot of the non-Brahmin movement. It emphasised not only the educational development of the Veerasaiva community, but also pledged to work for the integration of the group along with striving for progress in the spheres of employment, art, religion and culture (Souvenir of the 19th Conference of the Mahasabha : 1973). These were the main goals of the Sabha as it shared its ideals with Dayanand Saraswathi's Arya Samaj, Raja Ram Mohan Roy's Brahma Samaj and Sawarkar's Hindu Mahasabha (Sri Jagadguru Channabasava Niranjana Mahaswamigalu : 1981). The Mahasabha not only had definite goals but also clear-cut method of implementing them, a great part of which was learnt from similar efforts in the neighbouring states.

The subsequent meetings of the Sabha, commonly celebrated as caste conferences, were held at various towns and cities, both in Old Mysore and the Bombay-Karnataka areas, wherever Lingayats were predominantly found. This excluded the Hyderabad Karnataka area, despite the large presence of Lingayats there. It facilitated the awakening among Lingayats living in the neighbouring states of Andhra Pradesh, Tamil Nadu and Maharashtra. Propaganda was given to the activities of the Mahasabha and utmost interest was taken to introduce the donors and leaders hailing from the above two regions, to the community throughout the state. It is noteworthy that the movement was not popular in the Hyderabad-Karnataka area (as much as it did in the Bombay-Karnataka area) despite the presence of a large number of Lingayats there.

After its inception in the year 1904, the ABVMS met almost every year till 1909, presided over by Lingayat leaders belonging mostly to the Bombay-Karnataka area. We observe that, between the years 1909-1919, only four conferences were held. Subsequently, the meetings became irregular (see Appendix 4.3).

Economic dominance coupled with political power and religious control enjoyed by the upper strata of the Lingayat group was reflected in the composition and activities of the Mahasabha. But the process of caste mobilisation cannot be interpreted always in terms of sectarianism. The process which activated itself in the form of an association committed to the welfare of the whole caste group did not show characteristics of caste alone, but exhibited abundant class tendencies when it included among its leaders and beneficiaries only the upper strata of the group concerned.

Similarly, the lower caste groups among the Lingayats, except a few families of important upper castes, became resourceful enough to seek representation in the Mahasabha only recently. Nevertheless, intracaste inequalities with in the Lingayat fold have been under-emphasised or overlooked, even by the most conservatives like the Swamijis, strangely at a time when democratic and egalitarian values were not fashionable among even the few educated Lingayats. This is particularly visible at times when the Sabha suffered from any financial or moral crisis. During such events, the co-operation of all sub-castes was sought by the upper-caste Lingayats, irrespective of intra-caste barriers.

For example, the Mahasabha, within a year of its establishment proposed to start an educational fund at Bangalore, for which it faced some difficulty in obtaining the permission of the concerned authorities (Souvenir : 1973). The situation demanded the help of some one who hailed from the region with sufficient political enterprise to move things at higher levels. The officers of the Mahasabha were thus in a dilemma. By that time, Old Mysore was in the grip of the non-Brahmin movement which was led by Sri Basavayya, a Lingayat hailing from Tiptur of the present Tumkur district. Basavayya's father was under the service of the royal family at Mysore. After his higher education in Law, Basavayya was practicing at Bellary refusing to be under the mercy of the King of Mysore. His name ending with the suffix 'Ayya' denoting the name of a man from the priestly "Jangama" community was misleading to the upper caste Lingayats. However, they later discovered that he belonged to the "Sadu" Lingayat subcaste which was held as relatively a low caste among the Veerasaivas (Deveerappa : 1980).

The leaders of the Mahasabha and other Lingayat elite initially hesitated to seek the help of Basavayya, owing to his caste background. However, they found no alternative but to approach him for help due to his 'close contacts with the king and the administration at Princely Mysore'. Even the Swamiji of a leading mutt from Central Karnataka, viz., the Muruga Rajendra Mutt of Chitradurga, who was also one of the few donors of the MLEFA, received this 'leader' without any considerations of his (Basavayya's) inferior caste status among the Lingayats, and reportedly offered to him to sit next to him (Deveerappa : 1980).

The above account does not mean that the Sabha was totally inactive in Old Mysore area or that the people there were ignorant of it. The establishment of the MLEFA under the auspices of the Mahasabha at Bangalore in 1906 gave it a firm foundation in the Old Mysore area. Similar educational funds at Dharwar, Bagalkot and other places in the Bombay Karnatak area which were started around the same period, came to be strengthened subsequently. Thus, the educational interests of the Lingayat community came to constitute the chief functions of its caste association.

Veerasaiva Mutts and Caste Mobilisation

The Veerasaiva Mutts may be credited with spreading the seeds of caste mobilisation among the members of the community. Their contribution, apart from their welfare-oriented work, lied in the fact that the educational advancement of the community was given prime importance. A detailed account of the role of the Mutts in the field of education in Karnataka is covered in the next chapter. Suffice it to note here that the general process of caste mobilisation, including the functions of the ABVMS was considerably affected by these Mutts. A brief review of some of the salient features of this impact is made here to facilitate a thorough analysis of the process among the Lingayats in Karnataka.

The support of religious institutions like Mutts and Matadhipathis – whose role in the socio-political activities of the state is increasing – to the cause of the Lingayats is quite a complex subject to be analysed in a nutshell. There are more than four thousand Veerasaiva Mutts in Karnataka. The leading among them are Sree Murugarajendra Mutt of Chitradurga, Sree Muruga Mutt of Dharwar, Sree Murusavira Mutt of Hubli, Sree Thontadarya Mutt of Gadag in Dharwar district, the Ilkal Samsthan Mutt of Ilkal in Bijapur district, Sree Sharanabasaveswar Peetha at Gulbarga, Sree Taralabalu Bruhanmutt at Sirigere near Chitradurga, Sree Rambhapuri Mutt at Balehonnur in Chikmagalur district, Sree Suttur Mutt in Mysore and Sree Siddaganga Mutt in Tumkur.[29]

These multiple numbers of Veerasaiva mutts took keen interest in secular functions by either starting centres of education or by donating huge sums from the Mutt property towards the cause of Lingayat education. Such contributions generally assumed the form of setting up of free boarding-homes, granting facilities like scholarships and freeships to poor and deserving Lingayat students and so on. The gospel of unity and equality among all Veerasaivas, irrespective of subcaste differences, came to be mandatorily preached by the heads of the mutts in all the conferences of the Mahasabha (Souvenirs of the ABVMS : 1973, 1983 & 2005). This role made them distinctive in their mobilisation efforts as compared to their counterparts in the other caste groups. The credit for expanding the idea and efforts of private education in Karnataka through sectarian lines went to the Lingayat mutts, despite that a beginning had already been made by Dr. T. M.A. Pai, who founded the Manipal Academy of Education. Education, no doubt, came to be regarded by the non-Brahmins as an important variable in their activities. The model for this idea had been provided by the British, but more than them, it was the non-Brahmins, who came to influence many-a-non-Brahmin groups to emulate the former in working towards better social mobility. The British provided a general model which was first reciprocated by the Brahmins with no hurdles as they were traditionally allowed to both learn and to teach. English education provided them a new avenue for higher economic growth through seeking employment in British administration.

This benefit of obtaining English education was not only realised by the Brahmins, but it echoed at all the channels of caste hierarchy. Inspired by this new opening, there appears to be an upsurge of activity by all the non-Brahmin groups to spread the importance of education among their members. Caste associations were formed chiefly with this as an objective.

But not all caste associations were resourceful enough to implement whatever they visualised to be right for reforming the community. While some had to rest content with just campaigning for educational development, a few others were able to start a few caste-based hostels in important urban centres like Mysore and Bangalore. In a majority of such cases, the attempt by the caste associations to work for the educational upliftment of their caste-folk was not without the help from Dewans, administrators or businessmen-turned-philanthropists belonging to the respective caste groups.[30]

The Lingayat caste group stands out as the first caste to lay its hands upon the process of starting educational institutions of its own, as early as in the first decade of the twentieth century.

However, this pioneering task should be evaluated in the light of certain socio-economic factors characterising the community. To begin with, the community enjoyed, since a long time, a culturally and economically rich and secure religious patronage in the form of Mutts. In fact, these religious institutions have come to wield, through the centuries, remarkable influence over their "Bhaktas" (devotees), engulfing the economic, political and cultural facets of their lives. The position enjoyed and the role played by these Mutts has not only withstood the various socio-political challenges through the decades, but has also become a model for other (non-Lingayat as well as Brahmin) castes to emulate.

The answer for this lies, perhaps, in the fact that the mutts always developed a close liaison with their devotees by acting not only as their spiritual guide, but more as a regulator of their political and economic life. The mutts' lands were tilled by these Bhaktas and the Swamiji was traditionally considered as their living God, helping them to solve their litigation, both intra-caste and familial. This role played by the Mutts has continued even to this day, only with certain modifications. Independence and the changes that it subsequently brought upon the Indian society have only increased the role of these religious institutions, perhaps with a greater political orientation.

The original philosophies of Veerasaivism resting already on a firm foundation provided by the Mutts were strengthened by the adoption of Basava's principles of equality and humanitarianism. It gave the Sect a stable cultural footing with emphasis on charity and hard work. The concept of "Dasoha"[31] and the informal nature of religious ties must all be highlighted while analysing the role of Mutts in the mobilisation attempts by the Veerasaivas.

As already noted, the Mutts took upon themselves the added

responsibility of popularising English education, apart from their existing duty of teaching Sanskrit and heralding the principles of Veerasaivism. Both the duties appear to have been carried out with equal zeal and concern by them. Thus, the Educational Fund Associations and the educational institutions became rather more popular and useful to the community for their practical value and economic utility (Hiremath R. C. : 1983). The hostels and scholarship facilities offered by these Fund Associations proved to be of great help to the Lingayat students, especially those hailing from rural areas. After pursuing their education and obtaining thereby positions in the administration, these men were obliged to serve the Fund in varying capacities as a gesture of their gratitude to it.[32] This system benefited the association to grow in size and acquire stability, both in terms of money and time. Changes in the political structure did not cause much disruption or discontinuance of this practice by virtue of the 'dominance' of this community. Thus, the Lingayats who were hitherto leading a traditional life could achieve educational prosperity which only widened their control or 'dominance'.

The above account of Veerasaiva Mutts indicates that religious solidarity brings its own advantages to a community. By this, one should understand the economic, ritual and political security that it provides to its members. Secondly, the community is blessed with an equally well-knit, informal system of religious heads or 'Swamijis' who act as the protagonists of both tradition and modernity. These factors have contributed, in a large measure, to the growth and development of the Sabha and its members.

The above explanation is also intended to make clear the fact that the ABVMS, representing the Veerasaiva community in Karnataka, though a caste association like any other in the State, stands out as something entirely different, structurally and functionally. It has a highly complex but unique history.

During the pre-independence period, the caste mobilisation process among the Lingayats was characterised by their protest against the so-called Brahminical supremacy, which assumed the form of a Backward Classes movement. This period is notable for the formation of the ABVMS – the Lingayat Caste Association – and the attempts to stabilise it through organising caste conferences.

The Post-Independence Era

(a) The Pre-Reorganisation Period (1947-1956)

There appears to be not much of a change or progress in the educational and other welfare activities of the ABVMS during this period. Reorganisation led to a change in dominance as a result of which Mysore it came to be ruled by Veerasaiva Chief Ministers for more than a decade, i.e., till 1972. The Veerasaivas constituting a socially, economically and politically dominant group, such representation in politics made a strong dent upon the process of caste mobilisation. However, in comparison with the post-re-organisation period this impact is not that significant.

(b) The Post-Re-organisation Period (1956-1972)

The re-organisation of the State of Mysore (now renamed as Karnataka), in the year 1956, proved to be a turning point in the history of caste mobilisation by the Veerasaivas. Such a move meant a lot of political, economic and cultural significance to the group. The districts included from the northern region comprising the Bombay-Karnataka and Hyderabad-Karnataka areas contained large segments of Lingayat population thereby affecting the demographic composition of the State and its socio-cultural character. It also signalled a long and continuous process of rule by Lingayat Chief Ministers over the state (followed by a similarly long duration of rule by Chief Ministers from Vokkaliga caste from 1947-1956).

These events only gave a further facelift to the Sabha's

activities. With the State's administration being in the hands of Lingayats,[33] the Sabha worked as an agency of social mobility. Caste conferences organised by the Sabha emphasised both educational and economic development of the community. These became less in the frequency of their occurrence in the later years , i.e., to being held once in 5-10 years from the earlier frequency of 2-3 years' once (see, Appendix 4.3)unity. The agenda for discussion in these conferences and Sabha meetings concentrated upon the possible means and ways of obtaining sanction of professonal colleges (mainly Medical and Enginering) and a status of 'backwardness' to the community. They also discussed the issue of protecting the community from caste based exclusion and emphasised upon reserving seats for the youth in both educational institutions and in government employment. What the spokesmen of the Sabha disliked was that they had to share such backward status with the Vokkaligas, the other dominant caste (Proceedings of ABVMS meetings held at Mysore and Bangalore : 1982, 1993 and 2006).

The first phase of caste mobilisation by the Veerasaivas followed a different channel, when the generous help and support for this process came predominantly from the religious Mutts and a few philanthropists of the community. The MLEFA, established later than the ABVMS also played an important role here. The re-organisation of the state in 1956, no doubt, continued this process. An additional factor was the large-scale political support that they came to gain with the transfer of power to Veerasaiva Chief Ministers. But the Sabha's documents did not show evidence of any material gains from the government being run by their own community men (such as a site or a building). The need for such benefits came to be felt during the seventies (Souvenir of the ABVMS's 19th Conference, Bangalore : 1973), when attention was paid towards their strengthening their hold over private education. In addition to schools and colleges being run under religious mutts, few more professional colleges were also started under the patronage of these Lingayat Chief Ministers. Thus, the Veerasaiva caste association as an essentially "political-interest group" had a relatively less significant role when the state was headed by Lingayats as Chief Ministers and rose in its importance with the changes in political power in 1971 after the state came under rule by Devraj Urs.

© Post-Havanur Commission years (1972 and after)

The Seventies introduced a revival of activities on an entirely different plane for the Veerasaiva Mahasabha. The beginning years of the decade witnessed two major setbacks to it. One was the loosing of Lingayats' hold over the state politics with the dawn of rule by Chief Ministers from non-dominant castes beginning with Sri Devaraj Urs.[34] The second was the appointment of the Karnataka Backward Classes Commission by Urs in 1972 that classified the Lingayats as a 'forward group'. Being already disappointed by loosing political power, the reformist measures introdued by Urs like Land Reforms, abolition of bonded labour etc.[35], (the Lingayats were the chief target of such reforms being a dominant caste) only added more fuel to the fire.

As the policy of reservations was implemented with much political seriousness during Urs' time, anger against Urs' government reached its zenith at this time. The antagonism did not come as a surprise to both i.e., the Lingayats and the government, as it was never a sudden upsurge, but one that resulted from a combination of a number of preceding political factors .[36] It came to end their long cherished and uninterrupted 'backward' status under varying political regimes. The first blow was denial of reservation of seats in educational institutions and employment. The second was the threat of having to face greater competition from others, especially their immediate "inferiors" and staunch rivals – the Vokkaligas. The innumerable educational institutions, both small and big, started and run by the various educational societies as well as the pre-dominant hold this community enjoyed over government employment, judiciary and other fields[37] came to be affected by the new government's policies and programmes.

Thus a series of confrontations occurred between the government and the community's leaders, who resorted to protest movements to express their grievances particularly about the exclusion of Veerasaivas from the list of backwards.[38]

It was under these circumstances that the ABVMS regained its activities in the wake of the appointment of the KBCC (during 1972-73) pledging to work for restoring the lost backward status to the community (Souvenir : 1973). The changed circumstances leading to denial of reservation facilities to the community by the Havanur report provided a new footing upon which stood the Sabha's renewed functions.

Considering the prevailing need for a President who would suit the requirements of the day, the Mahasabha found a ray of hope in Sri J.B. Mallaradhya[39], a retired IAS officer. He belonged to the Aradhya subcaste (the priestly caste among Lingayats) and hailed from a small village near Mysore city. Apart from his high educational achievements and experience in government service as a senior officer, Mallaradhya was also an ex-member of the Representative Assembly formed by the Princely Government. His selection as the President of the ABVMS in 1973 also coincided with a reinforced, new phase of caste mobilisation activities by the Sabha, that started working with greater zeal and new ideas since 1973, set before itself the task of demanding from the government the return of the backward status to the community.

The above narration is a reflection of the strategies adopted by the Sabha. The events since 1970s offered a new channel or socio-political spring-board of opportunities for mobility. Losing of political power was an costly blow to bear for the Lingayat elite. As is common under such circumstances, group interest gained precedence over individual need and intra-group conflict was given a lesser importance. The call for unity among all the subcastes was mooted strongly.

Thus, the Mahasabha took upon itself the task of regaining to the Lingayats their "lost" status. The election of the new president in 1973 was the first step in this direction. It was also accepted perhaps owing to the inevitability of the situation[40] and the limited impact the Sabha hitherto had wielded on the heterogeneous Lingayat community. The ABVMS marched ahead with its campaign for ending of the discrimination meted out against the Lingayats. More appropriately, it condemned the government's treatment of the group as a 'forward' caste and sought continuation of reservation facilities conferred on the community since 1916. It emphasised that the ritual superiority of the lingayat caste or its upper caste status did not necessarily indicate its advanced status in the realm of education and government employment. Its main demand was to achieve continued reservation of seats in both education and employment, on the grounds that the community was still very backward in these respects.

The Mahasabha's campaign, under the leadership of its President and a group of supporters from a cross-section of the Veerasaiva population like traders, politicians and professionals constituting its elite, assumed the form of a protest movement against the government. The fact that the Swamijis of leading Veerasaiva mutts also offered their support to the movement added more strenght to it. The Sabha arranged a number of caste conferences commemorating its anniversary celebrations using them to place the demands before a large audience to gain confidence and support of its members (Proceedings of Conferences).

However, changes occured as a result of the amendments in the government's policy itself. The Urs government, perhaps owing to pressure from Lingayat legislators (also for certain of its own political interests), created a new category of backwardness known as the 'Special Group'. It accommodated the poorer sections among the Lingayats to benefit from reservations on grounds of income as the criterion. This category determined a family/individual, despite being 'upper' in caste status, as backward based upon considerations of occupation and income. It was meant to help those economically weaker sections falling within an upper caste (like Lingayats or Brahmins) by considering class and not caste as the criterion. Under this category, 15 per cent of seats in government jobs and educational institutions were earmarked to the poor among the upper caste groups. Any person whose parents'/guardians' income was below the ceiling fixed by the Commission, was declared eligible to claim reservation benefits, irrespective of her/his upper caste/tribe status. This step was "an excellent strategy for mobilising the forward groups......" and "for Urs to claim that his government had largely taken economic status as the determining factor" in granting reservations (Natraj and Natraj : 1982). Further, it could evoke the support of the lower sections among the Lingayats, especially the converts to Veerasaivism.[41]

Both the Mahasabha and the whole gamut of leadership among the Lingayats were not evidently happy over this concession. In other words, the criteria fixed by the "Special Group" category was based on income and occupation which apparently did not help the elite of the community who formed its leadership. The Sabha continued its protest at the instance of its President, taking recourse to law. It was pointed out that the Urs government had done great injustice to the group by overlooking many instances to prove the backwardness of the

Lingayats although it was an upper caste. The crux of its argument lied in the fact that the Havanur Commission had taken a wrong and incomplete census of the Veerasaiva population in the state. It was also alleged that the Commission had concentrated its work in a few localities in certain towns and cities, while the large majority of the community members lived in the rural areas. The Commission was also criticised as being misled in its data by the subcaste name of Lingayats which were based on the occupations they professed – like the Ganiga Lingayats (oil pressors), the Reddy Lingayats (an agricultural community distinct from the Reddis among the Vokkaligas), and other traditional village functionaries like the Barbers, the Washermen, etc. Memoranda, including all these factors, were submitted to the state and the Union governments demanding rescheduling of the Backward Classes in Karnataka (copy of the Memorandum : 1979). A delegation of Veerasaiva leaders, (who incidentally were not office-bearers of the Sabha) deposed before the Commission and gave memoranda (the KBCC Report : 1975). The Sabha also evinced keen interest in representing the woes of the community before the Mandal Commission appointed by the Government of India in 1977 (Memoranda : 1977). The Havanur Commission's classification of the group as 'forward' came to be challenged in the Supreme Court as a constitutional fraud (K. C. Vasantha Kumar and others Vs. *State of Karnataka*, Writ petition Nos. 1297-98 and 1407/79).

As noted earlier, during the decade 1972 to 1982, the state came under the rule of two different Chief Ministers. Consequently, even the Mahasabha's activities were influenced by the varying political policies of these governments. The rule by Devraj Urs from 1972-80 came to be viewed with contempt and was the target of attack because of its policy towards the Lingayats. The rule by the Gundu Rao government between the years 1980-83 also did not please the Lingayats, stemming mainly from the policy of even this government to continue the saga of reservations on the same lines, as the previous governments had done. What is more, the policy was implemented with much fanfare and political manipulation. It is important to note here that the Constitutional position of the Lingayats did not undergo any change. Instead, the government, yielding to pressure from the other non-Lingayat backward castes went ahead sanctioning a number of professional colleges. It became a highly controversial issue during 1980-83 and continued later also during the Janata government.

The beneficiaries of this turn of events were a few representatives of the backward communities who inadvertently set the trend for an untiring demand for medical and engineering colleges.[42] This also led to a state-wide agitation by students who were not only against opening of such colleges, but also demanded the abolition of the system of capitation fees. It was even alleged by a few backward caste leaders who started such new colleges that the agitation was instigated by the Lingayats, who were frustrated over losing their monopoly over private education; hence sought 'to block new ones so that they can collect capitation fee unabated' (Deccan Herald : February 2, 1981).

The year 1981 goes on record in the history of the Mahasabha, as it (Sabha) undertook a novel method to draw attention from the government to be identified as deserving reservation facilities to the Lingayats. It carried on a state-wide propaganda requesting the Lingayats to enlist themselves as "Veerasaiva", irrespective of their subcaste differences. Such a call was not new to the members of the community. But the Mahasabha demanded the Veerasaivas to be categorised in the Census of 1981 as a separate religious group – Veeasaivism – on par with Sikhism, Buddhism, Jainism and Zoroastrianism. Thus, the Veerasaivas or Lingayats were directed to register their religion not as Hinduism, but as Veerasaivism, by writing it under the 'other religions' category of the census form. The Registrar General of Census did not agree for this requisition of the Mahasabha. Therefore, in the Census of 1981, the Veerasaivas were included under the Hindus. It would be pertinent to recall here Justice Gajendragadkar's observation in the famous *Balaji's Case* (AIR 1963) that the Veerasaivas did not regard themselves as Hindus.

Such a separatist tendency on the part of the Mahasabha, as disclosed by its President, was to give religious autonomy to the group (Mallaradhya : 1977). The Sabha aimed at gaining both a non-Hindu status as well as access to reservation of seats under Articles 15 and 16. The idea was that separate enumeration would enable numerical strength and provide visibility to the Lingayats' educational and economic backwardness through such separate identity, than being grouped or compared with others. The Sabha and its President worked diligently during this period as this was regarded as a crucial stage in the mobilisation of Veerasaivas. The Sabha was also able to grow in its size as an institution, over the years since 1972 – the year which opened up a different horizon for it to operate upon. Sub-sabhas or branches of the Mahasabha established at important urban centres and taluk headquarters, where the Lingayats lived in large numbers, also came to play an active role in spreading this message of separate religious identity of Veerasaivas.

The Sabha was not alone in its fight for the welfare of the Veerasaivas. The religious foundation, upon which the Sabha relied for financial and moral support, was exploited in the present movement, predominantly, to gain recognition for its activities. The caste conferences and caste meetings held in various parts of the State (even in rural areas) were attended by people in large numbers at least to seek blessings from heads of local Lingayat Mutts who presided over them.

The caste conferences had also combined in themselves many other targets to be achieved. The issue of claiming autonomy through the Census was, no doubt, the prime concern of the above conferences. But it was also planned, at least indirectly, to serve two other purposes. The President of the Mahasabha, in his efforts to "reform" the group, had also mobilised political aspirations among his supporters, who formed a caucus around him wherever he went and addressed the people. The main idea behind such urgently arranged conferences was to collect, on the spot, funds for the Mahasabha's activities. These included, among other things, funds to meet the President's travel and other requirements to participate in the court proceedings at Delhi. This had caused, naturally, much resentment (however faintly expressed) at the President's style of functioning (Interviews with the office-bearers of the Sabha).[43]

The above discussion sheds light on the on-going process of conflict between the representatives of Veerasaiva caste and the state. It is too complex and detailed a subject to be explained in terms of any single factor. However, the interplay of the varied forces of modernisation, like education and the consequent spatial and occupational mobility that it had brought upon, have converted a hitherto homogeneous population (comparatively speaking), into a complex and heterogeneous one. Further, the process of protective discrimination has almost become institutionalised in Indian society, exhibiting many prospects of advantages to communities thereby encouraging the continuous process of fission. All this has resulted in a keen competition for the gains of development and an undeterred process of sectarian mobilisation.

The above explanation is only to substantiate the ineffectiveness of the ABVMS in its campaign during the census of 1981. Despite the extravagant propaganda given to the activities of the movement, it suffered from certain fundamental and inherent drawbacks, culminating from the very nature of the movement. The major demand of the Mahasabha, seeking

Veerasaivism to be categorised as a separate religion, failed to evoke much sympathy and support from the members of the community. Cross-verification of the information provided by the Sabha's authorities has pointed to the prevalence of an extensive feeling of discontentment and disagreement amongst the organisers and other associates of the conferences. It is too well established a fact that the ideals of caste system are strongly rooted in the cultural practices of the members of every caste. Lingayats were no exception to this. The different subcastes within this caste – a majority of which were the result of the process of conversion that is supposed to have taken place during and after Basava's time – are strictly endogamous. Such being the case, any call to overcome these differences which have stemmed out not only on caste-lines but portrayed inherent class tendencies, failed to lead to the desired results. The middle and lower sections of Lingayat caste practiced own caste occupations (as weavers, washermen, barbers, carpenters, smiths, oilmen etc.), even after conversion to Veerasaivism. They had realized pretty well that their inferior position within the caste hierarchy had not changed with conversion. They came to be attracted by the policy of protective discrimination under the "Special Group" category, which was not accessible to them if they identified themselves as just Lingayats. Instead, they sought backward status on par with their non-Lingayat counterparts in the same vocation and who had been already declared as either backward castes and sometimes scheduled castes (in other states). Whether such a rationale was acceptable to all the members of their respective subcastes or not and they consented to it then to what extent — are some of the questions that arise in this context and deserve further research.

Another explanation offered for the failure of the Mahasabha in taking all Lingayats into its fold during the campaign in 1981 related to the "economics" of such a change proposed by the Sabha. The advantages of reservation was much larger for a backward class beneficiary from Hinduism than what those from the non-Hindu communities would obtain in the bargain, owing to the pre-existing socio-cultural limitations. Secondly, the socio-economic security enabled and ensured by Hinduism was perceived to be any day stronger and more stable than trying to stand alone or outside it, independent status, in the long run, leads to insecurity and would be potentially shortlived. Thirdly, there was also lack of complete support from the upper strata of the community consisting of educated, urban-living government-employed Lingayats and the business group to these ideas. Worse, they had even turned apathetic towards them. For example, the proposal to categorise their caste as non-Hindu received very low — almost negligible response — from the community.

Further, the leadership pattern of the Lingayats was held to be incompetent and partial in its coverage. As stated earlier, the local leadership in each block or district came to be constituted by political aspirants. It was, in some cases, accompanied by a concrete backing by the Swamijis of local Mutts who tended to capitalise upon populism.[44] The Sabha's work in the rural areas benefited only such "aspiring" politicians, making little dent on the masses. This was evident in the caste conferences held by the Sabha in the later years. It could be concluded that, the ABVMS's campaign in 1981 gave a different channel to the movement to march on. It thus indirectly supported the government in power in its criticising the Urs' government.[45]

3. Karnataka Arya Vyshya Mahasabha

The Vyshyas are the important trading community of Karnataka constituting 0.59 per cent of the state's population and distributed throughout the state, in almost all districts. The community is known by their synonymous names like Komati and Setti. In Kollegal they are known as Chettis and in Kodagu district, as Baniyas. The significance of discussing their caste association lies in the fact that they are the only caste group who till recently had not expressed their desire for a backward status. The Karnataka Arya Vyshya Mahasabha, the caste association of the Vyshyas (or Vaishyas) came into existence in the year 1908 at Bangalore, almost along with the other upper caste associations. But the Sabha seems to have run on a different line of mobilisation trying to develop self-help and self-sufficiency among the Vyshyas. Over the decades, the association has extended its activities by opening branches in almost every district where the 'Vyshyas are found'. Educational institutions have also been established under its umbrella at Bangalore and a few other places. The institutions have been self-financing with no help sought from the government in this regard. This apart, the Sabha has started a number of hostels for poor Vyshya children including a few ladies' hostels. There are also a number of marriage halls/choultries established by philanthropists and businessmen to cater to the needs of the community.

The silence on the part of the Vyshya Mahasabha from making any claim over the community's backwardness was confined to pre-Urs regime and was, shortlived. Subsequently, the Mahasabha has been placing requisitions before the government and various Backward Classes Commissions in the last two decades for conferring increased backward status to the Vyshya community while at the same time promoting self-dependence by its members. This adds a uniqueness to its efforts to promote social mobility.

4. The Akhila Karnataka Bunts' Sangha

The Bunts are a minority caste in Karnataka with 0.68 per cent of population (KBCC Report : 1975), found mostly in the districts of Kodagu, Dakshina Kannada and Udupi. Their caste association was started in the 1940s at Mangalore, an important coastal city in Dakshina Kannada district. The Bangalore branch was a recent addition. Known as the Bunts' or Nadavars' Sangha, it was established in the year 1908. The fundamental driving force behind this, like many other caste associations, was the awareness among a few educated Bhunts at Mangalore and neighbouring places "to progress on the lines of their upper castes" (Souvenir of the Golden Jubilee of the Vokkaligara Sangha : 1961). To begin with, a hostel by name 'Sree Ramakrishna Vidyarthi Bhavana' was started for the benefit of students from outside residing at Mangalore for seeking education. The Vidyarthi Bhavana has opened many branches in the following years, at places not only in Karnataka, but also in Kasargod and outside the state like in Bombay, Tamil Nadu and Kerala. Apart from providing boarding and lodging to poor studens of the caste, the Bhavana has launched a number of welfare schemes, like provision of hostels and scholarships to poor students.

"The second notable step taken by the Bunts' Sangha was in the field of the economic development of the community. Besides opening hostels, a commercial bank was started to cater to the needs of the community. Being one of the nationalised banks now, the Vijaya Bank (as it was labelled) began functioning in the year 1931 with its head office at Mangalore." It has expanded with a number of branches in the subsequent years, not only in the state, but even outside it (Souvenir : 1961: 80). By the time the Sangha celebrated its silver jubilee in 1952 it had attracted Bunts living in different parts of the State as well as from Bombay (where it is well established) and Chennai to its fold. Recognizing the need for women's education, the "Sree Ramakrishna Vidyarthini Bhavana" was also added to the Sangha's hostels in 1941.

The sixties and the seventies marked the introduction of a new wave of activities by the Bunts' Sangha, a trait qualifying most of the caste associations covered in this book. As part of its educational programmes, the Sangha evinced much interest in establishing schools and degree colleges in Dakshina and Uttara Kannada districts apart from a degree college in Bangalore.

It was the classification of the Bunts as a forward group by the Havanur Commission that initiated a process of mobilisation by them through their Sangha, a process that was slow in the beginning and gained momentum since the year 1980. Like many of its contemporaries, the Sangha began to represent from time to time the grievances of the community in the form of memoranda to successive Backward Classes' Commissions. It began to consistently request the commissions — by forming alliance with the Vokkaligas whom it considered its synonymous group in Old Mysore — to consider their caste as a backward group.[46] This was more like a strategy to achieve the goal of claiming backwardness than an attempt towards integration of the two castes. The Bunts though a numerical minority, are quite enterprising and have made good progress in the fields of trade and industry (banking, hotel and others), apart from their high landownership. Added to this, they have also taken to higher and professional education settling in Mumbai and other important urban centres.

More than anything else, the Bunts claimed themselves to be superior to their counterparts – the Vokkaligas. Marital alliances between the two have been, if not numerous, not disallowed, Choultries (marriage halls) built by the Bunts are used by the Vokkaligas for conducting weddings considering Bunts as own caste. Alliances are sought to bridge gap between their Sangha and that of the Bunts'. Obviously, till the eighties such an alliance was more evident at only the leadership level of the two communities. Subsequently, it lost its tempo due to a number of politico-economic events. It is noteworthy that such efforts have taken a more pronounced path after the Vokkaligara

Sangha started its professional colleges in the year 1980. It is nevertheless true that the Bunts have always claimed a different and enhanced status than the Vokkaligas. The trend towards unity between the two castes is part of the process of fusion to gain certain benefits, as a united community against the other dominant caste – the Lingayats.

5. The Vokkaligara Sangha

The Vokkaligas constitute one of the two dominant castes of the state of Karnataka inhabiting a major part of the province of Old Mysore covering the southern part of the state. The term 'Vokkaliga' literally means 'a tiller or an agriculturist'. The members of this community traditionally practiced agriculture as their main occupation. In fact, this should be explained conversely; all those who tilled the soil either as land owners or as landless workers came to constitute this class. Thus the term, 'Vokkaliga' is a blanket term, not representing a single caste, but a group of communities following more or less similar vocation (Manor : 1977). They were listed under a common heading by the Census Commissioners both from the year 1799 to 1804 and from1871 onwards when decennial census operations were commenced, referring mainly to the similarity in the occupations these different groups professed. Under the banner of Vokkaligas were found communities like the Gangadikaras, Morasu, Haalu, Hallikaara, Namdhaari, Kunchitigas and Reddis and others like Dasa-Vokkaligas, Beralu-Kodo-Vokkaliga, Musaku Vokkaliga etc. These subcastes were small, endogamous, autonomous entities depending on agricultural work for their livelihood. Although some of them were found engaged in jobs like cow herding, trade (petty goods) and so on, it was only as a subsidiary occupation, along with agriculture. These groups were also found occupying distinct geographical regions, which is reflected in their occupation, food habits, language, religious practices and even ethnicity. However, it appears that at least since the year 1891, these different subcastes or groups have been brought under one category, viz., the "Vokkaligas" for purposes of census operations.[47]

The Vokkaligas are traditionally found concentrated in the districts of Mandya, Mysore, Hassan, Bangalore, Kolar, Tumkur and Shimoga, although they are not totally absent in the remaining districts. These districts also represent the Old Mysore area, which was under the Princely Rule. But their population is unevenly distributed in all these districts (see Appendix 4.6 and 4. 7).

Among the different subcastes found within the Vokkaliga society, the Gangadikaras are a major group, consisting of about 55 per cent of the total Vokkaliga population (Manor : 1977). They are found predominantly in the districts of Mandya, Mysore, Bangalore South and Bangalore (Rural). This subcaste has achieved considerable representation in the economy and polity of the state, including the establishment and managing of the 'Vokkaligara Sangha', the Vokkaligas' caste association.

The Pre-Independence Era

Just as the Lingayats came under the influence of the non-Brahmin movement that subsequently led to the formation of their caste association, the same process was emulated by the Vokkaligas. The Vokkaliga leaders who were interviewed for the study have provided an entirely egalitarian rationale as the reason or force behind the establishment of their caste association. Regionally strong communal forces operated to motivate a few urban, educated, rich Vokkaliga men to think on the lines of setting up of a caste association. The non-Brahmin movement of Tamil Nadu, on the one hand, and the establishment of a caste association and an educational fund association in Bangalore by the Lingayats, on the other, were the inspiring force behind the move taken by the Vokkaligas to mobilise themselves on similar lines. Being a basically agricultural community, access to education and urban-based employment was comparatively limited in their case. Popularizing modernisation among such people was a challenging task indeed to the few young men who came to the forefront of leadership to "bring about all-round development of the Vokkaligas" (Souvenir of the Golden Jubilee celebrations of the Vokkaligara Sangha, Bangalore : 1961).

The leadership of the community consisted of a few educated young men who were employed under the government in the capacity of Amaldar, Tahasildar and other important positions in the pre-independence period. They were not many in number. Of the only five educated men of the community at that time, three, who were in government service, viz., Shri B.N. Chennigappa, an Amaldar and Sri B.Nagappa, a barrister, along with another man who was a Tahasildar, gave serious thought to the improving of the living conditions of their brethren. One Sri T. Byanna (father-in-law of B.Nagappa), a leading contractor at the Oorgaum Gold Mines (Kolar Gold Fields), further strengthened this idea when he promised them of financial help in the starting of a caste association (Souvenir : 1961). The matter was discussed with a wider group consisting of a few other prominent men of the community including Sri M. Subbayya, a gardening contractor (popularly known as 'Lalbagh Subbayya') and Sri K.H. Ramaiah (who was instrumental in raising the Sangha to a higher level) at Subbayya's garden on April 1, 1906. This was followed by subsequent meetings of a few communities/ elite of Bangalore on the 8th and 15th of the same month and the first ever Vokkaliga conference was scheduled to be held in October that year. A Committee was formed for this purpose with Pleader Sri B. Kempanna and Sri K.H. Ramaiah as President and Secretary respectively (Souvenir of the Golden Jubilee Celebrations : 1961 and the Diamond Jubilee Celebrations : 1982 of the Vokkaligara Sangha).

The October Conference held on 7th, 8th and 9th of the month, was significant in many ways. It heralded, for the first time, the spirit of unity between the different subcastes and succeeded in bringing together "thousands of Vokkaligas" under a common platform (Souvenir : 1982). Though the term 'Vokkaliga' was not new to them, its different subcastes had followed endogamy particularly in marriage and inter-dining. Motivating them to come together under one banner was the first felt need to mobilise them. Thus, intra-caste differences were viewed as having implications for mobilisation. It was the hard and dedicated work of few leaders, especially by Sri K.H. Ramaiah, that oriented the community towards these threats. Along with a few of his associates, Ramaiah was so much involved in the Sangha's activities that he found his government job a nuisance and got rid of it to make himself free to work for the community. The conference helped in giving a further boost to the term Vokkaliga or 'Gowda', which hitherto was held as something derogatory (Souvenir : 1982).

Such organisational capacity of the Vokkaligas and the fact that a few of them held key roles in the Province's administration, resulted in wielding its influence upon the Princely Government which yielded to their demands (Mari Gowda : January 1982). This request of the Sangha was supported and granted by the Yuvaraja (Crown Prince) of Princely Mysore (Gundappa : 1971). The dominance of the community, especially in the rural parts of the kingdom, was another strong reason for its success in influencing the government for benevolent help (Hettne and Tamm : 1974).

Thus, the Vokkaligas did not lag behind the Lingayats in forming their caste association despite lacking the backing of a religious mutt, an edge that the Lingayats held over them. While the initial help in the form of financial contributions to the Sangha came from a few philanthropist men of the community (who were rich contractors), the greatest help and encouragement was from the then Maharaja, Sri Krishnaraja Wodeyar Bahadur and the Minister (Dewan) Sri V.P. Madhava Rao (Souvenir : 1961). The friendly relations the Dewan had with a few leaders of the Sangha (like with Sri B.Nagappa, Barrister), and the "Sympathetic support stand and the keen interest of the Dewan towards the establishment of the Sangha facilitated it to survive in the midst of all problems" (Souvenir :1961). The Dewan not only promised the leaders his support but even proved it by granting "as a gift on the occasion of the first Conference" of the Sangha more than 12 acres of land in the heart of Bangalore city. This land has been the prized possession of the Sangha where the buildings of its various educational institutions are located today. Apart from this, it has acquired from the Bangalore City Corporation, in return for its surrendering of a part of its land in the above area, another spacious land (site) in the vicinity of the office of City Corporation where the Sangha has constructed a fifteen storeyed building (Souvenir of the Diamond Jubilee Celebrations of the Sangha : Bangalore 1982).

The Dewan's concern towards the Sangha did not stop there. He made a reference to the starting of and the main goals set before the Vokkaligara Sangha in his speech at the Representative Assembly which met during the Dasara Celebrations the same month (October). He even emphasized that such an organisation would in the long-run benefit the whole province (Souvenir : 1961). His love for the development of the Sangha was so much that the Dewan even arranged for the transfer of Vokkaliga officials to Bangalore city on the request of the leaders as their services were required for the Sangha.

Another landmark in the history of the Sangha was the starting of a Kannada weekly by name "Vokkaligara Patrike" in Bangalore, from March 15, 1907, a year after the establishment of the Vokkaliagara Sangha. The Patrike was started under modest circumstances (it was originally published by a Brahmin, Sri Srinivasaiyengar, publisher of two newspapers – "The Standard" and "Nandegannadi" – in English and Kannada respectively). The effort received encouragement by the Dewan who was kind enough to inaugurate the launch. The publication were started in a house belonging to the President of the Sangha in Cottonpet near Bangalore city's railway station. By 1923 the Patrike was able to shift to its own building constructed on the land granted by the Dewan (Souvenirs : 1961 and 1982).

The years 1907 and 1908 marked the speedy development of the Sangha, whose annual conferences were inaugurated by the Maharaja and the Dewan respectively.[48] The Yuvaraja Sri Kanteerava Narasimharaja Wodeyar continued the tradition in 1910 who apart from making a munificent grant of Rs.2000 also became a patron to the Sangha, like the Maharaja.

In the 1920s, the Sangha made steady progress. Buildings were constructed for housing a students' hostel and also the printing press from where the Vokkaligara Patrike came to be published. Interestingly, the Sangha continued to obtain protection and financial assistance from Sir Albion Banerjee, the Dewan during 1920s, who arranged for a 'Matching Grant' – the system of the government granting an equivalent amount of what is collected by the Sangha. Incidentally, it may be noted here that Sir Albion Banerjee, as a member of the Council, was a staunch opponent of Sir M. Visvesvaraya (Gundappa : 1971). Further, he was also, like Dewan V.P. Madhava Rao[49], a 'foreigner' (Bengali-Brahmin). These factors are useful while understanding the Dewan's special concern towards the Vokkaligas. As an imported Dewan, he encountered trouble from the local Brahmins who were naturally aspirants for the post. To make his position secure, perhaps he turned to the non-Brahmins by encouraging their movement against the (local) Brahmins.

The popularity of the Sangha, more so its political and economic utility, appears to have spread over a wide area in the years before independence itself. The increasing number of donors and members to the Sangha and its welfare activities was a proof of this fact.

The decade between the years 1920-30 also witnessed a process of horizontal development of the activities of the Vokkaligara Sangha. Similar caste conferences were held in the neighbouring districts of Hassan, Mysore, Tumkur, Kolar and in small towns like Chikkaballapur, Kantharajapur, Maddur, Krishnarajapet and other such places. This resulted in the construction of Vokkaliga boys' hostels at these places. These hostels were managed and financed by the local Vokkaliga elite, headed usually by either a political worker or a leading landlord. Needless to state, majority of them hailed from the Gangadikara or Morasu sub-groups.[50]

The Vokkaliga Pathrike published under the auspices of the Sangha, did a good job of stirring up considerable awakening and awareness among the literate and urban dwelling sections of the Vokkaliga community. It also derived support in the form of guidance from the superintendent of the government press, who was very fond of the first editor of the Pathrike, Sri B.Puttaiah. The Pathrike gained popularity on communal grounds claiming to be the window to the external world about the Vokkaligas, who were then found to be liberally participating in the freedom struggle of the 30s and 40s. The publication of the Pathrike had to stop since February 1972 owing to financial loss (souvenir 1982). Later an educational trust named after the renowned poet late Dr. K.V. Puttappa hailing from this community (who was also the vice-chancellor of the Mysore University and Jnan Peeth awardee) bought the printing accessories of this press.

The Vokkaliga hostels which were established at taluk and

district levels did a yeoman service to the aspiring students of this caste, particularly in the early years of their education in rural areas, where, such facilities were non-existent. The fact, however, remains that most students came from the upper strata of landlords and contractors. With the support of the rich landlords of the caste and sympathy of the Maharaja and Dewan, it is quite expected that the Vokkaligara Sangha could make considerable progress. Much of this was by a few hostels for the benefit of the rural students. The starting of the degree and professional colleges is only a recent phenomenon.[51] Thus, it is clear that lack of resources to sponsor educational activities since its inception led to a situation of having to lag behind its dominant counterpart, the ABVMS in this respect.[52] The absence of a religious base to the community was soon realised by the Sangha. Sri K.H. Ramaiah its chief leader is remembered to this day by all the community for exploring the need for a religious base of the community to expand its educational, economic and political activities.

The Adichunchanagiri Mutt and Caste Mobilisation

Recognising fully well the lacunae of a religious mutt for the mobilisation of the Vokkaligas, Ramaiah, along with a few other leaders of the community, worked towards the revival of the history of the caste group. It is entirely with his and another important leader (who later became the President of the Vokkaligara Sangha), Sri M.C. Linge Gowda's efforts, that the religious institution "Sri Adichunchanagiri Kshetra", located at Nagamangala taluk of Mandya district (a district registering the highest Vokkaliga population in the state), was revived and developed. In fact, the Kshetra being very ancient in its genesis, had devotees from not only Vokkaligas but also various other caste groups like Brahmins, Lingayats, Kurubas, Besthas and Harijans (Souvenir : 1982). "On hearing about the untimely death of the Guru 'Sri Tejonatha' in 1926, who was the 67th Guru in succession and who died without naming his successor", the Vokkaliga leaders decided in a meeting held at Chunchanagiri village to fight for the continuation of the Mutt and for the appointment of a successor (Souvenir : 1982: 20).

They then sent a delegation of their representatives to request the Maharaja in Mysore to grant permission for their venture to revive the "Kshetra". The delegation consisting of leaders like Sri K.H. Ramaiah fought with the government for four years at the end of which the Maharaja appointed a four-member committee to probe into the matter of appointing a successor to the Mutt (Souvenir : 1982). The committee which met at the travellers' bungalow at Nagamangala declared that the Srimutt was headed by two Gurus belonging to the Vokkaliga community by name Sri Sampanatha (55th Guru) and Sri Sivanatha (59th Guru) and it was, therefore, lawful to appoint a Vokkaliga 'Yogi' (Saint) as the next Guru. Out of about twenty applicants who had aspired for the post, the leaders selected 'Sri Gururamayya', the Swami at Melkote ashram. At the instance of Sri K.H. Ramaiah, he came to be addressed as 'Sri Bhakthanatha Swamigalu' and was consecrated as the 69th Guru of the 'Sri Adichunchanagiri Mahakshetra (Krishnappa : 1982). Since then, the Mutt came to be fit into a suitable religious structure and was developed as an important pilgrimage centre for the Vokkaliga community.

Besides its religious work, the Adichunchanagiri Peetha also took upon itself the responsibility of providing the Vokkaligas with a base for holding their social work for the community. The first priority here was the attempt to herald unity and integrity amongst the diverse Vokkaliaga subcastes. The Mutt did not attempt, for a long time, to start any educational institutions.[53] Thus, the revival of the Mutt satisfied, at least partially, the intentions of the Vokkaliga leaders, who wanted it to unite the community and modernise it. The Mutt could not by itself contribute much towards this cause.

The fundamental reasons for this were some of the shortcomings of the mutt themselves. Being of a very recent origin (after its revival), it could not enjoy royal patronage and support in the form of assets and service by affluent devotees. Secondly, in the absence of any independent religious base, "dependence on a Brahminical model came up as a factor in underrating the importance of the Kshetra". This was in contrast to the advantageous position of Lingayats with their well-established and economically resourceful mutts to support them financially and politically in all their mobilisation initiatives. Thirdly, wide disparities did exist between the two Mutts, on the one hand, and its devotees, on the other. The professional pre-occupancy of the community with agriculture did not, under general circumstances, facilitate acquaintance with religious practice. Like the Brahmins, the community was not exposed to sanskritic learning and teaching. For the Lingayats who were also basically agricultural in profession, the fact that much of the lands were traditionally owned or controlled by religious mutts played a decisive role in linking the Mutt and the community.

When the Vokkaligas realised the significance of religious institutions, i.e., during the 20s and the 30s, the trend was towards greater Sanskritisation of one's ways of life. This took a deeper turn in the case of the Vokkaligas where the process of upward social mobility through Sanskritisation became more popular. The traditional caste practices "looked tribal in character" and failed to attract attention. They were held as preaching ideals of poor political significance and utility. The desire for the adoption of Brahminical ways of living, so much inherent in the mobilisation activities of the non-Brahmin groups (except the Lingayats for reasons specified earlier) is rated by the leaders as one of the factors responsible for the slow growth of these indigenous mutts.[54]

After 1934, the Vokkaligara Sangha had to undergo a thorough change in its leadership pattern. This was necessary since all the old leaders had to quit their posts owing to a government rule which declared as unlawful any person holding simultaneously a government job and being an office-bearer of any private organisation. This resulted in the stepping down from office by a series of Vokkaliga elite – landlords, contractors and politicians. The general atmosphere between the years 1930-50 was one of political disturbances when the country was preoccupied with the struggle for independence. In the early phase of this period, the non-Brahmin leaders in Karnataka were reluctant to join the Congress. This was due to the presence of other provincial parties like the Praja Mitra Mandali (Hettne and Tamm : 1974). Subsequently, most of these sectarian tendencies (irrespective of whether it meant developing one's caste association or the non-Brahmin movement) were directed towards the freedom movement,

The Post-Independence Era

More than the years immediately after independence, those following the re-organisation of the states in 1956, introduced many advantages as well as disadvantages to the Vokkaliga community. The State of Mysore, as it was then called, was unified with many parts of the Bombay-Karnatak and Hyderabad-Karnatak areas added to it. To the existing nine districts were added another ten districts, resulting in considerable demographic change.

Even the fact that the then government was represented by many Vokkaliga political workers and headed by Vokkaliga chief ministers, it did little towards promoting the Sangha's activities, excepting instances of small concessions in financial matters.

However, the programme of starting educational institutions was pioneered by the then President of the Sangha, Sri B.N. Vijayadeva, who was a barrister by profession, in the 1950s. The first step in this direction was taken when an Arts and Science College was started in Bangalore in 1966 followed by a Commerce College in 1967, later with branches as Day and Evening Colleges, in 1971. A Law College was added to the list in the year 1972.

Such a sudden upsurge of educational and other welfare activities undertaken by the Sangha after 1956 were not without strong push factors. Ever since its inception, the Vokkaligara Sangha and the entire range of Vokkaliga power elite had encountered limited competition by the other groups. Access to power between the years 1948-1956[55] and the economic dominance they enjoyed prompted the Vokkaliga leaders to develop an apathetic attitude towards strengthening the organisational base of their community through emphasising education as a stragtegy. They perhaps held that the Brahmins were not a threat to them being a minority caste although they were far superior with educational and intellectual pursuits. The consolation was that the other communities were also not a threat, considering that they were far too backward than themsleves to offer any competition.[56]

This situation changed with the reorganisation of the state and the changed political scenario in Mysore state. There was an unprecedented expansion of the Lingayat population with the newly-added districts representing a large percentage of this community. While earlier to it, the situation was one where both Lingayats and Vokkaligas enjoyed a dominant status in Old Mysore but Vokkaligas were more powerful. The Vokkaligas came to be confronted by the new-found dominance of Lingayats who were in a comparatively advantageous position supported by their religious mutts, through the decades. Not just that, they also had exposure to English education and could mobilise their interests in this direction quite early in history.

The third blow was when the Vokkaligas lost their hold over chief-ministership after 1956, which was a severe blow. It launched the beginning of a long period of monopoly over that seat by their staunch opponents – the Lingayats.[57] It is these factors that cajoled the serious functioning of the Vokkaligara Sangha, which reached its zenith with the celebration of the Golden Jubilee of the Sangha in 1961. It is observed that "The golden jubilee celebrations were held mainly to find solutions to the acute financial shortage that the Sangha was encountering at that time" (Souvenir of the Golden Jubilee Celebrations 1961). A south India Vokkaligara Conference was also held at Bangalore along with the Golden Jubilee of the Sangha. This was intended to give a facelift to the Sangha's activities.

The four-day golden jubilee celebrations held on a grandiose scale was an attempt at giving a new shift to the Sangha's activities. Although the celebrations did not result in any recognisable fund collection drive by the Sangha, they did succeed in reviving the ideals and goals of the Sangha which were an improvement over its earlier activities (Souvenir : 1961). Soon after the Golden Jubilee, the Sangha spent a critical period from 1964 -71. During this period, some part of its land had to be leased out to overcome the financial crisis. A cinema theatre was constructed in the place of the students' hostel and auditorium (these were demolished in the 1990s to be replaced by the magnificent buildings that house the Sangha's engineering and medical colleges).

As it was the case for a few other castes, the year 1972 also marked the beginning of a new awakening among the Vokkaliga leaders. This is evident in the activities of the Sangha. The year, rather, the whole decade was politically significant as it witnessed changes in the composition of the government when late Sri

Devraj Urs became the Chief Minister. The emphasis his government laid on the classification of the backward classes and the measures it subsequently took to ameliorate their living conditions laid altogether a different dimension to the process of social mobility hitherto in vogue among the Vokkaligas.[58]

The socio-political changes in the administrative structure of Karnataka introduced by Urs' rule provided the Vokkaligara Sangha and its leaders a different platform to function upon. The decade also heralded a shift in the leadership pattern of the Vokkaligara Sangha, when the son of late Sri K.H. Ramaiah, Sri K. R. Marudeve Gowda became its President. He is considered as the main spirit behind the extensive growth in the sphere of educational institutions managed by the Sangha (Souvenir :1961). His tenure from 1972-79 is remembered for contributing towards higher organisational integration of the Sangha. This included the systematic management of assets of the Sangha (i.e., its land/site, buildings, etc.,), establishment of educational institutions as well as the starting of more number of student hostels. More significant were the efforts of the Vokkaligara Sangha undertaken during 1973-76 in the direction of retaining 'backward' status to the community. A detailed report of its activities and vision was submitted to the Havanur Commission.

Any Backward Classes Commission could not possibly afford to exclude the dominant communities from the list of OBCs owing to their political and economic importance in the state. But this commission was bold in its decision and categorised only the Vokkaligas as a 'backward community' and included it as one of the OBCs, while it excluded the Lingayats by grouping them as 'forward'. Whatever may have been the other considerations, Constitutional guarantees were seen as advantageous to any caste or community. This move by the government decreased the extent of competition by the Vokkaligas with the

Lingayats, who now did not enjoy a backward status. Conversely, the former also came to benefit further due to lack of any strong competition from other castes in the OBC category. Either they were held traditionally 'inferior' in status and many of them lacked the numerical spread that the Vokkaligas commanded in the length and bredth of the state.

There was yet another interesting development which may be explained thus: the constitutional guarantees offered to the Vokkaligas, as recommended by the backward classes commissions, including that led by Havanur, only added momentum to the process of fusion with in the community. They have put all the subcastes among the Vokkaligas under the blanket category of the 'Vokkaligas'. The result was a merger of leaders from the different subcastes in the Sangha's activities that increased in intensity during the 1970's. The membership to the Sangha came to be increasingly sought by people from these subcastes. A glance at the list of names of the office-bearers and the members of the Sangha is proof of this fact. The trend was the essential trait of caste-mobilisation. The call for unity amongst all subcastes was a 'political necessity'[59]. Although the caste conferences of earlier years gave importance to this, the issue gained momentum only since the year 1970 (Souvenir : 1982[60]). Further, and as noted earlier while discussing the Bhunts' Sangha, a coalition was attempted by the Vokkaligas to link themselves with the Bhunts, who despite being agriculturists held themselves superior to the former. Such an alliance was forged considering that the Bhunts (at least a section among them) had achieved progress in the fields of education, trade, commerce and a lot of politicisation.

The Vokkaligara Sangha celebrated its Diamond Jubilee in 1982, reiterating its stand to work for the welfare of the whole Vokkaliga community at a macro-level. The years between its Golden Jubilee and Diamond Jubilee in 1961 and 1982 respectively, have seen the growth of a number of educational institutions. Many of these were the phenomena of post-1970s culminating in the opening of two professional colleges – one in Engineering and the other a medical college – in 1980, when the state was under the Chief Ministership of late Sri R. Gundu Rao. Its Platinum Jubilee was held recently at a time when the Sangha has accomplished still taller heights in its infrastructure supported very well by its richly spread diaspora.

The overall impression one gets from an analysis of the Vokkaligara Sangha is that it falls in line with similar other caste associations in its structure and activities. The programme and policies of the Sangha have been in tandem with the political changes at the state level and its changing nature of leadership. The nature and pattern of relations it was forced to establish with the other caste associations superior to oneself have also helped in shaping its programme. However, despite its ideals of intra-caste unity, rivalry and competition between the different subcastes and between the aspirants to leadership does exist. The opening of professional colleges in recent times has in fact accelerated this process of internal factions since these courses have opened up a resourceful avenue for further mobilisation.

The changing leadership profile of the Sangha reflects that it is characterised by the concentration of members of one or two subcastes among the Vokkaligas. These same subcastes (the Gangadikara and Morasu) have been in the leadership roles of the Sangha since its inception. A look at the social background of the leaders and others of relevance to the Sangha mirrors this fact.

After subcaste affinity, it is kinship that has determined access to positions of importance within the ranks of the Sangha. This phenomenon is evident in the religious activities of the Vokkaligas. One such was the rejuvenation of the religious shrine - Sri Adichunchanagiri Kshetra from its existence in the 1920s to its revival in the 1970s. The mutt is held with a lot of reverence as representing the Vokkaligas, irrespective of subcaste differences. However, close observation has shown that the Gangadikara subcaste of the Vokkaligas (who belong to the 'Bhyravara Okkalu' (meaning the worshippers of Bhyrava, a Shaivite God) owe special and sometimes exclusive allegiance to the mutt.

The above factors should not be understood as being peculiar to the Vokkaligara Sangha alone. They are general characteristics exhibited by almost all caste associations in varying degrees. It could be concluded that by encouraging two-fold developments – one on the sectarian channel in the form of the mutt and the other on the secular level in the form of educational institutions – the beneficiaries constitute a special group of Vokkaligas comprising the upper strata of the most articulate subcastes among them.

6. The Karnataka State Kunchitigara Sangha

While the Vokkaligas traditionally constituted the farming community in Karnataka, there are other similar farming castes but differing in their language and regional representation from Vokkaligas. For example, the Reddis and the Kunchitigas also profess agriculture like the Vokkaligas, but differ from the latter in certain aspects relating to their origin and culture. They are also endogamous groups like the Vokkaliga subcastes. The Vokkaligara Sangha tried to bring these other agricultural groups under the common banner of 'Vokkaligas' by making representations to the Census Commissions and other government channels in the pre-independence period itself.

The establishment of the Vokkaligara Sangha in the year 1906 (mainly through the efforts by the Gangadikara and Morasu subcastes, which excelled others in numbers and economic status) initiated [illegible] or generated a thorough process of mobilisation down the hierarchy. [illegible] in the same way the Vokkaligas themselves had been inspired by their upper castes in the hierarchy. The data collected from these associations pointed out that a number of caste associations other than those analysed so far also came to be formed, demanding a much higher status in the traditional hierarchy. The caste associations of the Brahmin, Lingayat and Vokkaliga castes were formed first, to be followed by those of the Kuruba (shepherd), Balija (trader), Devanga (weaver) and other professional groups. These in turn were followed by the associations of yet other groups like the Mudaliars, Karuneekars and Sadars, which were more or less immigrants from neighbouring provinces to the state. The numerical strength of a caste had a bearing on its attempts at social mobility. It was also true (as evident from the years of establishment of caste associations and the place where they were first located) that they were a phenomenon of the urban, politically awakened sections of the respective caste groups. It may also be interpreted that the spirit of the non-Brahmin movement led those leaders from the upper castes amongst the non-Brahmin castes, who, in fact, dominated the movement to initiate the setting up of caste associations amongst those castes lower than themselves in the hierarchy. For example, Sri K.H. Ramaiah, who was chiefly instrumental in the formation of the Vokkaligara Sangha is quoted as the main spirit behind the formation of many other caste associations belonging to castes like the Kunchitigas, Devangas and so on (Souvenir of the Devanga Sangha : 1972).

The Kunchitigas, who claim to be the original inhabitants of Mysore, speaking Kannada as their mother tongue, are a predominantly agricultural community living in the rural parts of the state. They are generally found in the Kannada-speaking portions of Karnataka, Andhra Pradesh, Maharashtra and Tamil Nadu. The term 'Kunchitiga' is described by the Census Commissioners and administrators as originating from the word 'Kunchiga', meaning one who used the 'Kunchi' (brush or fibre used in the manufacture of blankets) (Puttaiah : n.d.).

The community has various names attributed to it on a regional basis. For example, in Bangalore and Mysore regions, they are known as 'Kunchiga' or 'Kunchitigas'; in Tumkur and Chitradurga districts as 'Kunchiga-Vokkaligas', in Channagiri, Honali, Shikaripur taluks of Shimoga districts as 'Namdhari Kunchitiga' and in Hosadurga and Holalkere regions of Chitradurga and Poona, they are known as 'Karnati Kunchitigas' and in Cuddapah, Kurnool, Ananthapur and Chittoor districts of Andhra Pradesh as 'Kapu, Kamma Reddy Kunchitigas'. In the Madurai district of Tamil Nadu, especially in Periya Kulam, Dindigul, Palani, Kodaikanal and other places, they are known as 'Vokkaligas', 'Kapu Kappaliyar', 'Goundar', 'Kamakulada Vokkaligas', etc. (Puttaiah : n.d.).

In almost all government records they are called as Kunchitigas and the accompanying name Vokkaliga is common almost everywhere. Ethnographers have even placed them on par with the Reddis of Andhra Pradesh (Thurston : 1909). Even now, the Kunchitigas of Kalyanadurga, Thadapatri and other places keep the surname 'Reddy'. In Honali taluk in Chitradurga (central Karnataka) they are called as 'Namdhari Kunchitiga Reddy'.

Being an agricultural and rural dwelling group, educated people are a minority among the Kunchitigas. Those residing in urban areas, especially in the cities like Bangalore and Mysore (each being an important centre of administration both in the pre- and post-independence periods) are engaged in trade and commerce (in fact some Kunchitigas have made remarkable progress in this sphere).

The first generation of educated Kunchitigas was the product of the Backward Classes Movement that took place in Mysore, as an extension of a similar movement at Madras. The 'Kunchitigara Sangha', established in the year 1908 at Mysore, was an off-shoot of this movement. Dharmapravartha Gunja Narasimhanna of Mysore was its first president. However, the Sangha came to expand only during the twenties and the thirties.

This is evident from the fact that similar Sanghas were established at key centers (apart from Bangalore) during 1928 and 1935. Caste conferences and meetings to discuss the problems of the Kunchitigas and to decide the plans for their welfare were held only since 1924 (Puttaiah : n.d.).

Although the Kunchitigara Sangha was started in 1908, its real functioning, as seen above, began after the group came to be classified for the first time as 'backward' by the Miller Committee in 1918.

Mobilisation attempts by the Kunchitiga caste groups accelerated only after the government intervened in its welfare. An analysis of the history of the Sangha tells us that efforts were made after the year 1930 by a few leaders of the community to develop their caste association by encouraging Kunchitigas from all over the Province to become its members. The Sangha subsequently started a weekly by name "Kunchitigara Patrike" (on the lines of the Vokkaligara Patrike) that strove to propagate unity among all Kunchitigas through its columns (Muddulinganna : n.d.).

"Inspired by the government's encouragement to the Kunchitiga students in the form of backward class facilities, a few philanthropists belonging to the community came forward to help the poor and needy students through such schemes like scholarships, freeships, hostels, etc" (Puttaiah : n.d.). Most notable among them was Sri D. Banumaiah, a leading businessman and philanthropist of Mysore, who was also a member of the Representative Assembly, who started hostels for students at Mysore, which, apart from its educational duties, catered also to the unification of the community. In the absence of any other facilities the hostel at Mysore attracted students belonging to different Kunchitiga subcastes from the different parts of the state.

It is wrong to attribute the services of men like Banumaiah, to the cause of education as entirely communal, just because he hailed from the same community. His aristocratic background coupled with his close association with the ruling family of Princely Mysore and with the then Dewan, were the advantages that he possessed to get closer with both of them and also to convert that opportunity to work for the welfare of poor students of his community. But since the number of students who could make use of such institutions from within the Kunchitiga caste was abysmally low, he had to open it up for all others for purposes of financial viability, much against his desire to encourage large number of one's own community students to get in. This and the socio-political environment prevailing at that time (with Vokkaligas at the prime position) prevented Banumaiah from acting exclusively in the interests of his caste. He was declared leader of all non-Brahmins and lacked any alternate support. The weak socio-economic status of his own community suppressed any protest and in fact arrested or slowed down the expansion of the Kunchitigara Sangha during the pre-independence period.

Comparatively speaking, the Kunchitigas have been able to make much progress in the years following independence. This is mainly in the fields of trade, commerce and education, in the same order. The development in the sphere of education could, however, be attributed to the reservation benefits granted to the community by the Nagan Gowda and the Havanur Commissions in the post-independence era. The Kunchitigara Sangha, however, appears to have played a minor role in this, as the Sangha itself was not articulate in its demands till recently, perhaps due to lack of effective leadership. It is also probable that the elite of this caste showed little interest in pursuing mobility through the Sangha for two reasons: One, probably the treating of the Kunchitigas as synonymous with the Vokkaligas had underestimated the relevance of an independent

Sangha by the Kunchitigas. Second, the broader term 'Vokkaligas' proved egalitarian than the term 'Kunchitiga' and the latter would have preferred to remain within the broader category of Vokkaligas due to their socio-economic and political dominance.

The significant reason for the slow growth of the Kunchitigara Sangha lied in the political process of mobilisation. When the Vokkaligas and Lingayats were Chief Ministers of the state, it was highly impossible or difficult for the minor communities or subcastes to pursue autonomy in caste mobilisation. The right atmosphere was provided by the socio-political changes which took place after change of leadership when the rule by dominant communities was replaced by the one from a minority caste (Devraj Urs) in Karnataka politics. The Havanur Commission's call to depose before itself to claim backwardness accelerated the process of caste mobilisation among the Kunchitigas as was the case with several other castes, at that time.

Concurrently, the post-Havanur Commission days have witnessed a new wave of awakening amongst the Kunchitigas who are presently fighting for autonomous status through their Sangha. In their Caste Conferences they have been placing requisitions to consider them as more backward than the Vokkaligas and to sanction professional colleges (on the lines of those started by the Vokkaligara Sangha).

The alliance between the Kunchitigas and the Vokkaligas which began in the early years of the starting of the former Sangha did not, however, last long. Perhaps the political and economic benefits which the Vokkaligas gained in course of time, prompted the Kunchitigas to seek autonomous status. A demand was made in the 1930s in the Legislative Council debates by the leaders of the Kunchitigas to delink them from the Vokkaligas (Proceedings of the Mysore Legislative Council :

1931 and 1932). The apparently strict caste barriers are often relaxed whenever class interests dominate the situation, as in arranging alliances when upper class Vokkaligas and Kunchitigas intermarry breaking caste endogamy.

II

Introduction

The caste associations representing the various professional and service communities - like the Kurubas (Shepherds), Ganigas (oil men), Gangamathasthas or Besthas (the fishermen), Balijas (traders), Devangas (weaver), Edigas (toddy-tappers), Kumbaras (potters) - representing the professional castes - and the Madivalas (washerman), Nayanaja Kshatriyas (Barbers) - who are the service castes - all portray certain significantly diverse traits in their nature and functions from those of the castes traditionally above them in the social hierarchy, like the Brahmins, Lingayats and the Vokkaligas. By caste system is understood here not only a structural classification of the individuals into different groups on the basis of their birth into them, but also as a more complex system of allocation of definite politico-economic status to individuals as members of their respective castes. Thus, caste being a cultural entity, the relative growth or stagnation of individual caste groups, given the closed nature of the system itself, depends on the socio-economic restraints that operate in its (caste's) case.

Before embarking upon the details of the causes and effects of the variations existing between these associations of the 'upper' and 'middle' groups, a brief analysis is made below to identify their characteristics.

The professional and service communities constitute a major segment of Hindu society and are generally referred to as the middle castes. They are also universally represented in the sub-continent, in all states, with traditional duties, though constitute a small percentage of the population and are known by different names in different regions. These castes depend not only upon their respective 'caste occupation' or 'traditional occupation', but are invariably found engaged in agricultural wage labour also. Being predominantly rural dwellers, agriculture and agricultural wage work has provided them the subsidiary income to support their families, as their caste occupation alone is not economically rewarding. Traditionally, their service to the 'upper' castes was substantiated traditionally by an annual payment in kind or cash (Dube : 1955 and 1958). Perhaps, it is this phenomenon that inspired Charles Metcalfe to describe Indian Village Communities as self-sufficient entities, hence he called them "little republics".

Notable is that the process of moderisation is examined from the point of view of only its positive impact of promoting socio-economic mobility, while its negative impact has not gained significance. The goods and commodities produced by the village artisans were no doubt affected by industrialisation, but class distinctions between communities further affected them badly. They were forced to take up agricultural and casual wage work, or migrated to urban areas as unskilled labourers. Often, poor households worked as labourers under their own caste elite who continued the traditional occupation, like the Devangas with their powerlooms employing poor, immigrant caste brethren as labourers. Large numbers of 'middle' and 'lower' castes are dependent upon rich dominant[1] castes who most often were absentee landlords.

The position of the middle and low castes in the state is found to be influencing their participation in social mobility. Wide regional disparities and differences prevail in this. The number of these middle castes and their economic pursuits vary widely. The category is heterogenous and their occupations result in varying degrees of economic rewards. The Edigas and Kumbaras, the Devangas and the Ganigas do not have comparable income levels from their professions. There are economic, cultural and social diversities in their livelihood, making any generalisations about them difficult. 'Middle' and 'Lower' are thus blanket categories, incapable of containing all the characters that go in making of these caste groups.

A further point of significance before we discuss the caste associations of midle castes, is the presence of hierarchy, within the category. Disparities are strongly evident between, for example the Devangas the Balijas, the Kurubas and the Edigas who have a cultural advantage over the Barbers and the Washermen. The Kurubas enjoy a more widespread representation in all districts of the state. Besides sheep-rearing as traditional occupation, the community enjoys land ownership next only to the Vokkaligas and Lingayats. The Potters, Ganigas, and the Smiths are generally either landless or hold land in marginal extent only, and were highly affected by modernisation.

More vulnerable, however, are the Kaniyars (Sooth-sayers), the Jettys (Wrestlers), the Satanis (priests), the Thigalas (gardeners), the Bhatrajus (body-guards to kings and also to petty rulers) and the Komarpanths, all of whom constitute a small percentage of the state's population (0.18 per cent for Satanis; 0.74 per cent for Thigalas; 0.03 per cent for Bhatrajus and 0.06 per cent for Komarpanths). For many of the caste groups like the above, the policy of reservations kindled a lot of mobilisation efforts. From being excluded and segregated groups, they have made efforts to come together (through a process of fission), when government announced reservation of seats in educational institutions and in employment.

The above factor is actually the cause behind the significant rise in the number of caste associations in Karnataka. (see Appendix 4.4 and 4.5) A casual glance at the years of setting up of these caste associations would tell us that they are a phenomenon of the fifties and the seventies. While some were established during the time the Miller Committee functioned in 1916-18, others have followed suit. The process has accelerated after the setting up of the Havanur Commission in 1972. All this is perceived as a corollary of the numerical, economic and political status that they occupy in the social hierarchy. Higher the status of a caste in the social ladder, greater are its potentiality for establishing its caste association.

7. The Karnataka State Balija Sangha

The Karnataka State Balija Sangha, representing the community of the Balijas, came into existence in the year 1919. It was established at Bangalore, where already a number of caste associations had been established by that time. Authentic information on the circumstances leading to the origin of the Sangha was not available. The community is so backward even to have enough resources to document its own history. Moreover, none of the founding members was alive to provide us details on the Sangha's activities in the pre-Independence era.

The Balijas were traditionally traders in 'auspicious' articles such as flowers, saffron, red dye powder (Kumkum), bangles etc., and also sellers of betel leaves, cotton beads and rice. There are many subcastes among the Balija community in Karnataka, the predominant ones being twenty-two in number. Most of the subcastes are known by the name of the commodity they are engaged in trading. For example, the Balijas selling betel leaves are called 'Ele' (betel leaf) Banajigas, 'Akki Balijas', being rice sellers. 'Poosalu Banajigas', 'Poovalu Banajigas' and 'Gajalu Banajigas' meaning those selling beads, flowers and bangles respectively. The 'Dudi Banajigas' are cotton-sellers. Poovalu, Gajalu and Poosalu being Telugu terms, it suggests that large sections of the Balijas were immigrants from the neighbouring state of Andhra Pradesh (Memorandum submitted to the Mandal Commission, October 1979).

The Balijas also include subcastes called Velama Naidus (who claim descent from the Tirumala Naickers of Madurai. The leader of the non-Brahmin movement in Madras, E. V. Ramaswamy Naicker, was a Velama Naidu by caste), Kamma Naidus, Munnuta Kapu, Rajamahendraru, Jeedipalli, Naidu Banajiga, Ravut, Ralla, Choudhari Balijas are the names of major Balija subcastes in Andhra Pradesh suggesting names of townships there. Similarly, the Vaishnava Balijas claim superiority over others "on account of their Brahminic values though Balijas are generally Sudras or Dravidians" (*ibid.*).

The cultural variations amongst the Balijas suggest that they are a highly heterogeneous and widely distributed group. Majority of them speak Kannada as well as Telugu and reside almost throughout the State.

While the Balijas' occupation is given as trading in the commodities mentioned earlier, trade and commerce are carried out by the members of this group only at a moderate, petty level. In other words, like the village functionaries (Smiths, Ganigas and others), the Balijas traditionally had to cater for certain requirements of the people which were needed during auspicious occasions, such as marriages, festivals etc. Such celebrations being occasional, their trading activities also turned out to be seasonal in nature (at least in the olden days). With modernization and its impact over rural areas, the market for these traders dealing mostly in items of occasional or special use, or items of ornamental value like bangles and flowers, beads etc., has decreased substantially. Dependence on agricultural labour and migration to cities as workers was a result of such changed circumstances. Even this proved less beneficial as a number of Balija subsects like the bangle-sellers, flower-vendors, and Pusulu Balijas selling beads were basically wandering groups leading a semi-nomadic life. The nature of their caste occupation, viz., trade, necessitated extensive travel from village to village with no settled life which reflected itself on their socio-cultural practices. For example, "one set of Balijas, viz., Munnutu Banajigas, also known as Dandi Dasaris, are wandering peddlers and mendicants" have been reduced to a state of beggary by their weak economic base which lost its importance in a technological, scientific era (*ibid.*). They are considered by other subcastes as the lowest in the social scale among the Balijas. "The Dandi Dasaris and many other subcastes are treated as Sudras or low castes", a fact attributed by the Balija leaders to be the root cause of their backwardness *(ibid. : 4)*.

The above account of the Balija community highlights the major constraints for its mobilisation. On the basis of the information provided by the office-bearers of the Sanghas (discussions with Sri K.V. Aswathaiah, President of the Sangha), it is inferred that the lead given by the two dominant castes prompted some wealthy, Bangalore-resident members of the upper caste Balijas (not the Dandi Dasaris, in any case), who were traders and landlords to think on the lines of establishment of their caste association. Another possible explanation is that the Velama Naidus of the non-Brahmin movement of Madras inspired the Balija Velamas to organise themselves on sectarian lines. The appointment of the Miller Committee was another factor that influenced the Balijas to establish the Balija Sangha which came to obtain the full title of 'Karnataka State Balija Sangha' only in the mid-seventies.

There was virtually no progress in the Sangha's activities for more than fifty years after its formation in 1919. While this may be attributed to the problems the Sangha had to encounter during the beginning years of its establishment (like the extremely heterogeneous nature of the community coupled with its economic and educational backwardness and regional/cultural diversity in its composition). But the real reason was the changed socio-political circumstances in the post-independence era, especially after the appointment of the KBCC in 1972. It gave a boost to the various caste associations to revive their activities with a new objective and channel.

The above fact becomes clear when we look at the activities of the Karnataka State Balija Sangha (KSBS) during and after the 1970s. Lack of activities in the period earlier to it does not mean total stagnation or closure of the KSBS. It only means that the organisational drive by the leaders was restricted in its approach which was directed towards undertaking welfare measures like opening of hostels and securing own buildings of the Sangha.

In fact, emphasis on education and creating facilities for education were seen as the first step taken by these caste associations in general. The mobility aspirations of the caste groups though kindled by the movements against caste discrimination and the introduction of reservation benefits, perhaps, were short-lived in the sense that they did not exceed the period of the appointment of the Backward Classes Commissions and the immediate years of the implementation of their recommendations.

Thus the KSBS, irrespective of its comparatively early origin, is still in its 'developing' stage, when viewed from the angle of the established standards of caste mobilisation in vogue now (like starting of educational institutions, etc.). The Sangha owns the building where its administrative office is located, used also as a students' hostel and a choultry. It does not have any educational and welfare institutions of its own. It was only in 1972 that efforts were undertaken by a few leaders of the community, belonging to the upper cream of the rich, educated class under the leadership of a retired Balija Deputy

Commissioner, to create awareness among all Balijas about their 'social disabilities'. It appears that these people claiming to be the representatives of the community were the beneficiaries of the long drawn period of reservation policy who took to its revival realising the need for political representation to the group.

An important aspect of caste mobilisation, as shown by the data on caste associations, was an attempt by the caste leaders to bring together all the subcastes of the respective caste group. In doing so, attention was first paid towards conducting a caste census to demonstrate the demographic strength of the group and to strengthen its claims for government benefits. It does not mean, however, that the size of the caste group was any criterion in its classification as backward. Interesting it is to record here that while taking the census of the group, the Sangha tends to place emphasis on the most backward and small sects within the respective castes. This is because the economic condition of these small groups being very weak it tended to add weightage to the claims of the caste for a backward status.

Similarly, the KSBS organised a census drive throughout the State, which placed the estimated population of the community at 12 lakhs as against 4,72,409 assessed by the Havanur Commission in 1972 (KBCC Report : 1975). The Sangha has alleged in its memorandum to the Mandal Commission that the Nagan Gowda and the Havanur Commissions "have grossly underestimated its population which has increased over the years, especially, since 1921, from 122,035 in 1877 to 153,000 in 1930 and that the total variation of population between the decades 1901 and 1961 was +80.68 for every hundred due to migration from the neighbouring states" (Memorandum : 1979 : 6-7). Further, they have also alleged that the Nagan Gowda Committee had excluded the "caste from the list of backwards for purposes of Article 16 (4) of the Constitution on the principle that the Banajigas were adequately represented. The Havanur Commission had also upheld the adequate representation of the Balijas in government service", the excess being 0.36 per cent above the population percentage (Memorandum : 1979 : 7). Late Sri K.R.S. Naidu, a Balija leader and politician, as one of the members of the KBCC, even wrote a note of dissent in the Commission's Report against inclusion of Naidus among the omnibus category of the Balijas.

"However, the Sangha made representations to the Government who were pleased to issue Orders on the Commission's Report including the Balija community among others as socially and educationally backward under Art.16 (4)"(Memorandum : 1979 : 9).

"The High Court of Karnataka, while disposing certain writ petitions, has held the orders of the government as arbitrary basing such decision on the sole submission of the Advocate General that the Government has no other materials apart from those collected by the Commission. The Balija community were not parties in the Writ Petition and hence the decision of the High Court and the Government Order in this behalf have struck the community as a bolt from the blue" (Memorandum : 1979 : 9).

Apart from the census operations, the KSBS has been organising state-level conferences since 1972 on a regular basis. Impetus is being given to the branching out of the main Sangha into many sub-Sanghas to facilitate organisational work. This explains the new shape the Sangha's activities have assumed over the decades, especially during the post-independence era.

8. The Karnataka State Kurubara Sangha

Of the various middle caste associations, the association of the Kurubas, known as 'The Karnataka State Kurubara Sangha' is an important one. Its significance lies not only in that the Kurubas – the caste group of shepherds – were one of the earliest castes to start an association "for promoting the welfare of the community". The Sangha is significant also because it has been able to grow, over the years, in its size and activities.

The Kurubas whose traditional occupation is rearing of sheep, cattle and goat, are a predominantly rural dwelling population. As is common with many caste groups in rural areas, they are basically agriculturists. Both land-owners and landless labourers are found among the Kurubas, though the latter are a majority. They are traditionally placed at a slightly higher position than the so-called middle castes (like the Ganigas, Potters, Barbers and Washermen) in their economic level and social status.

Such a position of the Kurubas in Karnataka may be attributed to their comparative numerical supremacy over a majority of castes 'equal' and 'low' in status than themselves and to a certain percentage of land ownership among them. Rearing of sheep and cattle are not only the oldest professions of mankind, but are also held as one of the beginning invasions of human civilisation. Domestication of such animals is a common feature of all pastoral societies, as an economic necessity. The two – domestication of cattle and sheep and agriculture – are thus developed together as being complementary to each other.

Like many other caste associations, the 'Kurubara Sangha' is also a product of the non-Brahmin movement. It may be appropriate to include it under the list of those associations which came up following the establishment of the Vokkaligara Sangha in 1906. In fact, as it is in the case of the 'Kunchitigara Sangha', discussed earlier, the Kurubara Sangha was also a product of mobilisation led by a few Vokkaliga leaders, prominently by Sri K.H. Ramaiah. It was bifurcated from its support from and affiliation with the Vokkaligara Sangha in course of time.

As the province of Old Mysore contained more of Vokkaliga

population than the Lingayat, the former became models to the other castes, whose mobilisational activities generated similar tendencies among other castes of which the Kurubas were one.[61] The Vokkaliga leaders invited some land-owning or agricultural caste groups (like the Kurubas, Kunchitigas and Reddis) into their fold. But this tendency of the Vokkaligara Sangha to approach all agriculture based caste groups to get its fold degenerated in course of time. The Kurubas argued that they (and many like them) were used by the Vokkaligas to establish their own association. Once their efforts to secure government benefits bore fruit, they discarded identification with the Kurubas, who till then had given them all support and had even trusted them.

The Kurubara Sangha was started in the year 1921 at Bangalore, under the leadership of Sri Nilagiri Sanjeevaiah and a few other educated Kuruba elite of the area. Like the associations which preceded it, the opening of a students' hostel in Bangalore "encouraged poor and rural dwelling members of the community to educate their children" (Souvenir of the Kurubara Sangha : 1979).

Before proceeding with the analysis of the nature of and the role played by the 'Karnataka State Kurubara Sangha', it would be pertinent to understand the socio-cultural factors which have acted as the determinants of the living conditions of the Kurubas today. As one of the oldest caste groups of Karnataka, the Kurubas have developed a cultural history of autonomy unlike caste groups like the potters and the barbers. The socio-religious practices of the Kurubas have shown a tendency towards heterogeneity as the community itself is highly diffused and divided on the basis of its habitation in rural and urban areas. The differences between the so-called Halumatha Kurubas, Hande-Kurubas, Ooru (town) Kurubas, who are generally found living in both rural and urban areas, and the Kaadu (forest)

Kurubas, Jenu Kurubas (honey-collectors), Betta (those who dwell in hills) Kurubas, have reflected themselves in their cultural practices. The reorganisation of the State added more diversity to the demography of the Kuruba community when the members of the caste from the northern districts of Bijapur, Dharwar, Belgaum and Uttara Kannada (the then North Kanara district) joined their southern counterparts. The influence of Veerasaivism and Basava's philosophy were also responsible for the practice of Shaivite rituals and philosophy among the Kurubas of northern Karnataka. However, the Kurubas residing in the districts of Mysore, Mandya, Hassan, Bangalore and other southern districts chiefly worship Shiva, but by different names such as Revana Siddeswara, Beereswara and so on indicating the different manifestations of Lord Shiva.

The Kurubas have their own 'religious order' and monastery. Their religious heads or 'Gurus' are addressed as 'Odeyaru' who play the important role of sanctifying religious ceremonies like marriages. The impact of Veerasaivism is also seen in the institution of 'priesthood' and the 'Odeyaru' are held synonymous with the Lingayat 'Jangamas' in more than one respect (Murthy : 1979). But they do not constitute a separate subcaste, like the Jangamas or Aradhyas among Lingayats, but are a part of the Kuruba caste. In other words, they are not endogamous, but marry from amongst the various subcastes like Halumatha Kurubas and others.

The comparability of priesthood among the Kurubas and the Veerasaiva mutts and Swamis cannot be carried too far because the former do not enjoy the privilege of the rich and resourceful heritage of religious mutts. The Odeyars as 'Gurus' (teachers) of Kuruba caste group are generally found living in very poor conditions, professing their caste occupation like weaving of blankets, etc. as any other member of the group (Souvenirs of the Conference of Kuruba Weavers : 1979 &

1999). This may be considered as the major handicap the Kurubas of north Karnataka are encountered with, in contrast to the Veerasaivas of the same region who have built an educational empire with the support of their mutts and Swamijis.

The absence of an established religious order and the poor economic conditions of a large section of the Kuruba caste, coupled with the socio-political control exercised by one or the other dominant castes of the state, all these could be rated as the principal factors responsible for the stunted growth of the Kurubara Sangha in the pre-independence period. But a look at the organisational efforts of the Kurubas in relation to the development of their Sangha shows that it has earned far greater economic and political stability than a number of other 'middle' caste groups. The period marked the beginning of a long process of mobilisation by a section of the Kurubas who have made considerable advance in the field of education, government and professional employment and state politics.

The Kurubara Sangha is now a developed institution with many hostels and other welfare institutions at Bangalore and other key urban centres, established and managed under its pedestal. A co-operative bank was started in course of time but the most notable and interesting development is observed in the religious activity of the Kurubas restricted to those who have attained some level of socio-political status to be able to reach out for such mobilisation. In the beginning, the lacuna created by the absence of a monastery and religious leader was tried to be filled up by identifying few such personalities from mythology.[62] The data indicate that a programme for stabilising the religious origin of the community and in the absence of one discovering an ancestry for the caste from a sage or one of the gods or goddesses is a common and the most interesting process at work not only among the Kurubas, but also amongst a host of caste groups from the 'middle' and 'lower' levels of the hierarchy. 'Sanskritisation' may not be a significant term to explain this tendency of seeking autonomous cultural identity within a broader framework of Hinduism. While Sanskritisation was explained by Srinivas (1966) as a process denoting the attempts by the so-called lower caste groups to move up in the social ladder through the adoption of 'upper caste' cultural traits like vegetarianism, teetotalism, change of caste name to a more sanskritised form, the process of developing cultural identity by the middle castes appears to be reaching beyond this. For example, the claim to be the descendants of Kanakadasa, a saint, and Kalidasa, a renowned poet, are indicative of their efforts to establish a definite past to the community. They are found to be striving to create a culturally ancient and strong background to the caste group which had hitherto been either tribal in its religious character (like that of the Jenu-Kurubas and Kaadu Kurubas) or parasitic on the religious practices of the dominant castes of the area like the Lingayats and Vokkaligas. Interestingly, the sectarian channel of popularising the cult of demi-gods like Kanakadasa, Sangolli Rayanna (a war hero of Karnataka during British times)[63] or Kalidasa as hailing from the Kuruba community is also being used for purposes of creating an intellectual and patriotic background to the whole group.

What is true of a number of other caste associations with regard to the aspects of mobilisation apply to the case of Kurubas also. For example, the years immediately after independence did not result in the adoption of any far reaching developmental policies by the Kurubara Sangha. The reorganisation of the State in which many northern districts were brought under the province of Karnataka increased the Kuruba population of the state considerably. The districts of Bijapur, Dharwar, Belgaum and Raichur show a high percentage of this community. Though the increase in numbers did not bring about any change in the economic position of the Kuruba community, it added more strength (numerically) to the group when the Kurubas living in the newly added parts like the northern districts provided a stronger demographic base to it.

The actual mobilisation process amongst the Kurubas of Karnataka commenced with added emphasis and seriousness only after the two backward classes commissions (the Nagan Gowda and Havanur) were appointed by the government. Even here a distinction has to be made in the light of the differences existing in the politico-social set up under which they were appointed. More than any time earlier, the post-1970s have witnessed a greater degree of activity by the Kurubara Sangha. While this could be attributed to the change of leadership at the state level politics i.e., the shift in leadership from the dominant castes to the minorities, a certain amount of awareness developed over decades of politicisation amongst the leaders of the Kuruba community. This resulted in greater attention being paid to the activities of the Sangha.

When we say that the Kurubara Sangha became more active in the 1970s and later, it should be understood as a greater process of emulation of the activities of the Sanghas of the upper castes, especially the Vokkaligas. This is because, more than the Brahmins and the Lingayats, the Vokkaligas have provided a far informal role model to the Kurubas as well as to a number of other middle and lower castes. They were the immediate superiors of the Kurubas in the social hierarchy and also there were many similarities in the occupation of the two groups, which have to be considered while understanding this process of emulation.

It should not be concluded that the Kurubara Sangha functions only on the lines of the Vokkaliga's caste association. There have been some instances of inter-caste tensions and rivalry displayed in the activities of the Kurubara Sangha that were modelled after the Vokkaligara Sangha's activities. To begin with, the Sangha had taken up the task of seeking reclassification of the Kuruba population in the state on the plea that the Havanur Commission has not done justice to the community by including them under the backward caste category when they deserved backward tribe status! (Souvenir : 1979).[64]

The recent years, especially the seventies and the eighties, have witnessed an upsurge in the number of caste conferences and the multiplication in the number of branches of the Kurubara Sangha, which have been established at various urban and semi-urban centres of the State. A professional college – in engineering or medicine, or both – was promised to the Sangha by the Gundu Rao government which permitted the Vokkaligara Sangha also to start similar institutions in the year 1980 but in vain. This apart, wide publicity was given to popularise the newly founded religious base of the community at Kaaginele, as the birthplace of Kanakadasa, a popular saint belonging to the Bhakthi Movement in the state and hailing from the community. The Sangha, on par with many other such associations, has called for intra-caste unity amongst all the Kuruba subcastes to necessitate an integrated fight for securing a revised status to the Kuruba community.

But the most important of all its present activities, to which the Sangha is giving greater impetus and thought, is its demand for an increased share in the guarantees awarded to the Kurubas by the backward classes' commissions. The Sangha has been consistently requesting the successive governments to reclassify the Kurubas under the category of a 'tribe' from its present and commonly identified status of a 'caste'. Further, it is interesting to note that, even this demand has assumed different forms during the last 5-6 years. While the earlier (during 1979-80) demand was for a 'backward tribe status', sometime back there was a demand to classify the community as a 'Scheduled Tribe', a phenomenon of the post 1980s. The Sangha has claimed that the caste exhibits many tribe-like traits basing on the forest for livelihood (with honey collection etc.) by a section known as the Jenu Kurubas (meaning honey collectors). Behind these explanations are wider economic interests. The claim for a 'tribal tag' by not only the Kurubas but a number of other middle and lower caste groups is often due to the possibility of more benefits being available under that category.

The decision to establish the Sri Kanaka Guru Peetha at Kaginele was taken by ex-deputy chief minister of Karnataka, Sri Siddaramaiah, in February 1989. It was supported by Sri H. Viswanath, another leading Kuruba Political Leader and ex-Minister. Ultimately on 9-2-1992, it was established with Sri Beerendra Keshava Tharakananda Puri as the first Guru of the Peetha (Heggade : 2003).

The progress made by the Kurubara Sangha, sicne its inception, is categorized as follows :

- Initial stages (1921-1947) – establishment of the Sangha on 12-7-1921 and registration on 10-7-1923.
- Chief patrons of the sangha and instrumental in its establishement were Nilagiri Giriyappa, Nilagiri S. Sanjeevaiah, G. Muniyappa, Neeli Narasimaiah, Yele Angadi Thayappa, Mysore Akkimandi Doddaiah, Thammaiah and Javarappa & Brothers.
- Nilagiri S. Sanjeevaiah was president of the sangha for 5 years (1921-16) and G Muniyappa served as Secretary for a long time (1921-1955).
- N.S. Sanjeevaiah became President in 1928 with Yelahanka Patel Lakshmayya as vice-president and Halasur Contractor A Ramayya, Mysore Sahukar Dodda Javarappa as members, Sri S. Kariyappa as Treasurer, J. Muniyappa as Secretary, C.H. Shambulingappa as assistant secretary and T. Mariyappa as legal advisor.

- The Kurubara Sangha hostel in Gandhinagar in Bangalore city was established in 1955 in its own building.
- The sangha experienced slow stage of development between 1947-1971.
- The third president of the sangha was Dr. R. Nagan Gowda who assumed office on 10-11-1946.
- The fourth president was N.K. Siddappa from 27-11-1955.
- In 1958-59, poor merited students of the community were awarded scholarship of Rs. 500 which was raised to Rs. 800 in 1992.
- The fifth president was N.K. Siddappa from 1960 to 1963. By this time the sangha came to be headed by an MLA (Mr.T.K. Kambli) as the president of the Wool Products' Board.
- In 1956, Mysore Pradesh Backward Classes' Federation was formed under the auspices of the Mysore Pradesh Kurubara Sangha.
- 1971-1998 could be called as the period of expansion of the sangha's activities.
- In 1972, the name of the sangha was changed to Karnataka State Kurubara Sangha from Mysore State...
- The same year marked the donation by the then chief minister late Sri D. Devraj Urs a site in Banashankari in Bangalore for the sangha.
- In 1970, the central sangha at Gandhinagar was expanded, with S. Nanjundaiah IAS, as president, Sri B. Puttaswamy and S. Munisanjeevaiah as senior office bearers.
- In 1988-1992, K. Mallappa became the President and renowned physician Dr. Nandeesh as Secretary and R. Krishnappa as General Secretaries.

- In 1991-92, free boarding facility was offered to about 90 students in Gandhinagar's Kalidasa hostel and in the premises of Sri Beereswara temple in Sampigehalli.

9. The Devanga Sangha

The Devangas as another middle caste were the next to come up with forming a caste association after the Kurubas during the early years of the twentieth century. Being traditionally weavers of silk cloth, the Devanga caste group of Karnataka founded its caste association in the year 1923 at Bangalore with the aim of promoting education and business among the Devanga people. It also aimed at developing the power to establish representation in civic and political spheres to the caste, apart from striving for achieving unity within the group. Like many other caste associations, the Devanga Sangha was also an outcome of the Backward Classes Movement which had taken root in Princely Mysore and was generously guided in its establishment by leaders of the BCM (like Sri K.H. Ramaiah, Dewan Sri K.P. Puttanna Chetty and others).

The Devangas who believe to have descended from a sage by name 'Devala', "who was created by Lord Shiva to provide clothing to Gods and human beings" and "assigned to him the task of weaving and manufacture of cloth" (Souvenirs of the Akhila Karnataka Devanga Maha Sammelana : 1972, 1982 and 1999).[65] There are many caste groups among the weavers, of which the Devangas form a numerical majority. They constitute an important weaving community of Karnataka, the main pockets of Devanga settlement in the State being Doddaballapur in Bangalore rural district, the districts of Uttara Kannada, Gadag and Davanagere, taluk centres like Betageri, Hubli, Ilkal, Chikkanayakanahalli, Tarikere, Sakleshpur, Holenarasipur etc. They are also distributed moderately well in other parts of the state (see Appendix 7, 8 and 9).

As is common with any other caste group, there are many subcastes among the Devangas, based on their regional inhabitation and linguistic and cultural differences. For example, there are the Lingayat-Devangas, Kannada-Devangas (those who wear the sacred thread and constitute the Kannada-speaking Mysoreans), Andhra Devangas, Tamil Devangas, Hatagars and 18 Maneyavaru (people of the 18 houses).

Since the beginning of the last century itself, a number of changes have made inroads into the social structure of the Devanga community. For example, the number of subcastes has increased over the years. In their economic condition, the Devangas consider themselves very poor. The Sabha attributed poverty to educational backwardness. Since their profession does not necessarily demand education, the percentage of the educated is stated to be very low. Children are introduced to the profession at an early age. The introduction of spinning and weaving machines further caused considerable damage to the traditional handloom weavers rendering many of them unemployed and underemployed. This prompted a few rich, educated, prominent Devanga men and women "to analyse the problems of their community and take up some reform work" (Souvenir : 1972). Realising pretty well that any welfare work needs a certain amount of organisational footing, the Devanga Sangha was established in the year 1923 at Bangalore. It aimed, among other things, towards improving the educational prospects of the Devangas. The establishment and functioning of the Vokkaligara Sangha and also the educational advancement made by a few Vokkaligas became a model and inspired the Devangas, as it happened in the case of many other lower castes (Souvenir : 1972).

The cultural diffusion within the Devanga community found greater expression after the establishment of the Sangha and culminated in the separation of the Andhra Devangas from their Mysore counterparts. The Devanga immigrants from Andhra formed their own Sangha known as the 'Andhra Devanga Sangha' in the year 1924 at Bangalore (P. Bhuvaneswaraiah, President, December 26, 1981). Such a division, apart from its other threats, also brought about essentially a financial crisis in the Devanga Sangha as the Andhra group was comprised of rich and philanthropic businessmen who withdrew their support to the Devanga Sangha.

In course of time, the Devanga Sangha was able to establish similar Sanghas at various parts of the state where the community lived in large numbers. Quite remarkably, a bank was started to cater to the needs of the community. This was as early as in 1925 at Bangalore. Community hostels and choultries were the other institutions to be started about the same time. Emphasis was laid on the educational development of the Devanga children by opening schools not only in Bangalore, but also in other major centres of Devanga settlements. Many schemes for scholarships have been opened benefiting the poor and merited students of the community (Souvenir : 1972).

The educational and economic backwardness of the Devanga community was recognised by the Princely government in the pre-independence period. It was considered a 'backward' group and certain concessions in the fields of education and employment were granted to it (incidentally it should be noted that the Mysore Representative Assembly had a nominated member hailing from the Devanga community). Both the Nagan Gowda and Havanur Commissions have also classified them as backward communities. These constitutional provisions, although cannot be solely held responsible, became crucial agents of social change for the Devangas. A small percentage of those who obtained the privilege of education were able to manipulate certain socio-political forces both within and outside the group to the best of their advantage. As a result, the community produced a few eminent personalities in the fields of politics, education and business. In course of time, the Sangha could also increase its assets, a result of careful planning and munificent grants given by philanthropists from and outside the community. An Engineering College has come up in Nelamangala near Bangalore, where the Sangha owned about 40 acres of land. Apart from the student hostels established by the Sangha, a marriage hall (choultry), a market place, playground, a bank and a hospital, etc. wete the additions.

What was lacking for the community now was a religious mutt. The Devangas did not lag behind other middle castes in this venture. They soon established for themselves a religious order to culminate their attempts in emulating the upper castes. Lineage was traced to an ancient sage; and a package of rituals and ceremonies were evolved in an unique manner with the souvenir publishing the Gotras and Pravaras of the community. A religious head was appointed to the Mutt located at Hampi in Bellary district and is known as Sree Hampi Hemakoota Gayathri Peetha. Conducting ceremonies, celebration of the birth anniversary of their founder Guru, special pooja and car festival of the Gods and Goddesses are increasingly been carried out signalling the participation of the community in caste-based mobilisation. Conferences and community meetings are another significant feature in this context. However, it is to be noted that the emphasis laid on such meetings and organisations has gained momentum with time and has accelerated the process of caste mobilisation in the state.

As is common with many other caste associations, the Devanga Sangha in Karnataka protested strongly against the supposed under-enumeration of the community by the Nagan Gowda and the Havanur Commissions. Representations were made to the state government to re-assess the demographic strength of the community. The predominant demand of the Sangha is to reclassify the Devanga caste as a 'backward tribe', to facilitate it to avail greater quantum of benefits in the fields of education and employment. The tag of 'backward community' given to the Devangas by the Havanur Commission was resented by the Sangha, alleging that the government failed in protecting the interests of the community. The community was heterogeneous and comprised of many segments of extreme backwardness. The Sabha feared that being grouped along with the other (dominant) backward communities (like the Vokkaligas), the Devangas would get very little opportunity to obtain the reservation facilities. They lack the ability to compete with the major communities. These included the Vokkaligas and the Edigas; and service communities like the Darzis, Neygis and the Visvakarma - all in the same list of backward communities. Their plea was heard when the subsequent Government Orders categorised the various backward communities into further categories as backward community A, B and C.

Irrespective of these demands for a better constitutional status, the Devanga community is headed by a Sangha, which has attained considerable stability and growth both in terms of its financial assets and political manifestations. This development is attributed to a number of determinants operating in the economic and political spheres of the Devanga society. The fact that the Devangas, unlike many other weaving communities like the Kuruhina Settys, Padmasalis, Swakula Salis and Pattegars, are specialised in weaving of silk cloth, has benefited only a few enterprising, capitalist Devanga businessman, who have been able, with their economic resourcefulness, to mobilise themselves through the ranks of the Devanga Sangha, to demand higher political representation.

There is no doubt that the leadership of the community which includes its Sangha or caste association is dominated or monopolised by the elite as is true of any other caste. Secondly, the state politics is comparatively better represented by men and women from the Devanga caste than the other subcastes or weaving castes like Thogataveera, Kuruhina Setty etc. This is the class character of caste-based mobilisation as portrayed through its Sangha. Representation was given or achieved by men from this caste much before other weaving castes like for example, the case of late Sri K. M. Naganna, one of the ex-presidents of the Sangha, who was also nominated member of the Karnataka Backward Classes Commission appointed in 1972. A number of developmental schemes were started during his tenure as the President of the Sangha as well as when he held high positions like the Mayor of Bangalore City Corporation.

It is such factors that significantly added to the expansion of the Devanga caste association. The Sangha was soon able to build community hostels in the city of Bangalore apart from initiating a number of other activities. Its asset situation improved over the decades and there is a remarkable trend towards unification of the community with all subcastes brought together (process of fusion) for purposes of numerical strength. Caste conferences and meetings held in the recent decades are the manifestations of this increased political awareness (Akila Karnataka Devanga Maha Sammelanas : 1982, 1994, 1998 & 2004). Efforts are being made to maintain the unity among the different subcastes or the other weaving communities, like the Neygis, Swakula Salis, etc.

As noted earlier, the Devangas constitute only one of the many weaving caste groups of Karnataka. There are also a number of other small and not well identified castes which profess weaving as their caste occupation. They claim differences in their nature of work although all of them pursue weaving as their economic activity. These are based on technical isues like texture of the cloth that they weave (like silk or cotton), color of the thread (like white or black - Bilimagga and Karimagga) as also out of cultural differences like language, regional spread of the caste in question and so on.

The Havanur Commission classified the different weaving castes, apart from the Devangas, under the banner of 'Neygi', which means weaving (KBCC Report : 1975). There are about sixteen such caste groups under the category of 'Neygi' which is a backward community like the Devangas. While it is obvious that these groups are classified under a common heading due to the similarity in their caste occupation, it is interesting to note that each group is distinctively endogamous and homogeneous and is endowed with a caste association functioning from Bangalore as its headquarters.

The different caste groups coming under the category of 'Neygi' do not appear to be possessing equal mobilisational traits. The term 'Neygi', like the term 'Vokkaliga', may be treated as a blanket term including caste groups similar in occupations yet forming endogamous entities. It is also observed that the mobilisational efforts by these different groups have been kindled by certain socio-political developments in the days of post-Havanur Commission, as many of them, with Sanghas established nearly 50 years ago, have renewed their activities with a greater zeal and enthusiasm only then.

Among the castes categorised under the 'Neygi' group, the following have been predominantly active since the period noted above. Such an increased activity is detected on the basis of the number of caste conferences/meetings held and the propaganda given to the demands of the Sangha and its activities. These caste groups are the Kuruhina Shettys, Swakula Salis, the Padmashalis and the Thogataveeras.

10. The Akhila Karnataka Swakula Sali Sangha

The Swakula Salis or Swakula Sales are one of the weaving communities of the State. They are different from the Pattegars (with whom they are generally associated to be one and the same) in their cultural practices, though the occupation of most of the communities like that of the Padmashalis, Swakula Salis, Somavamsha Sahasrarjuna Kshatriyas, Aryavamsha Sahasrarjuna Kshatriyas, Kuruhina Shettys, Pattegars and others is similar (weaving). The Swakula Salis are distributed all over the State (there were about a lakh of them in 1972 when the Havanur Commission collected census data).

The first stage of caste mobilisation among the Swakula Salis was with the establishment of the Akhila Bharatha Swakula Sali Sangha, founded in the year 1913 at Hubli. It was then called as the 'Swakula Sali Vidyavardhak Sangha'. The first conference of the Sangha was also held at Hubli (where a large number of Swakula Salis reside) in the year 1916 (Souvenir of the Diamond Jubilee Celebrations of the Sangha : 1973).

The Bangalore branch of the Sangha was founded in 1931. Between the years 1913-54, the Sangha had a stunted growth and was able to raise limited funds towards the educational advancement of the community. Between the years 1954-68, which could be termed the second phase of the development of the Sangha, there was very little addition to the Sangha's assets (Souvenir : 1973). The appointment of the successive BCCs in the state since 1972 is seen as heralding a new wave of activity by the Sangha. The representatives have been asserting the backwardness of the community and pleading for a 'more backward' status. For example, the inclusion of the Swakula Salis under the 'Neygi' category as a backward community is viewed as affecting the group in the long run (Eswarappa S., President of the Sangha).

11. The Thogataveera Sangha

The Thogataveeras are yet another weaving caste group of Karnataka who are professionals in the weaving of both cotton and silk cloth. They are found, apart from Bangalore, in Tumkur, Kolar and Mysore districts. In addition to weaving, they are also found pursuing agriculture as an additional occupation.

Realising the extreme educational backwardness of the community, a few rich and philanthropic leaders of the community ventured to establish a Sangha at Bangalore to cater to the welfare of the Thogataveeras. Thus, the 'Thogataveera Sangha' came into existence in the year 1947 with the munificent donations made by the late Sri N.A. Munivenkatappa, a leading silk merchant and philanthropist from Bangalore and few others. To begin with, a hostel was started in Bangalore 'for the benefit of students who come from outside the city for purposes of education' (Souvenir of the Silver Jubilee Celebrations of the Akila Karnataka Thogataveera Sangha : 1973). As the pressure for greater accommodation increased, a site was bought near Sampangi tank (Bangalore) in 1961, and a hostel was constructed there in 1965. The hostel also caters to the needs of the community by acting as a marriage choultry. In the 1990s, a shopping complex has come up in the same premises.

The Thogataveeras claim to be economically more backward than the Devangas. This is attributed to their profession that is affected much more by industrialisation than that of the Devangas and to class-based oppression by the latter.[66] The appointment of KBCC led to an active process of mobilisation. This is clear when the Sangha chose to celebrate its Silver Jubilee on a grand scale in the year 1973, the year following the constitution of the Commission. A state-wide conference was held at Bangalore on July 13, 1973, to bring the demands of the Thogataveeras to the notice of the government. It was inaugurated by no less an illuminery than late Sri Devraj Urs, the then Chief Minister (Souvenir : 1973).

The Sangha's active role in representing the woes of the community increased in the years following the silver jubilee year. It demanded for classifying the Thogataveeras as the 'most backward community'. Their inclusion in the list of backward communities along with 'giants' like the Devangas and the

Vokkaligas was the foremost threat the Thogataveeras have alleged to be facing in securing their justified share in the reservation benefits (Ramaiah, Secretary of the Thogataveera Sangha : 1991).

Like any other caste group, the Thogataveeras are also divided into a number of subcastes which are endogamous units. Awareness as to the unity of the group for purposes of development of the community is a growing phenomenon of the recent years besides conflict between the leaders which is reflected in the chequered history of the Sangha.[67]

12. The Karnataka State Kuruhina Setty Sangha

The Kuruhina Settys are also among the weaving communities of the state found in the districts of Tumkur, Hassan, Bijapur, Dharwar and Bangalore. They are called by various names, like, Bilimagga, Jodu-Bomma, Hiriya-Bomma, etc., which are endogamous groups. But the Kuruhina Settys of Hubli and Dharwar are known as Lingayat or Veerasaiva Kuruhina Settys (Souvenir of the All-India Kuruhina Setty Maha Sammelana : January 11, 1981).

Throughout the State, most of the Kuruhina Settys follow weaving operations using both handlooms and power looms. Handlooms are a feature of villages while in cities power looms are used. The Sangha was mainly inspired by the starting of other caste associations, mainly the Devanga Sangha and founded a caste association in the year 1928 at Bangalore. It was predominantly "due to the initiative and pioneering efforts of Loka Seva Parayane late Smt.D.Sakamma, a coffee planter of repute of Somwarpet in Kodagu district (the erstwhile Coorg district) that the association took its birth. The main objectives of the Sangha were to strive for the social and economic advancement of the community and to promote education (Memorandum presented to the Government : 1981). Apart from this main Sangha at Bangalore, Sanghas were started wherever the community was preponderant. The founder, Smt. Sakamma, has donated a building at Bangalore, where a hostel for the community students is set up "without any government aid".

The Kuruhina Settys "being a largely unorganized group", do not seem to be having a mutt or monastery of their own. While the community has a Swamiji at Gadag in North Karnataka, the people of the Southern districts complained that they have no such Guru.[68] They also do not have a definite idea as to their demographic composition. However, on the lines of what the other communities have undertaken to mobilise themselves, even the Kuruhina Settys have attempted to take a census of their caste on their own. This is considered by them (and as believed by many other castes, to be the first step in the pursuit of mobilisation to facilitate bringing together the entire community under one shelter, thereby eliminating the subcaste differences) (Interview with the President of the Sangha).

The Sangha has continuously placed its demands before the government for sanction of a site at Bangalore to construct hostels and schools for the community's children. Its foremost demand has been to categorise the Kuruhina Settys as one of the Scheduled Tribes (Girijana). A memorandum to this effect was submitted to the BCCs, desiring to get recognition to their "very backward' position and to progress like the "Reddys", the Lingayats and the Vokkaligas.

13. The Karnataka Padmasali Sangha

The Padmasalis are yet another caste belonging to the family of weavers. Like the Swakula Salis, the Thogataveeras and the Kuruhina Settys, they represent a particular cultural tradition amongst the broader category of weavers. A brief note on the history of the community would be necessary to clarify the differences and similarities that tend to exist between these castes.

The term 'Sale' is a general term applied to a group of castes who have adopted weaving as their occupation. It is derived from the Sanskrit word, 'Salika', a weaver and its Kannada equivalent is 'neygi'.

While the Swakula Salis are immigrants from Maharashtra and predominantly the residents of the Bombay-Karnataka area, the Padmasalis are believed to have migrated from Andhra Pradesh and the Hyderabad-Karnataka Area.[69] They are also believed to have descended from a 'rishi' (sage) by name Markandeya. 'Padma' means the lotus flower and the mythology of Padmashalis tells us that a great saint by name "Bhavana Rishi" came out of the *Yaga* conducted by Markandeya, holding a lotus in his hand. When the latter was asked by the Gods to supply them clothing out of the fibre of the lotus flower, Bhavana Rishi and his 101 sons took to weaving of cloth, thus becoming the progenitors of Padmashali caste (Souvenir : 1980). They claim to belong to a caste similar to the Brahmins in its Vedic practices and quote the volume on Hindu castes and tribes by L.K. Ananthakrishna Iyer and H.V. Nanjundaiah (1930:559), where they are considered as being endowed with a fifth Veda by name "Padma Veda" and as belonging to the "Padma Shakha" and "Markandeya Sutra" (Souvenir : 1980). The above authors are also quoted as having emphasised upon the significance of the community by stating that the practices and mode of culture of the Padmashalis are analogous to the Shakhas, Sutras and Gotras of the Brahmins. They even quote a monographic study by S. C. Dube of the Shamirpet village in Andhra Pradesh (1955:36) where the Padmashalis are placed just below the priests and traders in the social hierarchy.

There are both Shaivite and Vaishnavite Padmashalis. As a caste, they are divided into one hundred and one exogamous units (Gotras) with many subcastes amongst them.

The all India population of the Padmashalis was estimated by the Sangha to be 75 lakhs (in 1983) and is mostly concentrated in the states of Maharashtra, Tamil Nadu, and Karnataka and in the states of Gujarat, Madhya Pradesh and Uttar Pradesh (Souvenir :1980).

The Karnataka Padmashali Sangha was established in the year 1927 at Bangalore. Apart from this main Sangha, there are Sanghas at places like Anekal, Doddaballapur, Kanakapura, Davanagere, Bellary, Hospet, Harihara, Ilkal, Banahatti and other such places where the community is represented well. These are independent associations, not branches of the Bangalore Sangha catering to the educational needs of the community by setting up hostels (Souvenir : 1980).

The 'acute backwardness of the people' is indicated as the prime reason for the slow growth of the Sangha with its membership drawn mostly from the Bangalore district in the beginning.

However, the Sangha is found trying to establish ties with the Akhila Bharat Padmashali Mahasabha, which is of a recent origin having held its first conference in 1961. In the succeeding years, the All-India Sangha has been quite active. Its tenth and last conference was held in Gujarat in the year 1971 (Thirumala R. Venkatesh, President and Bapu V. Munilakshmaiah, Secretary of the Karnataka Padmasali Sangha, Bangalore).

From the above, it could be derived that the Padmashali community being an immigrant and minority group is picking up roots in the state only of late and its Sangha, irrespective of its establishment in the twenties, is alert to mobilisational impulses since the 1970s.

The Golden Jubilee Celebration of the Karnataka Padmashali Sangha and the eleventh conference of the All India Sangha which were held in December 1980 had set before themselves the task of fostering unity and integrity among the community folk apart from aiming towards the eradication of certain evil practices like dowry. The fundamental target was set as the enhancement of the educational level of the community and its political representation.

Another feature of the Padmashali Sangha, which is common to many other caste associations, is the organisational spirit to hold All-India Caste Conferences. This is being attempted with a view to "bring about more unity and strength to the group". Despite the prevalence of wide cultural gaps, the Padmashalis of Karnataka are hoping to combine their interests with their counterparts in Maharashtra, Gujarat and Andhra Pradesh where they are present in large numbers.[70] In Kerala, they are known as Bahula Padmashalis. Such integration has been to facilitate mobilisation along political lines considering that Padmashalis in Andhra Pradesh and Maharashtra are reported to be politically well represented in the ranks of ministers and so on.

Like the other weaving caste groups, the Padmashalis are not satisfied with their inclusion under that 'neygi' group along with about a dozen weavers as the concessions are to be shared by all of them.

14. The Akhila Bharatiya Bhavasara Kshatriya Mahasabha

The Bhavasar Kshatriyas are a caste group whose occupation is associated with tailoring and printing of cloth. They are known by various names like Darzi, Simpi, Shimpi, Chippi, Sibbiliga, Namdev, Chippiga, Sai, Mirai, Rangari, Rangara, Nilari, Neelagar and so on (meaning a tailor). The community claims to have migrated from Baluchistan in Pakisthan and that there are many Bhahusar Kshatriya families in Karachi even today (Krishna Rao Sannesi, Secretary of the Mahasabha's Executive Committee, Bangalore : 1982). Three waves of immigrants are reported as having come to India towards North (Punjab), East (on the banks of river Ganges) and one towards Surat (Dwaraka). The presence of Bhavasara Kshatriyas in Karnataka is considered an outcome of migration from Gujarat and Maharashtra.[71]

The original occupation of Bhahusars was printing of cloth (hand-prints). In modern times, they have taken up dying of yarn. They were well-versed in this art which faced a setback when German dyes were introduced into the process. This deterioration in the economic rewards of one's caste occupation has been further strengthened by the introduction of many new dyes.

Although the Bhavasara Kshatriya Mahasabha was officially established in the year 1924, a state body known as the Mysore Bhavasara Kshatriya Sangha existed earlier to it, started around 1911 itself. This could be termed as the culmination of the efforts of the community's first graduate in old Mysore, Sri B.S. Ranoji Rao[72] who in fact started a caste association as early as in 1911 at Mysore. It was called "The Mysore Bhavasara Kshatriya Sangha". The data collected on the history of the Sangha show that it did not pass through continuous periods of activity, its revival co-inciding with certain socio-political events.[73] The Sangha remained dormant till the state's reorganisation and widened its horizon with the inclusion of new districts. It was titled 'Maha Mysore Bhavasara Kshatriya Sangha'. The state level conference was presided over by Sri B. D. Jatti, the then Chief Minister (Souvenir : 1980) and later the Vice-President of India.

Then followed periods of inactivity before the Sangha could think of any further role for itself, till 1973 when it was granted a small piece of land at Bangalore. It was sanctioned to a lady social worker by name Girijadevi Mahendrakar hailing from the Bhavasar Kshatriya community by the Maharani of Mysore. A temple was constructed on this site by her who was also the head of the Sangha's office for quite some time. Apart from the Sangha, there were more than eight Upasanghas (branches) functioning in the city of Bangalore alone, during the nineties.

Like its counterparts, the Mysore Bhavasara Kshatriya Sangha, having regained its political activities came to put forth the usual demand for a re-classification of its backward status. Its inclusion by the Havanur Commission under the 'Darzi' community was resented as the Bhavasara Kshatriyas claimed to be an altogether different caste than the Darzis despite both being tailors by profession, but claim superior status nonetheless[74]).

In addition to hostels for community students at Bangalore, Mysore, Hubli, Dharwar and Shimoga, the Sangha has also started a Co-operative Society converted as a bank in course of time. Welfare programmes like conducting mass marriages, organising anti-dowry campaigns, fostering unity within the group[75] etc., are taken up with zeal and concern by the Sangha in recent years.

15. Somavamsha Sahasrarjuna (Khatri) Kshatriya Sangha

The Somavamsha Sahasrarjuna (Khatri) Kshatriya Sangha represents the Pattegar caste group in Karnataka. It was founded in the year 1935 at Bangalore, on the lines of the Swakula Sali and other weaving communities. The Pattegars are also one of the weaving communities, generally engaged in the weaving and dyeing of silk cloth. They are known by the synonymous names of Patvekar, Khatri, Pattegar, Kshatriya, Shivaji and so on. But they claim and advocate their sanskritised new caste name as "Somavamsha Sahasrarjuna Kshatriyas".

The SSK Sangha's main activities centre on certain welfare programmes that it has undertaken for the community. This includes religious programmes (this is mainly oriented towards fund collection for the establishment of temples (like the one for Sri Rajarajeswara Sahasrarjuna, the "Moola Purusha" or founder of the SSKs), anti-dowry campaigns, encouragement to girls' education etc. Traditionally, educational advancement of children (especially higher education) was given less importance, since weaving formed their caste occupation passed on from generation to generation. However, the President of the Sangha – Sri Krishnasa Khoday, an industrialist and the owner of Khoday Distilleries at Bangalore – realised quite early that formal education was also necessary for the children of SSKs as the caste occupation was not solely dependable, especially under the changing situation imposed by globalisation and, earlier to it, modernisation. Thus the youth were encouraged to take to tailoring, petty trade, ribbon and label making and such other enterprises. Being predominantly urban dwellers, the community has no access to agricultural income or ownership of land. Hence, the request before the government is to consider it as "more backward" than the other weaving caste groups. The leaders have attributed the 'neglect' of this caste by the Backward Classes Commissions to the similarity found in the names of SSKs, Kalals, Tigalars and Rajputs – all of whom call themselves "Kshatriyas", which has affected the enumeration of the SSKs as a separate backward caste.[76]

The process of caste mobilisation among the weaving communities thus presents many diversities and it is difficult to form any generalisations. This is because of the very nature of the category, which is heterogeneous and complex. As seen above, the various weaving groups are not similar in their structure and resources for gaining socio-economic mobility. Of them, the Devangas appear to be better equipped with economic power and political representation besides being 'superior' in their occupation than their professional counterparts, majority of which are immigrants from outside (either Andhra Pradesh or Maharasthra). The comparative advantage that their specialisation in weaving silk cloth has provided them and also their numerical strength (0.93 per cent) over other weaving communities like the Neygi (0.74 per cent), the Darzi (0.37 per cent) and the Pattegar (0.041 per cent) are the important determinants of the Devangas' greater mobility than their professional counterparts.

III

Among the caste groups which came under the influence of the 'Backward Classes Movement' in the state during the 1920s and 1930s accelerating the process of caste mobilisation (of which formation of caste associations was a significant part), there were a few more communities that constituted the professional and service communities. The impact of the upper-caste patterns of mobility was evident even among these groups, which occupied the middle and lower levels of the social hierarchy.

As discussed earlier, the middle-castes as a category are diverse and complex in their social and economic characteristics making any uniform generalisation about them difficult. They too fit into the above process of caste mobilisation by forming caste associations, dependent on the upper castes for providing them the stimulus for doing so. Awareness about the benefits of caste association came much later for the above caste groups, a factor which should be attributed to their general socio-cultural backwardness.

Like the weavers, the traditional caste structure in Karnataka comprises of many other professional groups, of which the potters (Kumbaras), the oil-pressers (Ganigas), the fishermen (Besthas or Gangamathasthas), the toddy tappers (Idigas), the Smiths (Viswakarmas) and the cowherds (Yadavas) are important ones. The following is an analysis of these caste groups and their associations:

16. The Karnataka State Gangamathasthara Sangha

The caste group of fishermen known as the Besthas or

Gangamatha is the earliest among the above professional groups to start a caste association. This does not speak, however, of any advantages the Besthas have over the potters or the oilmen, but only an early adaptation of the upper caste formula of caste mobilisation.

'The Akila Karnataka Gangamathasthara Sangha (AKGS) was established in the year 1929 in Bangalore to organise the hetero-geneous Gangamatha people and to achieve their economic, educational and political development (Souvenir of the Golden Jubilee Celebrations of the Karnataka Gangamathasthara Sangha, Bangalore : 1980).

The Gangamathasthas are found throughout the state. A large concentration of them is in Mysore district (where they are known by a synonymous name Parivara Nayaka) and in the coastal districts of Uttara and Dakshina Kannada. They are worshippers of lord Shiva and goddess Ganga (the goddess of water and the name of an important river in north India) and have no religious mutt or 'Order' (Doddaveeraiah, Secretary of the Sangha : December 1981). Except for the starting of a small students' hostel, the Sangha has not been able to make much advance "Owing to the generally poor and backward state of the caste" (Suvarna Sanchike : 1980). Independence and the re-organisation of the state have resulted in adding to the number of Gangamathasthas in the state's population, when many districts with a large percentage of these people were included within the jurisdiction of the newly formed Mysore state.[77]

Subsequently, the Sangha has expanded in its size and activities. Although it does not have its branches, at least independent Sanghas have been started at places which show a considerably large concentration of the Gangamatha people. The districts of Chitradurga, Bijapur[78], Dharwar, Belgaum, Bellary, Bangalore, Uttara Kannada, Dakshina Kannada (Mangalore), Mysore, Mandya, Hassan, Kolar and Gulbarga have such Sanghas of Gangamathasthas.

The main occupation of the Gangamatha people is fishing, apart from which they also sell lime. This has led to another nick-name for them called as 'Sunnadavaru', meaning the people dealing in lime. The Sangha, which was reportedly inactive for years, submitted a memorandum to the Havanur Commission in the year 1973 stating its problems of backwardness (Lakshman Salian M., President of the Sangha : December 1981). The Commission classified the Gangamathasthas under the 'Backward caste' category. It has also enumerated as many as 27 names under the caption 'Gangamatha', as synonymous caste groups.[79] The fundamental goal the Sangha has set before itself "is to bring about unity between all the caste groups among the Gangamathasthas and to establish just a single name for the community" (Souvenir : 1980). A call to this effect was given firmly believing that it is essential to establish a common nomenclature for the group, since the development of any group depends on its unity.

The leaders of the fishermen association allege that the government, in its census enumeration and Backward Classes Commissions, has slowly degraded their caste status to that of a low caste and maintained a differential treatment to the varied fishermen caste groups, despite their common origin. The Gangamatha caste is believed to have descended from a great saint, Shakya Muni, of the 'Puranas'. Being originally Ambigas (boatmen) and fishermen, the 'Angadas' or descendants of 'Shakya Muni' came to be also known as Gangamatha. "Due to years of living together and the inevitable cultural interactions, they have adopted the culture of the people of the coastal belt", resulting in their varied culture and names (Suvarna Sanchike : 1980, 6). For example, in the districts of Uttara Kannada, like Raichur, Gulbarga and Bidar they are known as 'Kabbaligas'; in Shimoga, Chitradurga, Tumkur and Bangalore districts as Gangamathasthas and Gangakula Besthas; in Dharwar and

Belgaum districts as Ambiga, Sunagara and Barakera; in Dakshina and Uttara Kannada districts as Mogaveeras and in Bijapur as Koli and Mahadev Kolis.

The Gangamathasthara Sangha strongly denounces, through the memoranda it has periodically submitted to the state and central governments and in its caste meetings, "the tendency of differentiating between the subcastes of fishermen community". According to the memorandum, the Gangamathasthas and the Besthas are treated by the government as different groups and that "the Kabbaligas and the Kolis are not equivalent terms". "Even the Havanur Commission also, while making reservations for the different groups, has distinguished between the Besthas, Talwars and Boyas (who are enlisted by the Commission under the Backward tribe Category)" and the Gangamatha, Gangakula, Kabbiliga and others (who are categorised as Backward Castes) (Memorandum submitted to the KBCC : 1979).

It should be clarified here that the above caste groups functioning under the broader framework of 'fishermen community' have emerged out of a process of fission within the system, over the decades. This division appears to be resting basically on a combination of occupational and cultural factors. In other words, the Besthas, wherever they have settled in coastal areas, have taken to fishing and related occupations. In places where they are residing away from water due to migration and want of economic opportunities, the Besthas have taken to agriculture and other occupations. "This should not lead to any misconceptions about their original occupations and caste identity". Gangamathasthas and Ambigas are not two different groups. Gangamatha people are also basically boatmen along with which they had taken up fishing. Since their services were restricted only to a few royal families and zamindars or paleyagars who gave these fishermen some land as 'Inam land', by cultivating which the fishermen came to be identified as agriculturists and hence different from the Besthas. The Sangha thus strongly emphasises that the Gangamathasthas are not different from the Ambigas or Besthas. Such cultural diversities have arisen "due to occupational mobility among them". Apart from agricultural work, some have taken to modern jobs especially as messengers, 'Valikars', in the revenue department and Talwars.[80]

On the basis of the above explanation, the Gangamathasthara Sangha appears to be attempting strongly to establish the homogeneity of the community. The classification of the two fishing castes (tribes ?) viz., Beshtaar and Bunde Beshtaar, under the backward tribe category is also being criticised by the Sangha as the government's plan to introduce division within the group.[81] The main demand of the Sangha leaders is for a re-classification of the level of backwardness among them and thereby to assign to all the fishermen castes and subcastes a 'backward tribe' status, similar to that of the two groups which presently enjoy that privilege.

Another noteworthy development in the sphere of the Sangha's activities is the widening of the circle of leaders belonging to the fishermen community, characterised by a process of unification for administrative purposes amongst the various fishing communities. But the leadership of the Sangha is in the hands of the dominant castes like the Mogaveeras in the coastal belt and the Gangamathasthas in the north. The Mogaveeras, a subcaste among the various fishermen groups and inhabitants of Dakshina Kannada and Uttara Kannada districts are economically and politically the more advanced and mobile group than the other subcastes. The president of the AKGS at the time of this study was a Mogaveera. The Mogaveeras "being an advanced community than the Gangamathasthas" have also established their own Sangha, the Mogaveera Sangha, at Mangalore, which has many branches like the one at Mumbai. Many Mogaveera families reside there as migrants from Karnataka and enterprising in their economic and political activities due to opportunities available there than for their brethren back at Mangalore. "The Mogaveera Vyavasthapaka Mandali" at Bombay publishes a Kannada monthly by name "Mogaveera" with a good circulation among the local (Karnataka's) Mogaveeras.

The major problem facing the Gangamathasthas is the lack of any organised effort to tackle their problems since most of the enlightened and politically active people belong to the other group, the Mogaveeras.[82] This was evident in the manner in which the Silver Jubilee of the Sangha was celebrated as compared to its Golden Jubilee that was celebrated on a much grandeour scale. Each time a conference is held, a memorandum has been submitted to the government seeking political representation to the group and also assets like land or site in Bangalore to construct students' hostels or choultry for the benefit of the community.[83] But the notable demand is to re-classify the Gangakulas and all the castes under that category, irrespective of subcaste differences, as either Scheduled Caste or as Scheduled Tribe.

It is interesting to notice a change that has obviously taken place in the nature of the "demand" by the Gangamathasthas with the passage of time. In their memorandum submitted earlier to 1980, they had sought a backward tribe status. But by 1980, the demand rose for seeking a tag for greater backwardness — i.e., as Scheduled Caste or Scheduled Tribe. Different subcastes within this broad category have demanded different levels of tags of backwardness. While the upper strata of the community are demanding backward tribe status, the lower sections are seeking a Scheduled Tribe status.

17. Karnataka Pradesh Arya Idigara Sangha

The Karnataka Pradesh Arya Idigara Sangha was established in the year 1944 with headquarters at Bangalore and branches at Gulbarga, Mysore, Mandya, Tumkur, Hassan, Shimoga, Bellary, Davanagere, Hubli, Uttara and Dakshina Kannada districts.

The Idigas are also known by various other names due to the presence of a number of subcastes among them. Some of them are – Billava, Malayali Billava, Eliga, Iliga, Thiyan, Deevar or Devar and Devaru in Mangalore-Kollegal area. In Mysore area, they are known as Halepaik, in Gulbarga area as Kalal, Ediga, Goundla, Goundala and so on (KBCC : 1975). These subcastes are generally endogamous in nature.

The main aim of the Sangha is stated to be spreading of education among the Idigas. The hostels are open to students from all communities but preference is given to the Idiga boys. Like those of the dominant castes, the Idiga Sangha also aspired to open a professional college that would help a great deal in enabling the poor students of the community to access such education. A co-operative bank has been established at Bangalore to cater to the financial needs of the Idigas. The first conference of the community was held in 1958 (at the Race Course), the second in 1960 and subsequently at periodic intervals representing the problems of the community.

Prominent among the senior leaders of the Idigas included Sri S. Bangarappa, ex-chief minister of Karnataka, senior politician and founder of the Samajavadi Party in the state, Sri Kagodu Thimmappa, ex-minister, Sri H.R. Basavaraj and T.V. Venkataswamy, MP and MLC, respectively. The community is also represented by the Thespian, noted Kannada film star late Dr. Raj Kumar.

18. The Akhila Karnataka Pradesh Kumbarara Sangha

The caste groups of the Kumbaras (potters) and the Ganigas (oil pressers), share certain common characteristics in their mobilisation activities. As the middle castes of the social hierarchy they are traditionally a part of village functionaries (Srinivas : 1960). Like the weavers, smiths and the cobblers, the Kumbaras and the Ganigas are among those village professionals who are affected considerably by the introduction of the machine age (Marriott : 1955). With an agriculture-based economy, generally as landless labourers and rarely as owners of land, these groups were consistently reduced to more and more backward status reflected in their very low organisational capacity. They are numerically a minority among the various caste groups of Karnataka (0.73 per cent for the Kumbaras and 0.52 per cent for the Ganigas of the state population) (see Appendix 7, 8 and 9) and the absence of a monastery or religious mutt (as in the case of the Veerasaivas) and poor and insufficient political representation, have been held as the major handicaps for the absence of mobility in their case.

However, efforts for higher education, and through it, access to positions of a high rank in the administrative set up of Princely Mysore by a few members of these communities did provide at least a marginal political background to them, although the numerically and economically very weak and backward status of these groups (as in the case of many other middle castes) has hindered any attempt to mobilise caste support. This is evident when we see that it has taken nearly a quarter of a century for the castes to reach the fringe of organisational efficiency attempting to achieve socio-political status in an unequal society. Leadership in such caste groups, being middle and lower castes, is a product of the Constitutional Guarantees awarded since the Miller Committee days in 1918.

Of the two, it was the Potters or the Kumbaras (as they are known in the Kannada language), who were the first to establish a caste association, thereby giving a recognition to their organisational work. Whatever could be formed was a minor institution, limited in its activities to the capital city and only subsequently expanding in size and functions.

The Kumbaras trace their slow and weak organisational drive to the exploitative tendency on the part of the upper caste ruling-elite (A. Annayyappa, Hon. Secretary of the Sangha, Bangalore : 1990). They claim to be one of the earliest inhabitants of Bangalore city and as having resided in the central part of the city, i.e., the market area, as early as in 1537 when the city acquired a formal shape (Souvenir of the conference for the inauguration of the Kumbara hostel and the Fifth Kumbara Maha Sammelana : 1974).

This was the time when the different parts of the city were inhabited with migrants from neighbouring villages and the people following different professions resided in different parts of the city centre, "the streets where they lived came to be known by the occupations these people professed". The Kumbaras, once a sizeable majority, comprised approximately a hundred households in the city (a good number in those days) (Souvenir : 1974). But with the growth and expansion of the city, especially its commercial centre, the Kumbara families had to move away to different parts of the city for want of accommodation or residential space. Moreover, the city corporation also objected to the manufacture of pottery in the city centre, for reasons of atmospheric pollution. Thus, by 1920-30, all the land originally belonging to the Kumbaras had been taken over by the city corporation.[84] The Kumbaras, reportedly, did not get any compensation for the loss of land. The British government, however, developed an extension by name 'Pottery Town' at the Cantonment area during 1920. Even to this day at least 30-40 Kumbara families could be found living in that area (Souvenir : 1974). This account of the historical development of the Kumbara community throws light on some of the problems faced by the community.

There were efforts by some of the prominent men of the community to develop the Kumbara community and provide equal footing to it on par with the other upper castes. This was in the 1940s. Two leaders are conspicuous in their efforts and played a greater role than others. They were Sri N.M. Thirumalappa and Sri K. Bussayya. The former hailed from an elite family among the Kumbaras that practiced dyeing of pottery as its occupation. The idea of forming a caste association first occurred to him. It became a reality only in 1951, when the Kumbarara Sangha was established in Bangalore. The other leader Sri K. Bussayya also hailed from a village in Bangalore district. He was a renowned landlord and public works and military contractor. Being a member of the Mysore Representative Assembly, he had represented the Kumbara community during his tenure as its (Representative Assembly's) member during the years 1935-41 (Souvenir : 1974).

Sri Bussayya is remembered for the welfare measures that he undertook for the benefit of his community. Apart from constructing wells and houses at villages, many schools were also constructed by him. As a result of his and Sri Thirumalappa's concerted efforts the Kumbarara Sangha was started in 1951 and Bussayya became its first President.

Started thus with modest means, the Kumbarara Sangha continued through the years fundamentally out of the philanthropy of a few community elite and "has been able to make much progress" (Souvenir : 1974). Its membership, starting with 300 in 1951, has also increased substantially. The first conference of the Kumbarara Sangha was held under its auspices in 1955 at Chikkabanavara (near Hesaraghatta) in Bangalore district.

Irrespective of all this work, the Sangha made slow progress and did not achieve anything substantial. It took long for it to register itself i.e., only on October 14, 1964 - decades of its inception. Then with some more lapse of time it was in 1971 that a caste conference was organised by the Sangha in Bangalore.

This proved to be a landmark in the history of the Sangha despite many handicaps: it lacked a building of its own and organised conferences at the Thogataveera Sangha's building. The meeting "was attended by more than 2000 delegates from all over Karnataka". It was resolved to start a students' hostel in Bangalore as there was no such hostel for the Kumbara students till then while it was ready for their counterparts from the dominant castes. The backwardness is evident even today with the educational level of the community being very low.

A conference of all the Kumbarara Sanghas in the state was held in 1973 where the socio-economic problems of the community were discussed at length and a memorandum listing the demands of the community was submitted to the Havanur Commission. The city corporation, conceding to the demands of the Sangha, sanctioned a site for the construction of a students' hostel in an extension near the city market in the heart of the city. This place originally was owned by a Kumbara businessman who sold it after facing loss in hi s trade, "it was ironical." A building at an estimated cost of Rs.20 lakhs came up on this site during the eighties. The claim of the President of the Sangha is that admission in the hostel is open to poor and deserving students from any caste, not to Kumbaras alone.

All the sudden spurt in the activities of the Kumbarara Sangha could be attributed to two factors: the years both preceding and following the appointment of the Havanur Commission saw an upsurge in the sectarian activities by the various caste groups which were busy in either establishing caste associations or in activating the existing ones. The Kumbarara Sangha's efforts in this direction and their requests for the welfare of the group as portrayed in its 1973 conference (and the very timing of the conference itself) indicating that they had the only goal of attracting the attention of the government and the Commission to seek a backward status.

The second reason for the success in expansion was the assuming of leadership in the 1970s by a man with a lot of vision and socio-political contacts. This man, Sri B.V. Ramachandrappa, an aristocrat with lot of political clout deserves mention here for his capabilities of raising the Sangha to what it is today. He was a leading metal merchant in Banglore. The students' hostel and other such developmental works were his ideas and the result of his philanthropy. The idea of opening the gates of the students' hostel for students of all castes was his idea with the intention of promoting "cultural understanding" between various castes. However, he was also aware of the fact that students from only those castes lower to the Kumbaras in the social scale came to patronise the hostel.

The Kumbaras, like any other caste, are a heterogeneous community. The Havanur Commission has listed as many as eight subcastes among the potters. Its chairman, Sri L.G. Havanur, has written an article on the social background of Kumbaras in the souvenir of the Sangha in 1974. The subcastes are: (1) Kumbara, (2) Kummara, (3) Khumbara, (4) Kumghar, (5) Kusuvan, (6) Kulala, (7) Kulalar and (8) Moolya.

There are the Telugu speaking Kummaralu, Tamil speaking 'Odeyars' and the Kannada speaking Kummara or Kumbhara. The Kumbaras also call themselves 'Shalivahanaru'[85] (Souvenir : 1974). There is no independent religious order for the Kumbaras. Most of them follow Shaivism. In north Karnataka, they call themselves Lingayat Kumbaras and it is common to find them shifting from one status to the other. When the question of economic and social benefits to the community arose (like provision for education and employment) some of them forcibly claim Kumbara status, otherwise prefer to be identified as Lingayats. They are an endogamous group.

The Kumbarara Sangha is presently giving importance to the issue of promoting intra-caste unity. Apart from this, the major thrust has been upon obtaining reservations (a higher quota than what was earmarked) in the field of education, employment and in political position. The Sangha has made representations to the state and central governments requesting them to classify the Kumbaras as a "Scheduled Tribe". It held the inclusion samongst the backward castes as unjust. In that case they will have to share the benefits amongst many other castes in the middle and lower caste categories, like the Kurubas for example (Memorandum : 1980). The Kumbaras firmly believe that they deserve much better treatment in the hands of such commissions as they suffer many constraints for mobility; that are not operational in the case of the other backward castes.

On the whole, the Kumbaras hold their Sangha as being more resourceful in its activities and possessions than a few other middle castes like the Barbers and the Washermen. The success achieved by the Sangha as compared to the above service communities in advancing its mobilisational efforts cannot, however, be held as applicable to the whole caste-group as such. It is cornered by persons hailing from rich, elitist background (like leading businessmen and high ranking government officials belonging to the community), residing in the capital city, while a large majority of the poor and underprivileged members of the potter caste claim nothing much to do with the Sangha and its activities. This is not to be understood as typical of this caste alone, but should be taken as a general trait shared by almost all caste associations.

Attempts by the Kumbaras and the Ganigas to work towards caste interests led to their representation in the state legislature. The Kumbaras came to be represented in the state cabinet (when the Janatha Party formed its first government) in 1983 with the Law Minister, Sri A. Lakshmisagar who was a Kumbara by caste.

19. The Akila Karnataka Ganigara Sangha

The Ganigas are the oil-pressers or oil-men common to the

traditional village economy in India. Like the potters, weavers and the smiths, the Ganigas also constituted the village functionaries occupying the middle level of the social hierarchy. In Karnataka, they are concentrated in the districts of Bangalore, Mysore, Shimoga, Tumkur, Kolar and Uttara and Dakshina Kannada. A majority of them, all over the state, generally followed their traditional occupation besides agricultural labour. They have also followed the process of caste mobilisation through the formation of caste-based associations. The call was given by its leaders immediately after the government appointed the Backward Classes' Commission in the year 1973. Otherwise we have no evidence of the existence of a state level caste association representing the community, earlier to this period. The Akhila Karnataka Ganigara Sangha was established in the year 1972 in Bangalore. The real inspiration came when the Commission sought information about the Ganigas for purposes of determining its backwardness. This also led to the unification of the heterogeneous Ganiga community and the establishment of a united caste association.

The picture of the Ganiga community and its socio-political status earlier than 1972 is given as follows: the Ganigas of Karnataka are a minority community and are divided into many subcastes. The important subcastes are Jyothinagara Vyshya, Jyothipana, Vania, Hegganiga, Kiruganiga, Devaganiga, Ondeththu Ganiga, Yeradeththu Ganiga (one and two bullocks), Kallu Ganiga and Maradha Ganiga. It is difficult to accurately ascertain the years since when these subcastes have evolved, but their division is based either upon their profession or their regional origin. These subcastes are also endogamous groups. Apart from these divisions, the Ganigas living in north Karnataka have taken to Veerasaivism and claim superiority over the other Ganiga subcastes. Before the year 1972, these different subcastes had their own charities and maintained strict social distance between themselves following endogamy.

The Akila Karnataka Ganigara Sangha with its headquarters at Bangalore and with only one branch office at Mysore was all that existed in the initial stages of mobilisation. While the appointment of the KBCC came as motivation behind the expansion of the Sangha's activities. The movement was spearheaded further by Ganiga leaders to fight against "certain injustices allegedly done to the community by the same commission" (B.J Puttaswamy, President of the Sangha). The exclusion of the Ganiga community from the list of backward communities under Article 16 (4) of the Constitution of India, "considering wrong population and representation in services", was attributed to the failure of the Commission to document their population accurately. This lacuna had led to under-ennumeration of the Ganiga population in the state by the Havanur Commission (as 1,56,898 based on Census 1971, while in reality the population, as estimated by the Sangha, through the Census it had undertaken, was anywhere ranging from 3.5 lakhs to 4.4 lakhs). The Sangha placed the blame of such an under-enumeration upon the existence of many subcastes within the broader Ganiga community and the prevalence of intra-caste factions. The Sangha, therefore, conducted a house-to-house sample survey of the Ganiga community to establish its claims for a greater numerical strength than that arrived at by the Havanur Commission. The representatives of the Sangha gathered much more information about the backwardness of the community when they derived information about the population of the Ganigas. A detailed memorandum highlighting the above issues was submitted to the various BCCs appointed by the State and Central Governments.

These activities gave much significance to the Ganiga caste association. It is one of those associations, which owe their origin and expansion to the political and economic circumstances introduced by the appointment of the Havanur Commission. The Sangha's activities, though initiated in 1972-73, have gained momentum, especially after the year the Commission gave its report, excluding the Ganigas from the list of the backward classes under Art. 16 (4), while Art. 15 (4) considered them as backward. The Sangha's demands were placed before the Commission on the occasion of the first conference of the Ganigas held in 1974 at Bangalore. They were placed before the government two years later on the occasion of the second conference of the Sangha (Memoranda : 1974 & 1976). These were reiterated in the third conference of the Sangha held at Tiptur in 1982. The following demands were placed before the government:

1. To grant more educational concessions to the Ganiga students, like freeships, scholarships, reservation of seats in technical institutions and free hostels,
2. Political representation to the Ganiga community by way of nominations to statutory bodies, legislative council and other bodies,[86]
3. To give encouragement to the Ganigas to improve their economic status, in the form of grants, subsidies and loans to start small-scale industries, and
4. To grant aid for the construction of hostels for Ganiga students.

While placing the above demands for considerations before the government and the various BCCs, like the Mandal Commission set up by the Central Government during 1979, the demand for political representation had evidently been given more importance. This is supplemented by the demand for economic aid to the community. In the opinion of the President of the Sangha, political dominance by other castes (particularly the Vokkaligas) and the people from other communities are taking to oil-pressing (sometimes with advanced methods using the latest mechanical devices) the Ganigas are relegated to a very poor status. The Sangha has, therefore, called for the development of its economy through the establishment of corporations or federations on the lines of the Woollen and Silk Corporation which have benefited the Devangas and other class character weaving castes (Memorandum : 1979).

The above demands of the Ganigara Sangha are not unique to it but commonly constitute an integral part of mobilisational attempts by many castes. This fact is clearly evidenced from the data obtained from various caste associations in Karnataka. However, the lack of any form of own religious leadership and the heterogeneous nature of their cultural practices are regarded as severe handicaps which the Ganiga caste association claims to be encountering in its attempts to mobilise the caste group. In the beginning, Brahminic cults were being imbibed by a majority of Ganigas and it was common to find Brahmin priests officiating at ceremonies. The Ganigas living in the northern parts of the state, a Lingayat-stronghold, followed Veerasaiva cult and claimed themselves to be Lingayats following a conversion process during Basava's times. They kept a distance from the non-Lingayat Ganigas claiming superior socio-cultural status.[87] The barrier between these groups was so intense that during the time of data collection by the Havanur Commission, it was alleged by the non-Lingayat Ganigas that their Lingayat counterparts claimed a separate listing from the former, causing much ire among the former. They suspected that many non-Ganiga Lingayats but with socio-political clout used this opportunity to get into the list of Ganiga Lingayats, thereby misleading the authorities.

The non-Lingayat Ganigas are diverse in their caste structure and have many subcastes. However, leadership of the Ganigara Sangha is constituted by the dominant subcaste, viz., the Jyothinagara Vyshyas. In fact, the two hostels, which are the only assets of the Sangha and its whole officialdom for that matter, belonged to this subcaste. As alleged by the other subcastes, these hostels admit students only from the

'Jyothinagara Vyshya' or Jyothipana subcaste and none else from the other Ganiga subcastes. This reflects the class character of Ganiga mobilisation process.

An interesting trend found among many middle and lower groups is their desire to be listed as a SC or ST and not as an OBC. The Ganigas admitted that their profession does not carry any high status and is looked down upon by upper castes. "Even among the Ganigas, people performing jobs like oil-pressing and oil selling have got divided, by convention, into two groups. The oil-selling group assumed superiority and began to look down upon the oil pressing community as the latter is considered as a dirtier job than oil selling. In some states, like West Bengal, the members of the oil-pressing subcastes are treated as untouchables (interview with members of the non-Jyothinagara subcaste). These differences were highlighted by the leaders of the oil-pressing subcaste encouraged by the 'superior' Ganigas who sell oil, to join them)[88] claiming a SC status for themselves and evidently, separation from the oil-selling subcaste.

However, such a move is found to be opposed by the Lingayat Ganigas who are aspiring for a dual status - a backward position to claim reservation facilities, at the same time, preferring to remain unmixed with the other Ganiga subcastes in order to maintain their high ritual status. This appears to have led to serious obstacles in the process of unification of all subcastes attempted by the Ganigara Sangha.

The 'middle class' category, as noted earlier, consists of groups which include both the professional and the service communities. A further hierarchy is generally evident among those in the middle caste category. While the different professional groups are regarded as belonging to the upper and middle levels of the stratum, the service communities, which are chiefly divided into the barbers and the washermen, traditionally occupy a much inferior status as compared to the former owing to their profession considered as polluting. They are economically more backward than many of the middle castes. Culturally, they are ascribed a low status, which marks their separation from the other middle castes. These cultural differences have no doubt, arisen out of the professions that the barbers and washermen are traditionally ordained to carry out, which are considered highly polluting by the others. Their traditional occupation fetched them very little economic gains. The mode of payment being in "kind" form, it added to their uncertain economic position forcing them to undertake wage labour as a survival strategy.

The poor economic condition and ritually low status of the two communities has acted as the reason behind the comparatively slow growth of their caste associations. Having been started in the pre-independence era, they have gained momentum only during the seventies and more during the 1980s. This fact is clearly seen in the records of the respective Sanghas and also by an overview of the achievements and mobilisational trials by these associations in both the periods.

20. The Karnataka Madivalara Sangha

The 'Madivalas'[89] (Washermen) gain precedence over the barbers as far as the year of the establishment of their caste association is concerned. The Karnataka Madivalara Sangha was founded in the year 1933, presumably out of the efforts of a few educated, urban dwelling members of the washerman community who came under the influence of the non-Brahmin movement. The growth of the Sangha later came to be adversely affected by the poor and backward condition of the community. But the reorganisation of the state in the year 1956 had no far-reaching effects on the community at least till the seventies as it did for the Lingayats.

The Madivalas (more popularly known by the name 'Agasas') are numerically (and also socio-politically) a minority among the various Hindu caste groups. Constituting hardly 1.18 per cent of the state's population, they are one of those castes, which are found almost uniformly across all the districts of the state, but not in large numbers. Being a 'service community' and a part of the village's social structure, the Agasas are common to the social system of any village. Their traditional occupation being washing clothes, they constitute, traditionally, an essential component of the rural economy. Under the traditional jajmani relations, they were paid in kind for their services in agricultural work. Very rarely did they own any land and worked as landless agricultural labourers. Modernisation has disrupted the age-long caste economy of the Washermen group, forcing most of the people into unemployment and underemployment. Migration to nearby urban centres has followed this, where the members of the Washermen caste have either continued with their caste occupation or have taken to new jobs with a large percentage of them working as casual labourers.

As could be gathered from the above examination of the general living conditions of the Madivalas (which in fact is applicable to the caste group of the barbers who will be dealt with later), it is difficult to expect them to possess an established and resourceful caste association.

Thus, even after two decades of independence and constitutional guarantees, no marked change or development in the activities of the caste association of the Washermen in Karnataka was to be observed till the KBCC was appointed in the year 1972. These years should necessarily be taken as forming the preliminary stage of caste mobilisation among the Washermen elite. During this period, a slight increase in the level of awareness about the prospects of mobilisation among a few educated members of the Agasa caste seems to have come about. The otherwise, nearly defunct Madivala Sangha revived its existence through a series of activities after the appointment of the KBCC (D. Hanumanthaiah, President of the Sangha : 1982). These included, organising meetings of the caste members and discussing the general problems faced by the community. The Sangha also came to obtain an expanded title as the 'Karnataka Madivalara Sangha'.

The Havanur and other Commissions have grouped the Madivalas or the Agasas under the category of the 'backward castes'. Along with these groups, 8 of their subcastes have also been listed as synonyms of 'Agasa' or 'Madivalas'. They are: Sakala, Sakalavadu, Tskala, Chakala, Vannan (in Kolar district), Dhobi, Parit and Rajaka (in Mangalore) (KBCC Report : 1975, Vol. II).

The Sangha, despite its comparatively early year of establishment, has not been able to achieve as much growth as some other caste associations founded around the same period have. The fundamental reason behind this cannot be explained more satisfactorily than in terms of the low socio-economic status of the caste that has hindered any such process. Along with the economic factor, even the socio-ritual status of the community accounts enormously, for the drive it provides, or otherwise, for the mobilisational attempts by the community members. The Madivalas occupying the lowest rung among the middle castes suffer from age-old discrimination at the hands of all the castes above them, owing obviously to the ritually polluting caste occupation of washing clothes (Srinivas : 1960 & 1964).

The nature of mobilisation process among the Madivalas and the role played by their caste association will be analysed here basing on the above two (economic and ritual) determinants which are, nevertheless, interdependent and interrelated.

As noted earlier, an upsurge of mobilisation activities seem to have occurred in the Madivala Sangha on the occasion of the appointment of the KBCC. This move is decidedly one that was inspired by similar activities and attempts by a number of other caste groups. The Havanur Commission and others continued the backward status of the Madivalas, by further categorising them as a 'backward caste'.

The Madivalas were not very much pleased about the category the Havanur Commission placed them in. They considered themselves to be very low and stigmatised, "no less than any ex-untouchable caste" (Hanumanthaiah : n.d.) and their inclusion among the backward castes was considered by them as unjust since "they were more backward than the other castes included in the 'backward castes' category."

Hence, the Karnataka Madivalara Sangha, led by a handful of educated, Bangalore-based Madivalas who were working as high salaried government servants, made relentless efforts for the inclusion of their community in the list of SC or ST. The President of the Sangha at that time was a retired deputy commissioner who strongly asserted the claim of the community leaders to declare it as an inferior community and that facilities be given to it on par with the SCs (See Appendix 4.6). The representatives of the Sangha submitted memoranda to the various BCCs like the Havanur Commission, the Venkataswamy Commission and Chinnappa Reddy Commission appointed by the state and Mandal Commission of the centre. They demanded that the washermen community being "socially, economically and ritually very backward" had to be declared as a SC or ST. The demands included the following:

1 Inclusion of the Madivalas in the category of SCs or "at least" STs ;
2. Provision of representation in the legislature and the Panchayats ;
3. Provision of educational concessions to Madivala children in the form of scholarship, hostel facilities; and

4. Provision of other welfare schemes.

Of these, the demand for SC status was emphasised by the Sangha than anything else. Further, it has also been fighting for greater political representation to the community in the state legislature. These efforts by the President were considered by others as stepping stone to gain political positions for himself.

Thus, since 1979, the Madivalara Sangha has launched an extensive programme including organising of caste conferences and giving wide publicity to the demands of the Madivalas in order to obtain the above modifications in its constitutional status. Lack of funds and the highly unorganised nature of its membership (the community is spread throughout the state as one of the essential services castes) (see Appendix 7, 8 and 9) are the fundamental handicaps that the Sangha is encountering in this regard. The extent of backwardness of the group and the absence of any substantial economic and political strength needed for its advancement were evident in the activities of the Sangha that have been quite limited in their number and irregular in their occurrence. For over a span of more than 70 years since its inception, the caste association of the Washermen has been able to invest its resources upon the construction of only a small hostel for the community's students. This was also a post-1970 achievement. The highly deplorable living conditions of the washermen throughout the state could be attributed to the changes brought about by the process of modernisation which has, reportedly, "uprooted the very concept of caste occupations" by introducing occupational mobility.

This situation should be understood here not as benefiting the lower caste groups to move up in the social ladder by making use of the processes of industrialisation and urbanisation, which were expected to provide them occupational mobility (Srinivas : 1960). But the processes did the opposite of rendering many middle and lower caste groups go deprived of their traditional occupation. They had to loose these to the "more enterprising" upper castes which were able to practice the same job by giving it a face-lift. For example, occupations like leather-work, laundry or hair cutting came to be carried out using advanced technology by upper classes that did not affect them with impurity.

The main grouse of the Madivala leaders was that their caste occupation was dominated, if not monopolised, by the more enterprising, 'traders or Seths' and 'Muslims' who have taken over the laundry profession from the poor Madivalas. Although, this trend is commonly found operating in urban centres, like the taluk headquarters, towns and cities, with the village Washermen left untouched by these changes, there were certain other factors that affected the profession in rural areas. The impact of urbanisation in the form of easy access it has provided to the cities and the comforts it has offered through the network of transportation facilities have helped in meeting the daily needs of the villagers. In the olden days, the services of the Washermen were expected rather compulsorily on ceremonial occasions. During such events, he was traditionally required to supply clean cloth for ritual uses (both auspicious and inauspicious) on occasions like birth, marriage and death (Srinivas : 1951). This need is also found diminishing in its utility in the present times with modernisation influencing the institution of marriage. Even during the ordinary days, the washerwomen's services are demanded to a far lesser degree. With the disintegration of the traditional village economy, the service castes and professional groups have been exposed to modernity. For example, cash payment has replaced payment in kind. This and a variety of other elements of modernity are given as reasons by the Madivala caste members as leading to their backward status. For example, introduction of synthetic and woollen fabrics is viewed as having "ruined" the Madivalas, obviously because these textiles are easily washable and offer inexpensive laundry both in terms of cost and time. Similarly, the invention of detergents and cleaning agents like washing powders, whitening solutions etc., have sufficiently reduced the demand for washermen's services both in villages and in towns and cities. Even where their services are required, especially in urban areas, generally the Washermen are found owning petty laundry shops mostly catering for a limited section of the population. This is because the demand is more for ironing of clothes than washing them. Further, the more 'sophisticated' and 'modern' dry-cleaning shops are beginning to be owned by non-Madivalas. "Ironically, the poor members of the Washermen community are working in such shops as labourers."

The Karnataka Madivalara Sangha is, therefore, demanding representation in government service and a greater share in educational concessions to the Madivala children. It is in the light of the above problems that the leaders of the Madivalara Sangha have demanded scheduled caste or scheduled tribe status to the Washermen caste. They justify their claim by quoting instances where it is classified as a 'Scheduled Caste' in many north Indian states and as a scheduled tribe in eleven states of India (Memorandum : 1980). This was first highlighted at the "Dhobi Conference" held in Delhi in the year 1980 and emphasized in the state level caste conferences held at Bangalore.[90] The main contention of the Sangha was that the Madivalas were like the ex-untouchables as they also suffered from the stigma of untouchability. "The upper castes look down upon the Madivalas as the latter are engaged in the stigmatising job of washing dirty clothes and hence are polluting and inferior." The only difference between the ex-untouchables and the Madivalas was that "the former (ex-untouchables) use broomstick to clean and the latter (the Madivalas) clean all filth without it, but with their bare hands. It is more horrifying to learn that in some parts of the state; even the ex-untouchables treat the washerman as ex-untouchables, especially on some auspicious and inauspicious occasions.

This demand led to the Sangha encountering strong opposition to their demand for a 'Scheduled Caste' tag to the Madivalas. The major dislike for this move has come from those washermen who, because of their living in the northern districts of the state, have got converted to Veerasaivism and hence claim superiority over the rest of the community. Labelled as Lingayat Madivalas, they have strongly objected to the demand for a SC status, as they feared ritual degradation by doing so. They even did not wish to be identified as mere Madivalas or Agasas, but wished to be called and identified as just Lingayats, since it gave them a sense of superiority over the other Agasas. This self-proclaimed superiority is also increasingly becoming popular among the rest of the Madivalas who, in the absence of any alternative established religious order, are attempting to adopt to the Veerasaiva fold.[91] Books and pamphlets were distributed by the Sangha as well as by caste leaders highlighting the life and contributions of the 'Sharanas' (devotees) who lived during Basava's times.[92] Even amongst the non-Lingayat Madivalas, 'there is a gap between the educated and the uneducated on the issue of Scheduled Caste status to the community.[93] The idea was welcomed by the educated, obviously for its socio-economic rewards, while it was strongly resented by the ignorant and uneducated sections of the Madivalas.

It should be made clear here that the 'Agasas' were not alone in making such an interesting claim for a more backward status. The other service community, viz., the barbers, fell closely in line with the former in undertaking such initiatives.

21. The Karnataka State Savitha Samaja

Like the Agasas or Washermen, the caste group of the Barbers constituted one of the lower-middle castes of the Hindu social hierarchy. As a numerically minor group (economically and politically as well) its population was estimated to be around 0.44 per cent (the Havanur Commission Report). This was refuted by the leaders of the community who claimed that their caste strength was much more than that. The barbers are, as is common to any other caste in India, sub-divided into many subcastes and sub subcastes. The following subdivisions amongst them exist as local terms of the same caste. They are:

Nayinda, Bhanjantri, Arya Nayanaja Kshatriya, Nayi Brahmin, Bhandari, Navaliga, Navi, Kelasiga, Napitha, Hadapada, Kshourika, Neniyabaradava, Kasta Maduvava and so on.

The chief occupation of the barbers is Ayushkarma or Kshurike (hair-cutting) along with which they also render services like 'piping' (playing on the Dolu and Nadaswaram) – both being musical instruments.

Comparatively speaking, the barbers traditionally occupied a slightly more inferior or degrading position in the social scale (socio-ritual) than what the washermen caste does. Their caste occupation, although constituting an essential service, is considered ritually polluting and unclean. Occupational mobility in the case of the barbers has shown a different pattern. While it is sometimes seen that members of the upper castes are also taking to the caste occupations of groups below them in the hierarchy (normally due to economic incentives under the cover of modernisation), such a phenomenon appeared to have rarely occurred in the case of the occupation professed by the Barbers. (The only exception to this is the opening of beauty parlours and sophisticated hair-dressing saloons, etc., by a few members of the other castes). For example and as noted earlier, the traditional occupation of laundry is no longer the prerogative of the Agasas alone, but has been tried by others, but using machines. They have changed the entire process with the help of mechanisation in such a way that it has a touch of sophistication which has exempted those who follow it from the fear of ritual stigma, at least partially (similar are the professions of *chappal* making and oil-pressing).

But the profession followed by the barbers (i.e., hair-cutting) has failed to attract the attention of these enterprising caste-Hindus who have not ventured to follow it owing predominantly to the stigma that is attached to the profession. Moreover, the job also does not appear to give much scope for profit unlike professions like weaving, oil-pressing, etc. Changing fashions and the emergence of beauty parlours have posed as competitors to the old-styled barber. Occupational mobility among the barbers (from their caste occupation to other non-polluting jobs) has also not occurred on an appreciable scale. The small percentage of such mobile population may generally be found working as blue-collar workers in factories and mills, while salaried jobs are opted only by a few for want of educational qualifications.

The prime reason for the insufficient number of educated people among the Barbers is a natural corollary of their economic backwardness. Predominantly rural based, functioning as an important village 'service community' (Srinivas : 1951), with certain ritual and economic roles to play in the village social structure, the Barbers are, since ages, looked down upon as a stigmatising, low and unclean caste. This attitude is evident to be in practice among those castes, which are lower than the barbers in the social ladder, as the ex-untouchables and the tribal communities are. Their role as pipers was no doubt an essential service providing the 'Mangala Vadya (auspicious music)' during occasions like birth, marriage, festivals and so on. But this ceremonial role had always been a subdued one adding virtually nothing to boost their ritual ranking. Like the other village functionaries, the barbers are supposed, rather traditionally ordained, to serve the entire village (except serving of course the ex-untouchables and other exterior communities) for which service they received payments annually in cash or kind. "Since ages, the members of the barber community are found working under the 'Ayam' system and are known as one of the 'Ayagararu' (Ayam means payment made in kind form). Even today one can see the system prevalent in many villages. Under this system no money is paid for the service rendered. In turn, a small levy of agricultural produce is given at the time of harvest from a family in proportion to the number of people the Barber has served in that family. No specific quantum is fixed for his service, but it mainly depends upon the good harvest and the generosity of the people who do so. Consequently, any failure of crops will affect the payment" (Anjaneyalu B.K., President of the Samaj 1981).

The most unfortunate experience which the barbers had undergone in the 'Ayam' system was the upper castes' treatment that their (barbers) duty is a 'must' and the reward is only a 'gift'. These Ayagararu are supposed not only to go to the customers for rendering service than the customers themselves coming to them (in a traditional set up) but they have also to go over literally "as beggars" (as painfully felt by Sangh's Secretary), to their customers at the time of harvest to seek remuneration for their services. "The system is so designed that the barbers dare not raise their voice against this since they do not have any other ways and means to survive."

"The great impact of this system in general and barbering profession in particular is that the 'giver' (the customer) is made to have a feeling of 'superiority' while the 'Ayagara' is made to feel inferior, submissive and obedient. This is keeping in tune with the traditional Brahminical penal codes, thus blocking all ways to economic progress."

The fact of the barbers living in urban centres is stated to be different, but nothing to be envied about. "In towns and cities,

95 per cent of the community leads a hand-to-mouth existence. Many of the professional and non-professionals are liquor-addicts because of the contemptuous attitude of the upper caste people and the prevalence of professional stigma. The plight of the professional pipers is still worse. They will be earning only during the auspicious months and during the marriage season. The income from only these sources, obviously, is not sufficient. Adding to this, both the professional barbers and pipers will generally be discarded of their services, mainly because they are thought to be out of touch. This additional blow, which they receive at old age, hits the very root of their survival."

Furthermore, the advancement made in the fields of science and technology has contributed its share to the problems of professional barbers and pipers who are struggling very hard to come up. "Safety razors and electric shaving equipment have already crippled the economy of professional barbers. Added to this, the recent hippie mania is also posing a big threat to their already sinking profession" (Memorandum submitted to the KBCC : 1979).

The economic problems encountered by the Nayanajas are closely related to their social structure and cultural practices. The barbers are given a very inferior status in society leading to their highly deplorable living conditions. Though their services are indispensable they are treated as a socially stigmatising group "relegated almost to the level of the untouchables." The barbers allege that while they render "honest, humble and loyal service to the society, they will in turn get contempt, abuse and mockery from the society." "Even today, many of the rural folk consider it a bad omen, if they see the face of our caste people, especially early in the morning. In some parts of the state, the people will not even think of our caste people after sunset, as it is considered inauspicious for them." As a result of this, the barbers in certain parts of the state like in Tumkur and Chitradurga districts are called as "Neneyabaradavaru" (those who should not be thought of) (Memorandum : 1979 : 5).

Thus, the Barbers allege that their position is almost comparable to that of the ex-untouchables being only slightly higher than what they are. They argue that nobody need feel astonished about this since this is the naked truth which anybody can observe in villages and towns. Many rules of untouchability, like physical pollution etc., are observed in their case too. Another example is the dropping of coins from a certain height to avoid pollution while paying the barber for his services, etc., are in vogue among the caste Hindus. "Except the SCs no other caste people eat in the house of or accept any food from the barbers" (Memorandum : 1979).

It is fundamentally on the above issues that the 'Karnataka State Savitha Samaj' has been basing its battle for a changed constitutional status to the community. Founded in the year 1946, as the Mysore State Savitha Samaj, this organisation is named after 'Savitha Maharshi' a legendary seer who is said to have "done the first Ayushkarma to Lord Soma Brahma as per legends" (History of the Nayanaja Kshatriyas or the barbers, as narrated by a leader of the community).

Possessing comparatively lesser organisational potentialities and politico-economic resources than the Agasas, the Barbers' caste association shares no doubt many of the characteristics of the former as far as the nature of the activities of the Samaj goes. To begin with, the Samaj seems to have gained momentum in its activities especially in the late 1970s, that is, after the Havanur Report's recommendations were implemented by the state government. Secondly, like the Agasas, the Barbers' association has also submitted a memorandum highlighting the socio-ritual backwardness of the community and requesting the government and the various Backward Classes Commissions to consider its case for greater share with reservation facilities. "As we (the barbers) have been subjected to humiliating social disabilities and are treated as untouchables, next only to the Harijans, our caste is to be included in the list of scheduled castes of the state for our overall development" (Memorandum : 1979 :13). In addition, "we (barbers) should be assured of equality of opportunity, social security and status without any stigma or disabilities attached to us ...... and impose effectively penalty against those who practice and perpetuate this act....." (Memorandum : 1979 :13).

The justification for their claim to an 'untouchable' status was provided by the barbers thus: the Gollaru and the Thigalaru who have organised conferences to put forth their problems before the Karnataka Backward Classes Commission have claimed themselves to be the most backward groups. But the Secretary of the Barbers' association insisted that even these 'most backward' groups including the SCs did not eat in the houses of the barbers. This practice is prevalent even in the towns and cities of the state. He further added that the stigma attached to the barber community is conspicuous in situations like the barbers trying to get a house for rent or commercial places to run their profession. "The professional barbers", i.e., those who practice hair cutting, he alleges, "especially suffer from this social ostracism and are subjected to mental agony and made to lead a secluded life, with psychological torture."

Apart from this, the barbers complain of another type of discrimination. Members of their caste group are not generally entertained in private organisations, commercial establishments or business houses because of certain social stigma that are tagged on to these people. A common superstitious belief is prevalent in the minds of many (upper caste, i.e., non-barber communities) people, that if they associate with the barbers in business or industry the firm will never prosper. In other words, their profession (hair-cutting and shaving) is looked down upon as something derogatory and as indicating, always, "loss".

Although with the march of globalisation such superstitions have come down but not totally not-existent.

The Samaj has therefore launched a massive agitation for the eradication of this stigma attached to the barbers and their profession. The general economic and political backwardness of the community has reflected itself in the nature and activities of the Samaj. With only two offices in the state (one at Bangalore and the other at Mysore), the Savitha Samaj's only assets were a hostel each at these places in the early nineties. The Samaj has included in the list of its demands, among other things, certain professional facilities and concessions to the community from the government. A few of them are presented below as they are expected to provide an understanding of the problems facing the community :

1. That the government should consider barbering as a cottage industry and give all encouragement to it by starting a diploma in barbering, hair dyeing, wig manufacturing and other connected courses (as it is found in some advanced countries). This is expected not only to attract the people of the superior castes to take up this profession, but to also see that the barbers will improve their professional efficiency with a variety and modern touch to it keeping in tune with the changing times. This is expected to help the improvement of their economic condition.
2. That the government should immediately come to the rescue of the worst affected professional barbers by announcing cash subsidies and also to subsidise the rent paid by all the professional barbers, besides assuring them of business places such as shops for carrying out their profession normally and without any stigma in obtaining such places.

3. That all landless and homeless people of this caste should be given lands and houses or financial aid.
4. That the government should extend all help regarding the educational development of this caste. Apart from the giving of scholarships and freeships and hostel facilities, reservation in admissions to technical courses is also sought.
5. That encouragement must be given to the fast waning traditional instrumental music (piping) of this caste.
6. That political representation must be given to the members of the barber community, to voice the feelings and woes of nearly 5 lakh people of this caste throughout the state. This must be done either by nomination or by reserving some constituency for them, as they are not able to contest any elections.
7. That as many members as possible from this community should be appointed to the Sangeeth Natak Academy in the state and the centre.
8. That the barbers must be assured of adequate representation in all the strata in the legislative, executive and judicial services in the state and the centre, proportionate to their numerical strength (on the lines of facilities given to the SCs).
9. That special coaching facility which is given to the SCs and STs are to be extended to this caste also, especially for IAS and other competitive examinations.

The above demands constituted the fundamental goals of the Savitha Samaja, which have been placed before the Mandal and other backward classes' commissions for consideration since a long time but to no avail.

The Samaja has been active in celebrating its anniversaries and holding of caste conferences in Mysore and other parts of the state. By doing so, the Samaj has shared a trait that is currently more in vogue among the castes – at all levels of the hierarchy – and which forms a popular aspect of mobilisational attempts by them. But one point has to be highlighted here, which is significant. It refers to the call given to the community by its leaders to develop "self-help". In other words, instead of relying entirely on governmental help and sympathy, the members of the Barber caste were advised to organise themselves to become self-dependent taking the help of the Sangha (meeting of the Sangha :1984). This call, in its broader connotations signified shedding of even reservation facilities by the barbers, in course of time.

IV

Below are discussed a few caste groups and their associations, which come under the category of the 'newly-emerged caste groups'. They are called 'new' here, because, they have emerged encouraged by the socio-political pressures prevalent in the society at present as a result of the 'system of reservation' based on caste. Many of them were offshoots of subcastes of a broader community or caste. Others were very minor groups (to the extent of being even non-existent a few decades ago), usually recognised as an occupational category like the 'Karuneekars' (accountants), 'Kaniyars (sooth-sayers) and so on.

22. The Karnataka Karuneeka Sangha

The Karuneekas, who may be categorised as the immigrants from the neighbouring state of Tamil Nadu, have established their caste association in Bangalore during 1970-71. The 'Karnataka Karuneeka Sangha' as it is known, also falls in line with its counterparts representing other communities in demanding a 'backward status' to the Karuneekas. The Sangha with its head office at Bangalore is linked with the 'Tamil Nadu Karnikar Sangha'. Claiming to be the descendants of 'Chandra Gupta', a Mourya king, the Karuneekas are constituted by a number of subcastes like the Kanaka Pillai, Seer-Karnika, Sunnambu Kannakar and so on, which have come under one banner after the formation of the Sangha.

The fact that the Karuneekas are one of the 'newly-emerged' castes is proved when we take into account that no mention is made of them in the Reports of the earlier Backward Classes Commissions. Even the Havanur Commission has not recommended their case. Subsequently, upon the Sangha's request, the Mandal Commission appointed by the Government of India in 1979 has classified the Karuneekas as a 'backward caste'.

23. Sadara Vidyabhivrudhdhi Sangha

Similarly, the Sadara Vidyabhivrudhdhi Sangha in Bangalore is one of those Sanghas or caste associations, which are noticeably more active and articulate only since the 1970s. Despite its establishment as early as in 1943, this association representing the caste group of 'Sadar' (an agricultural community of Karnataka) has not made much progress in its mobilisational activities (discussion with Sri Mallaiah M. S., ex-secretary of the Sangha). However, this inactivity was only until they were not considered for a backward berth by the Havanur Commission. It was only in the late 1970s that the President of the Sadara Vidhyabhivrudhdhi Sangha signalled the revival of the Sangha by submitting a representation for the community's inclusion in the backwards' list.

The fundamental idea behind the representation "was to make clear to the government and others about the existence of a community by name 'Sadar' and to highlight its socio-economic backwardness" (Ramamurthy, A. M., Secretary of the Sangha : 1982).

The Havanur Report has, admittedly, discarded the inclusion of the 'Sadars' as a backward caste mainly because of its low-demographic profile in the state. Like many caste groups which were not considered by the KBCC for purposes of reservations (like the Kaniyars – sooth sayers-for example) as they all constituted numerically minor communities with very meager populations, the Sadars' plea for separate identity as a backward group was not taken into account by the Commission. One of the reasons for such a treatment by the Commission was as stated by Sri A. M. Ramamurthy, the Secretary of the Sangha, the confusion that would have probably arisen regarding the name 'Sadar'. Among the caste group of the Lingayats are found, at least in the northern districts of the state, a subcaste by name 'Sadar Lingayat'. The enlisting of their name as 'Sadar' by both the castes has led the Commission to conclude that they were one and the same (ibid.).

The Sadara Sangha, therefore, asserted that the Sadars did not wear 'Lingam' and were not to be taken as 'Sadu Lingayats'[94] (Memorandum : 1978).

Secondly, the Sadars were not recognised as a distinctive group due to their inclusion under the Jains by the earlier censuses. In a letter to the Director of Census Operations, submitted in 1978, the Sadara Sangha has stated that the censuses of 1911 and 1941 have categorised the Sadars as a subcaste under the Jains (Copy of the letter : 1978). Representations were made since then seeking separate caste status to the Sadars along with Constitutional guarantees to them by the 'Sadu Mathada Sangha' which came into existence in the year 1943. On the basis of the representation made earlier, the "government were pleased to consider the glaring injustice done to our community and ordered in G. O. No.E 1897-9 EDN. 0-30-60 dated 1-12-1939 that the schedule/ of castes were eligible for backward status. This was, reportedly, confirmed through the government's letter to the Sangha in 1942[95] and 1955[96] respectively" (Memorandum : 1978).

Thus, the Sangha has presently taken up the challenge of securing individual caste status and constitutional provisions to the Sadars in Karnataka. Its efforts are concentrated on the issue of proving that the Sadars are greater in proportion than assessed by the Havanur Commission. Alleging that the Sadars are underenumerated by the various Census Commissions, the Sangha has presented facts and figures about the population of Sadars in the State, derived out of census conducted by it.

24. The Karnataka State Jattigala Sangha

Of the communities which have set up associations in the post-Havanur Commission era, the Jetties are a significant one. Being a numerically minor group, 'they are wrestlers and body-builders having enjoyed royal patronage till recently'. After the abolition of princely privileges in late 1960s and early 1970s by Mrs. Indira Gandhi, they had to seek employment as labourers as most of them were not educated and were landless (spokesman of the Sangha : 1982).

While the Nagan Gowda Committee recognised the Jettis as a 'backward' and 'more backward' group – vide Government Orders in 1951, 1952 and 1961 respectively – the Havanur Commission classified them as a community "whose population cannot be ascertained" (KBCC Report : 1975). "When some members of the community requested him (Havanur) to include them under the list of nomadic, semi-nomadic tribes, he pleaded his inability to do so on grounds that he had not received any representation from the recognised association of Jettis" (Memorandum : 1979). Therefore, to fill this gap, "the Jetti community of Karnataka formed an association known as 'the Karnataka Jettigala Sangha' in February 1977 at Mysore".

25. Kaniyara Seva Sangha

The Kaniyars or Sooth-Sayers are represented by their caste association known as "the Kaniyara Seva Sangha". Founded in the year 1942, the Kaniyara Seva Samaja seems to have also awakened to the call of mobilisation only in the post-Havanur era. Comparatively speaking, the Kaniyars are a more institutionalised community than the Sadars and the Karuneekars as they constituted the traditional sooth-sayers or fortune tellers. Yet, being a mobile group, owing to their caste occupation, which demanded their wandering from place to place, the Kaniyars may be considered as having missed the census operations as a group. The existence of a large number of subgroups and the predominantly rural-dwelling nature of the community, coupled with their ignorance, illiteracy, and the poor socio-economic conditions of the people may be held as the factors responsible for the general backwardness of the Kaniyars.

The lack of accurate figures about the demographic strength of this community prompted the Havanur Commission to categorise the Kaniyars amongst the 396 castes whose population could not be ascertained (KBCC Report : 1975). The previous Commission (the Nagan Gowda Committee) had, accommodated them as 'backward' and 'more backward' groups[97] (Report of the Mysore Backward Classes Committee : 1961).[98]

Since then the Kaniyara Samaja, amidst much disunity amongst its members, has been attempting to secure a backward status to the community.[99]

26. The Mysore Rashtreeya Vishvakarma Samaja

The above account of the functioning of the different caste associations does not however complete the picture. There are many others for whom data were not available because of lack of proper functioning and disorganisation of the Sangha. The 'Akhila Karnataka Vishwakarma Samaja' was one such association representing the Goldsmith community in the state. It was founded in Bangalore in the year 1942 by the late Sri B.G. Shankarayya, a Viswakarma leader.[100] The name 'Vishwakarma Brahmana' is a sanskritised form for the 'Acharis' or 'Akkasales' who constitute an important middle caste group (2.3 per cent of the state's population) (KBCC Report : 1975) – one of the village functionaries like the oilmen or the weavers (Srinivas : 1960). Nevertheless, active participation in the process of mobilisation to secure backward tag was rather slow and lacking much propaganda and leadership. But it is not totally lacking among the Smiths. This is in no way covering up the development of the Samaja through the years. The assets of the Samaja include a building in Seshadripuram, Bangalore, which is used partly as a students' hostel and partly for commercial purposes.

27. The Karnataka State Yadava Sangha

The caste associations of the 'Yadavas', 'the Raju Kshatriyas' and 'the Thigalas' all share certain common characteristics. Of them, the Yadavas were numerous (1.49 per cent) than the Raju Kshatriyas and the Thigalas (0.03 per cent) (KBCC Report : 1975). More familiar with the name 'Gollas' meaning cowherds, they are generally found all over the country, at least in the plains. Their caste occupation is cowherding to which at times is added sheep-rearing. The Gollas are basically a rural-dwelling group sharing all the problems of a backward community. In recognition of this fact, the Nagan Gowda Committee and subsequently the Government Orders have classified them as a nomadic and semi-nomadic tribe along with other 48 communities and granted educational and other benefits to them.[101]

After the acceptance of the Havanur Commission's Report, the government, in an Order, included another 13 communities to the list of nomadic and semi-nomadic tribes bringing the total to 62 communities. This has, as complained by the leaders of the Golla community, lessened their share in the benefits, which is only 5 per cent as no increase was recommended by the Commission.

The Karnataka Yadava Sangha came into existence in the year 1942.[102] The Sangha's demands have been for a change in category from being a backward tribe, to that of a Scheduled Tribe. It has drawn support for such a claim from the prevalence of a few nomadic and semi-nomadic sub-divisions amongst the Yadavas, which are in a very backward condition. The 'Haavu Gollas' are the professional snake-charmers living in the northern districts of the state living by catching snakes and selling their skin. Another sect called the 'Kaadu Gollas' are living in the outskirts of villages. The 'Vaidyakeeya Gollas' are traditionally endowed with the task of administering herbal medicines to the village folk.

These subcastes among the Yadavas are being quoted by the educated, urban-dwelling Yadava leaders to project the backward status of these groups to their own advantage, thereby to seek a Scheduled Tribe tag to the whole group. They argued that while the SC and ST Amendment Act of 1976 "categorised the Bhovi, Lamani, Koracha, Korama, Nayaka and other communities either as SC or ST, the Yadavas are omitted in spite of their miserable living conditions which are equal to that of the SCs and the STs" (Memorandum submitted to the Mandal Commission : 1980).

28. The Raju Kshatriya Sangha

The Raju Kshatriyas also come under the communities whose mobility aspirations kindled more after the implementation of the recommendations of the Havanur Report. The 'Raju Kshatriya Sangha' whose existence was revived during the late seventies is now busy organising caste meetings and conferences "as the circumstances have necessitated such a move now" (Gopalaraju, Secretary of the Sangha, Bangalore : 1982).

The Sangha's main contention was that during the Princely Rule, the Raju Kshatriyas were employed in the royal army, which came to an end with independence proving to be an economic blow to the community. The Nagan Gowda Committee categorised the Rajavar (Rachavars as enumerated in the report of the Committee) as more backward. But the Havanur Commission put them under the non-backward group including only Bhatrajus – another Kshatriya group – under the backward list. This appears to have kindled much antagonism towards the Commission's Report and the then ministry responsible for it. The then Chief Minister, Sri Devraj Urs, who was instrumental in appointing the KBCC, was commented for his caste prejudice, "that though belonging to another Kshatriya caste, he refused to help the Rajus while he included his caste, the Arasus, in the backward category". Participation in the Rachavar Caste Conferences has shown that the leaders intended to utilise the then political set up headed by Sri Gundu Rao and also the services of two of their leaders in charge of Backward Classes Commissions – one at the centre and the other set-up by Sri Gundu Rao.[103]

29. The Thigalara Sangha

Similarly, the 'Thigalas' constituting the caste group of Gardners show much complexity and in-fighting amongst the various subcastes under them. The Havanur Commission has grouped the Tigala, Thigala, Vannikula Kshatriya, Dharmaraja Kapu, Kuravan and Palli sub-divisions under the common heading of Thigalas as a backward caste. In the latter years, that is after 1975-76, we observe that at least 3 or 4 of the above subcastes of Thigalas have mobilised themselves and formed separate associations. The Shambukula, Agnikula and Vannikula Kshatriyas claim separate caste status and have established independent caste associations. Each group claims to be more backward than the other two. The Shambukula Kshatriya Students' hostel in Seshadripuram, Bangalore, proclaims to include the other two sub-divisions also, which reads as "The Mysore Shambukula (Agnikula, Vannikula) Kshatriya Sangha." However, this is refuted by the members of the Vannikula Sangha as they claim superiority over the rest.[104]

CASTE ASSOCIATIONS AMONG THE SCHEDULED CASTES AND SCHEDULED TRIBES IN KARNATAKA

As noted already, it is difficult to consider all the existing SC and ST organisations because of the fundamental reason that most of the existing associations do not fit into the definition of caste associations envisaged by the present study. First of all, the innumerable 'SC/ST Welfare Organisations' operating within institutions like banks, factories, industries and universities as welfare bodies (like the Canara bank SC/ST Welfare Association or the HAL, ITI, BEL, SC/ST Welfare Associations or the University SC/ST Teachers' Association and so on) share certain similarities and dissimilarities with each other. For example, they are all alike as far as their structure is concerned but differ widely in the nature and intensity of their functions. They also differ widely in the extent of their political influence, participation and the type and characteristics of leadership. Some of them function as autonomous bodies while others exist as branches of bigger organisations (especially the ones representing central government sponsored institutions).

Apart from these, we have the second set of SC/ST associations that have sprung up in the residential areas of the Scheduled Castes and Scheduled Tribes particularly in rural areas.

It is shocking but at the same time true that despite its legal abolition more than three decades ago the practice of untouchability has survived in all its forms even to this day. What is more, it is present in its worst form of residential segregation between the caste-Hindus and the ex-untouchables. The practice is present in this worst form not only in the rural areas but in alarming proportions in towns and cities. These associations represent only a small section of the SC/ST population in the residential zones where they have sprung up, hence micro in nature.

Further, in most of the towns and cities different castes among the SCs have started their own associations that function as autonomous units protecting the interests of these castes within the SC fold. In their genesis, they present a combined picture of being organised by both outsiders (non-SCs) and by their own leaders.

The analysis of caste associations among the SCs and the STs is divided into two parts indicating their two major dimensions. In the first category, an attempt is made to cover, as completely as possible, those associations, which were founded by individual SC/ST groups and which were found to be functioning as state bodies. This includes the Sanghas representing 'single-caste' groups from within the blanket category of SCs and STs like for example, the Voddas, the Lamanis, the Nayaks and so on. There are a number of such associations representing the SCs and STs of which only two for which data was available (and which have an all-state footing) are discussed below:

30. The Korama/Koracha Sangha

The Koramas are one of the scheduled castes of Karnataka who established their caste association as The Korama (Koracha) Sangha at Bangalore as early as in 1935, representing them along with their synonymous groups like the Koracha, Korava, Koravar and Yarakula. The main occupation of the Koramas is basket making along with which they also pursue petty business and palmistry.[105] The leaders of the Korama Sangha at Bangalore claim that it is the state organisation although the existence of similar Sanghas in the other parts of the state cannot be denied.

The Sangha was started in one of its buildings in the Journalist Colony in Bangalore, which is used as students' hostel and also aided by the government (through periodical grants). The main goal of the Sangha was to see that the reservation benefits to the community were not disturbed or discontinued for another 2-3 decades as it believed that so far the community had been able to make little progress in educational and political fields.[106]

31. The All India Nayak Sangha

The All India Nayak Sangha, the association representing the Nayakas (a tribe) of Karnataka was established at Bangalore in the year 1972, almost as a direct consequence of the appointment of the Havanur Commission.[107]

The Nayakas are a highly diffuse community with a number of synonyms. In fact, any attempt to analyse the associations among this tribal community has been hampered by the presence of many sub-divisions and sometimes most of them being represented differently. The following groups are the 17 synonyms of Nayakas:

Beda, Bedar, Bendar, Beord, Boya, Nayaka, Naikmakkalu, Naikwadi, Paleyagar (Palegar), Ramoshi, Talwar, Valmiki, Valmikimakkalu, Vedan, Walmiki, Naik and Nayak.[108]

The second category of SC/ST associations covered by the present survey related to those which went by the blanket label of 'dalit'. They were not representative of any single caste/tribe within the SC/ST category but of all the communities within those categories.

Field work conducted in different parts of the state has brought out certain significant features of the dalit movement in Karnataka. Conspicuous is its characteristic of regional variation. The associations (of a micro and unorganised nature) of the old Mysore area differed from their north-Karnataka counterparts. The latter, which were established in the erstwhile Bombay-Karnatak and the Hyderabad-Karnatak areas seemed to be more familiar with the Ambedkar phenomenon than in southern Karnataka where the people were getting aquainted with Ambedkar since the 1970s.

A further division was also noticed prior to 1980s, among the SCs in their patronising the philosophies of Gandhi and Ambedkar. While Gandhi was found to be popular among the left-hand division (the Madigas) of the ex-untouchables, the right-hand division consisting of the Holeyas (the Adi-Karnatakas) and other 'upper' ex-untouchable castes appreciated Ambedkarite thinking and considered him as the saviour of SCs (Report on the SCs/STs : 1976). This demarcation in leadership was also further evident and put to practice while naming the different zones where the two groups lived. For example, the areas in many towns and cities where the Madigas, Chamars and other left-hand castes resided were then known as Gandhinagara and Bapujinagara. While among the right-hand ex-untouchable castes, names like Siddartha, Ananda were more prevalent. Siddhartha and Ananda were the names of Gauthama Buddha (in his early life) and his disciple respectively. This should be understood in the context of Dr. Ambedkar's conversion to Buddhism. Further, the preference for leaders had made its impact on the names of the caste associations of the two groups and of the journals published by these caste associations.

However, since the past few years, more than Gandhite ideology is replaced by Ambedkarite philosophy and the word 'dalit' has become universally popular in leading the mobilisational activities of the SCs.

Of all the ex-untouchable (SC) organisations functioning

in the state since the 1980s, this study had looked into the working of few which were found to be more articulate in putting forth their demands and were more open and systematic in their working at that time.[109] These three major dalit associations were the Dalit Sangharsh Samithi (DSS), the Dalit Action Committee (DAC) and the Dalit Action Forum (DAF).

Although all these organisations profess the title 'dalit', they differed in the degree to which this term was in usage within their network of activities and membership. Here it should be made clear that the word 'dalit' as a connotation for ex-untouchables has been popularly used increasingly by many individuals, organisations and even political leaders in the recent decades. As noted earlier, the word dalit had its roots in the state of Maharashtra where the movement by ex-untouchables was named as Dalit Panthers.

In its broader connotation, the term 'dalit' should include any person (or group) who is oppressed, depressed, exploited and discriminated against by the rest of the society. Thus, dalits are to be found theoretically among all castes, tribes and religious groups including the Brahmins and other upper castes.

But in course of time, the term dalit came to have a significant relation to the cause of ex-untouchables and heir movement for equality and justice. The term was used by the protagonists of dalits in Maharashtra but soon gained popularity as a common title for the downtrodden in India. Most of the organisations started or led with the goal of emancipation of ex-untouchables have come to designate themselves as dalit organisations. More than its universal feature, it also lets an air of radicalism and revolt around itself that has made it a popular slogan.

32. The Dalit Sangharsh Samithi (DSS)

The popular caste association of the SCs in Karnataka that aimed to "function up to the full meaning of the term 'dalit' was hailed to be the Dalit Sangharsha Samithi" (B. Krishnappa, March 22, 1982, Mysore). Emerging in the state of Karnataka during the mid-seventies, the DSS may be termed as a 'semi-revolutionary' organisation working towards the welfare and protection of dalits in the state. It began as a non-party organisation, which shuns any structured organisational form within itself. Compared to the other dalit organisations of Karnataka like the Dalit Action Committee or the Dalit Action Forum, the DSS was more popular in rural area in the 1980s, in Karnataka due to its largely rural-based and rural-oriented programmes and actions. It was also comparatively well-organised and highly decentralised. The DSS was composed of one state secretary and many organising secretaries at district and taluk levels. Apart from this, it consisted of a band of volunteers at district levels. These workers were generally young, educated and spirited, drawn not only from the ex-untouchable groups, but also from a few lower-middle (touchable) castes and tribal groups (at least in the eighties).

The main activities of the DSS, which was able to achieve a considerably strong footing and an all-state stature in a comparatively short period, centred on:

(1) Representing cases of atrocities and persecutions against, and the problems faced by, the dalits to the government and fight towards rendering justice and liberation to them. In doing so, the DSS organises protest morchas, meetings and conferences to press its condemnation of such incidents. These were also expected to gain public support and create awareness about the incidents of assault on dalits. Although other organisations are credited with similar kinds of activities, the DSS stands outwith certain specialities. The approach sought by the DSS is direct. The case was taken into its hands and fought. Further, the DSS, as noticed in a few cases, has

not stopped after referring the problem to the government, but has continued its active support and fight till justice is achieved.

(2) Another chief dimension of the DSS lied in its rural oriented programmes – like organising camps in different interior villages of the state. This activity may be termed as carrying the forces of social change to the doorsteps of rural dalits. The camps acted as training-cum-model institutions to impart messages of liberation from bondage to upper castes, economic independence improvement, entitlement and so on. This also included programmes meant for the growth of the intellect and awareness about their surroundings on the part of the dalit families in villages, thereby aiming to empower them and to provide opportunities for all-round development of dalits.

(3) Another noteworthy aspect of the DSS with respect to its above-mentioned activities is observed in the interest it has taken in developing dalits' knowledge about socio-economic policies of importance. Generally, in the rural camps organised by the DSS, lectures and discussions on current social, economic and political matters were held.

With these ideals and activities that began in the early 1980s, the DSS in Karnataka has been able to make considerable dent over the Dalits and non-dalits alike. Its alienation from active identification with any political leader or party for long and its work and the success it has achieved in resolving some cases of assault[110] on SCs have also helped in elevating its stature.

One of the novel types of protest organised by the DSS in the 1980s was its opposition to the "silence and inaction of SC legislators, MPs and ministers in the face of growing and alarming attacks against dalits all over the country" (Natraj and Natraj : 1982). Processions and morchas to register their ire over their own community leaders' apathy and negligence towards the problems of the ex-untouchables were carried out by a section of the dalit youth on February 27, 1982 (Natraj and Natraj : 1982). Demonstrations were held before the SC and ST legislators' houses in Mysore, Bangalore and other places, demanding their resignation from the political seats they occupied as they were accused (by the DSS) of alienating themselves from their own kin-group (caste) in order to achieve certain political (class) interests.

The action of the DSS came to be lauded by quite a few social scientists dalit workers as "indicative of a healthy and radical attitude towards some of the most serious social and economic problems" facing the country. It was hailed and encouraged as it constituted the first (in decades) attempt by "a downtrodden section" of Indian society to resort to "serious introspection" and it was hoped that by continuing the same 'set of attitudes', 'the dedicated dalit youth can achieve' a "truly liberating force in a society where almost everyone is relentlessly pursuing the path of political manoeuvring to gain a share of the spoils" (Natraj :1982). This demonstration did not receive the sympathy it deserved from caste-Hindu leaders as a whole although there were exceptions. The above action of the DSS is remarkable in that it signalled a unique self-introspective attitude on the path of a set of (though a minority) awakened, alert Dalit young men and women. Thus, it heralded a new era or 'milestone in the history of dalit movement in Karnataka' (Natraj : 1982; Yadav : 1988).

References

1. Irschick makes a reference to this community while dealing with the social structure of Tamil Nadu with reference to the non-Brahmin

movement there. The community in Bangalore might have migrated from Madras a few decades ago (1969: 10).

2. Generally, the Secretary was a more knowledgeable person than the President, who would normally be either a landlord or a noted businessman.
3. Like the Miller Committee in Princely Mysore, appointed in the year 1916 and the Mysore Backward Classes Committee and the Karnataka Backward Classes Commission appointed in the years 1960 and 1972 respectively after the State's reorganisation grouping the Brahmins under forward castes category.
4. Late Sri P.H. Krishna Rao and others.
5. Interviews with K.S. Suryanarayana Rao and H.K. Nanjundaswamy, Presidents of the Sangha at Mysore and Bangalore, respectively.
6. One of the oldest educational institutions started during Princely Rule.
7. The Sabha remembers with gratitude the munificent support by Rao Bahadur B.K. Garudachar, an engineer and an administrative officer under the Princely State of Mysore.
8. The Madhwas have well-established Sanghas in Dakshina Kannada district as compared to other parts of the state, where their Guru Sri Madhwacharya lived and preached his philosophy.
9. It was initially started at Benne Govindappa Choultry in Basavanagudi, Bangalore, and was registered in 1943.
10. Souvenir of the Sangha's Maha Sammelan, 1978.
11. Sri H.S. Venugopal, Bangolore
12. The name is held to be highly derogatory and disliked by the community. It is alleged that the name 'Satani' is somehow included in the government records, and claim that the Madras Government had reserved an Order in 1940, calling them as Sri Chatinada Sri Vaisnavas in the George Gazette, Part B, page 214, March 5, 1940.
13. Synonym subcastes of Satanis are: Chathada Sri Vaisnava; Khadri Vaisnava; Sameraya; Venkatapurada Vaisnava; Chikka, Dodda and Bettadapurada; Aravathumaneyavaru; Jamkhanadavaru; Prapanna Vaisnava; Satvika Vaisnava; Ippathanaalku Maneyavaru; Prathama Vaisnava; Telugu Vaisnava; Varaveera Vaisnava; Kulashekhara; Shathada Srivaisnava; Ramanuja Vaisnava; Dasanambi; Ekakshari; Chatuakshari; Ashtakshari; Andhra Vaisnava, etc. [Memorandum : 1979].
14. He was also a minister in the Hyderabad State before 1956.
15. Krishna Rao, as the President of the Maha Sabha, was very conscious of this fact.
16. The details of these aspects of educational mobilisation among the

Brahmins and their protest against the system of reservations have been dealt with subsequently in chapters V and VII.

17. Subcaste differences loom large when sharing the benefits of development; class formation is another issue besides factionalism, points noted by the present leaders who preferred to remain anonymous.
18. Agaram Rangaiah, a veteran octogenarian Brahmin journalist from Mysore, who edited "Sadhwi" a local Kannada daily.
19. He was a retired Mysore Civil Service officer and the Census Commissioner for Mysore, during the year 1941.
20. He hailed from the Madhwa subcaste among Brahmins.
21. Like inviting representatives from all three subcastes to share the dias during caste conferences or meetings. Important members to the Sabha were selected exercising much caution and concern, to give a good profile to it.
22. These names are used here synonymously.
23. Discussed in the subsequent chapters also.
24. The first being the Vokkaligas
25. Now the state of Tamil Nadu
26. Discussion with Prof. R.C. Hiremath and Prof. S.S. Wodeyar, Vice-chancellors of Karnatak University and with several senior office-bearers of the Sangha and KLE Society, Belgaum.
27. The Desais are village headmen or rulers of small towns - petty kings.
28. Like Rao Bahadur Aratal Rudra Gowda, Rao Bahadur Gilaganchi Gurusiddappanavaru, Sirsangi Lingarajaru, Vantamuri Desai Raja Lakamana Gowdaru, Vaarada Mallappanavaru, Deputy Chennabasappanavaru, Dewan Brahadurs M.Shantaveerappa and P. Mahadevaiah, G. Shanthaveerappa, H.K.Veerabasavayya, Gurubasavappa Halakatti and others.
29. All of them have championed the cause of private education and hostel to students from rural areas in the respective districts/provinces.
30. There is evidence to this observation: the souvenir of the "Madhwa Yuvaka Sangha", a subcaste Brahmin association, speaks about the help and benevolence of Dewan Pradhan Shiromani Nyapathi Madhava Rau to the Sangha. Similarly, the efforts of a few leaders belonging to the Babbur Kamme subcaste (also a division among the Brahmins) were sympathetically and encouragingly supported by Dewan Bahadur Rajakarya Prasaktha, K. Ramaswamy (Brahmana Sammelana : 1978). Coming down the scale, we find the Vokkaligara Sangha, the caste association of the Vokkaligas, encouraged and helped by Dewan V. P Madhava Rao (Archives of the Sangha).

31. The philosophy preached by Basava, emphasising charity.
32. The case of how highly educated members of the Lingayat community sacrificed opportunities of better occupations and dedicated themselves to the interests of the community and worked in the institutions founded by the Mutts and Swamijis is of relevance here. Men of eminence like D. C. Pavate and S. C. Nandimath joined the KLE Society of Belgaum, their benefactor, refusing the offer of Pandit Madan Mohan Malaviya to work as Professors at the prestigious Banares Hindu University.
33. In the sense that the chief ministers for a continuous period of time of 16 years (from 1956-1972) were Lingayats.
34. The Urs Government did contain a good number of Lingayat and Vokkaliga ministers in it. Its "significance" lies in the fact that it gave representation to a few hitherto unrepresented minority groups (Natraj and Natraj : 1982).
35. The Lingayats were affected by such policies as among them were a number of landlords and businessmen.
36. In fact, during Mrs.Gandhi's election from Chikmagalur in 1978, there was an expectation that Lingayats would go against her. Veerendra Patil, the ex-chief minister of Karnataka and a Lingayat was the Janatha candidate against her in the political fight.
37. See Manor (1980) for a discussion on the effects of land reforms on the Lingayats, especially Sadar Lingayats.
38. Booklets and pamphlets were published by the Sabha and articles were published in local dailies written by the President and other critics of Urs' policies.
39. A retired IAS officer. He was the Census Commissioner of Mysore for the Census of 1951 besides being the opposition leader in the Mysore (State) Legislative Council during the late fifties.
40. J.B.Mallaradhya was not a very popular leader among the members of the community. This has been ascertained by interviews with a few Lingayat leaders and members of the trading community. The latter was apathetic to many of his ideas like claiming a separate religious identity to Veerasaivas. Further, his sophisticated mannerisms and lifestyle alienated him from the rest of the Lingayat masses. This was when he called upon the Lingayats to claim a non-Hindu identity and to register themselves in the Census of 1981 as a separate religious group, viz.,Veerasaivas.
41. The leaders of the "Lingayat Ganigas" have formed an association at Bangalore – called as the Akila Bharatha Hindu Ganigara Sangha – to discuss the problems they encounter as minorities.
42. Even the Lingayats had a share in the state governments' benevolent

step. A few educational institutions were also sanctioned to the Lingayats by the Rao Government at that time (1979-81). They are :

(i) The Hyderabad Karnatak Education Society's Engineering College at Ranebennur in the then Dharwar district.

(ii) Rural Technical Education Society's (founded by late Sri K.H. Patil, Veteran politician from Reddy-Lingayat caste) Engineering College at Hulukoti near Dharwar,

(iii) The Vijayanagar Engineering College of Veerasaiva Vidyavardhak Sangha of Bellary, and

(iv) Jagadguru Murugarajendra Institute of Technology founded by the Sri Swamij, of Murugarajendra Mutt at Chitradurga.

43. Discussions with Lingayat Leaders M.L. Mallamma, Chennappa among the important traders of Mysore city; Late Sri. D.M. Chandrashekar, Ex-Chief Justice, Karnataka High Court, academicians like late Dr. Parasivamurthy, Late Sri B. Sivamurthy Sastry, renowned Sanskrit Scholar and spokesman of the Mahasabha - all had opposed (privately) Mallaradhya's campaign. The protest also had come from the participants in the "Aradhya - Meet" held at Mandya in January 1981, who had resolved to protest aginst his policies, and threatening to oust him from their community (of Aradhya sub-caste of Lingayats). (*Deccan Herald*, January 19, 1981).

44. Late Sri K.P. Shantha Murthy, President of Mysore District unit of ABVMS, hailing from Hanur in Kollegal taluk (now part of Chamarajnagar district) used the platform to contest elections on a Congress ticket in 1986, later defected to Janata Party in 1988.

45. The Gundu Rao government, apart from assuring of a reclassification of the Backward Classes in the state, promised to sanction a Medical College to a leading educational society at Mysore, under the control of a local powerful mutt, the Suttur Mutt.

46. The Bunts made no representation to the Havanur Commission. Leading Vokkaliga leaders of the times like Sri K.R. Marudeve Gowda the then President of Vokkaligara Sangha and Son of its founder Sri K.H. Ramaiah Sri J. Lingaiah, Ex-Mayor of Bangalore City Corporation and Mr. Guthala Gowda, Secretary of the Sangha deposed before the Commission stating that "Bunts of South Kanara have now become members of the Sangha" [Souvenir, KBCC Report, Vol. I, pp. 254, 1975].

47. The Census of 1891 brought out the following: "Appropriate" distribution of Vokkaliga subcastes; Gangadikars probably over 50 per cent, Morasu 15 per cent, Kunchitigas 9 per cent, Reddy 8 per cent, Halu 3 per cent, Hallikara probably 3 per cent (Manor : 1977: 35).

48. For example, its second conference was inaugurated by his Highness Sri Krishna Rajendra Wodeyar Bahadur IV, on Octobar 17, 1907 who assured the community "all help and support in their efforts to develop" (Souvenir : 1980: 30). On April 8, 1908, its third conference was inaugurated by Dewan Bahadur Sri V.P. Madhava Rao (Souvenir : 1961).
49. Dewan V.P. Madhava Rao was an "imported" Brahmin (Madrasi Mahratta Brahmin) "and Rangacharlu's youngest protégé" (Hettne : 1978 : 78).
50. This is evident from the articles in the Souvenir, 1961. Moreover, the above places are also those where these subcastes are found in large numbers. Gangadikaras and Morasus constitute the majority among the Vokkaligas, with 50 and 15 per cent of the total according to the Census of India 1891 and the Report on the Mysore Census of 1881, quoted in Manor 1977.
51. The Sangha's first college was founded in the year 1966 and its engineering and medical colleges in 1980.
52. The first college started by the Sangha was in 1966 in Bangalore city, otherwise, all its attention was given to starting students' hostels (for boys).
53. An engineering college was established by the Mutt in Chikmagalur in 1981.
54. Nevertheless, the Adichunchanagiri mutt continued to function in its traditional pattern till recently. It has gained more importance since 1974, particularly after it came to be headed by its 71st Guru, Sri Bala Gangadharanatha Swamiji, under whom many educational institutions have been established.
55. There were 3 Chief Ministers during this period – Kyasamballi Chengalaraya Reddy, Kengal Hanumanthaiah and Kadidal Manjappa – all Vokkaligas.
56. This is so even now, but for the fact that the political importance laid on the minorities and the backwards has caused concern among the upper groups regarding safeguarding their hold over the system of reservation.
57. The state came under continuous Lingayat Chief Ministers during 1956-72, viz., Siddavanahalli Nijalingappa, Basappa Danappa Jatti, S. R. Kanti and Veerendra Patil.
58. The reaction of the Vokkaligas to Devraj Urs requires some complex analysis. They were classed under the other backward class category, but in view of the general atmosphere created by Urs they probably felt insecure.
59. The Sangha has stated during the early years after independence that all

the groups which have taken to agriculture as the predominant occupation like Gangadikara, Morasu, Reddi, Hallikara, Kunchitiga, Namdhari, Bhunt, Kamma, Halakki, Dasa, Vellala, Nadavar, Badaga and so on – are Vokkaligas (Souvenir : 1982).

60. Intra-caste or inter-subcaste unity was stressed during the Princely Government also when the Sangha was in its initial stages of growth. Being endogamous entities, the different Vokkaliga subcastes practised separation (cultural and other forms) from each other and tried to maintain their separate identity. The Kunchitigas, for example, prevaricated on the issue of being put together with the Vokkaligas in the 1930s (Representative Assembly Debates).
61. In fact, there were many Kuruba members in the Vokkaligara Sangha prior to the starting of the Kurubara Sangha (Discussions with the office-bearers of the Sangha).
62. Like sages and gurus. This is discussed here in the light of the observation that possession of Mutts and Swamijis by castes is being recognised increasingly in the recent decades, as an important key for mobilisation. Perhaps, the effective role of Veerasaiva mutts in the field of private education has kindled similar aspirations among castes down the hierarchy.
63. The Kurubas of Belgaum have established an educational trust at Belgaum which runs hostels and schools. The trust was managed by Gavisiddappa Siddappa Belvadi an ex-MLC and leader of the community. The fact that Rayanna hailed from the district (Sangolli, a village in Belgaum district) is held with great pride by the above and other leaders of the Kuruba community who are eulogising him and feel proud of their patriotism.
64. The Vice-Chairman of the KBCC Sri Y. Ramachandra was from this caste. He was also an ex-Minister.
65. This had been arranged rather hurriedly. The Gundu Rao government had encouraged holding of caste conferences inaugurated by him and in most cases, promising to grant professional colleges to castes and communities.
66. This is in the light of the following allegation made by a few representatives of Thogataveerara Sangha; since the Mayor of Bangalore City Corporation (K. M. Naganna, who was also a member of the Havanur Commission), the President of the Bangalore Silk Weavers' Association and Silk Development Corporation (B.G. Veerana) during the sixties and the seventies were Devangas, the Thogataveeras allege that all the benefits (in distribution of and concessions for silk thread

and other weaving accessories) and grants by the government were "swallowed" only by the Devangas who are the dominant group. As a result, their (Devangas) Sangha grew. Its president from 1967 for nearly a decade was K. M. Naganna, who in the capacity of the Mayor and an MLA is alleged to have sanctioned sites to the Devanga Sangha. Such assets have been well-developed in the later years where schools and other educational institutions of the Sangha have come up. The tradition continued with the election of B.G. Veeranna an industrialist who had held posts like, among others, the Directorship of the Vijaya Bank as the President.

67. The litigation was on the issue of converting the hostel near the City Corporation into a marriage choultry and to further remodel it as a shopping complex. The fact that with such asset formation, a few office-bearers would derive financial benefits, had led to internal conflicts among the members. As a result, the hostel, which used to cater for the immigrant Thogataveerara boy students, had been closed for sometime. It was very difficult to contact the office-bearers as a result of all this who normally functioned in the same building where the office of the Sangha was situated. Pamphlets indicating the "corrupt activities" of the office-bearers were also circulated by the opponents drawn from few subcastes of the Thogataveeras.

68. Interview with B.V. Thimmappa, ex-President and an important donor to the Sangha. Apart from silk industry, he has also ventured into small scale industry to become a noted industrialist in Bangalore. On acknowledging the lacuna in the sphere of religious mutt to the community, Thimmappa has not only worked towards that direction, but has also sponsored his younger brother as a Guru for a mutt near Tumkur.

    It is noteworthy that the Kuruhina Settys of North Karnataka have formed one's own religious mutts. The community in Bijapur is stated to have been divided into 14 parts in its allegiance to the 14 mutts there. It is not rare that many a caste conferences organised in the eighties and nineties came to be postponed due to infighting between the two mutts – at Gadag and at Hubli (Thimmappa : 1981).

69. A Padmashali from Uruvakonda in Andhra Pradesh has narrated that they migrated from Hampi in Vijayanagar during the times of Kempe Gowda (Souvenir of the Golden Jubilee of the Karnataka Padmashali Sangha : 1980).

70. For example, in Sholapur, in Maharashtra, 50 per cent of the population has claimed to be Padmashalis (the Padmajas) while in Bombay, there

are stated to be as many as 8 Padmashali Sanghas. (Bhiwandi is the place in Bombay where Padmajas are largely found. It is called as the Lancashire of India).

71. The Akila Bharatiya Bhavasara Kshatriya Mahasabha, as the name indicates, claims to be an all-India association of the Bhavasara Kshatriyas. Its President was (in 1981) Manohar Dhondiba Mahendrakar from Bijapur in Karnataka. L. N. Pissey the vice-President hailed from Bangalore, while the state (Karnataka) Committee consisted of, among other elite of the community, Prabhakar Telkar, MLA representing Gulbarga district.

    The history of the community proudly records that the Goddess 'Hingulambika', the caste deity of the Bhavasara Kshatriyas is worshipped both in India and in Baluchistan. But majority of Bhahusars have become "Vittal Bhakthas", i.e., the followers of Vittal of Pandarpur (Souvenir of the 19th Conference of the Akila Bharatiya Bhavasara Kshatriya Mahasabha, Bangalore : April 1979).

72. Who is held as the "Father" (Pithamaha) of the community who championed the cause of his community by organising meetings and conferences of Bhavasara Kshatriyas of Mysore, Bangalore, Dharwar, Bagalkot, Ankola, Gadag, Bombay and other places as early as in the year 1911. He was the President of many conferences held by the Mahasabha. He was awarded many medals (like the Public Service Medal as it was called, awarded in recognition of outstanding community and public service) for his service to the community (and others) by the then Maharaja of Princely Mysore, Krishnaraja Wodeyar Bahadur IV, and also by the Government of Bombay (where he was under service apart from other places in northern India). After his death in 1959, the road in Bangalore, where he was dwelling, was named after him.

73. Like the setting up of Backward Classes' Commission or changes in the caste pattern of political rule in the state.

74. A delegation of leaders of the Akila Karnataka Bhavasar Kshatriya Samaj (as the Mysore Bhavasara Kshatriya Sangha came to be known by that time), consisting of its then President, Kripashankar N. Zhingade (he was also the President of the Samaj when the survey was conducted), Prabhakar Telkar, MLA, BM K Rao, the Secretary of the Samaj deposed before the KBCC and presented a memorandum requesting backward status. Subsequently, the Samaj represented its case to the Gundu Rao government as well as to the Mandal Commission in 1979.

75. Apart from the subcastes amongst the Bhavasara Kshatriyas like 'Simpi', 'Simpiga' and 'Darzi' there is another subcaste by name 'Namdev', which

is held by the former as an inferior group than themselves. Namdevs have obtained, the story goes, their name from "Pandarpur", where a Bhavasar Kshatriya saint lived (in Maharashtra), who is said to have converted ex-untouchables and included them into his religious fold.

76. The details of the social conditions of the SSKs have been obtained through the KBCC Report 1975. A delegation of SSK leaders, including its President had deposed before the Commission and stated their problems. This information had to be only "substantiated" with the data given by Krishnasa Khoday, the President, Magaji Subbanna (owner of silk thread factory in Bangalore), the vice-President and Krishnasa Gujarati, the Secretary of the Sangha, January 4, 1982.
77. The important areas united with the state and which contained large number of Gangamathastha people were the districts of Uttara and Dakshina Kannaada, Bijapur, Dharwar, Belgaum and a few other small urban and rural centres in Uttara Kannada district.
78. Where the fishermen caste is known by the synonym 'koli' which in Marathi means a fisherman. Suffixes like 'Rao', 'Choudhari', and 'Koli' are also added to the names of the caste members. The Gangama-thasthas' Sangha at Bijapur is called as the 'Koli Sangha' or as 'Mahadev Sangha' (another synonym being Mahadev Koli).
79. They are Gangakula, Gangaputra, Gangemakkalu, Gowrimatha, Ambig, Ambiga, Bestha, Kabbaliga, Kabbili, Kabber, Kabbera, Koli, Kharvi, Bhoi, Bhoyi, Boyi, Thoreya, Harakanthra, Harikanthra, Kahar, Meengar, Mogaveera, Kharia, Sunnagar, Siviyar, Barki and Parivara. Incidentally, Beshtaar and Bunde Beshtaar, also fishermen groups, are included under the backward tribes.
80. 'Valikars' are traditionally the village messengers and the Talwars are the village guards, who act as the policemen to the village, appointed by the Panchayat. Generally, the Thotis (another commonly used term for the village messengers) hail from the ex-untouchable groups and the Talwars belonged to lower groups, if not to the ex-untouchable communities.
81. Interestingly, this demand is made despite these various subcastes being strictly endogamous.
82. This may be true, but only partially. The Mogaveeras at that time had few leading personalities in state politics like Mrs. Manorama Madhwaraj, for example, a lady Minister in the Ministry of late Devraj Urs, who continued in the Gundu Rao Government also. The Gangamathasthas of Uttara Karnataka were represented by Sri Devendrappa Ghalappa, also a Minister in the above two governments. Among the other important political representatives of the community were K.B. Choudhari, M.P.

from Bijapur, D. T. Ramu, MLA from Channapatna taluk in Bangalore (R), now Ramanagaram district) and a few others.

Owing to their political and economic backwardness, presence of a few individuals who have made remarkable achievements in various public activities has been held with great pride by the community. For example, the souvenirs of the anniversary celebrations of the Sangha present photographs of well-known musician, Padma Vibhushan Dr. Gangubai Hangal, famous cartoonist late R. Ramamurthy, writer Chennanna Valikar, administrator and Kannada scholar Muddu Suvarna and many others as they hailed from this caste.

It should, however, be noted here that the above tendency to honour important people was also a trait of almost all other caste groups, particularly the middle and lower castes.

83. The AKGMS in Bangalore owns a site in Nagarthapet, where, apart from a students' hostel, a temple of Goddess Ganga Devi, the caste deity of the Gangamathasthas has been constructed. The building also acts as a marriage choultry for the community.
84. The Kumbaras claim to have owned the whole area now called Kalasipalyam and the market area where presently the Town Hall is constructed.
85. Shalivahana, a king is said to have defeated Vikramaditya (another north Indian king) in a war in which he prepared an army giving life to the toys he made. Thus, the potters claim Kshatriya status (Souvenir : 1974).
86. Since it was believed that only political power in the hands of the community can solve their problems.
87. The Veerasaiva Ganigas, alleging discriminatory attitude and treatment by the Veerasaivas have formed Sanghas to protect their interests. One such is the Akila Bharatha Hindu Ganigara Sangha of Bangalore (V. D. Ganiger : 1982).
88. This encouragement for intra-caste unity is to obtain greater share in the quota of reservations by including all the subcastes, not only enhancing the numerical status of the community, but also by presenting a more critical socio-economic status of the group when the subcastes at its lower fringe are accounted for. Such a situation is expected to retain the status of 'more backwardness' (even as a SC or ST) to the group.
89. The term Madivala, Agasa and Washermen are used here synonymously.
90. In 1980, the 'Karnataka Dhobi Conference' was held in Delhi which was attended by a delegation from the Karnataka Madivalara Sangha of Bangalore. The Conference is quoted to be the second of its kind. However, the reasons for holding it at Delhi could not be ascertained. The Sangha leaders give the explanation that due to the non-availability

of organizational support no caste conference was held at the state level. However, a conference was proposed to be held during 1982 and at the time of the interview even the 'Souvenir' was ready. It should be noted here that 1982 was an important year in the recent times when a number of caste conferences were held.

91. Attempts are being made to construct a temple for Madivala Machideva (a follower of Basava, the social reformer, and a protagonist of Veerasaivism in the eleventh century) in Bangalore (on the banks of a small tank which is used as a 'Dhobi-Ghat', the public washing yard). Machideva who hailed from the Madivala caste is worshipped by the Lingayat Madivalas who claim superiority owing to their caste (Veerasaivism), vegetarianism and teetotalism over the non-Lingayat Madivalas. The same site, where the temple is planned, is expected to be later converted into an educational complex.
92. For example, Nanjundayya's Kannada booklet 'Madivalamachideva' was mentioned as a religious text of the community by the Lingayat-Madivala respondents.
93. The leaders of the Sangha (the President and others) expressed their problems in convincing this uneducated section among their brethren "about the positive aspect of obtaining an SC status".
94. However, such identical caste names were also used at times to claim a higher socio-ritual status to the community, the maintenance of barriers and clarifications sought on caste names being only a means to gain more facilities under the reservation system.
95. Vide No. E 2258/R & P 32-42-2 dated 5-12-1942 list of SCs, STs and OBCs (part 12 Mysore, page no. 40, Sl.No. 58).
96. Ministry of Education, GoI (Part 12 Mysore, page No. 40, Sl.No. 58).
97. The memorandum submitted to the Mandal Commission by the Samaja also stated that "in 1942 the erstwhile Government of Mysore had included" the Kaniyars "under the backward classes vide G. O. 6590, Census 14, 42-2 dated 26-11-42"(Memorandum : 1979).
98. In page Nos. 48-50-53 (Memorandum : 1979).
99. Lelah Dushkin (1980), in her analytical article on the 'Caste Associations in Bangalore' has made an exclusive study of Kaniyara Seva Samaj, particularly its leadership.

    Note: The office-bearers of the Samaja did not lend co-operation to the research team in parting of information as they had many internal feuds and quarrels. A copy of their memorandum submitted to the Mandal Commission was shared with us.
100. Interview with M. Neelakantan, President and S. Krishnachari, General Secretary of the Samaj, Bangalore.

101. Interview with Sri Siddappa, a prominent Yadava caste leader and ex-Secretary, Karnataka Backward Classes, SCs, STs and Minorities Cell, and Secretary of the Yadava Sangha, Bangalore. He was also the Additional General Secretary for the All-India Yadava Maha Sabha.
102. Known then as Akhila Karnataka Gollara Sangha. The change of name to 'Yadava' is an indication of the alignment the local Gollars or Gollas are seeking to establish with the Yadavas of Uttar Pradesh, in an effort to link themselves with them, thereby aiming to achieve an all-India footing. It should be added that when this change was adopted, the Yadavas of Uttar Pradesh were represented in the Central Government by the Minister Chandrajit Yadav.
103. Late Professor K.H. Cheluvaraju, former vice-chancellor of Gulbarga University and a Professor of Political Science, was appointed as a member of the Mandal Commission at the Centre and a Committee appointed by Gundu Rao was headed by Muniraju, the two prominent men from the community during the eighties.
104. It may be pertinent to mention here that it is the subcaste of Vannikula Kshatriyas, who carry the famous 'Karaga' festival in Bangalore. Hence, their claim for superiority over the other subcastes is justified according to them.
105. Interview with Sri Govinda Swamy, Secretary of the Sangha, January 5, 1982.
106. It was represented by K. Yenkatappa, a minister in the Gundu Rao government and a few MLAs.
107. C. Narayana, the General Secretary of the Sangha agreed in the interview with him that the starting of the Nayak Sangha was inspired and encouraged by Havanur himself, the Chairman of the Backward Classes' Commission who hailed from the Nayaka community.
108. The Government of Karnataka, in its Order No.SWL 104 SAD 81 Bangalore, dated September 1, 1979, clarified that the above "Communities" were recognised as Backward Tribes throughout the state.

     In another letter, the Government further clarified that "in the Government Order No.SWL 104 SAD 81 dated September 1, 1981, the Sl.No. 14, 'Naik' be renumbered as Sl. No. 16 'Naik'" and Sl.No.15 'Nayaka' deleted.
109. No consolidated survey has yet been conducted on all these associations despite its strong need and significance for research on the SCs and STs. Whatever generalisations are drawn here are derived out of field-work in a few sample towns like Bangalore, Mysore, Belgaum, Gulbarga

and Tumkur. Apart from these sources, conclusions are drawn out of some of the paper clippings relating to the activities of these associations and general observations.

110. Some of them are: (a) the Hunasikote episode of 1976-77; (b) the Devarasanahalli clash near Mysore during 1983 (*Deccan Herald :* January 23, 1983); (c) land-grab incident at Devalapura in H. D. Kote taluk in Mysore district, *Deccan Herald* : Feb 25, 1983 and (d) riots in Bhalki in Bidar district, *Deccan Herald* : April 22, 1981.

Appendix 4.1 : Details of Caste Associations in Karnataka (till 1985)

Sl. No.	*Name of the Caste Association*	*Year of Establishment*	*Place of Establishment*
1.	Akila Bharathiya Bhavasara Kshatriya Mahasabha	1924	Mysore
2.	Akhila Bharatha Veerasaiva Mahasabha	1904	Dharwar
3.	All India Nayak Sangha	1972	Bangalore
4.	Akhila Karnataka Bhunts Sangha	1908	Mangalore
5.	Akhila Karnataka Korama (Koracha) Sangha	1935	Bangalore
6.	Akhila Karnataka Brahmana Maha Sabha	1971	Bangalore
7.	Andhra Devanga Sanghamu	1924	Bangalore
8.	Arya Vyshya Mahasabha	1908	Bangalore
9.	Badag Anadu Sangha	1943	Bangalore
10.	Beitadapurada Sankethi Sangha	1945	Bangalore
11.	Brahmana Yuvaka Sangha	1971	Bangalore
12.	Dalit Sangarsh Samithi	1973	Bangalore
13.	Devanga Sangha	1923	Bangalore
14.	Kaniyara Seva Sangha	1942	Bangalore
15.	Sadara Vidyabhivruddhi Sangha	1943	Bangalore
16.	Somavamsha Sahasrar'una (Khatri) Kshatriya Sangha	1935	Bangalore
17.	Sri Madhwa Yuvaka Sangha	1945	Bangalore
18.	The Akhila Karnataka Ganigara Sangha	1972	Bangalore
19.	The Akhila Karnataka Pradesh Kumbarara Sangha	1951	Bangalore
20.	The Akhila Bharath Swakula Sali Sangha	1913	Hubli
21.	The Hebbar Sreevaishnava Sabha	1918	Mysore
22.	The Hoysala Karnataka Sangha	1908	Mysore
23.	The Karnatakaa Dalit Action Committee	1977	Bangalore
24.	The Karnataka Dalit Action Forum	1980	Bangalore
25.	The Karnataka Karuneeka Sangha	1970	Bangalore
26.	The Karnataka Madivalara Sangha	1933	Bangalore
27.	The Karnatak Pradesh Arya Idigara Sangha	1944	Bangalore
28.	The Karnataka Padmashali Sangha	1927	Bangalore
29.	The Karnataka State Balijigara Sangha	1919	Bangalore
30.	The Karnataka State Gangamathasthara Sangha	1929	Bangalore

(Contd...)

Appendix 4.1 : (Contd...)

31.	The Karnataka State Jettigala Sangha	1977	Mysore
32.	The Karnataka State Kunchitigara Sangha	1908	Mysore
33.	The Karnataka State Kurubara Sangha	1921	Bangalore
34.	The Karnataka State Kuruhina Setty Sangha	1928	Bangalore
35.	The Karnataka State Savitha Samaja	1946	Bangalore
36.	The Karnataka State Yadava Sangha	1942	Bangalore
37.	The Mysore Rashtreeya Vishwakarma Samaja	1942	Bangalore
38.	The Mysore State Chathada Sri Vaisnava Association	1940	Bangalore
39.	The Raju Kshatriya Sangha	1942	Ban galore
40.	Karnataka Thigalara Sangha, Karnataka Thigalara Vidyabhivrudhi Sangha & Karnataka Thigalara Okkuta Samsthe, Karnataka Shambhu Kula Kshatriya Sangha	1966	Bangalore
41.	The Thogataveerara Sangha	1947	Bangalore
42.	The Vokkaligara Sangha	1906	Bangalore

All the associations have their headquarters at Bangalore.

Many of the above associations have opened their doors to women from their castes by 1990s which is a progressive development.

The following table provides details of those associations which have women cells or divisions as part of their mobilisational activities.

Appendix 4.2 : Details of Caste Associations & their Representatives

Sl. No.	*Name of the Caste Association*	*Year of Establishment*	*Place of Establishment*	*Name/s of the office bearer/s interviewed*
1.	Akhila Bharathiya Bhavasara Kshatriya Mahasabha	1924	Mysore	B. M. Krishna Rao Sannesi, Secretary
2.	Akhila Bharatha Veerasaiva Mahasabha	1904	Dharwar	J.B. Mallaradhya, former President
3.	All India Nayak Sangha	1972	Bengaluru	Chandrasekar Guddakayi, Ex-MLA and President
4.	Akhila Karnataka Bhunts' Sangha	1908	Mangalore	V. Thimmappa Shetty, a senior leader
5.	Akhila Karnataka Korama (Koracha) Sangha	1935	Bengaluru	A. M. Shamprasad, R.td. DC & President
6.	Akhila Karnataka Brahmana Maha Sabha	1971	Bengaluru	P. H. Krishna Rao, former President H. K. Nanjundaswamy, President G. Lakshmipathaiah, Secretary
7.	Andhra Devanga Sangham	1924	Bengaluru	P. Bhuvaneswaraiah, President
8.	Arya Vyshya Maha Sabha	1908	Bengaluru	K. S. Vittal, President
9.	Badaganadu Sangha	1943	Bengaluru	G. Lakshmipathaiah, President B. N. Rama Rao, Secretary
10.	Bettadapurada Sankethi Sangha	1945	Bengaluru	—
11.	Brahmana Yuvaka Sangha	1971	Bengaluru	K. N. Venkatanarayana, Spokesperson
12.	Dalit Sangharsha Samithi (DSS)	1971	Bengaluru	B. Krishnappa, Secretary
13.	Devanga Sangha	1923	Bengaluru	K. Maganna, ex-President B. G. Veeranna, President K. V. Bhaskar, Secretary
14.	Kaniyara Seva Samaja	1942	Bengaluru	President
15.	Sadara Vidhyabhivruddhi Sangha	1943	Bengaluru	M. S. Mallaiah, Secretary A. M. Ramamurthy, Spokesman

(Contd...)

Table 4.2 : (contd...)

16. Somavamsha Sahasrarjuna (Khatri) Kshatriya Sangha	1935	Bengaluru	Krishnasa Khoday, President Krishnasa Gujarathi, Secretary
17. Sri Madhwa Yuvaka Sangha	1945	Bengaluru	P. H. Krishna Rao, President
18. Akhila Karnataka Ganigara Sangha	1972	Bengaluru	B. J. Puttaswamy, President
19. Akhila Karnataka Pradesha Kumbarara Sangha	1951	Bengaluru	B. V. Ramachandrappa, President A. Annayyappa, Secretary
20. Akhila Bharatha Swakula Sali Sangha	1913	Hubli	S. Eswarappa, President Jnanoba, Secretary
21. The Hebbar Srivanshnava Sabha	1918	Mysore	Lalitha Parthasarathy, President
22. The Hoysala Karnataka Sangha	1908	Mysore	K. S. Suryanarayana Rao, President
23. Karnataka Dalit Action Committee	1977-78	Bengaluru	D. M. Thimmarayappa, Convener
24. Karnataka Dalit Action Forum	1980	Bengaluru	K. Chandrashekar, Secretary
25. The Karnataka Karuneekara Sangha	1970-71	Bengaluru	K. Chandrashekar, President R. Nagaraj, Secretary
26. The Karnataka Madivalara Sangha	1933	Bengaluru	D. Hanumanthaiah, President K. Appayyanna, Vice-President Dr.Gangayya , Vice-President G. Varadappa, Vice-President M. Rudrappa, Vice-President
27. The Karnataka Predesh Arya Idigara Sangha	1944	Bengaluru	H. R. Basavaraj, ex-MP, & President T. V. Venkataswamy, ex-MLA, Vice-President K. P. Appaji Gowda, Manager
28. The Karnataka Padmashali Sangha	1927	Bengaluru	Tirumala R. Venkatesh, President B. V. Munilakshmaiah Secretary
29. The Karnataka State Balija Sangha	1919	Bengaluru	K.V. Ashwathaiah, Secretary

Table 4.2 : (contd...)

30. The Karnataka State Gangamathasthara Sangha	1929	Bengaluru	H. Lakshman Salian, President H. Doddaveeraiah, Secretary
31. The Karnataka State Jattigala Sangha	1977	Mysore	Spokesperson
32. The Karnataka State Kunchitigara Sangha	1908	Mysore	S. G. Srinivasan and IYluddulinganna, Spokespersons
33. The Karnataka State Kurubara Sangha	1921	Bengaluru	H. Chikkanna, ex-President S. Nanjundayya, President Munisanjeevayya, Secretary
34. The Karnataka State Kuruhina Setty Sangha	1928	Bengaluru	B. V. Thimmappa, ex-President D. Shankarappa, President B. R. Shantappa, Secretary
35. The Karnataka State Savitha Samaj	1946	Bengaluru	B. K. Anjaneyulu, President K. Venkataswamy, Secretary
36. The Karnataka State Yadava Sangha	1942	Bengaluru	S. Siddappa, Secretary
37. The Mysore Rashtreeya Vishwakarma Samaja	1942	Bengaluru	M. Neelakantan, President S. Krishnachari, Secretary
38. The Myscre State Chathada Sri Vaishnava Association	1940	Bengaluru	K. N. Muthuraju, President H. S. Venugopal, Secretary
39. The Raju Kshatriya Sangha	1942	Bengaluru	Gopalaraju, Secretary Venkatachala Raju, Secretary
40. The Thigalara Sangha	1966	Bengaluru	Spokesperson
41. The Thogataveerara Sangha	1947	Bengaluru	Ramaiah, Spokesperson
42. The Vokkaligara Sangha	1906	Bengaluru	M. H. Mari Gorda, President Guthala Gorda, Secretary

All the Sanghas covered by the study have their HO at Bengaluru. The office bearers interviewed were representatives of the HO; otherwise the branch they represent has been indicated.

Appendix 4.3 : Conferences of the Akhila Bharatha Veerasaiva Mahasabha

Sl. No.	Place	Year	Name of the President	Conference Number
1.	Dharwar	1904	Sirsangi Lingaraja Sirdesai	I
2.	Bengaluru	1905	Sirsangi Lingaraja Sirdesai	II
3.	Sholapur	1907	Sir K. P. Puttana Chetty	III
4.	Bagalkot	1908	Raja Lakshmana Gowdaru Basavaprabhu	IV
5.	Bellary	1909	Varada Mallappa	V
6.	Belgaum	1911	Bullappa Basawanthraya Handiganoora Desai	vi
7.	Nippani	1913	Rao Bahadur Aratal Rudra Gowdaru	VII
8.	Davanagere	1917	Sir K. P. Puttana Chetty	VIII
9.	Birur	1919	Dewan Bahadur Shanthaveerappa Menasinakayi	IX
10.	Bengaluru	1927	Sir Siddappa Kambli	X
11.	Dharwar	1933	Rao Bahadur F. G. Halakatti	XI
12.	Raichur	1934	Sir Siddappa Kambli	XII
13.	Hubli	1938	Prof. S. S. Basavanal	XIII
14.	Kumbakonam	1940	Barrister M S Sardar	XIV
15.	Tumkur	1945	C. C. Hulukoti	XV
16.	Basavakalyan	1955	Sri Sanganabasava Swmigalu, Banthanal	XVI
17.	Shivayogamandir	1960	Dr. D. C. Pavate	XVII
18.	Bombay (Mumbai)	1969	Sri Sri Sivakumaraswamigalu	XVIII
19.	Bengaluru	1973	J. B. Malaradhya	XIX
20.	Mysore	1983	Eswara Mallappa Magdum	XX

Appendix 4.4 : Details of Caste Associations having Specific Activities for Women (till 1985)

Sl. No.	Name of the Caste Association	Place of Establishment
1.	Akila Kamataka Viswakarma Sangha (Women's Division)	Bangalore
2.	Kamataka Ganga Mahila Balaga	Bangalore
3.	Karnataka Pradesha Arya Edigara Mahila Sangha	Bangalore

Appendix 4.5 : Caste Associations established after 1982

Sl. No.	*Name of the Caste Association*	*Place of Establishment*
1.	Kamataka Rajya Uppara Kalyana Sangha	Bangalore
2.	Kamataka Rajya Arasu Sangha	Bangalore
3.	Nagartha Community Welfare Association	Bangalore
4.	Khila Kunchitigara Maha Mandali	Bangalore
5.	Kamataka Rajya Shuddha Shaiva Shivacharya (Thammadi) Maha Sangha	Bangalore
6.	Sindhi Federation of Bangalore	Bangalore
7.	Kamataka Helava Jananghadha Sangha	Bangalore
8.	Akhila Bharatha Sadhuchetty 24 Mane Telugu Shetty Sangha	Bangalore
9.	Kammavari Sangha	Bangalore
10.	Kamataka Rajya Namdev Simpi Samaj	Bangalore
11.	Kamataka Vanniyar Sangha	Bangalore
12.	Kamataka Vahnikula Kshatriya Seva Sangha	Bangalore
13.	Sri Somavamsha Arya Kshatriya Seva Sangha	Bangalore
14.	Kamataka Dombidasara Kshemabhivrudhdhi Sangha	Bangalore
15.	Mudaliar Sangha	Bangalore
16.	Karnataka Bomta Maha Sangha	Bangalore
17.	Beda Jangama, Budga Jangama, Mula Jangama Samaja	Bangalore
18.	Byari Chetiar Sangha	Bangalore
19.	Karnataka Digambar Jain Maha Mandali	Bangalore
20.	Karnataka Jogi Samaja Sudharaka Sangha	Bangalore
21.	Karnataka United Sourashtra Association	Bangalore
22.	Karnataka Christian Progressive Front	Bangalore
23.	Karnataka Maratha Parishat	Bangalore
24.	Bengaluru Edigara Vidyarthi Nilayadha Old Students Association	Bangalore
25.	Karnataka Bhavsar Kshatriya Yojana Mahasabha	Bangalore
26.	Karnataka Rajya Kshatriya Sangha	Bangalore
27.	Karnataka Swakula Sali Sangha	Bangalore
28.	Karnataka Devadigara Sangha	Bangalore
29.	Karnataka Gondhali Samaja	Bangalore
30.	Kulala Yuvakara Sangha	Bangalore
31.	KSCSV Association (Satani)	Bangalore
32.	Karnataka Billava Samaja	Bangalore
33.	Karnataka Arasu Samaja	Bangalore

Appendix 4.6 : Demands of Caste Associations in Karnataka (formed after 1980) placed before successive Backward Classes' Commissions

Sl. No.	*Name of the Association*	*Description of Demand*
1.	Karnataka Rajya Aradhya Jangama Yuvajana Samithi, Mandya	Represented the subcaste of Jangama Lingayats to be included as a Backward Caste (BC)
2.	Arya Kshatriya Yuvaka Sangha, Bangalore	Demanding BC status
3.	Arya Maratha Kshatriya Sangha	Demanding BC status
4.	Kodagu Ayiri Samaj	Demanding BC status
5.	Bomman Valekar Samaja Seva Sangha	This is the caste of Messengers, demanding BC status
6.	Akhila Karnataka Bestar (Bunde Besar) Sangha, Bangalore	This is the caste of Messengers, demanding BC status
7.	Karnataka Bajantri Kshemabhi-vrudhdhi Sangha	To be included as a SC
8.	Daivagna Brahmins Samaj or Sonegars	To be included as a synonym of the Visvakarmas
9.	Desh Bhandari Samaj	BC status
10.	The Bunts' Sangha (Nadavaru)	BC status
11.	Akhila Karnataka Banrarara Sangha	Demanding ST status
12.	The Banjara Society, Shikaripur	Demanding ST status
13.	Brahmana Maha Sabha, Hubli	BC status on economic criterion
14.	The Karnataka State Gondali Samaj	Seeking shift to SC status from BT status
15.	The Gejjagara Shettaru (Blacksmiths), Mysore	To be separated from other blacksmith castes and claiming separate ST status
16.	North Kanara Gamokkal Samaj Development Organization representing Gond, Gouda and Patgar tribes	Demanding ST status
17.	The Gollar Sangha, Bangalore	Demanding ST status
18.	All India Gudigar Samaja, Sagar, Shimoga District	Demanding BT status
19.	Hugar or Hoovadiga Samaj	Demanding BT status
20.	The Helavas, Helawas or Holavas Samaj	Demanding ST status
21.	The Haranshikari Samaj (Hunters)	Demanding BT status
22.	The Hatagars	Seeking separate BC status and not as a synonym of the Devangas
23	The Jain Association, Bangalore	Seeking BC status
24.	Karnataka Jettigala Sangha	Demanding BC status
25.	The Kawali Community	Seeking BC status
26.	The Akhila Karnataka Komarpanth or Komarpaik Parishat, UK district	Demanding separation as subsect of Idigas and classification as a separate BC

Appendix 4.6 : (contd...)

27.	Vaishya Konkanastha Jathiya Abhyudaya Sangha	Seeking inclusion of Galada Konkani community as separate BC
28.	The Karnataka Acharara Sangha	Konkani Acharis to be treated as separate BC
29.	Karnataka State Shivaji Educational and Social Welfare Trust	To include Kshatriya Marathas as BC
30.	The Kotegar, Kote Sherugar, Ramaraja Kshatriya or Rama Kshatriya or Kshatriya Sherugar Community	Separate BC status than Sherugars
31.	The Karnataka Kuruba Jagruthi Samithi	SC status to Kurubas (declaration in Bangalore on Nov. 14, 1982, *Times of Deccan*
32.	The Karnataka State Kurubara Sangha, Bangalore	Seeking ST status
33.	Krantiveera Sangolli Rayanna Yuvaka Sangha community as	Representation in State Cabinet to 2 members of their Ministers
34.	The Khatik Samaj conference held at Hubli	To include its 22 subcastes under BC category
35.	Kembatty Association, Kodagu	Seeking BC status
36.	Mysore Samsthana Kshatriya Ladara Sangha	Seeking BC status
37.	Akila Bharatiya Lad (Yeligar) Samaj	Seeking BC status
38.	Karnataka Kshatriya Maratha Parishat	Seeking BC status
39.	The Lingaveeraru or Lingavvaru Community	Seeking BC status
40.	The Karnataka Pradesh Medara (Mahendra) Sangha, Dharwad	To consider Gauriga, Burud Budda as synoyms of Meda
41.	Mogera Caste of UK district	Seeking SC status
42.	Karwar Meengar (Harikanthra) Seva Samithi	Seeking SC status
43.	Akila Karnataka Madivalara Sangha	Seeking SC status (demanded in the State level conference held in 1981 in Chikmagalur)
44.	Mysore Maratha Yuva Mandali	Seeking BC status
45.	Karnataka Maratha Yuva Kendra	Seeking BC status to Marathas
46.	Nagarthas	Plea for deleting Namdhari Nagarthas from Lingayat caste and to include them as BCs
47.	Narvekar Samaja Kalyana Sangha	Seeking BC status
48.	Nolambar Parishath	BC status to Nonaba or Nolamba Veerasaivas
49.	Neygi Samaj	BC status to Lingayat weavers

Appendix 4.6 : (contd...)

50. Akila Karnataka Nayak Sangha	To include all Nayak subcaste like Beda, Valmiki, Talawar, Palegar and Nayak-Makkalu as STs
51. Nayari Community of DK District	Seeking BC status
52. Padati Sangha	Seeking clarification between Padati and Padit and Padarthi as BCs
53. Parivara Bunt Sangha	Reclassification as ST or most BC
54. Panjukars'	Plea to be treated as a BC
55. Palegars Sangha	Plea to be treated on par with the Nayaks.
56. Sri Gajanana Pattashale	Seeking BC status to subsect Pattashale
57. Mysore Andhra Raja Kshatriya Maha Mandali	Seeking BC status
58. Somavamsha Arya Kshatriya Samaj	Seeking BC status
59. Sthanikaru	Stressing not to be included as BC
60. Karanataka SC Christian Sangha	Seeking BC status
61. The Sourashtra Association, Bangalore	Request to recognize their name
62. Upparara Sangha	Seeking BC status
63. Valmiki Sangha	Plea to consider its synonyms like Valmiki while listing for BC status.
64. Mysore Rashtreeya Vishwakarma Samaj, Bangalore, Akhila Bharatiya Viswakarma Mahasabha, Bangalore, Mysore District Vishwakarma Shaiva Brahmana Samaja requesting for BC status.	
65. Mudaliar Sangam	Requesting BC status to Velamas, Vellala Mudaliars
66. The Arya Vaishya Mahasabha	Plea to not take their caste as the critierion

Appendix 4. 7 : District-wise Distribution of a few castes/subcastes/tribes in Karnataka (estimated for 1972 by the Havanur Commission)

Sl. No.	Districts	Adi Andhra		Adi Dravida		Adi Karnataka		Agasa		Arasu	
		Population in the district	*% to the district population*	*Population in the district*	*% to the district population*	*Population in the district*	*% to the district population*	*Population in the district*	*% to the district population*	*Population in the district*	*% to the district population*
1.	Bengaluru	14,399	00.41	1,71,575	4.92	2,99,896	8.61	49,237	1.41	2,990	00.08
2.	Belgaum	–	–	–	–	–	–	1,341	0.05	–	–
3.	Bellary	7,116	00.62	6,311	0.55	58,027	5.08	22,292	1.95	–	–
4.	Bidar	–	–	–	–	–	–	6,934	0.82	–	–
5.	Bijapur	–	–	–	–	–	–	2,665	0.13	–	–
6.	Chikmagalur	213	00.28	12,681	1.68	76,452	10.14	9,384	1.24	168	00.02
7.	Chitradurga	55	00.04	20,157	1.40	1,41,981	9.88	22,218	1.54	–	–
8.	Dakshina Kannada	–	–	4,619	0.23	552	0.02	14,355	0.72		–
9.	Dharwar	–	–	–	–	–	–	9.021	0.37	–	–
10.	Gulbarga	–	–	–	–	–	–	15,123	0.85	–	–
11.	Hassan	337	0.03	17,913	1.59	1,34,791	11.95	20,408	1.80	1,856	0.16
12.	Kodagu	–	–	1,378	0.35	9,122	2.35	3,622	0.93	32	0.008
13.	Kolar	2,297	0.16	1,05,048	6.81	1,96,305	12.72	26,674	1.72	89	0.005
14.	Mandya	605	0.05	19,141	1.61	1,20,452	10.14	18,520	1.56		
15.	Mysore	4,996	0.23	44,839	2.10	2,94,886	13.85	33,152	1.55	15,268	1.28
16.	Raichur	–	–	–	–	–	–	28,493	1.95	–	–
17.	Shimoga	357	0.02	10,114	0.75	73,047	5.46	30,520	2.28	424	0.03
18.	Tumkur	48	0.003	50,938	3.07	1,69,199	10.20	29,376	1.77	423	0.03
19.	Uttara Kannada	–	–	–	–	–	–	11,861	1.36	–	–

(Contd...)

Appendix 4. 7 : (Contd...)

Sl. No.	*Districts*	*Balija*		*Bbanjara*		*Beda*		*Bhatraju*		*Bhunt*	
		Population in the district	*% to the district population*	*Population in the district*	*% to the district population*	*Population in the district*	*% to the district population*	*Population in the district*	*% to the district population*	*Population in the district*	*% to the district population*
1.	Bengaluru	1,30,897	3.76	13,929	0.40	63,784	1.83	624	0.01	–	–
2.	Belgaum	–	–	2,927	0.11	1,17,457	4.74	59	0.002	–	–
3.	Bellary	26,415	2.31	35,780	3.13	2,14,382	18.77	353	0.03	–	–
4.	Bidar	14,893	1.76	10,938	1.29	4,396	5.20	–	–	–	–
5.	Bijapur	–	–	44,663	2.20	63,550	3.13	4	0.0001	–	–
6.	Chikmagalur	15,383	2.04	17,853	2.37	10,052	1.33	55	0.007	–	–
7.	Chitradurga	12,000	0.83	38,138	2.65	2,33,459	16.25	212	0.15	–	–
8.	Dakshina Kannada	2,033	0.10	11	.0005	13	.0006	–	–	2,02,617	10.00
9.	Dharwar	–	–	26,566	1.11	1,42,678	5.97	–	–	–	–
10.	Gulbarga	45,895	2.57	57,820	3.24	1,22,779	6.89	4,583	0.24	–	–
11.	Hassan	7,427	0.65	19,462	0.92	11,140	0.98	172	0.01	–	–
12.	Kodagu	2,809	0.72	233	0.06	214	0.05	–	–	2,576	0.66
13.	Kolar	90,626	5.87	3,859	0.25	1,17,270	7.60	642	0.04	–	–
14.	Mandya	14,885	1.25	219	0.01	6,104	0.28	10	0.0005	–	–
15.	Mysore	26,834	1.26	1,417	0.06	6,104	0.28	10	0.0005	–	–
16.	Raichur	33,296	2.28	17,632	1.21	2,23,683	15.35	1,074	0.07	–	–
17.	Shimoga	14,565	1.08	50,627	3.78	62,538	4.67	–	–	–	–
18.	Tumkur	34,351	2.07	16,637	1.00	1,21,508	7.32	489	0.02	–	–
19.	Uttara Kannada	–	–	4,181	0.48	2,576	0.29	–	–	–	–

(Contd...)

Appendix 4. 7 : (Contd...)

Sl. No.	Districts	Brahmin		Darzi		Devadiga		Devanga		Gabit	
		Population in the district	% to the district population	Population in the district	% to the district population	Population in the district	% to the district population	Population in the district	% to the district population	Population in the district	% to the district population
1.	Bengaluru	1,85,062	5.31	20,561	0.59	–	–	46,949	1.34	–	–
2.	Belgaum	63,955	2.58	6,445	0.26	490	0.01	12,649	0.51	17	.0006
3.	Bellary	20,262	1.77	3,823	0.33	–	–	6,862	0.60	–	–
4.	Bidar	19,3	2.29	3,489	0.41	–	–	14,545	1.72	–	–
5.	Bijapur	50,446	2.49	1,933	0.09	–	–	22,012	1.08	–	–
6.	Chikmagalur	45,160	5.99	3,995	0.52	–	–	18,003	2.38	–	–
7.	Chitradurga	22,632	1.57	8,176	0.56	–	–	16,211	1.12	–	–
8.	Dakshina Kannada	1,78,663	8.99	141	.007	50,266	2.53	8,493	0.42	198	.009
9.	Dharwar	75,653	3.16	9,428	0.39	–	–	21,888	0.91	–	–
10.	Gulbarga	49,461	2.77	10,859	0.60	–	–	27,816	1.56	–	–
11.	Hassan	43,277	3.83	3,224	0.28	–	–	18,823	1.66	–	–
12.	Kodagu	6,547	1.69	291	0.07	156	0.04	4,048	1.04	–	–
13.	Kolar	50,844	3.29	2,090	0.13	–	–	3,901	0.25	–	–
14.	Mandya	30,128	2.53	1,466	0.12	–	–	1,999	0.16	–	–
15.	Mysore	1,04,405	4.90	6,648	0.31	–	–	11,770	0.55	–	–
16.	Raichur	57,847	3.97	11,320	0.77	–	–	15,145	1.03	–	–
17.	Shimoga	88,932	6.64	12,302	0.91	–	–	13,352	0.99	–	–
18.	Tumkur	42,179	2.54	4,243	0.25	–	–	15,826	0.95	–	–
19.	Uttara Kannada	1,34,595	15.49	1,128	0.12	16,528	1.90	272	0.03	6,568	0.75

(Contd...)

Appendix 4. 7 : (Contd...)

Sl. No.	Districts	Gangakula		Ganiga		Halwakki Wakkal		Holeya		Hoovadiga	
		Population in the district	*% to the district population*	*Population in the district*	*% to the district population*	*Population in the district*	*% to the district population*	*Population in the district*	*% to the district population*	*Population in the district*	*% to the district population*
1.	Bengaluru	37,637	1.08	26,802	0.76	–	–	–	–	–	–
2.	Belgaum	27,058	1.09	164	0.006	–	–	72,213	2.91	1,029	0.04
3.	Bellary	9,922	0.87	5,936	0.51	–	–	–	–	–	–
4.	Bidar	40,560	4.80	3,802	0.45	–	–	33,132	3.92	3,819	0.45
5.	Bijapur	61,448	3.03	1,906	0.09	–	–	79,499	3.92	272	0.01
6.	Chikmagalur	8,653	1.14	1,829	0.24	–	–	–	–	–	–
7.	Chit.:adurga	16,389	1.14	1,025	0.07	–	–	–	–	–	–
8.	Dakshina Kannada	6,863	0.34	21,225	1.07	–	–	–	–	–	–
9.	Dharwar	60,581	2.53	559	0.02	97	.004	5,375	0.22	135	.005
10.	Gulbarga	53,092	2.98	7,155	0.40	–	–	1,36,942	7.68	8,137	0.45
11.	Hassan	16,663	1.47	5,501	0.48	–	–	–	–	–	–
12.	Kodagu	820	0.21	851	0.22	–	–	9,816	2.53	–	–
13.	Kolar	7,361	0.47	13,004	0.84	–	–	–	–	–	–
14.	Mandya	46,765	3.93	14,619	1.23	–	–	–	–	–	–
15.	Mysore	2,16,911	10.19	27,955	1.31	–	–	4,033	0.18	–	–
16.	Raichur	42,511	2.92	10,539	0.72	–	–	6,925	0.47	–	–
17.	Shimoga.	29,125	2.17	1,191	0.08	–	–	–	–	–	–
18.	Tumkur	10,994	0.66	8,519	0.51	–	–	–	–	–	–
19.	Uttara Kannada	20,468	2.35	4,316	0.49	45,735	5.26	–	–	–	–

(Contd...)

Appendix 4. 7 : (Contd...)

Sl. No.	Districts	Idiga		Komar Paik		Koracha		Koraga		Korama	
		Population in the district	% to the district population	Population in the district	% to the district population	Population in the district	% to the district population	Population in the district	% to the district population	Population in the district	% to the district population
1.	Bengaluru	12,488	0.35	–	–	1,524	0.04	–	–	9,801	0.28
2.	Belgaum	33	.001	5	.0002	2	.00008	–	–	9,219	0.37
3.	Bellary	10,171	0.89	–	–	4,275	0.37	–	–	2,445	0.21
4.	Bidar	5,728	0.67	–	–	–	–	–	–	1,179	0.13
5.	Bijapur	8	.0004	–	–	–	–	–	–	12,794	0.63
6.	Chikmagalur	18,495	2.45	–	–	686	0.09	–	–	2,429	0.32
7.	Chitradurga	10,583	0.73	–	–	3,609	0.25	8,102	0.40	3,272	0.22
8.	Dakshina Kannada	3,08,968	0.007	–	–	–	–	–	–	–	–
9.	Dharwar	177	1.03	–	–	115	0.004	–	–	12,057	0.50
10.	Gulbarga	18,446	0.68	–	–	–	–	–	–	16,750	0.94
11.	Hassan	7,715	2.65	–	–	699	0.06	–	–	2,250	0.19
12.	Kodagu	10,266	0.36	–	–	22	0.005	–	–	321	0.08
13.	Kolar	5,565	0.36	–	–	4,817	0.31	–	–	2,584	0.16
14.	Mandya	6,074	0.51	–	–	–	–	–	–	2,647	0.22
15.	Mysore	11,469	0.53	–	–	11	.0005	2	.00009	3,057	0.14
16.	Raichur	23,608	1.62	–	–	–	–	–	–	6,779	0.46
17.	Shimoga	1,13,966	8.52	–	–	2,869	0.21	–	–	3,579	0.26
18.	Tumkur	14,278	0.86	–	–	917	0.05	–	–	5,058	0.30
19.	Uttara Kannada	97,618	11.23	17,352	1.99	618	0.07	1,179	0.13	1,834	0.21

(Contd...)

Appendix 4. 7 : (Contd...)

Sl. No.	*Districts*	*Kumbara*		*Kuruba*		*Ladar*		*Madiga*		*Kotegar*	
		Population in the district	*% to the district population*	*Population in the district*	*% to the district population*	*Population in the district*	*% to the district population*	*Population in the district*	*% to the district population*	*Population in the district*	*% to the district population*
1.	Bengaluru	19,578	0.56	1,32,733	3.81	222	.006	–	–	–	–
2.	Belgaum	10,794	0.43	1,58,947	6.41	1,984	0.08	9,297	0.37	11	.0004
3.	Bellary	5,234	0.46	1,19,250	10.44	–	–	–	–	981	0.08
4.	Bidar	6,252	0.74	58,040	6.87	–	–	15,326	1.81	–	–
5.	Bijapur	5,726	0.28	2,36,558	11.68	1,051	0.05	3,245	0.16	–	–
6.	Chikmagalur	7,015	0.93	67,411	8.94	423	0.05	–	–	–	–
7.	Chitradurga	5,908	0.41	94,218	6.56	272	0.02	–	–	–	0.52
8.	Dakshina Kannada	50,403	2.54	382	0.02	–	–	166	0.008	10,338	–
9.	Dharwar	682	0.03	2,04,471	8.56	1,360	0.05	240	0.01	–	–
10.	Gulbarga	12,580	0.70	1,55,984	8.75	–	–	98,369	5.52	–	–
11.	Hassan	7,843	0.69	88,031	7.80	172	0.01	–	–	–	–
12.	Kodagu	1,915	0.49	16,214	4.19	–	–	1,223	0.31	57	0.01
13.	Kolar	9,345	0.60	73,646	4.77	101	0.006	–	–	–	–
14.	Mandya	16,442	1.38	79,328	6.68	–	–	–	–	–	–
15.	Mysore	25,941	1.29	2,23,511	10.50	982	0.05	4,891	0.23	–	–
16.	Raichur	13,417	0.92	1,61,462	11.08	–	–	96,207	6.60	–	–
17.	Shimoga	6,480	0.48	63,326	4.73	29	.002	–	–	–	–
18.	Tumkur	10,018	0.60	96,050	5.79	299	0.02	–	–	–	–
19.	Uttara Kannada	2,826	0.32	2,464	0.28	258	0.29	–	–	1,320	0.15

(Contd...)

Appendix 4. 7 : (Contd...)

Sl. No.	Districts	Mahratha		Nayaka		Nayinda		Neygi		Padit	
		Population in the district	*% to the district population*	*Population in the district*	*% to the district population*	*Population in the district*	*% to the district population*	*Population in the district*	*% to the district population*	*Population in the district*	*% to the district population*
1.	Bengaluru	47,855	1.37	–	–	30,879	0.88	35,209	1.01	–	–
2.	Belgaum	4,05,834	16.38	62,708	2.53	8,493	0.34	1,193	0.05	–	–
3.	Bellary	4,513	0.39	–	–	8,543	0.74	25,431	2.22	–	–
4.	Bidar	1,51,887	17.99	–	–	7,804	0.92	3,637	0.43	–	–
5.	Bijapur	42,423	2.09	8,393	0.41	8,131	0.40	7,820	0.38	–	–
6.	Chikmagalur	6,459	0.85	–	–	1,994	0.26	5,921	0.78	–	–
7.	Chitradurga	10,094	0.70	–	–	5,013	0.34	15,698	1.09	–	–
8.	Dakshina Kannada	–	–	–	–	10,842	0.54	8,154	0.41	–	–
9.	Dharwar	1,01,903	4.26	11,966	0.50	1,024	0.04	18,838	0.78	–	–
10.	Gulbarga	83,399	4.68	–	–	16,856	0.94	15,569	0.87	–	–
11.	Hassan	3,877	0.34	–	–	6,424	0.56	10,597	0.93	–	–
12.	Kodagu	4,717	1.21	–	–	1,757	0.45	4,376	1.13	–	–
13.	Kolar	11,950	0.77	–	–	19,556	1.26	18,597	1.20	–	–
14.	Mandya	3,254	0.27	–	–	10,032	0.84	8,658	0.72	–	–
15.	Mysore	17,312	0.81	–	–	17,375	0.81	4,039	0.18		
16.	Raichur	22,075	1.51	–	–	18,584	1.27	23,562	1.61	–	–
17.	Shimoga	37,852	2.82	–	–	5,004	0.37	5,517	0.41	–	–
18.	Tumkur	8,973	0.54	–	–	10,002	0.60	8,826	0.53	–	–
19.	Uttara Kannada	71,960	8.28	4,689	0.53	3,189	0.36	83	.009	6,694	0.77

(Contd...)

Appendix 4. 7 : (Contd...)

Sl. No.	Districts	Patvekari		Satani		Thigala		Upara		Veerasaiva	
		Population in the district	% to the district population	Population in the district	% to the district population	Population in the district	% to the district population	Population in the district	% to the district population	Population in the district	% to the district population
1.	Bengaluru	–	–	10,787	0.30	1,32,699	3.81	5,620	0.16	1,56,578	4.49
2.	Belgaum	636	0.02	–	–	–	–	35,041	1.41	5,58,901	22.56
3.	Bellary	–	–	1,679	0.14	9,540	0.83	17,462	1.52	1,19,879	10.49
4.	Bidar	–	–	3,407	0.40	–	–	1,661	0.19	1,20,624	14.29
5.	Bijapur	926	0.04	–	–	–	–	18,007	0.88	5,81,265	28.71
6.	Chikmagalur	–	–	2,359	0.31	1,205	0.15	26,044	3.45	1,42,628	18.92
7.	Chitradurga	–	–	1,910	0.13	661	0.04	32,356	2.25	3,04,570	21.21
8.	Dakshina-Kannada	–	–	11	.0005	717	0.03	2,180	0.10	1,352	0.06
9.	Dharwar	10,234	0.43	–	–	1,152	0.05	12,124	0.50	7,23,118	30.26
10.	Gulbarga	–	–	–	–	–	–	10,379	0.58	3,36,330	18.88
11.	Hassan	–	–	6,943	0.61	1,157	0.10	16,779	1,487	1,60,150	14.20
12.	Kodagu	–	–	142	0.03	–	–	501	0.12	16,621	4.29
13.	Kolar	–	–	2,497	0.19	24,206	1.56	5,312	0.34	25,401	1.64
14.	Mandya	–	–	5,809	0.48	2,023	0.17	7,448	0.62	70,963	5.97
15.	Mysore	–	–	5,787	0.27	1,171	0.05	1,11,247	5.22	3,72,890	17.52
16.	Raichur	–	–	–	–	–	–	27,598	1.89	2,26,613	15.56
17.	Shimoga	–	–	3,364	0.25	387	0.02	22,985	1.71	2,66,246	19.90
18.	Tumkur	–	–	8,314	0.50	48,271	2.91	29,792	1.79	1,99,255	12.01
19.	Uttara Kannada	–	–	–	–	90	0.01	4,037	0.46	9,815	1.12

(Contd...)

Appendix 4. 7 : (Contd...)

Sl. No.	Districts	Vishwakarma		Vodda		Vokkaliga		Vyshya		Yadava	
		Population in the district	% to the district population	Population in the district	% to the district population	Population in the district	% to the district population	Population in the district	% to the district population	Population in the district	% to the district population
1.	Bengaluru	57,460	1.65	65,759	1.88	8,96,631	25.75	32,134	0.92	65,177	1.87
2.	Belgaum 0.07	44,316	1.79	18,460	0.74		13,670	0.55	–	–	1,947
3.	Bellary	28,185	2.46	22,636	1.98	71,259	6.23	13,100	1.14	39,518	3.46
4.	Bidar	24,130	2.85	–	–	2,724	0.32	8,441	1.00	1,417	0.16
5.	Bijapur	44,788	2.21	23,156	1.14	28,641	1.41	–	–	2,954	0.14
6.	Chikmagalur	17,578	2.33	12,588	1.67	90,625	12.02	4,584	0.60	7,702	1.02
7.	Chitradurga	25,153	1.75	58,381	4.06	90,070	6.37	11,637	0.81	1,08,409	7.54
8.	Dakshina Kannada	62,503	3.14	29	0.001	74,495	3.75	2,355	0.12	1,492	0.07
9.	Dharwar	45,103	1.88	40,472	1.69	25,657	1.07	5,717	0.23	9,478	0.39
10.	Gulbarga	37,514	2.10	15,424	0.86	64,546	3.62	11,946	0.10	6,250	0.35
11.	Hassan	29,533	2.62	13,844	1.23	3,77,374	33.46	4,669	0.41	12,340	1.09
12.	Kodagu	5,552	1.43	280	0.07	56,108	14.50	776	0.20	1,957	0.50
13.	Kolar	21,606	1.40	64,556	4.18	3,28,625	21.30	23,145	1.50	39,307	2.54
14.	Mandya	34,554	2.91	9,489	0.80	5,95,795	50.18	1,470	0.12	2,447	0.20
15.	Mysore	65,984	3.10	11,698	0.55	2,42,021	11.37	8,847	0.41	4,775	0.22
16.	Raichur	46,510	3.19	12,831	0.88	75,836	5.20	21,952	1.50	31,023	2.13
17.	Shimoga	38,443	2.87	47,191	3.52	1,06,990	7.99	6,209	0.46	7,991	0.59
18.	Tumkur	27,200	1.64	37,633	2,27	4,05,007	24.41	16,270	0.98	1,02,124	6.15
19.	Uttara Kannada	34,577	3.98	4,133	0.47	87	0.01	5,328	0.61	185	0.02

(Contd...)

Appendix 4.8 : Distribution of a few Castes/SubcastesITribes in Karnataka (estimated for the year 1972 by the Havanur Commission/KSBCC) State Population (then): 3,00,08,876

Sl. No.	*Name of Caste/Subcaste/Tribe*	*Population in the State*	*% to the State Population*
1.	Adi Andhra	30,623	00.10
2.	Adi Dravida	4,64,714	1.59
3.	Adi Karnataka	15,74,712	5.37
4.	Agasa	3,55,246	1.18
5.	Arasu	21,245	00.07
6.	Balija	4,72,409	1.57
7.	Banjara	3,53,882	1.18
8.	Beda	15,19,621	5.06
9.	Bhaata: Bhatraju	8,227	00.03
10.	Bhunt	2,05,193	00.68
11.	Brahmin	12,69,455	4.23
12.	Darzi	1,11,567	00.37
13.	Devadiga	67,440	00.22
14.	Devanga	2,80,564	00.93
15.	Gabit: Gapit	6,783	00.02
16.	Gangakula (Bestha)	7,12,922	2.38
17.	Ganiga	1,56,898	00.52
18.	Halwakki Wakkal	45,832	00.15
19.	Holeya	3,88,348	1.32
20.	Hoovadiga	13,392	00.04
21.	Idiga	6,75,656	2.25
22.	Komar Paik	17,357	00.06
23.	Koracha	20,164	00.07
24.	Koraga	9,283	00.03
25.	Korama	98,055	00.33
26.	Kotegar	12,707	00.04
27.	Kumbara	2,18,399	00.73
28.	Kuruba -	20,32,032	6.77
29.	Ladar	7,153	00.02
30.	Madiga	2,28,964	00.76
31.	Mahratha	10,36,337	3.45
32.	Nayaka	87,756	00.29
33.	Nayinda	1,91,502	00.64
34.	Neygi	2,21,725	00.74
35.	Padit	6,694	00.02
36.	Patvekari	11,796	00.04
37.	Satani	53,459	00.18
38.	Thigala	2,23,279	00.74
39.	Uppara	3,86,573	1.29
40.	Veerasaiva	43,92,699	2.30
41.	Viswakarma	6,90,689	2.30
42.	Vodda (Bhovi)	4,58,560	1.53
43.	Vokkaliga	35,46,171	11.82
44.	Vyshya	1,78,580	00.59
45.	Yadava	4,46,893	1.49

Source: Report of the KBCC, Vol. II 1975.

Appendix 4.9 : Details of Caste Associations formed after 1980s (in response to the setting up of successive Backward Class Commissions in Karnataka)

Sl. No.	*Name of the Sangha*	*Description*
1.	Karnataka Rajya Aradhya Jangama Yuvajana Samithi, Mandya	Represented Jangama Lingayats to be included as a BC.
2.	Arya Kshatriya Yuvaka Sangha, Bangalore	Demanding BC status
3.	Arya Maratha Kshatriya Sangha	Demanding BC status
4.	Kodagu Ayiri Samaj	Demanding BC status
5.	Bomman Valekar Samaja Seva Sangha	Caste of Messengers, demanding BC status
6.	Akhila Karnataka Bestar (Bunde Besar) Sangha, Bangalore	Caste of Messengers, demanding BC status
7.	Karnataka Bajantri Kshemabhivrudhdhi Sangha	
8.	Daivagna Brahmins Samaj or Sonegars	To be included as a synonym of the Visvakarmas
9.	Desh Bhandari Samaj	To be included as a synonym of the Visvakarmas
10.	The Bunts' Sangha (Nadavaru)	To be included as a synonym of the Visvakarmas
11.	Akhila Karnataka Banjarara Sangha	Demanding ST status
12.	The Banjar Society, Shikaripur	Demanding ST status
13.	Brahmana Maha Sabha, Hubli	BC status on economic basis
14.	The Karnataka State Gondali Samaj	SC status from BT status
15.	The Gejjagara Shettaru (Blacksmiths), Mysore	To be separated from other blacksmith castes and separate ST status
16.	North Kanara Gamokkal Samaj Development organization representing Gond, Gouda and Patgar tribes	ST status
17.	The Gollar Sangha, Bangalore	ST status
18.	All India Gudigar Samaja, Sagar, Shimoga district	BT status
19.	Hugar or Hoovadiga Samaj	BT status
20.	The Helavas, Helawas or Holavas Samaj	ST status
21.	The Haranshikari Samaj (Hunters)	BT status
22.	The Hatagars	Seeking separate BC status and not as a synonym of the Devangas
23	The Jain Association, Bangalore	Seeking BC status to Jains
24.	Karnataka Jettigala Sangha	BC status
25.	The Kawali community seeking BC status	—
26.	The Akila Karnataka Komarpanth or Komarpaik Parishat, UK district	Not as a subsect of Idigas but as separate BC
27.	Vaishya Konkanastha Jathiya Abhyudaya Sangha	Seeking inclusion of Galada Konkani community as separate BC
28.	The Karnataka Acharara Sangha	Konkani Acharis to be treated as separate BC
29.	Karnataka State Shivaji Educational and Social Welfare Trust	To include Kshatriya Marathas as BC

Appendix 4.9 : (Contd...)

30.	The Kotegar, Kote Sherugar, Ramaraja Kshatriya or Rama Kshatriya or Kshatriya Sherugar Community	Separate status than Sherugars
31.	The Karnataka Kuruba Jagruthi Samithi	SC status to Kurubas (declaration in Bangalore on Nov. 14, 1982, *Deccan Times*)
32.	The Karnataka State Kurubara Sangha, Bangalore	ST status
33.	Krantiveera Sangolli Rayanna Yuvaka	Representation in State Cabinet to 2 members of their community as Ministers
34.	The Khatik Samaj conference held at Hubli	To include its 22 subcastes under BC category
35.	Kembatty Association, Kodagu	BC status
36.	Mysore Samsthana Kshatriya Ladara	BC status
37	Akila Bharatiya Lad (Yeligar) Samaj	BC status
38.	Karnataka Kshatriya Maratha Parishat	BC status
39.	The Lingaveeraru or Lingavvaru Community	BC status
40.	The Karnataka Pradesh Medara (Mahendra) Sangha, Dharwad	To consider Gauriga, Burud, Budda as synoyms of Meda
41.	Mogera caste of UK district	SC status
42.	Karwar Meengar (Harikanthra) Seva Samithi	SC status
43.	Akila Karnataka Madivalara Sangha	SC status (State level conference in 1981 in Chikmagalur)
44.	Mysore Maratha Yuva Mandali	BC status
45.	Karnataka Maratha Yuva Kendra	BC status to Marathas
46.	Nagarthas' plea for deleting Namdhari Nagarthas from Lingayat caste and to include them as BCs	—
47.	Narvekar Samajada Kalyana Sangha	BC status
48.	Nolambar Parishath	BC status to Nonaba or Nolamba Veerasaivas
49.	Neygi Samaj	BC status to Lingayat weavers
50.	Akila Karnataka Nayak Sangha	To include all Nayak subcastes like Beda, Valmiki, Talawar, Palegar and Nayak-Makkalu as STs
51.	Nayari Community of DK District	BC status
52.	Padati Sangha	Seeking clarification between Padati and Padit and Padarthi as BCs
53.	Parivara Bunt Sangha	Reclassification as ST or most BC
54.	Panjukars' plea to be treated as BC	—
55.	Palegars Sangha	Plea to be treated on par with the Nayaks.
56.	Sri Gajanana Pattashale	Seeking BC status to subsect Pattashale
57.	Mysore Andhra Raja Kshatriya Maha Mandali	BC status
58.	Somavamsha Arya Kshatriya Samaj	Bc status
59.	Sthanikaru	BC status
60.	Karnataka SC Christian Sangha	Stressing not to be included as BC
61.	The Sourashtra Association, Bangalore	Request to recognize their name

Appendix 4.9 : (Contd...)

62.	Upparara Sangha	BC status
63.	Valmiki Sangha	Plea to consider its synonyms like Walmiki while listing for BC status.
64.	Mysore Rashtreeya Vishwakarma Samaj, Bangalore, Akhila Bharatiya Viswakarma Mahasabha, Bangalore, Mysore District Vishwakarma Shaiva Brahmana Samaja requesting for BC status.	
65.	Mudaliar Sangam	Requesting BC status to Velamas, Vellala Mudaliars
66.	The Arya Vaishya Mahasabha	Plea not to take their caste as the critierion

5 EDUCATION AS A STRATEGY FOR CASTE MOBILISATION

Introduction

Formal education, with its fast expanding areas of knowledge is gaining importance as a prerequisite for development. It has become an indispensable tool in achieving social mobility by hitherto backward castes. Sociologists have referred to it as a 'lever of social change' (Moore : 1965) due to the advantages that it has in store for promoting social mobility and social transformation.

India never lagged behind other developing nations in realising this importance of education as an instrument for social and economic development and went on designing a number of plans and policies to popularise education, especially among the downtrodden sections. Earlier to the efforts of the Indian government, the system of education introduced by the British was popular only in a limited way. It was instrumental in giving a push to the initiatives of the post-independence days. Although it was initiated to meet the needs of the administrative staff of the East India Company, the education system introduced by the British is hailed for laying the foundation of formal education in India and for providing opportunities for employment. This and few other reforms, like introduction of transportation and communication network, expansion of urban areas etc., came to have a role in changing the traditional Indian social structure from being a 'closed' one to an 'open' one (Srinivas : 1966). In course of time, the importance attached to formal education also came to be best exemplified in, or identified with, the stirring up of the historical 'backward classes movements' in various parts of British India.[1]

Education in Pre-British India

Access to education in the traditional Indian society was the prerogative of only the Brahmins being held as the most superior caste in the social ladder. Education was Sanskritic in nature, including the learning and teaching of Vedas and the Upanishads, the sacred Hindu religious scripts. Learning them and becoming proficient in their use in daily social, economic and religious life was considered as the duty of the Brahmin than just a habit he was traditionally ordained to carry out. All non-Brahmins were denied access to such education[2] and had to profess their own traditional caste occupation that never required any such Sanskritic learning. Basing on the occupational theory of caste, the non-Brahmins not only were restricted to following their caste occupations, but were also addressed by their caste names. Agriculture and allied occupations came to be associated with non-Brahmins who had access to its ownership based on their position in the caste hierarchy. Brahmins owned agricultural lands but were traditionally prohibited from cultivating it by themselves. Touching of the plough was a taboo for them. Since the Brahmins' duty was to teach and offer priestly services, their knowledge of religious texts and practices became mandatory.

Education in British India

When the British introduced education in their schools for the benefit of the children of the British officers of the East India

Company, the gates of such institutions were opened to those Indians who could afford its cost and for those who matched the British in status. Thus, the rich, politically articulate, urban-living Brahmin elite could utilise this opportunity by sending their sons to British schools. These children later grew up to be officers and clerks in the Company that led to significant changes in their life-styles and ideology. Thus, from being Sanskritic, the new-found status was also one that came to be associated with English speaking, reading and working with the English people.

There is no dearth of sociological literature on the social transformation caused by education in British India (see, Srinivas : 1960; Patwardhan : 1973; Chitni : 1981; Bradford 1995). The fundamental idea mooted by the above works is the link that existed between formal education and the resultant economic gain in the form of employment or service under the government. They have argued that under the changed situation with the emerging industrialisation and consequent urbanisation processes, the traditional services of most of the non-Brahmin communities were eroded as being not relevant in the changed circumstances. Brahmins' access to English education was largely owing to their culturally and socially advantageous position by virtue of superior status in the social hierarchy. This was followed by access to salaried employment. Gradually, the educated Indians came to be aware of their subjugation to the aliens. The seeds of ideas of freedom and democracy were sown in the minds of these young and educated Indians who participated in the movement for the country's independence.

These ideas affected the fringe of Hindu social structure in the beginning and gradually penetrated the system as a whole engulfing caste in all its dimensions. Thus, the so-called middle and lower castes also came under its spell, though gradually. However the *modus operandi* of this process of caste mobilisation underwent transformation due to modernisation but the change varied between the upper castes and the middle castes and between them and the lower castes.

The Brahmins came to be looked upon as the models to all the castes, which were below them in the traditional caste hierarchy, in which each caste group followed a procedure where it acted as a model to castes lower to itself, while aspiring to achieve the status of the caste above itself. While this process was aptly labelled as 'Sanskritisation' by Srinivas (1956 b), a combination of this and the process of Westernisation characterised the efforts of the non-Brahmins in their mobility aspirations. Besides the cultural practices like food habits, religiosity, language etc., even aspects of occupational mobility were impacted by Westernisation. Thus, the striking development in the years following independence was the combination of the two polaric processes by a number of caste groups for purposes of social mobility.

Education as a means of Mobilisation

While it was hoped that the twin processes of Sanskritisation and Westernisation would lead to an enhanced socio-ritual status to the aspiring caste group, it was doubted whether this would suffice to enable the concerned caste community to achieve the desired goal? It came to be feared that mere changes in the external appearances like dress or behaviour pattern or in the name and type of God/Goddess that is worshipped, or change in the name of one's caste - would not result in any drastic transformation in the public image of a caste group. It was realised that change in social status is, necessarily, a result of changed economic status. Mere earning a higher quantum of money would not fetch a social status when the society attached social value to the type of one's work. Improved economic conditions caused by better earnings but with the same occupations (often stigmatised and impure) would not succeed in enhanced social status. Stigma traditionally attached to occupations professed by ex-untouchables, for example, has not vanished with changes in occupational changes (Parvathamma : 1976; 1989; Gayathridevi : 1989; 2003).

It is in this context, that, education came to occupy a place of centrality in the mobilisational aspirations of especially the backward classes. It certainly is an important dimension of social mobility characterising them. Therefore, the system of English education introduced by the British is held by social scientists as a promoter of social change as it facilitated occupational mobility in a closed system where work was ascribed, fixed and hierarchised. Access to government service that formal education was expected to train an individual was the chief attraction such career possessed for the members of the so-called middle and lower castes in the hierarchy. Irrespective of whether for group or individual mobility, the system of education introduced by the British in Princely Mysore initiated a process of mobilisation amongst an array of aspiring caste groups.

Thus, we find that education during the British times paved the way for two different streams of mobilisation: the idea of spreading education in order to boost the spirit of patriotism was mooted by a group of national leaders among whom Brahmins were a majority (Desai : 1966), the idea of securing higher educational standards as a token of their equality with Brahmins was popularised by a group of non-Brahmin leaders of the BCM. It was the latter move that culminated in the wider establishment of 'private education' in the country.

Education and the Backward Classes Movement

It is for the various seasons that the BCM gave primacy to education (as a 'lever of social change') in the movement for social equality. This movement launched by the backward classes in different states, like, Bihar, Maharashtra, Tamil Nadu and Karnataka, was chiefly characterised by the protest against the Brahminical supremacy, particularly in matters of education and government employment. As a remedy to the Brahmin oligarchy, the leaders of the movement demanded representation in educational institutions and in government service. Emphasis was placed upon government service and the former was only a means to achieve that end.

Emergence and Role of Private Educational Institutions in Karnataka

The idea of starting private schools and colleges came into vogue in Karnataka (even in India) roughly around the early part of the 20th century. While there may be variations in the years of establishment of private educational institutions in different parts of the country, the above argument is nonetheless applicable everywhere. In the beginning these institutions or the educational trusts that sponsored them even proposed that it was a move to bring about equity in resources that all the members of a caste could benefit from. However, as we shall see in the chapter, the institutions have moved quite away from their original ideals, a tendency accentuated by the prevailing socio-political trends characterising education as a political subject. Thus, today there is more complexity and heterogeneity in the system than before.

It is in the case of Karnataka that the above factor has been very much true. Education has emerged as an important competitor to the government-sponsored schools and colleges. Furthermore, it has come to wield considerable influence over the social and political dimensions of the educational scene in the state. There is no doubt that education has a serious role and responsibility in carving the economic development of any society. But the fact that private education in Karnataka, since the beginning, is in the hands of a few dominant caste groups, has made it a matter of greater social significance. The social and politically advantageous position that these castes enjoyed, over the years, by virtue of their traditional control over resources has facilitated their hold over professional education. What came to be the effort by the dominant castes to gain access to socio-political power in the state, by using education as a lever, has come to be adapted by the entire system, in course of time making the whole situation complex and not possible to be viewed from only caste-based perspectives.

What follows is a detailed analysis of educational societies started and managed by certain caste groups in Karnataka. In some areas of the state, wherever non-Hindu organisations were playing significant roles in such mobilisation, even they have been included in the sample. Considering the popularity of professional education in the current scenario of mobility in the state/country, the study covered only a select list of educational societies. With the ever increasing commercial value of education, that too higher education, professional education presents more complexities. It has become the centre of political controversy on the one hand, and on the other, has succeeded in making the state the 'IT Hub' or hightech state in the last 2 decades or so. Despite their high cost, professional courses like engineering and medicine, in particular, have become immensely popular across the country and many SAARC nations, pulling students from there to Karnataka. The fact that a large number of these colleges offering these courses are under private management has made the issue significant as well as complex. The Common Entrance Test (CET), which is in vogue since nearly 2 decades, has led to a decline in unequal access to these institutions by many students, and has upheld 'merit' as the only factor to seek admissions. Yet, the private colleges have continued with their system of charging heavy capitation fees or donations to admit students in their institutions.

An important outcome of this process is the rising value of the institutions offering such courses owing to the economic value attached to these professional courses. The educational trusts of such caste groups, which have started them have also likewise become popular and rich—both. This has obviously led to a keen competition among the so-called middle and lower castes to emulate the former in a bid to mobilise their own status upwards. The result has been a keen fight and competition for establishing such educational institutions that would offer engineering, medical, management and such other courses, by the galaxy of caste groups in Karnataka. What need to be captured are the social and political circumstances that have paved the way for such a demand. The various aspects of caste mobilisation that education as a variable of social mobilisation has stirred up in the state needs to be looked into for drawing conclusions about the role of caste in this whole, complex process.

This chapter presents the results of the study of almost all such first generation educational trusts and the professional colleges that were started in Karnataka, to obtain insights about the process of caste mobilisation using education as a strategy, for development.

The Beginning

Karnataka ranks first in the whole of India in its number and history of private professional colleges. Such a status and the so-called proliferation of institutions has not come about in a shorter period of time, but is a long process covering two centuries, viz., the 19th and 20th. While the private educational institutions or at least student hostels were initiated during the last part of the 19th and the first half of the 20th centuries, professional education made its appearance in a big way only in the 1980s. As noted already, the emphasis placed upon technical and medical education is an indication of the growing complexity and market value of education in the present society. But the starting of private educational institutions was, definitely, a move in the direction of asserting their rights for equality by the members of what are known as the backward classes. Although the movement by the BCs was not uniform across the regions within the state, there nevertheless was a concerted effort to promote a broad-based one inspired by the one that occurred in Princely Mysore.

Regional Disparities in Education and Caste Mobilisation

Discrepancies are evident in the nature and effects of the BCM or Non-Brahmin Movement (NBM) across different regions of the state. Of the two regions in the north, viz., the Bombay-Karnatak (BK) and the Hyderabad-Karnatak (HK) areas[3], the former presented greater traces and tendencies of a BCM than the latter. The social composition of the two areas is responsible for this. It had encouraged or deterred the people from participation in such mobilisational activities. The Bombay Karnatak area was administered by the Bombay Presidency where a general sprinkling of non-Brahmin officials participated in the administrative work provided by the non-Brahmin leaders of the area, with an edge over their counterparts in the HK area that was under the Nizam of Hyderabad. The non-Brahmins (i.e., chiefly the Marathas of the BK area) were vehement in their protest against Brahminical supremacy, a fever that caught on the people in the BK area soon.[4]

The HK area, being devoid of any such influence, included the districts of Gulbarga, Bidar and Raichur.[5] It is argued that the communal attitude of the rulers deterred the development of Kannada language and Hindu culture; that Urdu was imposed on educational institutions where Hindus were students, since Kannada schools were totally non-existent[6] at least till the year 1919 (Patil : 1979). In the light of these circumstances, it should be assumed that the occurrence of any sort of protest within the Hindu-fold was a lesser possibility when the danger was greater from the alien's (Muslim's) rule. While the people of BK area and the remaining parts faced the threat of the British, the people of the HK region were doubly disadvantaged. Thus, despite the presence of Lingayats in both areas, protest against the so-called Brahminical supremacy was higher in the BK area, as for those in the HK region, the challenge of Islamic domination was greater. Moreover, there was no support from the backward class counterparts in the state of Andhra Pradesh, since its non-Brahmin leaders joined hands with those from Madras in launching a BCM (Irshick 1969). On the whole, the HK area remained without much noticeable educational development at least till independence and later till its merger with larger Mysore State in 1956, to dream anything like establishing private educational institutions.[7] This excludes the work by Veerasaiva Viraktha Mutts and other private bodies, which had started few schools and community hostels earlier than 1956.

This leaves us with the BK area, the Old (Princely) Mysore and those parts under rule by the Madras Presidency. Of these, it is found that the people of South Kanara and Coorg districts[8] generally migrated to Madras[9] to seek higher education, as the areas came under the jurisdiction of the Madras Presidency. The two dominant communities of the state, viz., the Lingayats and the Vokkaligas were also not present in large numbers as elsewhere in the state. However, between the two, i.e., the BK area and the Princely Mysore, attempts to open private educational institutions were first made by the former. "The Lingayats constituted the bulk of the population in the 4 districts of the area and they started many educational institutions to popularise education among the Lingayats" (Report of the KBCC : 1975). The BCM chartered demands for both reservations of seats in educational institutions and in employment, as it held education as the chief criterion of social mobility (Manor :1977 and Dushkin : 1974). Urban centres were chosen in both the regions to locate these institutions, viz., Dharwar & Belgaum cities (BK area) and Mysore & Bangalore (Princely Mysore). The first educational societies of the respective regions came to be established in these cities. Since the societies aimed at popularising education among the masses, hostels were started for poor students as an initial effort.

The BCM in the BK area was led by veteran freedom fighters like Sri.Hardekar Manjappa, Sri F. H. Kattimani etc., who were also the champions of the NBM. The presence of a large percentage of Marathas[10] in the population of districts of the BK area was a deterrent in popularising the BCM of Princely Mysore in the BK area.[11] In their caste structure, the two regions are different with the Lingayats being the commonality in both regions. The Marathas and the Vokkaligas are the other dominant community in the BK and PM regions respectively. Otherwise, the content and impact of the movement was similar in the two regions. The lead taken by the BK area in initiating private educational institutions was the importance that education had already received in the Bombay state.

Yet, one could ask, as to why Old Mysore lagged behind the BK area in establishing private educational institutions? Why did it, with its strong sectarian force with the presence of both the dominant castes (of Lingayats and the Vokkaligas) delayed in materialising the dream of starting private institutions for heralding education for the BCs? What drawback or constraints prevented them from doing so and forced them to rest content with the starting of a few students' hostels for the respective communities?

It is not that the leaders of BCM in Old Mysore failed to receive any external assistance to support their fight for private education. In one way, they were in a more advantageous position than their counterparts in the Bombay-Karnatak and the Hyderabad-Karnatak areas. The most valuable and benevolent benefit to them came from the Princely Government itself, which had appointed, as early as in 1916 itself, a backward classes commission by the then Maharaja, Sri Krishnaraja Wodeyar Bahadur-IV. His initiative had already been preceded with a munificent grant in the form of a site in Bangalore to the Vokkaligara Sangha, the caste association of the Vokkaligas.

The Veerasaiva Educational Institutions and the Role of Mutts

The Lingayats of the BK area were not deprived of such support as received by their counterparts in old Mysore in their attempts to herald higher education among the backward communities. What is lacking was any link between the two areas, at least till the formation of their caste association in the year 1904. The administrative and political set up in which the two regions had to survive did not leave much scope for unification of activities. While the movement had similar goals, the resources to achieve them were different at least in the beginning.

Prior to the starting of private educational institutions, particularly professional ones, like law colleges, the cities like (Bombay now called as Mumbai), Poona and Madras were the only resort for pupils from the BK and HK areas as well as PM to seek higher education. Thus, those students who went to either Bombay or Madras came under the influence of the BCM in these places. The cue was taken from well known leaders of the freedom movement and those who had already established such institutions there, like the Deccan Education Society at Poona.[13]

But the real force behind the move to open private educational institutions by the Lingayats was the benevolent donation made by the Lingayat petty rulers ('Desais' as they were known in North Karnataka) and the religious mutts there. This complimented the process of formation of caste associations along with private educational trusts - both of which are crucial to mobilisation. Thus, in both spheres, we find the lead taken by the Lingayaths.

Veerasaivism as a Social Reform Movement

The movement for social equality heralded by Basaveswara during the 12th century in the northern parts of present state of Karnataka was basically a form of protest and reform in Hindu society. The details of its historical development are too elaborate to be dealt with here. After Basava, Veerasaivism developed into a sect with autonomy and complexity. As a rebel sect against Brahminism, it succeeded in providing an alternative religious system to many middle and low castes of the hierarchy[13], by opening its doors for them for conversion.

The presence of religious mutts as centres of Veerasaiva philosophy engaged in spreading and institutionalising their sectarian interests that really strengthened the spread of Veerasaivism. Possessed with a strong literary base, in the form of Vachanas, in simple Kannada and with a general emphasis on education - these have led to importance placed by the mutts on opening of schools and colleges for the community.

The mutts' educational activities in the initial years mainly centred on providing food and shelter to poor students drawn from rural areas. They enjoyed royal patronage under kings and petty rulers, more prevalent in north Karnataka. In some cases, the mutt also enjoyed landed property that further enabled its reform work for the poor.

The mutts of Veerasaivas are numerically so preponderant that it is difficult to provide an accurate account of them. They are also complex in nature. Except the district of Dakshina Kannada, almost all other districts have one or two such mutts. It is north Karnataka that has the largest number of and some of the oldest religious mutts of the Veerasaivas. They vary in the economic resources at their disposal, year of origin and activities. But most of them have been preaching the philosophy of philanthropy, where every Lingayat man or woman is supposed to be contributing to the mutt from one's earnings. Known by the name 'Dasoha', this practice is found in most mutts (Sri Sharanabasavappa Appa, Gulbarga).

The contributions made by the devotees are used to provide free boarding and lodging to the poor students. Thus, each mutt has come to be attached with a 'Prasada Nilaya' (dining home) which caters to the needs of the visitors and devotees of the mutt (discussions with Swamijis of the Muruga Mutt, Dharwar and Moorusaavira Mutt, Hubli). This also helped in strengthening the religious base of the community (Prof. S. S. Wodeyar, Ex-Vice Chancellor, Karnatak University, Dharwar). This Dasoha cult in a way laid the foundation for the establishment of private educational system of Veerasaiva mutts in north Karnataka. The real beginning was made with the starting of the 'Sivayogi Mandir' in 1909 near Badami in Dharwar district. The Mandir was established due to the chief efforts of 'Hanagal Kumaraswa-migalu' who was the founder of the Akhila Bharatha Veerasaiva Mahasabha, the caste association of the Veerasaivas. A band of dedicated Lingayat leaders were also involved in this work.[14] The Shivayogi Mandir was endowed with the duty of giving religious training to the Swamijis of Veerasaiva mutts (R. C. Hiremath, ex-Vice-Chancellor, Karnatak University, Dharwar).

The situation of students from poor Veerasaiva households was pathetic as there were no colleges in north Karnataka at that time. The aspirants had to go to either to Poona or Bombay, but it was not affordable by all, rendering poor boys incapable of pursuing college education.

Further, there was not a single master degree holder from the community at that time. Therefore, to encourage the students to do their master's course, a prize of Rs.100, and Rs. 200 was instituted by the leaders of the community to act as an incentive for students to join postgraduate courses. This was the situation in 1910 in north Karnataka and the leaders were a cross-section of community elders and heads of religious mutts. Known as the 'Victoria Jubilee Prize', it had governmental link and patronage with the Collector also as one of the trustees.[15] These efforts had been preceded by the establishment of the "Veerasaiva Vidhyabhivrudhdhi Samsthe" at Dharwar in the year 1883.

Much earlier, in 1878, Sri Vaaradha Mallappa (Shivanand : 1977) started a Sanskrit school at Sholapur. Only two schools existed in the whole of Karnataka at that time. They were the "Sakkari Karadeppa's Sanskrit School" at Bellary and in the Maharashtra border was the school founded by Varada Mallappa. Both specialised in imparting Sanskritic education to Veerasaiva boys, especially in training the prospective religious gurus (heads) of Lingayat mutts. A number of present Lingayat Swamijis, Poets and Pandits received their education there.

Thus began the efforts of Veerasaiva leaders to popularise education – both English and Sanskritic – among their caste brethren. At least till 1910, there appears to have been no sign of starting private schools by them, though one cannot deny the idea being discussed often among leadership circles (Sri Sharanabasappa Appa). Lack of educated men belonging to the community to take leadership roles and the existence of monetary problems were the reasons that deterred the starting of private institutions at that time (Souvenir of the Society : 1969). Rich and powerful Lingayat leaders like Sri Varada Mallappa, Aratal Rudra Gowda, Rao Bahadur and others as leaders of backward classes were the chief workers behind such move to open private educational institutions in this region.

It was due to the efforts of all such committed leaders that the seeds of private education were sown in north Karnataka. The first step in this direction was taken by Vaarada Mallappa by opening the "Veerasaiva Ashram" at Bombay around 1915. The Ashram was used to provide shelter to 'poor and clever' Lingayat boys who went for higher studies to Bombay. It was formed on the lines of similar hostels at Bombay representing various other caste groups.

I. PRIVATE EDUCATIONAL INSTITUTIONS OF THE PRE-INDEPENDENCE PERIOD

(A) Bombay-Karnatak Area

1. The Bijapur Liberal District Education Association (BLDEA)

Of all the existing private educational institutions of north Karnataka, the Bijapur Liberal District Education Association (BLDEA) founded at Bijapur in 1910 is the oldest. However, the Karnataka Liberal Education Society (KLES) founded in the year 1916 is a more developed and leading institution than the former. A few leaders of the Kannada and the BCMs laid the foundation for private education, when they founded the "Bijapur Lingayat District Education Association" at Bijapur.

The establishment of both the BLDEA and the KLES could be attributed to a combination of Kannada movement and BCM in the BK region, during the latter half of the 19th century as well as in the early years of the 20th century. It appears that the Kannada movement (in a Marathi-dominant area) was led and activated by a group of non-Brahmin leaders of the area (invariably Lingayats who were the majority of non-Brahmins) as the Brahmins generally spoke Marathi as their mother tongue.

Peshwa rule influenced the region much more than the one by the Muslim rulers. Maratha Brahmins constituted the culturally dominant group (Interview with Sri Kanakanady, a Lingayat leader from KLE Society). It could be inferred that the non-Brahmin movement inspired the leaders of the Kannada movement, like F. G. Halakatti and others, to think on the lines of opening private schools to facilitate the Kannadigas of the region to study in their mother tongue. The Kannada movement first aimed at introducing Kannada as a language in the school curriculum and at encouraging the study of Kannada when Maratha schools were in the majority.

To this linguistic issue was added the caste issue when the non-Brahmin movement echoed itself in this region. The movement championed the cause of the advancement of the backward classes, keeping education as the primary criterion of progress or mobilisation. Inspired by the prospects of English education with respect to jobs and social status (as it was supposed to have occurred in the case of the Brahmins), the leaders of the BCM in this region also tried to herald the ideals of education among their fellow caste people. As a result of the efforts of a few persons, prominent among whom were F. G. Halakatti, a freedom fighter and literary figure of the early 20th century, the BLDEA was established in the year 1910 at Bijapur. It was originally started with a view to giving scholarships to Lingayat students and only later a school was founded.

The real growth of the BLDEA began in the post-independence period. Till 1950, the Association seems to have made tardy progress, acting just as an institution for primary education. It was in 1950, when the association obtained a munificent grant of a landed property consisting of 54 acres from a rich and philanthropist Lingayat widow, Smt. Bangaramma Sajjan, that it was able to expand its institutions. The campus of the educational institutions run by the BLDEA was shifted to this new site in Bijapur in 1957 (Souvenir of the Golden Jubilee Celebrations of the BLDEA : 1969).

Thus the establishment of the BLDEA could be traced to the combination of the NBM and linguistic movements in the state. Its founder F. G. Halakatti even founded the Siddeshwar Co-operative Society and the Siddeshwar Bank, reportedly as anti-Brahmin associations (Kabbin, ex-principal, BLDEA's Arts College, Bijapur). Added to this was the idea to counter Maratha dominance of Peshwa rule. Halakatti started Kannada schools, the first of their kind in the region. He even organised a backward classes' conference and published a paper heralding the goals of the NBM.[16]

The educational institutions started by the BLDEA expanded only in the post-independence period.

2. *The Karnatak Liberal Education Society*

The establishment of the 'Veerasaiva Vidyabhivrudhdhi Samsthe' in 1883 at Dharwar, the 'Shivayoga Mandir' in 1909 and the 'Veerasaiva Ashram' in Dharwar and the 'BLDEA' in 1910 in Bijapur - all contributed towards kindling the educational aspirations of many young Lingayats. Four Lingayat students[17] of the first batch passed their post-graduate course from the Furguson College, Poona in 1916. "They were inspired by the ideals of self-sacrifice, service and dedication to the cause of spreading education in the then educationally backward northern Karnatak of Bombay state". They received education at places where idealists like Chiplunkar, Ranade, Agarkar and Tilak had laid solid foundation for similar work by starting the "Deccan Education Society" (Souvenir of the Golden Jubilee of the KLES : 1969 : 2).

The first four graduates also joined hands with local leaders like P. R. Chikkodi, Rao Bahadur R. C. Artal, V. A. Angol and

V. G. Naik Desai of Chachadi, H. P. Kattimani etc., in starting an Anglo-vernacular school, later on known as the G. A. High School in Belgaum. The year 1916 was thus not only a landmark in the history of educational development of north Karnataka but also in other parts of India, when it saw the birth of the Mysore, Banares and SNDT Universities (Souvenir of the KLES : 1969 : 1). "These leaders voluntarily and happily embraced a life of hardship and poverty with a view to educating their illiterate and backward brethren. All of them could have very easily secured well-paid government jobs; but they willingly chose the hard and lonely path of struggle against great and innumerable odds. The entire Karnataka is grateful to them for having sown the seeds of private enterprise in the field of education in spite of insurmountable difficulties" (*ibid.*).

The life members of the foundation started the high school in 1916 but the educational society came into being on July 20, 1917. The expansion of the KLES with many educational institutions was facilitated by the property granted by Raja Lingaraj Sirdesai of Sirsangi.[18] The huge sums of money and other assets owned by the Raja prompted some of the Veerasaiva leaders of the times to request him to donate them for building educational institutions under the KLES and promote education among Lingayats in the region. The Desai, who was a known philanthropist donated his entire property in the form of Dana Patra (Letter of Donation) to be made as a trust, used and maintained for the said purpose. Thus, the Sirsangi Trust was formed (Somannavar, Secretary of the KLES, Belgaum).

Having started thus, the educational society took up the cause of education among Veerasaivas with much zeal and enthusiasm. It was this society that was responsible for sending Dr.D C Pavate and Dr. S C Nandimath, who became eminent educationists and scholars in later years, to England for higher studies. As a result, poor and talented Lingayat boys were encouraged to pursue higher education, but with the condition (as a legal bond) that they would serve the institution (KLES) after they returned from abroad.

To begin with, the KLES started a students' hostel that was a boarding home. This was because, by then, higher education had achieved considerable attraction as a passport for better employment. With Dharwar becoming the district headquarters, the people demanded a college there. Philanthropists like Artal Rudra Gowda collected money from "people from all communities" and Rudra Gowda contributed Rs. one lakh out of the total Rs. 2 lakhs collected to start the Karnataka Arts College in 1926.

In Belgaum, the KLE Society's Gilaganchi Artal High School[19] was not functioning well. The establishment of the Karnataka Arts College was like that of the Deccan College at Poona. It compensated for the absence of any college in the whole of North Karnataka region. Till its establishment in 1926, there was no college in the districts of Belgaum, Dharwar, Bijapur and North Kanara.

Therefore, in 1930, the life members of the KLES thought of starting a college at Belgaum. Dr. Pavate who had just then returned from England after a brilliant academic career was chosen as the first Principal of the college. In fact, Pavate had been offered the Professor's post at the prestigious Banares Hindu University at Varanasi[20] by no less a person than its vice-chancellor, Pandit Madan Mohan Malaviya. Pavate refused the offer and decided to abide by his promise to the Sirsangi Trust that had sponsored his trip to England for higher studies and that he would serve the institution after having received from it financial and moral support to pursue higher education. Later, the Bombay University did not grant permission for the starting of the college till 1933 by which time Pavate had joined government service.

Dr. Nandimath who came back from abroad six months later was also offered an important post. It was that of the Deputy Director General of Research in Delhi. This offer was made even while he was in England. But he had decided to return to India and to consult the Sirsangi trust authorities about his career. At that time, Mr. Vakil was the Inspector General for Schools for the southern division. Nandimath met Vakil who complained that the schools managed by the KLES were in a bad condition and just because of his (Vakil's) concern for education of non-Brahmins (he was a non-Brahmin himself) that he had protected them from being taken over by the government. This moved Dr.Nandimath who henceforth decided to devote the fruits of his education and training abroad to the cause of Lingayat education. He took the school under his control and saw to it that it received affiliation. He also became a life member of the KLES in the year 1931 (A. B. Kotrasetti, President of the KLES and Somannavar, Secretary and other office bearers of the KLES : 1983).

All this also kindled the interests of the members of the society to start a college at Belgaum. The atmosphere was 'favourable' to do so with the appointment of Sir Siddappa Kambli[21] as the first Lingayat Minister in the Government of Bombay. The non-Brahmin movement was also active then. Despite staunch opposition, the movement spread to Dharwar also. As the Education Minister in the Bombay Presidency, Kambli was very sympathetic to the progress of his community (the Lingayats). People like Mahajan and Paranjape, who were able administrators and workers of the Deccan Education Society, assisted him in this. Kambli convinced Mahajan about Lingayat's efficiency in work and appointed more and more of them as lecturers in the Presidency's colleges.

The above account of the history of the origin of private educational institutions in north Karnataka shows how the

Lingayats, even as a dominant caste, had to encounter various obstacles to start their own institutions. Two factors have emerged from this: one was the difficulty that organisations like KLE.S had to face in terms of strong opposition from the Brahmins. The Lingayats alleged that the Brahmins complained to the British administration about a freedom movement being generated by them by starting educational institutions. The Deputy Commissioner inspected the school, upon orders from the British government. To his surprise, he found that all the students were dressed in their own traditional styles with red or blue turban and blue or brown coats with silk or cotton dhotis. When he entered the classroom, he was greeted with the traditional head-dress (not with the Khadi-Gandhi-caps). All students were in this dress and there was no trace of Khaddar or Khadi. The DC was surprised and left without a comment. But in reality this was just a drama planned by Sardar Veeranna Goud and V.V. Patil.[22]

The second difficulty was the problem created by the British in giving recognition to the KLES and its affiliation to the Bombay University. The KLES applied for starting a college at Belgaum with affiliation from this University. The latter, in turn, appointed an enquiry committee consisting of people from the Deccan Education Society. The proposal was finally approved since one of the seven founding members was a student of one of the members of the committee. But when the proposal was put for voting, it did not succeed in winning the required support. Dr. Pavate, who was at that time shown as the Principal Designate, had to join the Banares Hindu University since the college was not sanctioned even after three years.

After a year, permission was again sought (on December 31, 1932) when the same story of refusal was repeated. When it was put to vote, it turned out again to be equal. "But luckily the vice-chancellor, Sri Chandravarkar cast his vote in the Society's favour[23] (Souvenir of the KLE Society : 1969 : 5). Permission was then granted to the opening of the college and on September 29, 1933, the college was started. It was named after the late Lingappa Jayappa Sirdesai of Sirsangi and Navalgund, in recognition or memory of his contribution to the educational progress of the community. The inauguration of the 'Lingaraj College' was performed by Sir Fredrick Sykes, the then Governor of Bombay (Archives of the Lingaraj College, Belgaum).

The first college under the auspices of the first private educational society of North Karnataka contained staff members who were highly qualified, but very lowly paid. But they were taken from different communities and caste groups. In other words, the imposition of the caste factor restricted itself only to the intake of students in the hostels run by the society. But in the selection of both the students and staff, the pattern was more secular than sectarian.[24] This was perhaps inevitable in view of the non-availability of educated, qualified staff within the community.

With the formation of the Karnatak University in the year 1950, the KLES expanded its educational activities much more broadly. The University itself owed its coming into existence to a movement in Poona led by leaders like Sir Siddappa Kambli and others. Kambli demanded that since Sindh, Maharashtra, Karnatak, Gujarat and Kutch were all separate regions, separate universities must be given to them. A resolution to this effect was pursued in the Bombay Legislative Assembly in 1932 and the Karnatak University was started in 1950. Subsequently, we find not only the KLES adding many new institutions to its fold, but even the emergence of a few other private educational societies in the state. The stability achieved in course of time by the KLES, in the form of expansion of its colleges and the introduction of the system of capitation fees, no doubt, facilitated the growth of the society. But it also led gradually to a keen intra-group competition amongst the members for a share in the total gains. As early as in 1941, when the society had not yet established its professional college at Gadag, we find evidence of intra-community agitation for power within the leadership circles of the KLES. It is to be noted here that more than in the south, northern Karnataka presents a highly diverse Lingayat community with many sub subcastes. These divisions have arisen out of the differences in the occupations they pursue. Also these differences naturally surface when the community is in a majority as in North Karnataka. The feelings of jealousy and competition surfacing the behaviour of the different Veerasaiva subcastes, though not manifest, may be traced to the fact that these caste groups have hailed from different Hindu lower and middle castes. The socio-ritual ranking enjoyed by them earlier to their conversion to Veerasaivism continued even after, thereby leading to internal hierarchy within the Lingayat community.

Likewise, factions between Sri M.R. Sakhare, the General Secretary of the Society, who was a Devanga (weaving caste) Lingayat and Dr. S.C. Nandimath, an Aradhya or Jangama Lingayat (priestly class) led to a series of clashes within the society culminating in changing the Constitution of the society. The matter was even taken to the Bombay High Court in 1943. Sakhare won the case and continued his office of the Secretaryship of the Society. Infuriated by the Court's decision, Dr. Nandimath resigned from the life membership of the Society and joined the Basaveswara College at Bagalkot (Souvenir of the KLES : 1969).

The above incidence led to the changing of the Constitution of the KLES. The administration of the Society came to be vested in the Board of Management in which adequate provision for representation of all classes of members was made. With the coming into effect of the new Constitution, "a new chapter started in the history of the Society" (Souvenir : 1969 : 7). Instead of landlords, Dewans, retired Collectors and similar others, educated people came forward to become its members and to occupy important seats in the society. This account shed light on the existence of intra-caste tensions and conflicts ever since the first private educational society of Karnataka was established and even before they started professional colleges.

The period from 1910 to 1920 was characterised by the rise of a movement for education in north Karnataka. This seems to be also an aspect of caste mobilisation by the Lingayats, who are the dominant caste of the region. We find the leading six out of the twelve educational societies founded by the Lingayats, coming into existence during this decade. They were:

(1) The Bijapur Lingayat District Education Association (1910),
(2) The Karnatak Liberal Education Society (1916),
(3) Shri Basaveswar Vidya Vardhak Sangha (1906),
(4) The Veerasaiva Vidyavardhak Sangha (1918),
(5) Sri Sharana Basaveswara Vidya Vardhak Sangha (1918), and
(6) Sri Siddaganga Educational Trust (1917).

While the first five were established in different towns of the Bombay Karnatak and Hyderabad Karnatak regions, viz., at Bijapur, Belgaum, Bagalkot and Bellary respectively, the Siddaganga Educational Trust was founded at Tumkur, which was under the Princely government of Mysore.

3. *Shri Basaveshwar Vidya Vardhak Sangha*

The oldest private educational trust founded not only in this region but also perhaps, in the whole of Karnataka was the Basaveshwar Vidya Vardhak Sangha (BVVS).[25] It was founded at Bagalkot, a taluk[26] in the Bijapur district, in 1906 by His

Holiness Shri Gurubasav Mahaswamiji of Bilur Mutt. "The establishment of this trust was a historical step taken in this area and its sole objective has been to spread education amongst the rural masses of north Karnataka."

As part of a historical step, the establishment of the trust had spreading of education among the rural masses as its sole objective. Priority was given to the starting of a "Sanskrit Patashala". Then, a free boarding home was started to enable poor and meritorious students to continue their education, with liberal grant of aid by a renowned merchant and philanthropist of Sholapur by name Appasaheb Varad, popularly addressed as Varada Mallappa. Along with this, a free library and reading room were also started.

By 1917, the Sangha was able to start its educational activities on a stable foundation. A first grade middle school was started in the year 1917 which was upgraded into a full-fledged high school in 1923. From then onwards, the Sangha has been extending its activities with generous donations of the public (S. S. Kuppasat, General Secretary, BVVS, Bagalkot : 1983).

By 1938, the Sangha started, realising the need for providing primary education to rural masses. 200 primary schools were opened in 200 villages of Bijapur district. A Teachers' Training College was added to the list in the year 1942 (Report of the BVVS : 1981 : 1).

The starting of the Sree Basaveswar Arts College in 1944 was a landmark in the history of the region. This was because till its establishment, there was only one Government college (Karnataka College at Dharwar) and only one private college (Lingaraj College in Belgaum) in the whole of North Karnataka or BK area. Students desirous of receiving higher education had to go to Dharwar, Belgaum in this region or to Kolhapur and Sangli in the erstwhile Bombay state. The college was also the first to be started at the taluka (block or below district) level in the Bombay Presidency. The late Shri B.C. Kher in 1946, who was then the Chief Minister of the erstwhile Bombay state made the inauguration of the degree classes in Arts subject. Late Shri V.V. Giri, the then Vice President of India inaugurated the addition of the Science College to the campus, in the year 1967. The college also came under the concerned support of the State government during this year headed by Sri S. Nijalingappa and a noted Lingayat of the region, Shri Veerendra Patil who was the PWD Minister then (Report of the BVVS : 1981 & S.G. Hubballi, Principal, Sree Basaveswar Arts College, Bagalkot : 1983).

(B) Madras Presidency Area

Veerasaiva Vidyavardhak Sangha

The fourth educational society to be established in the chain of institutions during the period 1910-1920 was the 'Veerasaiva Vidyavardhak Sangha' at Bellary in 1916. The initiative was taken this time by a Jagadguru (a senior religious head of a Mutt) of Ujjaini Peetha, who inspired the local Lingayat leaders to start a hostel and a school for the children of the community. The Sangha began its activities in this regard by starting a 'Sanskrit Patashala' with the intention of imparting training to heads of Lingayat religious institutions (mutts) on the lines of the Shivayoga Mandir at Dharwar. It was later on converted into a regular school admitting students from the Lingayat community. Since the institution did not generate sufficient financial returns, the organisers thought of other means of financing the educational institutions. A Kannada elementary school was started initially, the first of its kind in Bellary city which was a predominantly Telugu-speaking area. Sri Y. Mahabaleswarappa, President of the Bellary District Board, was instrumental in starting it with the mission to spread Kannada as the medium of instruction in all high schools of the district's headquarters.

This move came under severe opposition by the erstwhile Madras government, on grounds that it was a communal institution that should not be encouraged. By that time, the NBM was in full swing there. Maheswarappa could gather courage to question in turn as to how the Christian institutions had been permitted to do so. The main objection by the government was to the prefix of the books and name of the institutions as 'Veerasaiva', which was permitted to be continued after considerable debate with Mahabaleswarappa.[27]

(C) Old Mysore Area

Sree Siddaganga Mutt

Sree Siddaganga Mutt[28], another Lingayat educational trust, was established at Sree Siddaganga Kshetra (a religious shrine of Lingayats) near Tumkur in southern Karnataka in 1917.[29] It is not clear whether it was influenced by the starting of the KLE Society or the BLDEA referred to earlier, in launching its educational institutions.

But, the mutt and its educational institutions have gained enormous popularity over the years both in relation to their establishment as well as for their work. The rise and popularity of the mutt should be chiefly traced to the efforts of its head, the centenarian, Dr. Sree Sivakumara Swamigalu, "who is a great idealist, educationist and disciplinarian". The growth of the mutt is coincidental with his initiation into it in 1930. He has served the cause of education on secular grounds without restricting it to only students of Lingayat caste, in that part of the state and was awarded honorary doctorate by the Karnatak University way back in 1965 itself.

A large number of educational institutions ranging from pre-primary to graduate education were started under the Mutt to begin with. "Almost all these are located in the most interior parts of the state where higher education was otherwise a dream" (Swamiji of the Mutt). Its Sanskrit college was the biggest in the country started as a school in 1917 that grew to become a college in 1937. Subsequently, engineering and business administration courses followed as important institutions attracting students from far and wide.

Charity work of the mutt has surpassed its educational activities. Free boarding for poor students and devotees was started way back in the year 1909 by Sri Uddama Sivayogi Swamigalu. Its significance lied in it not following any caste rules for inter-dining and treating all students as equal. The mutt allowed even converts to Veerasaivism from various non-Brahmin communities to sit together with Lingayats for such communal dining.

(D) Hyderabad Karnataka Area

1. Sri Sharanabasaveshwar Vidya Vardhak Sangha

The Dasoha cult preached by Veerasaivism has been stressed by many as the main reason behind the charity activities followed by their educational institutions. The district of Gulbarga as part of the Nizam-ruled HK region has many shrines of importance to Lingayats. Sri Sharanabasaveshwar Peetha is one such popular Lingayat Dasoha mutt that attracts thousands of devotees everyday of the year, from not only Gulbarga, but from different parts of north and south Karnataka, Maharashtra and Andhra Pradesh. The Sharanabasaveshwar Vidya Vardhak Sangha (SBVVS) was established under the auspices of this mutt in the year 1918 at Gulbarga.

The SBVVS oriented itself more towards Dasoha culture by opening residential schools for poor Lingayat students. It did not attach much significance to the starting of educational institutions in the pre-independence era. A Kannada school was started by the late Poojya Sri Doddappa Appa (the former head of the mutt) in the year 1934 at Gulbarga. High schools in rural areas of the district followed this. This slow growth of private education initiative in HK area was a reflection of the general backwardness of the region itself that was for long ruled by Muslims (Bahmanis and then the Nizam). When Sri Doddappa Appa started the women's college known as 'Mahadevi Kanyashale', there is reported to have been severe protest from the Nizam. There was also a lot of opposition to Kannada being introduced in schools as the medium of instruction. Thus, the SBVVS, though started in 1918 itself, was busy with other welfare activities than starting educational institutions and had to wait till 1934 when such activities were started by it (M.B. Oni, Principal, SBVVS's College, Gulbarga).

The above discussion about the five educational institutions that represented the different regions in the state shows that their establishment during the decade 1910-1920 is indicative of their relation with the non-Brahmin movement then in vogue in the state. It also proves the place of education as an important variable in mobilisation. Secondly, such a move was the monopoly of the Lingayats who constituted the dominant caste of the state and invariably led the NBM too. Although their counterparts, the Vokkaligas a dominant caste in the south (of Karnataka) had formed their caste association as early as in 1906, there was no educational institution founded by them yet during this period. The main factor behind the success of or the lead taken by the Lingayats was the constant support and financial assistance given by their religious organisations known as the mutts that were lacking in the case of Vokkaligas then. When the NBM was at its peak in the state, influencing the government to go ahead with the appointment of a commission to look into and classify backwardness, all the five educational institutions discussed above took their birth supported by various religious mutts. In cases where the institutions came into existence due to the non-religious factors like the philanthropic grant by nobles and rulers, like in the case of the Lingaraj College of Belgaum, the initiative of Sirsangi Desai was supported by the Swamiji of Hanagal mutt.

In addition to the above forms of expression of mobilisation, the movement for Kannada in an environment of compulsion to learn alien languages like Marathi and Urdu led to starting of Kannada schools in both BK and HK areas. However, the institutions in the latter area were slow in their growth and expansion due to its backwardness.[30] Lingayats being the dominant community in these regions made it look like a caste-based movement.[31] Thus, the mutts and their Dasoha cult, the Kannada movement and the opening of schools and hostels by private trusts of Lingayats marked the BCM in this area during the early part of the 20th century. Dominance of Maratha Brahmins in education and official matters, and imposition of Marathi as medium of instruction in schools was what inspired the movement.

While these problems were common to both BK and HK areas, in the case of the latter, there was an additional problem. The so-called 'decay' of Hinduism in the face of Muslim rule gave way for the coming in of Arya Samaj during this time, and started its campaign for conversion of Hindus into its fold. There was the alleged attempt on another quarter too. Religious leaders like Swami Ramananda Theertha with an idea of reestablishing the fading Hinduism and protect it from Muslims, advised the Lingayats to adore the sacred thread (Janivar) in the place of their Shivadara (the wearing of Linga). At this juncture, two leaders of the region by name Udgir Sangramappa and Prabhuraoji Kamblivale had to carry out a fight to arrest such forced conversions. The head of the local mutt supported and guided them in this venture (Souvenir of the Shanthivardhak Educational Society : 1978)

Thus, here too, external factors like threats of imposition of Marathi and Urdu on the one hand and the domination of Maratha Brahmins and Muslims in general administration are supposed to have intensified and spread the BCM and expressed in the form of private educational institutions. Added also was the effort to 'save' Veerasaivism' from being suppressed by the Marathi-Brahmins.

2. *The Shanthivardhak Educational Society*

The beginning of this society in 1940, also striving to bring about educational advancement among the Lingayats in HK area, is thus attributed to the BCM. As noted already, the head of a leading mutt in Bidar district[32] was responsible for its genesis. It grew to be an important institution over the years, with headquarters originally at Kamalnagar (now in Andhra Pradesh). A number of schools, hostels and colleges were started in course of time. An engineering college was added in 1982. Subsequently, few other societies were also initiated under its umbrella. Some of them were (a) the Amareshwar Education Society at Aurad, (b) the Udgir Education Society, (c) the Karnataka Rashtreeya Education Society at Bidar founded in 1954 and managed by Sri R.V. Bidap, ex-Chairman of the Karnataka Public Service Commission and (d) Sri Veerabhadreshwar Education Society at Humnabad founded by Sri Basavaraj Patil (Discussion with Mastapur, advocate and President of the Society).

Notable is that despite their coming into existence under the same circumstances as those in the BK area, these institutions did not make steady progress. Their slow pace of work could be attributed to the economic and cultural constraints on the one hand and the political climate then prevailing in it as compared to the BK area.

While the above discussion has covered the three districts in the HK area, it excludes the district of Raichur in it. As a part of the HK area even at that time, Raichur did not lag behind other districts in joining the race in opening private educational institutions. However, its situation was not comparable with other districts in the quantum of the presence of private educational institutions. This was despite the presence of a considerable large number of Lingayats in the district besides many religious mutts acting as charitable institutions. On the contrary, it was a few local Brahmin leaders who founded the 'Taranath Educational Trust' to commemorate the constructive work done by Pandit Taranath, an educationist and social reformer, who was also associated with the upliftment of the backward classes in the region. The institution came to be managed by Lingayats in course of time is besides the point (D. Mariappa, retired principal, Veerasaiva College Bellary : 1983).

Non-Lingayat Educational Institutions in the Pre-independence Period

The above process of starting own educational institutions by the Lingayats led to a trend that set in motion similar efforts by other castes too. The Marathas of the BK area were one non-Lingayat group to do so quite early. Besides the institutions started by them, one by the Muslims, three by Brahmins and three new ones by the Lingayats were also started during the last two decades before independence. This raised the number founded by Lingayats alone to eight. Out of the total five institutions started by non-Lingayats, three were established at Belgaum. They consisted of two by Brahmins and one by Marathas. Obviously the KLES founded in 1916 at Belgaum had inspired these to come into existence.

(i) The Bombay-Karnatak Area

(a) The Karnatak Law Society

The earliest educational trust to be started out of the above five was the "Karnataka Law Society" (KLS) founded by a few 'nationalistic minded Brahmins' at Belgaum in 1939. It was, in fact, an offshoot of the Kannada movement in the BK area, especially in Belgaum. Earlier, the students from the region had to study at law colleges located in Poona, Bombay, Kolhapur or Madras as the state had no college of its own. This inspired a group of lawyers consisting of Sriyuths Kelkar, B.N. Datar (who later became a union minister), Yashwant Rao Lele, V.A. Majumdar, Belavi and others to promote legal studies locally. They had also in mind the idea of giving a Kannada orientation to the Marathi-dominated area. Hence they approached the local chieftain Raja Lakhamgoud Sirdesai of Wantmuri[33] who was an outstanding philanthropist of the area. The Raja was working as a judicial officer in the government but more a landlord than being a barrister. He was in the habit of making contributions to public cause, without any discrimination on the basis of caste or creed and had donated much of his property towards it. He readily obliged the leaders of the Kannada movement and granted enormous amounts of money towards the starting of private[34] educational institutions, of which the KLS was one (B.M. Gogte, the President of the KLS and also a leading industrialist/businessman of the area :1983).

The KLS started a law college at Belgaum with Sri Kelkar as its first Principal, who was an able administrator and eminent lawyer. The Society was his brainchild. Justice N.S. Lokur became its first President. As the first institution of its kind in the state, the Raja Lakhmgoud Law College heralded law education in that region besides catering to the need for law education in southern Karnataka. A number of leading legal practitioners of the present times, including the ex-Chief Justice of Karnataka and Kerala High Courts Justice V.S. Malimath were products of this great institution.

The KLS was initially affiliated to the Bombay University, despite the starting of the Karnatak University in 1950. It took 6 more years for it to be brought under the latter's jurisdiction. To the law college were added, in course of time, few more institutions like an Arts and Commerce[35] College. Its financial position continued to be very weak till 1960, after which donations came flowing to it. For example, in 1964, a grant of Rs.50 000 was made to the society by Sri B. M. Gogte, a Brahmin lawyer and an aristocrat businessman and industrialist of the area (Souvenir of the KLS : 1980). He served as its President for long and was responsible for obtaining sanction from the government to start an engineering college in the year 1979.

(b) South Konkan Education Society

Following the Raja, came another munificent grant, this time by a benevolent lady by name Rani Parvati Devi of Sawantwadi.[36] Another educational society came into existence in the year 1945, first at Bombay and later shifted to Belgaum in 1948. It was inspired by not the BCM but by the freedom movement and sponsored by Sri D.P. Thakur a freedom fighter, Sri A. B. Latte, ex-finance minister of Bombay, Sri Gangadhar Rao Deshpande, a national leader from Karnataka and many others. An industrialist from Bombay Sri Govindaram Seksaria contributed donation to be used for the said purpose, which was combined with the one made by the Rani. The SKES was started with the establishment of the Rani Parvatidevi College and Govindram Science Institute.

The establishment of the SKES connotes not just another

private educational trust in the state, but it reflected the emotions and socio-cultural backwardness of the people in these regions, in the form of a rift between Kannadigas and Marathas. There is no evidence to the motive behind its establishment. But there is no doubt that the step taken by the Lingayats inspired, out of at least sheer competition, many other dominant castes of the region, Marathas being the primary group in that context. Caste rivalry and linguistic hatred contributed to these. Thus, the KLES was able to prosper by opening professional colleges. The others in the race, like the SKES failed in catching with it immediately, but had to wait for long till the 1980s to do so. This was when the domination of Lingayats in state's political power structure came to be contested with the inclusion of many others in such berths by the then Chief Minister Sri Devraj Urs.

(c) Sanmati Shikshan Sahakari Samiti

Like the KLS & SKES, that were initially founded by the efforts of Brahmins, one more institution by name Sanmati Shikshan Sahakari Samithi (SSSS) was established at Shedpal in Athni taluk of Belgaum district in the year 1941. It aimed at promoting the educational interests of the rural students, inspired by the ideals of Mahadeva Govind Ranade, the well known freedom fighter. However, owning to problems like drought in Athani taluk, it had to be subsequently shifted to Belgaum in the year 1973 (B.M. Hurakadli, Principal of the Commerce College : 1983).

(d) Janatha Shikshana Samithi

There was yet another serious move to meet the educational needs of Kannadigas as against the Marathas in this region, which was fulfilled by the establishment of the Janatha Shikshana

Samithi (JSS) at Dharwar. It was first called as the 'Karnataka Education Board' (KEB) by a few highly educated freedom fighters of the Bombay-Karnatak area belonging to the Brahmin community, during the 1940s. By 1944-45, it stood the test of time compared to other similar institutions. This was one institution founded by the minority Brahmin caste that had stood the test of time and the dominant caste groups (Lingayats) of north Karnataka.

But the inspiration to start it came actually from one such domination – that of Marathas over the Kannadigas. In contrast, it was the initiative of the Brahmins to counter the increasing access gained by the non-Brahmins to higher education which culminated in the efforts of a freedom fighter, social worker and also the Chairman of the Bombay Legislative Council, Sri Hukerikar Ram Rao to start this institution. The high school that the KEB started were first located at Dharwar in the Vidyaranya High School there. Known by the name Rashtreeya Vidyalaya, it was founded by Rajakarya Prasaktha Sri N.S. Gubbi, the late Sri Krishna Rao Kabbur and others. Later in 1947, the whole campus was shifted to Vidyagiri, a small hillock on the outskirts of Dharwar, where the engineering and other colleges came to be located (Souvenir of the Sangha). Beginning with the Banashankari Arts College (first located in a rented building in Dharwar City as an intermediate college) started in the year 1944, the number of institutions went on increasing. In 1952, the management of the college was handed over to Shri R. S. Hukerikar, "a pioneer freedom fighter and constructive worker" of the times. The college came subsequently under the principalship of such eminent academicians like Prof. B.M. Srikantia as its first Principal. "Against all odds and undaunted by difficulties", Hukerikar added a Law College in 1955, an Engineering diploma institute in 1956 and a few vocational training centres to the list of educational institutions of the JSS, "all established on the lovely campus of Vidyagiri"[37] (Souvenir of JSS Banashankari Arts College : 1969-70 : 2).

Once Hukerikar retired, the Samithi came under heavy economic pressures and crisis. The situation reached a climax with the taking over of the Samithi by an educational trust belonging to Sri D. Veerendra Hegde, the Dharmadhikari of Dharmasthala[38] in the year 1973. Sri Hegde is the Chairman of the trust and at the time of this study its President was the Swamiji of Pejavar Mutt Sri Visveshatheertha Sripadangalu at Udupi (N. Vajra Kumar, Principal of the Engineering College and Secretary of the trust : 1983).

(ii) The Hyderabad Karnatak Area

Nutan Vidyalaya Society

The Nutan Vidyalaya Society was founded by the late Sri Vittal Rao Deulgaonkar, a freedom fighter of Gulbarga, with a view "to imparting education to the children in their own mother tongue and instilling national spirit and patriotism in the minds of the youth (Chandrike, MP and Chairman of the society, Gulbarga : 1983). This was a courageous act when any public activity was viewed with suspicion in the then Nizam government.

The establishment of the NV Society in the year 1907 at Gulbarga indicates one of the earliest private institutions founded with the nationalistic spirit. The society, which is a Maratha-Brahmin institution, was followed by the starting of the "Vivekvardhini Educational Trust" at Hyderabad in the year 1907.

While the NVS of Gulbarga and the Karnataka Law Society of Belgaum were the major institutions founded by the Brahmins in the two regions, they were also branded with linguistic chauvinism. Founded by a few leaders of the freedom movement who belonged to the Maratha-Brahmin community, they heralded the cause of education through their regional language-Marathi. These institutions are to be demarcated from those founded by the Kannada-Brahmins at Dharwar as their headquarters.

Likewise in Bidar, a Sikh leader started the Gurudev Education Society, and the Maratha caste group started a few schools under the leadership of one Manik Rao Pulekar, Ex-MLC, hailing from the Kuruba community.

Later years found the active interest taken by political leaders belonging to Lingayat and other caste groups to establish colleges, especially money-spinning ones, offering professional courses. Until such permission to start engineering and medicine courses was obtained, the trusts started diploma courses in engineering and polytechnique subjects. For example, is the Rural Polytechnic College started at Kushnoor in Thana taluk in 1982 by Manick Rao Patil, an ex-minister and Chief Whip in the Legislative Assembly during Gundu Rao's Chief Ministership in 1981. In HK area too, before the establishment of the HKES, the Nutan Vidyalaya was started by Sharanabasaveshwar Vidya Vardhak Sangha and another by a Muslim Trust by name Kwaja Hazrat Bande Nawab Educational Trust both at Gulbarga.

(iii) Madras Presidency Area

Academy of General Education Manipal Academy)

The Academy of General Education was founded in Manipal in Dakshina Kannada district in the year 1942. Apart from being another private educational trust like the others, the Academy marked the acceleration in the phases of starting of professional colleges (medical and engineering) in the state by private management. Its founder was Sri T. Madhava Anantha Pai, an adventurous industrialist and pioneer in banking profession. He is known as 'Maker of Manipal'. Pai was a physician turned banker turned educationist. While practicing at Udupi as a doctor, he founded the Canara Industrial and Banking Syndicate Limited (now known as the Syndicate Bank). As its managing Director for 36 years, he literally built it up from scratch to the present position of one of the 14 nationalised banks in the country.

The vast amount of suffering that Pai came across during the course of his private practice in Udupi was mainly responsible for motivating him to devote his time "for starting an institution to give medical education which will make possible availability of hundreds of qualified people to play their role in the field of medical relief" (Alse : 1979: iv). "Money was flowing and had to be pooled somewhere. This is how the idea of starting of professional (medical) college at Manipal came to his mind" (Souvenir of the Academy : 1989). Subsequently, Pai approached the Karnatak University to obtain permission to start a medical college. To the news item published in Madras Mail about his idea, he got within a week of the advertisement, about 8,000 applications from various parts of the country from students who had out of disappointment joined various other courses.

Pai approached the Karnatak University as he knew that "there was a provision that wherever Kannadigas wanted to start any college, they could seek affiliation with it, provided the concerned provincial government had no objection" (Alse : 1979: iv). Pai did not expect any objection from the Bombay and Madras governments. He was also confident about the co-operation from his friends in both the governments. However, the objection did come from no less a person than the Vice-chancellor of Madras University, Sir A. Lakshmanaswamy Mudaliar, who was a devoted non-Brahmin. His opposition to the starting a medical college by private trust were given lent in his speeches where he made "random remarks touching on the consequences that might result as an offshoot of the proposed private medical college" (*ibid.*). Pai was able to convince the Director of Medical Service, Madras, Dr. Vasudeva Rao, who questioned him as to why he was "making such statements and embarrassing the government and the University". Even the Mysore University replied in the negative to Pai's request. The reason for such opposition by the two universities was that in both places (Madras & Mysore), the NBM had just passed and Pai was a Brahmin by caste.

Pai's crusade for obtaining permission for starting professional colleges under private management gained momentum in the course of the next 4 years (1949-1953) and he succeeded in his mission. "The Madras government was able to extend its co-operation since the Karnatak University decided to give affiliation and thereafter the Bombay government blessed the whole project by their consent" (Alse : 1979: vii). However, such permission was given only on an experimental basis and on the condition that if the private management failed in shouldering the responsibility of the college, the same would be surrendered to the university (R. C. Hiremath, a senate member at that time and later the Vice-Chancellor of the university).

Thus came into existence the Kasturba Medical College in Manipal in 1953 when there were no other private medical colleges in the state. It became an inspiration to other educational trusts to start similar colleges in future. Pai is also credited for initiating the process of capitation fees paid for seats in such private colleges. He even asked the university to "select the students qualified for medical education" and his responsibility was only to run the college by being allowed to charge a prescribed sum of money for the seats on the students.

Today the Academy has grown under the dynamic leadership

of Dr. Pai and his successors. Starting with a few vocational training courses and schools, the Academy entered the field of collegiate education in 1949 when the Mahatma Gandhi Memorial College was established at Udupi. The Manipal Institute of Technology (1957), the Law College (1957) and a number of other colleges followed soon.

(iv) Old Mysore Area

The National Institute of Engineering

Among the other educational societies founded by private trusts in the pre-independence period, mention must be made of the 'National Institute of Engineering' (NIE) founded by a group of veteran engineers[39] hailing from the Brahmin community. They founded the NIE in the year 1946, at Mysore, intending to spread and encourage engineering education among the community's students.

II. Origin and expansion of Private Educational Institutions in the Post-Independence Period

The process of setting up of schools, hostels and colleges by private bodies gained greater momentum in the years after independence. This is clear from the emphasis that came to be laid upon the starting of mostly professional colleges during this period. The increase was a direct consequence of the encouragement given to technical education in the plans and programmes of the government, particularly by the five-year plans. Important it is to note that the educational societies that were till recently content with the starting of only hostels and schools, or at the most, degree colleges, began demanding professional colleges from the government and started a few on their own. The new societies began by starting (directly) such professional colleges based on capitation fees for financial support.

The socio-political changes accompanying the declaration of independence to the country had its impact on the administration and structure of these private educational institutions. Democracy came to be combined with legislative action to deal with issues like inequality and backwardness.

The post-independence period is divided here into two periods, comprising the years 1947-1970 and 1970-1990. In the first period, political power in the state was vested with the two dominant castes, which formed the ministries alternately, from 1947-1956 and 1956-1972. The second period was characterised by the changes introduced by the government led by the first time non-dominant ministry of late Sri Devraj Urs.

This study covered 39 educational societies of which as many as 13 belonged to the Lingayat community. Of these 10[40] owed their origin to the pre-independence period, some of which have been discussed already. While 8 of them have been discussed earlier the details of other two are provided as below:

1. *Jagadguru Sree Suttur Shivarathreeswara Mahavidyapeetha, Mysore*

Forming an important Lingayat Educational Trust in Old Mysore, the JSS Mahavidyapeetha was established in the year 1933 at Mysore under the auspices of the Sree Sree Suthur Jagadguru Veerasimhasana. The origin of the mutt dates back to more than 1,000 years to the 11th century or so (Malledevaru : 1984). It was founded by Sree Sree Shivarathreeshwara Bhagavathpadaru on the banks of the river Kapila in Suttur, in Nanjangud taluk of Mysore district.

The mutt had restricted its activities in the initial days of its formation to only religious activities like construction of temples, establishing its branches etc. with the assumption of office by the 20th Swamiji Jagadguru Sree Shivarathreeswara Mahaswamigalu,[41] the Srimutt began expanding its activities in the sphere of education, realising the needs and demands posed by the changing society. The Swamiji therefore envisaged certain new welfare activities for the Mutt to undertake. Providing good education became its prime goal. A beginning was made with the starting of the Kyathanahalli Sahukar Sree Siddalingayya's Students' Home at Mysore. Along with it a Sanskrit Patashala was also started at Mysore in the year 1933.

The Swamiji's efforts to spread education among the masses did not stop there. After consulting the community leaders, like Kothegalada Puttamalledevaru, Harsiddappanavaru and K.P. Mallayyanavaru, a free boarding home was started in the year 1944 in a rented home belonging to one Sri Gundappa in Mysore as the Mutt had no building of its own then. Subsequently, in 1946, a house was bought on Vani Vilas road where the hostel was shifted.

By this time (1940), the next head of the mutt, Sree Shivarathri Rajendra Mahaswamigalu had come to Mysore from Suttur seeking education. He evinced keen interest in expanding the educational activities of the mutt. On seeing his enthusiasm the Inam land belonging to the mutt was donated for maintenance of the Vidyarthi Prasada Nilaya (students' hostel) by the elder Swamiji. This facilitated the smooth functioning of the hostel, which in turn, encouraged more and more Lingayat students from rural areas in the district to pursue their education.

The real growth of the mutt or Peetha took place after 1950. Till 1953, only hostels were founded in the different parts of Mysore district. The educational empire of the mutt has expanded thoroughly with an engineering college in 1963 and medical college in 1984 besides a number of other institutions.

2. *Sree Jagadguru Jayadeva Murugarajendra Vidyapeetha*

This institution represented another Veerasaiva Educational

Trust founded after independence. Located in Chitradurga, this was founded by Sree Jagadguru Jayadeva Murugarajendra, the Swamiji of the Sree Murugarajendra Mutt of Chitradurga, one of the important, oldest mutt and centre of Veerasaivism. It is known to have played an important role in the history of the Durga since more than 1000 years, when it was ruled by Paleyagars and petty kings. It has also engaged itself in many welfare activities. Along with spreading Veerasaiva Dharma, the mutt controls the political and economic activities of the region.

The mutt started to evince interest in the community's educational activities from the 20th century itself, by starting the 'Prasada Nilaya' or mass feeding centres in different parts of the district. It started to expand its educational work once its own person, Sri S. Nijalingappa became the state's Chief Minister after the reorganisation of state in 1956, thereby also ending the long rule by the Vokkaligas as chief ministers. Being a fervent devotee of the mutt he made all arrangements for its prosperity.

The main institutions run by the mutt were a few undergraduate colleges, student hostels, and engineering colleges.

3. The Taralabalu Jagadguru Vidyabhivrudhdhi Samasthe

The Taralabalu Jagadguru Vidyabhivrudhdhi Samasthe is another educational association started in the same district – Chitradurga but by a subcaste among the Lingayats viz., Sadar Lingayats. It was founded in Sirigere in the year 1962 under the auspices of the Sreemaddujjayani Saddharma Simhasana (Taralabalu Brihanmutt) which was established at Sirigere in the year 1910. The first institution to have been started by the mutt was the Sree Taralabalu Jagadguru High School in the same year. The credit for starting it and taking the mutt's activities to great heights goes to its Swamiji Sree Sivakumara Shivacharya Mahaswamigalu, the 20th Swamiji of the mutt.

With the founding of the Taralabalu Jagadguru Vidyabhivrudhdhi Samsthe, the educational activities of the mutt expanded with more than 100 high schools, 20-25 colleges, 60-80 hostels and so on (Souvenir of the Samsthe : 1997).

4. Sri Dharmasthala Manjunatheshwara Educational Trust

The Sri Dharmasthala Manjunatheshwara Educational Trust was established in the year 1965 at Ujire in Dakshina Kannada district by the initiative of Sri D. Veerendra Hegde[42], the Dharmadhikari of Sri Kshetra Dharmasthala. With the intention of providing higher education facilities to children of poor families of Belthangady taluk in this Malnad (Western Ghats) region of the state, he sought support from a group of leading citizens of the area and started the Sri Dharmasthala Manjunatheshwara Educational Trust (DMET). The trust has expanded very well over the years with a number of schools, hostels, degree and professional colleges, both here as well as at Dharwar, Bangalore and so on.

Notable among the initiatives of these trusts that were started after independence was the degree of autonomy that they could attain with regard to economic resources needed to start and run colleges, especially professional ones. Till then, the institutions had been managed by the mutts with whatever resources that they could generate. The question of collecting donation or capitation fee from prospective students in engineering and medical colleges, was absent till then. This does not mean that the process was totally devoid of support by mutts in the post-1947 era. What is notable is the rising commerciality of the system of private education and the practice of collecting capitation fees as started with T. M. A. Pai's Academy, becoming an inseparable part of private education in Karnataka.

5. Bapuji Educational Association

The establishment of the Bapuji Educational Association (BEA) at Davanagere was the result of the efforts of a group of merchants of the same town (now a district headquarters). It was part of the effort to convert the upcoming Davanagere city as an educational centre besides being a commercial center. The BEA was the offshoot of a trust that became full-fledged only in 1958[43] with a delay of 11 years that was due to internal cleavages between different Lingayat subcastes.

Once started, the association has established a number of basic and professional educational institutions of repute.

6. The Hyderabad Karnatak Education Society

The Hyderabad Karnatak Education Society (HKES) was established in the year 1958 at Gulbarga by the Lingayats of the area particularly to set right the lacunae in the case of professional education. Before its establishment, the students from the districts of Bidar, Gulbarga and Raichur had to migrate to other regions seeking professional education. It was Sri N.S. Hirannayya, the then divisional commissioner (DC), who recommended the starting of an engineering college in Gulbarga and the idea crystallised when Sri G.N. Nagaraja Rao was the DC in 1957.

Thus, the HKES was formed with Sri Rao[44] as the Chairman and Sri Mahadevappa Rampure, Member of Parliament (MP), as its Secretary. It received a grant of Rs. 5 lakhs by the government to start an engineering college. Although the amount was insufficient, 'undaunted' by the mammoth bulk of the sum required, Rampure went ahead organising support when every cultivator of the region paid additional revenue that year to start the college (Souvenir of the HKES : 1982-3 :1). The institution was hailed not "as a gift from above, but (it) was a growth from below. The common people of the region, who cannot be regarded as well-to-do but were vested with sacrifice and generosity, responded to the call of collection of the money" (the late Dr. S. Radhakrishnan, presidential address upon laying of the foundation of the engineering college on October 15, 1958, quoted in the Souvenir : 1982-3 : 1).

Mahadevappa[45] continued to work and inspire the society for a long time (13 years) as its President till his death in 1973. Rapid strides were made by the society during this time, establishing many institutions in the region with support from philanthropists like Sri B.V. Bhoomraddi, Seth Rameshchandra Lahoti, Sri Basanna Gangasiri, Sri Sharanappa Gangasiri, Sri Homi Irani, Sri S.S. Margol, Sri Yakoob Ali Maniyar and others.

The HKES has a number of institutions in all the four districts of the region besides in Bangalore. Its dream of starting a medical college was realised in 1960 itself when the "perseverance and constant efforts of Sri Rampure and other members" bore fruit and the government gave permission to start one as part of the third five year plan. But the society was to deposit Rs. 20 lakhs with the government and Rs. 30 lakhs with the University. Since it was a great burden on the society, the latter waived off the precondition. At this time, Sri Veerendra Patil, the PWD Minister and later Chief Minister in the government, gave 'liberal assistance' to the society that 'deserves an honourable mention' (Souvenir of the HKES : 3). The Mahadevappa Rampure Medical College came into existence in the year 1963. It flourished later under the leadership of both religious heads (Poojya Sri Sharanabasappa Appa) and local landlords (Sri Agadi S. Anganna). The government had taken over its administration for a brief period during 1976-79 following internal quarrels for power. Not much progress was made in starting of new institutions during this troubled period.

But in its third phase of growth, the HKES managed to again develop itself under the leadership of Dr. A.S. Malaka Reddy, an ex-minister and a senior political leader. The activities expanded to reach other districts of the area like starting a homeopathy college in Gulbarga and an engineering college at Raichur etc. Later, Dr. B.G. Javali, son-in-law of Veerendra Patil became its President in the 80s.

There are a few educational institutions in Karnataka that have been started by individuals with their own efforts and not associated with any mutt. Some of the important ones are discussed as under:

7. Rashtreeya Shikshana Samithi Trust

This is a private educational trust founded at Bangalore owing to the efforts of few Lingayats led by one Sri M.C. Sivananda Sharma[46], of T. Narasipur taluk of Mysore district in 1940. A school in Bangalore was started initially with only 8 students in a small rented room, which gradually developed into a big educational institution. As its founder secretary, Sharma was the key figure responsible for all the initial activities of the Trust. The first batch of trustees included prominent businessmen and industrialists who have made heavy contributions to it. They hailed from the leading business communities like the Vyshyas, Lingayats and Banajigas. Vyshyas have been heading the trust continuously while many other business families have represented the trust like Raju Kshatriyas, Christians and so on.

A number of institutions have been started by the trust including a leading engineering college, dental college and others all at Bangalore, most of which have not received any financial aid from the government and are relying 'purely upon the co-operation of the people' (Prospectus of RVCE : 1981-82: 4).

8. Sri B. M. Srinivasaiah Educational Trust

Sri B.M. Srinivasaiah Educational Trust (BMSET) was the brainchild of late Sri B. M. Srinivasaiah[47], started at Bangalore in the year 1957 with the intention of promoting higher education. Srinivasaiah donated a site to enable the trust to achieve this end, where a soap factory existed earlier owned by him. A women's college, an engineering college (day and evening), a law college were also located in the same premises. As a public body, the trust has eminent educationists, members of the syndicate and professors of the Bangalore University and political leaders as its members. The engineering college is a grant-in-aid institution with 80 per cent of seats filled through government quota and only 20 per cent left to the management.

9. Mahatma Gandhi Vidya Peetha Trust

The Mahatma Gandhi Vidya Peetha Trust was founded by late Sri R. Dayanand Sagar, ex-MLC and ex-minister of Karnataka, in 1962, at Bangalore. As admitted in a discussion with him and recently with his sons who are continuing the leadership to the trust as well as in state politics, was the dominance of Lingayats in the field of professional education that motivated him to start his educational trust it to break this monopoly. It has a number of colleges ranging from law, to polytechnic, engineering, management and teachers' training. Its engineering college was started in 1980 with support from Gundu Rao, the then Chief Minister.

10. Gokula Education Trust

In the same year, Late Sri M.S. Ramaiah founded the Gokula Education Trust in Bangalore, to encourage poor students to seek higher education. Ramaiah was "a leading citizen of

Karnataka and an engineering contractor of all India repute". He founded the Trust solely with his own resources. It began with the M. S. Ramaiah Institute of Technology, without looking for any financial aid from the state or Central Government with a view to impart technical education to students from all over the country and even abroad without provincial barriers (Prospectus of the Trust : 7).

After the establishment of the above foundation and the Engineering College, Ramaiah established the Gokula Education Foundation to start the M.S. Ramaiah Medical College in the year 1979. He went on to build massive structures to house all his colleges and called it Vidya Soudha on the lines of the Karnataka government's secretariat building viz., Vidhana Soudha. The college has an attached hospital that has gained popularity with many special treatment facilities catering to many villages and towns in Kolar and Bangalore Districts.

Thus, besides caste and commercial interests, the spirit of regionalism and patriotism has been the driving force behind few academic institutions and the societies that started them. These came to be regional as well as communal in character. Special mention is made here of three societies started for driving higher education to local levels. They were the Malnad Education Society at Hassan, the People's Education Society at Mandya and the National Education Society at Shimoga.

1. Malnad Education Society was started with the efforts of a few leaders of Lingayat, Vokkaliga and Brahmin castes of Hassan culminating in the starting of the Malnad Engineering College in 1960 (Thammanna Gowda, spokesperson : 1983).
2. The People's Education Society and the National Education Society

The above two institutions, started at Mandya and Shimoga,

respectively, were also the results of efforts of castes like Vokkaligas in the former and Brahmins in the latter. The former society started its engineering college rather early in 1962; it took several years for the other to follow (1980).

The above description of the various private educational institutions in the different regions of Karnataka is proof of the stability, adaptability and variety that the issue came to acquire amidst the changing social and political life of Karnataka. Glaring was the sectarian character displayed during their beginning stages, gradually disintegrating into commercial and class character, in course of time, by succumbing to capitation fees as a survival strategy.

Another feature of this process was that a few of these institutions were able to make remarkable progress in the pre-independence period, succeeding in establishing themselves, over the years. Many representatives of the societies, especially formed by the Lingayats, have reported that the changes in the political leadership in the state after 1956 proved advantageous to them to expand their institutions. The situation also led to a number of instances of inter-caste conflicts or those between subcastes of a bigger caste. Upper sections of social hierarchy became forerunners of socio-political achievements claiming to represent the whole group. For example, among the Lingayats, the upper castes among them founded educational trusts in the beginning years, with those who were converts or from lower cadres following them. This applied to Lingayat subcastes like Reddy Lingayats, Devanga Lingayats, Gowda Lingayats, Ganiga Lingayats, Nonaba Lingayats, etc., who could form exclusive educational trusts of their own in the last 20 years or so. The Taralabalu Mutt started its educational institutions only recently, as compared to the ones founded by older mutts in the state. Exposure of small sections of Lingayat subcastes to such mobilisation processes have made them to get exposed to increased political participation. Small castes or subcastes of bigger ones started emulating the latter in course of time.

11. Vokkaligara Sangha

Next to the Lingayats, the Vokkaligas stand out as the caste, which has imbibed the secular channel of caste mobilisation through the opening of educational institutions. Earlier to 1972, there were three chief trusts viz., the Vokkaligara Sangha, Malnad Education Society and the People's Education Society, which had started engineering colleges. After 1972, the more articulate members of the Vokkaligara Sangha started to think on the lines of mobilisation on a different horizon, apart from just the formation and strengthening of their caste association. The Sangha had already started a number of student hostels and degree colleges in Arts and Science subjects in many parts of old Mysore area. Now it started to give importance to the opening of professional colleges with zeal and enthusiasm. They realised that there was a fundamental lacuna in their organisational effort as compared to that of the Lingayats. It related to the absence of a religious organisation or Mutt which the Lingayats were blessed with in large numbers and spread over the different parts of the state. The Vokkaligas realised that the mutts gave enormous support to the Lingayats in their spreading the cause of education among the rural brethren and more importantly in the opening and successful managing of professional courses.

Beginning with the early decade of 20th century, the Vokkaligara Sangha had become a centre of support not only for heralding education but was also a stepping stone for members of the community to emerge as active politicians. However, in the next few decades, it had to loose leaders of eminence like Sri K.H. Ramaiah, who joined the freedom movement representing the Congress Party. After independence, the community had to succumb to the Lingayats taking over political power following the re-organisation of the state in 1956, causing an unprecedented increase in their population due to the merging of the 8 Lingayat dominant districts of the BK & HK areas. However, by then, owing to continued benefits of reservation policy the community had achieved quite a good representation in government service and politics. The first chief minister hailed from it, so was the trend till the merger of the BK and HK areas in 1956 when the state was reorganised and Lingayats became the numerically and politically significant community. It was then that the second generation leadership in the Sangha formed by Sriyuths H.K. Veeranna Gowda, a minister, K.R. Marudeve Gowda, a civil servant and others took keen interest in expanding the Sangha's educational activities. Few more colleges and students' hostels came to be added to the list, but the important ones were the starting of professional colleges (engineering in 1979 & medical in 1980).

The most significant event was the revival of interest in the religious mutt of the community, viz., Sree Adichunchanagiri Kshetra, located in the Vokkaliga stronghold, Mandya district. Further importance was given to spreading of education through the mutt and few more colleges (both professional and non-professional) were started in all those districts with a heavy Vokkaliga population.

The process of starting professional institutions this time by 'using' the religious mutts did not stop with the Vokkaligas, but influenced others in the hierarchy, both upper and lower. Take for example, the mutts of Brahmins. They have also been actively engaged in encouraging educational advancement of the community, not just Sanskritic education but also to match the changing commercial value of education. Since the beginning, there was no effort to start own schools and colleges, since their children were able to get into regular government institutions on merit basis. The government institutions were enough to cater to their needs as there was no competitor.

But the BCM and its aftermath did necessitate a serious thinking among Brahmins about facing the challenge posed by the growing competition among the backward communities to access by education and government service. The students of Brahmin community came to encounter serious competition from others in respect to admission to professional colleges. The situation was made worse off by the increasing number of government policies favouring the non-Brahmin and SC/ST students. All these jeopardised the chances of Brahmin students in accessing higher education as before.

The above process inspired Brahmin leaders (both religious and political) to think of starting own professional colleges through private educational trusts or societies in different parts of the state. There were three of them, initially, each with its own set of reasons behind such a move. They claim to have resulted from reasons peculiar to each one of them than being supported by a single uniform cause. For example, the KLS of Belgaum and the National Education Society of Shimoga came into existence due to the Kannada movement in the BK area, rising patriotism during British rule and to support regional development. The desire to popularise the utility of professional education brought the NES of Mysore into existence, while the desire to provide education to the poor masses of DK district necessitated the formation of the Sri DMET of Ujire.

The caste association of the Brahmins known as the Akila Karnataka Brahmana Maha Sabha became active since 1979 in its educational drive. 'Sringeri' in Chikmagalur district, where the Sharada Peetha of Adi Shankaracharya is situated, was chosen as the site for the setting up of the Dhanvanthri Maha Vaidyashala (medical college) by the Sabha. It is a matter of conjecture as to whether this interest evinced by the Sabha was guided by the then chief minister of the state and a Brahmin himself, Sri Gundu Rao's liberal policy towards private professional education.

Two educational trusts belonging to the SCs also came into existence during the same period. They were the Siddartha Education Society of Tumkur and the Ananda Social and Education Trust, Bangalore. Both the trusts were founded by leading political figures in the state, representing the SC category. They were influenced by the process of mobilisation that was prevalent all around them, and as found among the other castes, this was the initiative taken by those who belonged to a higher class among the SCs.

The Muslims, on their part, also started educational trusts, four of them, two in Bangalore and the rest in Uttara Kannada and Gulbarga districts respectively. They directly went ahead with the formation of professional colleges (engineering), resulting in the Ghousia Engineering College of Ramanagaram and the Islamia Institute for Technology at Bangalore. In Bhatkal (in UK district) was started the Anjumaa-Hami-E-Muslimeen's Engineering College, founded by Sri S. M. Yahya, an ex-Minister from the same place. The fourth college was started by Khaja Educational Society of Hazrat Khaja Bande Nawaz Trust in Gulbarga – all in the year 1980.

Thus, 35 private colleges of engineering and 10 of medicine were started in the years following independence till 1990. Of them, 22 engineering and 3 medical colleges were founded during the period 1978-82 alone symbolising the congenial atmosphere provided by the then government led by Sri R. Gundu Rao. Among them a majority of private trusts came into being purely for purposes of starting engineering and (if not succeeded) or medical colleges.

The second interesting character of this process is that as compared to the pre-independence era and the first two decades following independence, after 1972, the subcastes of major communities began emulating the forming of trusts and educational institutions.

A third phenomenon in this regard was the entry of ministers and other politically important people into the fray. Most of them were beneficiaries of the reservation policy in their own upbringing. Second, they benefited from Urs' policy/strategy of recognising members of backward classes, Minorities and SCs to occupy ministerial berths in his cabinet.

Some of the educational trusts that the latter category founded were as follows:

(a) Karnataka People's Education Society

This society was founded in 1974 at Gulbarga by Sri Mallikarjun Kharge, an ex-Minister and now leader of the opposition in the Karnataka Assembly, hailing from the SC category. The society was inspired in its existence by the one founded by Baba Saheb Dr. B.R. Ambedkar and owns a large number of schools and colleges in north Karnataka and a B.Ed. college in Bangalore too.

(b) Sri Siddartha Education Society

A visit to Gollahalli, a village in Tumkur district, by the Bhoodan leader late Acharya Vinoba Bhave is supposed to have inspired the establishment of the above society. The initiative was taken by late Sri H.M. Gangadharaiah, a social worker of much repute and also a MLC of Tumkur. Beginning with a few schools and a hostel for SC students, the society grew to start its own medical and engineering colleges. It came to be led by a band of distinguished SC politicians, like late Sri M. Mallikarjunaswamy and after his death by Sri Mallikarjuna Kharge, currently President of the State Congress Party and a senior politician. It was later that Kharge founded the People's Education Society at Gulbarga. There was another charismatic leader, Sri M. Maruthi Male, during whose tenure the engineering college of the society was established, as the addition to the district's single engineering college started long time back by the Siddaganga mutt representing the Lingayats.

(c) Ananda Social and Educational Trust

Founded by a noted politician of Kolar and state head of the Republican Party of India (founded by Dr. Ambedkar) late Sri C.M. Armugam, the Ananda Social and Educational trust came into existence to start the Dr. Ambedkar Institute of Technology and the Ambedkar Medical College in Bangalore during 1979-80. The former is administered by a separate trust, viz., Panchajanya Vidyapeeth Welfare Trust.

Rural Technical Education Society

Besides the above educational trusts representing the SCs, one more was added to the existing Lingayat Trusts, which went on to form professional colleges. Founded in the year 1980 by late Sri K.H. Patil[48], a veteran politician from Gadag (a district in north Karnataka) and a staunch opponent of Devraj Urs, the RTES began an engineering college as its first institution. It also aired the intra-caste factions in that region. Hailing from the subcaste of Reddy Lingayats, Patil crusaded against the so-called Panchamasale and Jangama subcastes to set up this institution.

Karnataka Progressive Educational Institution (KPEI)

The KPEI was yet another institution to have joined the list of private educational trusts in Dharwar. Founded in 1975 by a group of political leaders under the guidance of late Sri K.H. Patil, it went on to start a law college.

The following are few of the leading politicians of the

seventies who also evinced interest in starting educational trusts in the regions from where they hailed. For example, Sri Sudhidra Rao Kasbe, an ex-minister in both Urs and Gundu Rao cabinets tried for a medical college at Raichur but it failed to materialise. Sri Bheemanna Khandre in Gundu Rao's cabinet, who headed the Shanthivardhak Educational Society in Bidar, succeeded in starting an engineering college at Bhalki, a taluk headquarter, in the district.

Late Sri L.G. Havanur, Chairman of the Karnataka Backward Classes Commission and an ex-Minister in Urs cabinet founded the Bharatiya Adimjati Sevak Sangha at Ranebennur in Dharwar district to start colleges for women.

Sri R.V. Bidap, ex-Chairman, KPSC, started the Karnataka Rashtreeya Education Society at Bidar with pharmacy, law and commerce colleges to its credit.

Sri Basavaraj Patil another politician started the Sri Veerabhadhreswara Education Society at Humnabad in Bidar district; Sri Manick Rao Patil founded in 1981 the Rural Polytechnique college at Kushnoor in Bidar; S. M. Yahya founded an engineering college at Bhatkal; and so on. A number of others like M.Y. Ghorpade, Azeez Sait, Visvanatha Reddy Mudnal and others also ventured to start private educational trusts at Bellary, Bijapur and Bidar.

Thus, while a single engineering college functioned in the pre-independence era (started by Lingayats), its number rose to nine by 1972. Out of these, 5 were by again Lingayats. Two were started by Vokkaligas and one by Brahmins. Likewise 3 medical colleges were started, between the years 1947-72, by three Veerasaiva Educational Trusts. Only one was by a non-Lingayat, viz., The Academy of Liberal Education's College at Manipal.

The fifties and sixties present a picture of dominance by Lingayats in private education particularly in the north. The

Vokkaligas came on the scene after independence with colleges in Old Mysore and the Brahmins (with Pai) representing the coastal Karnataka.

III. The Post-1970 Scene

The practice of starting private educational trusts became intense with the march of time, but facilitated the growing mobilisational tendencies of the backward and SC population/leaders. In their view, development and progress of their communities was possible only when they attained autonomy in higher education. As students of these communities were not recognised for admissions to government run colleges or by those started by other castes, the idea was to start their own colleges to safeguard the interests of their community's students that too the poor and the needy. Holding of caste conferences to address people about the backwardness of their community vis-à-vis others and to seek benefits became a habit and continues even to this day. While some have successfully started professional colleges, others have been in the fray. The state had only four engineering colleges in 1947. One was added between 1947-51; one more between the years 1951-56, 4 during 1956-57; 6 from 1961-66, 3 in 1969-74 and one between the years 1974-78. Come 1980, 9 more emerged. 1980-81 added 12 more to the list. Thus, by the end of 1982 itself Karnataka could boost of 44 engineering colleges.

Undoubtedly, the credit for this went to the Gundu Rao ministry, but the process had begun much earlier. The practice of starting private educational institutions came as a significant aspect of caste mobilisation in Karnataka. It shed light on the fact that a certain amount of socio-economic and political awakening is needed to this initiative, so was the case with education. The successive backward classes commissions have provided graded backwardness to a number of castes and communities, over the decades. It shows that a certain amount of socio-economic and political awakening was also necessary for caste mobilisation.

However, the process discussed above also sheds light on the fact that not all castes have been able to participate in it. Barring the ones founded by Lingayats (with the backing of their religious mutts), the others have been the Vokkaligas as the other dominant caste of the state, the SCs (elite among them) and the Brahmins. This was a sign of a combination of economic, social and political strength, gathered over a period of time.

Between the years 1979-82, as many as 8 Lingayat, 3 Vokkaliga, 2 SC, 3 Brahmin, 2 Sikh and 4 Muslim educational trusts had started engineering colleges in the state. The Lingayat based institutions topped the list as is evident, showing that caste based economic and social status mattered even here. Deep-seated economic initiatives led to their participation and older an institution (and earliest the effort of a caste) more was the number and type of institutions founded by them. With the government constituted by such sectarian tendencies, the state attained national fame for its liberal policy towards private education.

Conclusions

Was this a strategy adopted by successive governments at least in the past, to remain in power? Did the governments aimed for a longer and stable political survival by granting such benefits to caste or sectarian demands? This is the essential element of caste mobilisation in the state. Educational development plans came to be used as the mask behind fighting political battles and accessing socio-economic status by successive band of leaders – representing both caste and political interests.

For the Lingayats, the mutts controlled their representation in state politics to a large extent. Showing gratitude to the mutt by way of granting affiliation to its demand for professional colleges became almost a political habit. This was because in many cases, the leaders were sponsored candidates of the former. Not just that, mutts sponsored efforts for the education, employment and mobility of many of their followers. As a result, politicians continued to make submissions of patronage to religious or caste based organisations. For example, the HKE Society started colleges of engineering and the KLE Society its medical college, during the regime of S. Nijalingappa. Likewise, the ones at Bagalkot and Bijapur came up when B. D. Jatti and S. R. Kanti were Chief Ministers.

All this is a mirror to the rising sectarian character of secular development through education. Caste based private education became a label for Karnataka in the whole of India. This 'vehicle' for upward mobility propounded by the NBM of the pre-independence times continued even today, the difference being whatever was the prerogative of only few upper castes earlier, has now spread to other castes.

A number of social, economic and political factors have moulded the private education scenario in Karnataka to become what it is today. Dominance of a community in economic, political and religious terms has been challenged by others in the hierarchy using development as the strategy. Thus, in the last nearly 35 years since Urs introduced the policy of reservations for the OBCs with rigour, we find a number of changes in the social standing of these communities. Despite its many drawbacks, Urs regime thus gave a fillip to the castes in the middle and lower levels of the hierarchy to attempt for social mobility. This is a major difference between pre and post-1972 socio-political climate in the state. The so-called policies of the Urs government as heavily leaning towards the OBCs and minorities, besides the SCs and STs, was clearly absorbed by the cream of the social groups to which they were aimed at, resulting in the creation of small leadership clusters amongst them.

These elite groups within the OBCs have been following the model of the castes above them in the social hierarchy in their ambition for mobilisation. Starting of private colleges was one such. The strength provided by the policy of reservation received further boost with the state governments becoming actively engaged in such mobilisation and Urs' successors taking the issue to a point of no return. It gathered more storm after the fall of Urs government when his successor Ramakrishna Hegde took the issue to greater heights by adding more number of colleges and the collection of capitation fees by them.

However, no private educational institution has been able to transform into action the ideals it had set before itself, i.e., taking education to the reaches of the poor and the needy amongst their community. At least there may be some truth in this tall claim made by them in regard to education at lower classes but certainly not at the level of professional education. With all its glamour and popularity it is an expensive one hence beyond the reach of the poor of one's own caste. Maintenance of institutional infrastructure and the socio-economic value that they carry along with them have almost institutionalised the practice of capitation fees. This has expanded the student population beyond the (leave alone the caste boundaries which never was true) state to a wider area – the only requirement being the ability to afford it by paying huge sums of money as donation to build the institutions. Before the system of Common Entrance Test was introduced by the Veerappa Moily government, the students in these private professional institutions comprised the rich and creamy layer of various communities of the state and also from outside it. The management of such colleges took shelter under the unrealistic statement that without substantial income in the form of donations, it would be impossible for them to run the colleges and they cannot run them as substandard ones.

Initiated into the system of professional education as a supportive means for the working of the institutions, the practice of collecting capitation fees has attained maximum heights as an inseparable aspect of higher education in Karnataka, as well as in India. This has rendered education more and more vulnerable to politicisation and corruption. Opposition to the practice by way of series of protests led finally to the idea of holding a Common Entrance Test to admit students into professional colleges on the basis of graded merit based selection. Any other move to abolish the system of capitation fees was made difficult considering that many of these colleges had been started by the minority, backward and dalit-based organisations.

However, the difficulties encountered by the newly founded caste-based professional colleges in the state do not appear to have deterred the other castes from following the others in the process. Many intermediate caste groups had not realised their dream of obtaining permission for professional colleges. Perhaps those who had permitted the private colleges to rely upon capitation fees for their survival were not in a position to foresee the gigantic growth of the practice turning to be a bane of the education system in the state.

REFERENCES

1. Like the Provinces of Madras, Bombay, Bengal and the Princely State of Mysore.
2. The Manu Dharma Shastra justifies that a Brahmin and only a Brahmin can undergo religious training of learning and teaching of the Vedas. Even the traditional theory of caste signifies that a Brahmin, since he is born out of the mouth of Lord Brahma, should profess Sanskritic education and no other caste is eligible for this (See Kane : 1974).
3. The state's reorganisation in 1956 led to the creation of a unified state of Karnataka (known as Mysore State till 1973 when it came to be

renamed as Karnataka by the then Chief Minister late Sri Devraj Urs). The following erstwhile areas were added to it: (a) 9 districts of the Princely Mysore state (after 1950, Part B State), (b) 4 districts of the Bombay State, (c) 2 districts of the Madras State, (d) 3 districts of the former Part B State of Hyderabad, and (e) the centrally administered State of Coorg (now Kodagu district). This made the State consists of 20 districts. Later, in 1997, some of the districts were bifurcated increasing the number of districts to 27. Again in June 2007, two more districts were added by bifurcating the Bangalore (Rural) district into Bangalore (Rural) and Bangalore South districts (the latter as Ramanagaram district also) and bifurcating the district of Kolar into Kolar and Chikkaballapur districts. This leaves the state with 29 districts today.

4. These are field observations and there is no satisfactory literary evidence to support this view. However, Gail Omvedt (1976) makes a reference to the impact of BCM in western India as having had some impact upon similar movements in the BK area.
5. Bellary, now a part of this region, was at that time (before reorganisation) part of Madras Presidency.
6. "In the HK area, due to the autocratic nature of the Nizam's government and the relative domination of the Muslims, the Brahmin-non-Brahmin backward cleavage did not surface until after 1956, i.e., when these areas were merged with Mysore" (*Report of the KBCC, Part II, Vols. III-VII, 1980, p. 151*).
7. Revealed during discussions with Mrs.Mahadevappa Rampure, widow of the founder President of HK Education Society 1983 and later, with office-bearers in 2005.
8. Now called as Dakshina Kannada and Kodagu districts.
9. Now called as Chennai.
10. Marathi speakers as a linguistic category.
11. Due to various historical reasons the non-Brahmin movement in the then composite Bombay Presidency did not gather momentum. The Lingayaths in the Bombay area did not enjoy the advantage of caste reservation until 1941 when they were grouped along with the Marathas into an intermediate group which was given some job concessions. Even this reservation benefit did not last long. The leaders of the Lingayat community were particularly affected and "constrained" in their mobilisational activities "because of the control of the Gujarathis and Maharashtrians in the Bombay administration". They were also agitated over the domination of Brahmins in the Pradesh Congress Committees whose jurisdiction included the Princely Mysore State also.

12. Souvenir of the Golden Jubilee of the KLES, 1969; interview with the President of the Society, Belgaum.
13. Despite contradictions and differences in the opinion that exist amongst Veerasaivas regarding the relevance of 'Basava' in the origin of the religious sect, there are divergent views on its origin: One claiming that it is an offshoot of the social movement stirred out by Basava and the other claiming that it preceded even Basava in its origin (Naganna : 1943: 28).
14. Like Vaarada Mallappa, Lingaraj Desai of Sirsangi and Navalgund Samsthana (Provinces) (who later converted his entire property consisting of his province or Samsthana into an educational trust for the sake of the educational development of the Veerasaiva community), Aratal Rudra Gowdaru and a few others.
15. In 1919, two Lingayat men (who later became community leaders and were instrumental in raising the KLES to a great height) by name S. S. Basavanal and M. R. Sakhare secured their post graduate degree (Master of Arts) together from the Deccan College, Pune, and had to share the prize amount.
16. The Brahmin newspapers described the conference as a Lingayat Conference. "Papers (edited by Brahmins) played a prominent role in kindling hatred against the non-Brahmins". Halakatti was called as being anti-nationalistic and pro-British by these papers and it was even rumoured in the Brahmin circles that he was given the title of "Rao Bahadur" because of his pro-British activities (Sri B.D. Karur, Principal, BLDEA's Commerce College, Bijapur). Also, quoted from M. Ed. Dissertation by Managonda on the BLDEA, Karnatak University, Dharwar. Books like F.G. Halakatti by the Thontadarya Mutt, Gadag and collection of articles on Halakatti published by the Bijapur District Literary Development Association.
17. S.S. Basavanal, M.R. Sakhare, B.S. Hanchinal and B.B. Mamadapur.
18. Sirsangi was a small Samsthan (province) in the present Navalgund taluk of Dharwad district. It was ruled by one Raja Lingaraj Sirdesai who had no offspring. He owned enormous property that was donated to the KLE Society.
19. Named after the renowned social workers and leaders Sriyuths Gilganchi Gurusiddappa and Rao Bahadur R.C. Artal.
20. Dr. Pavate was a renowned mathematician.
21. He was also the Deputy President of the Bombay Law Council.
22. Interview with Sri Kanakanady, one of the founders of the KLES, Belgaum. This incident was no doubt helpful in shielding the KLES from being affected by British administration, but gave way for critics

of the NBM to call it an unpatriotic attitude of the leaders of the society. See, also, Irshick (1969) for details of a similar trend in the non-Brahmin movement in Madras. Even in Old Mysore, the non-Brahmins joined the Congress rather late (see, Hettne and Tamm : 1974 and Manor : 1977).

23. Justice Chandavarkar was from Karwar, in Uttara Kannada district. His support to the Lingaraj College arose from his personal affinity to the area he hailed from.
24. The college had Brahmin staff members like Sri Srinivasa Iyengar, who later became the Vice-Chancellor of Andhra University (Sri S.G. Kallur, Principal KLES's Arts College, 1983) .
25. It is highly doubtful whether the year of establishment of a private educational trust (in terms like the most developed also being the oldest in the rank) is of much help in rating its socio-economic standing in comparison with similar trusts. The oldest trusts have not always been able to establish professional colleges immediately after their formation, though it is true of many trusts of the post-reorganisation years. It is also necessary to note here that private educational trusts of the pre-independence period came into existence, keeping solely in mind the starting of professional colleges. At the time when education itself was a new phenomenon, starting of schools and gradually establishing colleges assumed much significance, perhaps the significance that professional education holds today.

    In the above case, the BVVS, though founded earlier by the KLE Society of Belgaum, has been a 'smaller' institution compared to the latter, for a variety of socio-political reasons, which have been discussed in the course of this chapter.
26. Now a district in its own right.
27. Information about VVS at Bellary as a premier institution was difficult to elicit as the Sangha experienced long period of internal factions among the office-bearers. Litigation spurred the issue of capitation fee in the professional colleges started later by it, one such being the Vijayanagar Engineering College at Bellary.
28. It is an ancient ashram fostering a continuous line of illustrious "Siva-yogi Siddapurushas" (Saints with yogic and extraordinary spriritual powers) dating back to 15th century AD.
29. It was established by Sri Gosala Siddarameswara Swamiji, who belonged to the 'Shunya Simhasana' (a spiritual academy of fame during the days of Lord Sri Basaveswara of the 12 century AD).
30. No literary evidence is available on this. What is presented here is based on discussions with the following persons:

(a) Sri Channabasava Swami Pattadevaru of Bhalki Hiremath & founder, Shanthivardhak Education Society, Bhalki;
(b) Jayadevi Thai Ligade, Basava Kalyan, noted literary person;
(c) Sri Bheemanna Khandre, ex-minister in Gundu Rao's cabinet hailing from Bidar, associated with the above Vidya Sangha;
(d) Prabhuraoji Vakil Kamblivale of Bidar who gave information that Annapoornayya Swamigalu was responsible for the formation of educational institutions in that area;
(e) Sri Viswanatha Reddy Mudnal, ex-minister and Shankar Shetty Kamblapur, ex-MLA of Gulbarga;
(f) M.B. Oni, Principal, Sharanabasaveswar Commerce College, Gulbarga;
(g) S.M. Kappikeri, Department of Hindi, Gulbarga University, Gulbarga.

31. In Telangana area of Andhra Pradesh, especially in taluks like Narayankhed, form Lingayats the major caste. In Aurad and Bhalki taluks, the term Kannadiga invariably meant a Lingayat since it was they who supported the Kannada movement as opposed to the Brahmins' support for Marathi as the official language and medium of instruction.
32. He is Sree Channabasava Swami Pattadevaru of Bhalki Hiremath. It is interesting to note that he did not hail from the priestly subcaste among Lingayats from where heads of religious mutts are drawn. In fact, he hailed from the Devanga (weaving) caste. He converted many lower caste Hindu communities including the ex-untouchables to Veerasaivism. The society is headed by Sri Bheemanna Khandre, a veteran politician and ex-minister, since 1958.
33. Wantmuri was a Samsthan in Belgaum like Sirsangi.
34. Who incidentally is the son-in-law of Sri S.C. Nandimath, one of the main personalities behind the growth of KLES of Belgaum and later, the Vice-Chancellor of Karnatak university.
35. Commerce was then considered a professional course as in the Bombay pattern and it was not intermixed with Arts subjects (D.A. Hegde, Belgaum : 1983).
36. A petty province under the Marathas which is now in the state of Maharashtra.
37. Originally known as Mylara Gudda.
38. An important Hindu pilgrimage centre in Dakshina Kannada district.
39. Like D.V. Narasimha Rao, retired chief engineer of railways, T. Rama Rao, retired executive engineer and S. Ramaswamy retired superintending engineer and 16 others.

40. Viz., (1) Shri Basaveshwar Vidya Vardhak Sangha, Bagalkot, 1906, (2) the Karnatak Liberal (Lingayat) Education Society, Belgaum 1916, (3) the Bijapur Liberal District Education Association, Bijapur, 1910, (4) Sree Siddaganga Mutt Tumkur, 1917, (5) the Veerasaiva Vidya-Vardhak Sangha, Bellary, 1918, (6) Sree Sharanabasaveshwar Vidya Vardhak Sangha, Gulbarga, 1918, (7) Sree Shanthi Vardhak Education Society, Bidar,1940, (8) Taralabalu Education Society, Sirigere, Chitradurga, 1946, (9) Jagadguru Sree Suttur Shivarathreeswara Mahavidyapeetha, Mysore, 1933 and (10) Jagadguru Jayadeva Murugarajendra Vidyapeetha, Chitradurga.
41. Popular also by the name Manthra Maharshi.
42. Heggade is the President of DMET, Janatha Shikshana Samithi, Dharwad, Academy of General Education, Manipal and several other academic and social service organisations. He is addressed as "Abhinava Chavundaraya" (Prospectus : 1979).
43. Information collected from late Dharma Ratnakara Rajanahalli Madduraayappa, the then President and with Shamnur Shivashan-karappa, Honorary Secretary of the BEA.
44. Discussions with family members of Rampure, Gulbarga.
45. Described as a politician, parliamentarian, statesman, doyen, educa-tionist, who brought HK area under the renaissance movement after state's reorganisation. As Prof. N.C. Ranga described him, he built of half the Gulbarga University. The late Dr. D.C. Pavate, ex-vice chancellor of Karnatak Univeristy called him "Madan Mohan Malaviya of HK.
46. Discussions with late Sri D.A. Pandu, Secretary of RV Educational Trust, Bangalore.
47. From the Chatadha Srivaisnava Caste.
48. Whose son H.K. Patil is also a minister. K.H. Patil is well known as the architect of the co-operative movement in Karnataka and to have changed the map of Gadag through cotton co-operatives.

6 Political Aspects of Caste Mobilisation

Introduction

The role that the state as the political institution plays in achieving social transformation in a backward society is no less significant than economic reforms. The interaction between state and society has become increasingly complex in the present decade when the millennium development goals (MDGs) have to be achieved. The government as the agency of implementing the policy of reservation for the backward, SC, ST and other weaker sections is bound to face many challenges in this complex scenario.

The policy of reservations is the child of political planning, having come into existence when the British introduced political reforms in the country. The communal character of the policy linked it to politics, making the former the basis of granting facilities to the backwards. The resting of the policy upon the phenomenon of 'caste' has resulted in far-reaching consequences. With the dual policy of aiming at the eradication of caste as an evil of Hindu society and the other using it as the foundation upon which developmental programmes have been chalked out - the situation is challenging for the government to see that both co-exist. As a result, the interplay of caste, class and politics is noticeable in all forms and stages of the process of mobilisation in the state.

The discussion on the caste associations and the

establishment of private professional colleges in the preceding chapters has explained the limitations of a caste approach to the examination of social mobilisation and necessitate a class approach.

The process has led to at least two outcomes: one is the continued process of mobilisation along socio-political lines and the other is the emerging conflict that such sectarian and class-approach has led to. This chapter attempts to make a critical evaluation of the role of the political institutions in the history of sectarian mobilisation in Karnataka. It is an effort at locating how the problems of the society and the efforts of the people to overcome or resolve them have been used by political leaders for "purely temporary political and electoral gains". The crux of the subject was aptly described by Namboodiripad thus: ".... Most of the present day caste and communal organisations ... use the political leverage they have, the support of the particular caste and communities to which they cater, for making political bargains with this or that bourgeois political party. The leaders of the latter, in their turn, are making opportunist use of such caste and communal organisations, raising or opposing the particular slogans raised by these organisations not on the basis of any principle, but for purely temporary political and electoral gains" (Namboodiripad : 1979b: 335).

The reciprocity with which the interaction between social and political factors of social change occurs is an important characteristic of the BCM in Karnataka. This interaction had two phases: one was in the form of a sectarian movement started by one or the other pressure group as an attempt to alter the existing form of political control. The second was one where the political system itself resorted to encouraging sectarian feelings in order to remain in power.

Taking the first, we find the case of the BCM protesting against the domination of Brahmins as an example. As power (political and economic) is considered as an indicator and determinant of higher status, its achievement became the goal of the BCM. Gaining access to office under the state was one of its principal demands. Penetrating what was a virtual Brahmin monopoly required state intervention and therefore the leaders of the BCM sought such intervention with vigour.

The structure of leadership in the several BCMs across the country bears further evidence to this fact. Invariably, everywhere the movement was led by the locally dominant caste/s for demanding equal representation in education and government employment. The movement in Princely Mysore (true elsewhere also) suffered from the serious disadvantage of being totally urban in character. Its main participants were drawn from towns and cities, particularly from the cities of Mysore and Bangalore. Notwithstanding that these leaders hailing from the dominant Lingayat and Vokkaliga communities, were immigrants from rural Mysore, they were not new urban life. Being highly educated and cosmopolitan in outlook and manner and with an ambition towards westernisation, these leaders departed extensively from their rural counterparts, both in their attitudes and actions.

This substantiates that the BCMs were generally class-oriented and caste-based. Beneath the mask of caste inequality was fought deeper, significant class or economic interests. The fact that the movement did not reach the rural masses, the marked absence of other groups in it and the nature of demands made by its leaders – all testify its 'class' orientation.

In their attempts to fight for such class interests but from a sectarian platform, these dominant castes took to certain extreme steps that gave them the label of being anti-nationalistic in their spirit. This was a drastic generalisation about their mobilisational attempts, but not totally untrue. Taking the example of the BCM in Madras, Irschick points out that the non-Brahmins went against the efforts of the local nationalistic leaders who sought and fought for 'Home Rule' supported in their cause by Dr. Annie Beasant. They expected that British Rule would be replaced by Brahmin rule as majority of the leaders in the freedom movement invariably belonged to that caste. Their movement against the Brahminic domination in the political system reached its zenith with the non-Brahmins forming their own autonomous political party on August 27, 1944, which came to be known as Dravida Kazhagam (or DK party) (Irschick : 1969: 347).

In Princely Mysore also, there were attempts to favour the British Raj to win support and sympathy to the cause of the non-Brahmin movement. It is more conspicuous in the Bombay-Karnatak area, than in Princely Mysore, as the latter was not directly under British Rule, but was administered by the Maharaja under the general supervision of the British. On the other hand, in the BK area, mobilisational activities by the Lingayats were encouraged by the British. The Marathas as the other dominant caste in the region represented the Marathwada area in the movement. Thus, the Lingayats had to fight two opponents: the Brahmins and the Marathas.

In Princely Mysore too, the dominance of the two communities, viz., the Lingayats and the Vokkaligas was visible in deriving benefits from the rulers for their mobilisational activities. The Arasus (a community) as kings were a minority and wielded less influence as a caste than the Lingayats and the Vokkaligas particularly in the rural parts of the province (Hettne and Tamm : 1974).

This brings us to the second angle where the political system is understood to have owing to its own built-in weaknesses, encouraged sectarian tendencies. The establishment of caste associations and private educational trusts in Old Mysore bears testimony to this fact. The encouragement that these activities received from the kings and their ministers was a reflection of their own insecurity as a minority community (the Arasus) or "imported" Dewans (from Tamil Nadu). Much before the BCM showed any beginning in Princely Mysore, the Brahmins of Mysore indulged in fighting against the "Import" of Brahmin Dewans from Madras. Intra-Brahmin feud on this matter even made some of the Brahmin Dewans feel threatened. Sometimes indigenous help by such sources, which were anti-Brahminic in tempo, was sought by such 'imported' Dewans. The economic and social status of the two dominant castes was utilised to gain security against one's own problems by those in political power. Rich tributes have been paid by the Vokkaligara Sangha, to Dewan V. P. Madhava Rao for his munificent grant of a site in the heart of the Bangalore city to the Sangha to build its institutions (Souvenir of the Vokkaligara Sangha : 1961).

The action of Madhava Rao is quoted as a measure to seek support for himself as a member of a Brahmin subcaste, the Deshasthas, in the wake of intra-Brahmin rifts. Even the appointment of the Miller Committee to classify and grant benefits to the backward classes and the inclusion, later, of the Muslims and Christians, as BCs, may also be termed as an insurance against the possible threat by the dominant castes and these minority groups. Significantly, the policy of reservations came to be implemented by a non-Brahmin Dewan to begin with.

This interface between caste-based mobilisation and the state is discussed below dividing it as falling between certain periods:

1. Years between 1947-1956

The trend set in motion during the British Rule by identifying caste as a basis of classification for backwardness and the consequent reform policies continued even during the post-independence period. As already noted, the movement for equality with Brahmins was active till about the thirties after which it was merged into the freedom movement led by the Congress (Manor : 1972). After independence, the Vokkaligas gained an upper hand over the Lingayats as their number was more in the BCM.

A cursory look at the debates in the Representative Assembly indicates that as the BCM altered its character ever so slightly – from that of a pure non-Brahmin movement to one of a movement for the nation's independence (which inevitably and incidentally brought the non-Brahmin leaders in close touch with leaders at the national level) there appears to have been a gradual increase in the 'class' character of the movement. The leadership then came to be composed of young men who may be termed as the products of the reservation policy, especially in their educational achievements. They were also more sophisticated and modern in their outlook, as most of them were born and bred in urban areas unlike the first batch of leaders who hailed from rural areas (Manor : 1972).

These leaders representing mostly the two dominant castes, laid emphasis on a macro-approach to the problems of inequality. Their concern for the ex-untouchables and others was only superficial. It reflected their due recognition of the importance laid on the welfare of these downtrodden sections at the national level by leaders like Gandhi and Ambedkar. The Government of India Act, 1935 provided communal representation to the Muslims, Sikhs, Anglo-Indians, Indian Christians, Depressed Classes, and Aborigines etc. It did not take long for its effect to reach all the states, where the SCs began to organise with a greater zeal, obviously inspired and encouraged by the leadership of Dr.Baba Saheb Ambedkar. The non-Brahmin leaders of Mysore, perhaps realising this, have extended their support to the demands of the scheduled castes, although the latter continued to feel swamped by the other backward classes.

The role played by a group of Vokkaliga leaders in the freedom movement during the 30s and 40s brought them to the forefront of political leadership in the State even after independence. In other words, the first Ministry in free Mysore state came to be headed by Sri K. C. Reddy, a prominent Vokkaliga leader of the second generation. 1947 to 1956 was a period that saw successive Vokkaliga Chief Ministers that laid the foundation for a new chapter in the history of caste mobilisation in Karnataka. However, the comparative picture that emerges here is that the Vokkaligas' attempts at caste mobilisation have acquired wider dimensions since 1972.

The first is the greater significance attached to intra-caste solidarity in the years after independence. Since the beginning of the non-Brahmin movement and the establishment of the Sangha in the year 1906, power –political and social – is almost vested in the hands of a minority Vokkaliga subcaste elite, viz., the Gangadikaras who are numerically and economically at a higher level than the other Vokkaliga subcastes like the Morasu Vokkaligas, the Halumatha Vokkaligas, the Namdhari Vokkaliga and so on. These subcastes share almost the same caste-culture with the former group, but are endogamous.

Such subcaste barriers have been underplayed by the Sangha in the recent years. However, it is not inspired by any move to relax caste feelings. On the contrary, it is the result of the classification of the community as a whole as backward, by the Miller and other Backward Classes Commissions. Since the backwardness of the community lies in its lower ranks more than at the top, the socio-economic level of the Vokkaliga subcastes acts as an important component in the maintenance of the backward status of the whole group. Therefore, the Sangha is campaigning for the establishment of unity within the community by discouraging the process of fission among its subcastes.

Apart from the call for fusion, the Sangha's other chief activities included, the expansion of its organisational network, reviving of the religious mutt and the starting of educational institutions. It is rather strange that despite the power vesting with the community for nearly a decade (1947-1956) its caste association has not noticeably paid much attention to the above issues till the year 1972. Although educational activities received attention during the above period, it was limited to the opening of a few students' hostels at some important urban centres. Thus, sectarian activities have been active against hidden class interests.

2. Years between 1956-1971

The reorganisation of the state brought in its wake many changes in the nature and composition of its political leadership. There was a shift in the caste composition of political control where the Vokkaligas came to be replaced by the Lingayats after sixteen years of their control over state politics. This period may be regarded also as one that is remarkable for the pace at which mobilisational attempts in the Lingayat caste association as well as among the upper strata of the community gained momentum.

Notable among the factors which characterised the Lingayats' efforts to stabilise their socio-political strength in the years after 1956 were: the establishment of a few new private educational societies and the strengthening of the old ones by adding 'money-spinning' professional colleges to them, the expansion of the educational activities of the religious mutts and an improvement in their assets and the efforts to capture greater monopoly over administrative and judicial posts in the state by installing as many Lingayats as possible.

The above new activities do not suggest that mobilisational activities on these lines began and ended with the Lingayats holding the position of chief minister for long. Instead, they should be understood in terms of the advantages political hold or authority offered to the Lingayat elite. The discussion on the private educational trusts established by them shows that even among the Lingayats it was only the upper subcaste of the Panchamashales and the Banajigas (landowners and traders respectively) who have benefited most during this regime and not the whole group as such. This is particularly true of the lowest Lingayat subcastes like Madivalas, the Kurubas, the Ganigas, the Sadars and the Devangas, who are a group of middle and lower Hindu castes which are supposed to have converted to Veerasaivism during Basava's time. These groups are, nevertheless, endogamous and do not form the mainstream of the Lingayat community.

Another significant event of this 'Lingayat regime', among others, is the appointment of a backward classes commission in the year 1960. It was sought to reclassify the list of backward classes since the existing ones did not contain castes and communities of the newly added districts after state's reorganisation. Called after its chairman, Sri R. Nagan Gowda, it classified the castes on the basis of their representation in government service and divided into two categories, viz., "backward" and "more backward", basing on their educational backwardness. The Mysore Government, upon the submission of the Nagan Gowda Report passed orders in 1961 treating about 90 per cent of the state's total population as backward, inclusive of the SCs and STs. It reserved only 30 per cent of seats or posts to the OBCs, as against the Committee's recommendation for 50 per cent. But this order was, however, overruled by the Order of 1962, which increased the quota for the OBCs to 50 per cent. A note of dissent was issued by one of the members of the Committee, Sri M.S. Patil, who was a Lingayat (the report of the MBCC : 1961 : 33-36).

This decision of the Nagan Gowda Committee is significant as it grouped the Lingayats as forward. They had till then enjoyed a backward status. This was altered very soon due to the increasing pressure from the political elite of the community.

The Committee's support to their inclusion, in the face of strong judicial opposition, is clearly indicative of the role played by the two dominant communities in the state. An Order was issued by the government in the year 1962, under Art.15 (4) reserving seats in the medical and engineering colleges in the state for the backward classes, the SCs and the STs. A total of 68 per cent was reserved leaving only 32 per cent to the merit pool.[1]

The validity of the above Order was challenged by candidates who could not secure admissions only by the reason of the Government Order. Along with this, even the basis adopted in 1961 to specify the educationally and socially backward classes was also challenged in the *Balaji case* (AIR 649, Mys 1963).

The main contention of the petitioner in the *Balaji case* was that the provisions made in the Order were "ultra vires" and constituted a fraud on the power conferred by Art.15 (4). The reservation up to 68 per cent was simply inconsistent with Art. 15 (4). The court held that Art. 15 (4) speaks of a special provision, it is not a provision which altogether excluded the advancement of the rest of the society.

On the striking down of the Government Order in the *Balaji case*, the Mysore Government, "purporting to go by the decision of the Supreme Court, issued an order in July 1963 as a temporary measure" (KBCC Report, Vol. I, Part I : 1975 : 131). It took the family with its economic condition and occupation as a unit for purposes of Art.15 (4). This GO was also challenged in the Mysore High Court in the *Viswanatha Case* by Sri L. G. Havanur (AIR 1964, Mys.132). "The High Court observed that caste was a relevant, nay, an important factor, in the determination of backward classes and that classifying individuals as backward was a very imperfect classification which had harmed the Hindu backward castes that the state government should soon make a proper classification lest its bona fides should be questioned" (KBCC Report, Vol.I, Part I : 1975 : 132).

The years before change of rule by the dominant castes were turbulent with a number of processes. Changes introduced by the Devraj Urs ministry, including the appointment of the KBCC, did not, emerge from a vacuum. This is particularly true of the backward classes among whom the seeds of mobilisation along economic and political channels had been sown already and developed substantially. It was the system of protective discrimination, in vogue since 1935, that had led to all this. As the forerunners in this process, the Lingayats and the Vokkaligas had influenced a number of middle and lower castes in the scale to follow them.

By 1960, we find most of the middle and lower castes including the SCs sporting leaders who were striving towards the improvement of their respective castes. Many of them followed the upper castes by forming caste associations, and thereby attempted to strengthen their base through government help.

Thus, these new forces among the backward classes led by a batch of educated men hailing from these groups gathered more strength and resources so as to pose a threat to the government where the Lingayats dominated the scene. In addition to this, major political changes at the national level like the historic Congress split in 1969 and the emphasis laid on the welfare of the weaker sections of the society by the Congress ® Party led by Mrs. Indira Gandhi – all these contributed to a deepening crisis in state politics.

On the reservation front, the Congress government had not appointed any commission nor did it collect any data, despite the centre's directives to do so. This was needed to "supply the deficiencies in the Kalelkar Commission Report" and "in spite of the stand it took in *Viswanatha case* before the Mysore High Court and in the *Chitralekha case* before the Supreme Court that the July 1963 Order was only a temporary measure pending elaborate collection of data" (KBCC Report : 1975, Vol.I, Part I. 9). The then Chief Minister, Sri S. Nijalingappa is reported to have declared his intention that "caste and community factors shall not be taken into consideration" (*ibid.*, 8).

This attitude of the government instigated protests and agitations by some of the backward castes. For example, on 13th September 1970, a delegation of their leaders and sympathisers[2] presented a joint memorandum to the President of India on his visit to Bangalore requesting him "to direct the state government to appoint a commission on backward classes" or to derecognise caste or to implement the recommendations of the Kalelkar Commission (*ibid.*). The memorandum presented by the delegation to the President warned that if its demands (to appoint a BCC) were not met, "a situation may arise when", the President "may be called upon to impose" his "rule in the state" (*ibid.*). Reiterating their demand, the above leaders along with a few others like Sriyuths B. Basavalingappa, M. Mallikarjunaswamy, Kalle Shivothama Rao, B.T. Parthasarathy, N.N. Kallannavar and T.V. Venkataswamy convened a Scheduled Castes' and Scheduled Tribes' and Other Backward Classes' conference at Bangalore on 8th November, 1970.

The conference stressed the need for the appointment of a new BCC to classify and list the backward classes in Karnataka. The reaction of the Chief Minister, Sri Veerendra Patil to this movement is notable. Just two days before the conference, he stated that "reservations to the SCs and the STs in the IAS and IPS should be done away with" (*ibid.*). Within a few months, i.e., in the mid-term polls of March 1971, President's rule was imposed on the state dissolving the Veerendra Patil's Ministry.

The above examination of reservations, caste mobilisation and the political scene in Karnataka during the rule by the dominant castes throws light on the interrelationship between the social and political aspects of change. It also points to the impact of the changing role of caste on the political structure. The downfall of the Lingayat Ministry is viewed here as an indirect evidence of the inter-caste feud that was manifested in a political framework. In the coup against Veerendra Patil's Ministry, a few leading Vokkaliga politicians played their part in expressing animosity over the "dominant caste hegemony". The retorting of non-Lingayat backward castes is a crucial aspect of the process of mobilisation in which political participation and control over political resources is proved as an important goal of all mobilising castes. There is no need to stress that beneath such political ambitions there were always economic interests.

The convention of the OBCs, SCs and the STs during the above period ultimately resulted in the takeover of power from the dominant castes by the backward classes. This is significant to any study of caste mobilisation in Karnataka. Such incidents are occurring at regular intervals, affected by an intermixture of political and economic determinants. The class character of the whole process that led to the downfall is discussed briefly in the following pages :

> Certain questions are relevant to begin with. Are sectarian movements representative of only caste interests? Could we explain the BCMs in terms of a single factor, i.e., caste or class? The answer to these questions could be attempted by having a look at the socio-cultural composition of the first batch of the backward class leaders. They were the first batch of beneficiaries of the reservation policy too. They hailed from economically more resourceful and socially a higher level than the middle castes but lower than that of the Brahmins and Lingayats. They are the Vokkaligas, the Reddys, the Naidus, the Billavas and the Deevars. Except a few leaders of excellence, like Sri Devraj Urs, in whose case

there were other determinants of charismatic leadership, the rest constituted the upper class elite of the respective caste groups that was their strength to gain access.

3. Post-1972 Years

The seventies could be hailed as marking the beginning of a new era in the social map of the state as it significantly brought to a halt the dominant caste leadership of nearly quarter of a decade. Much has been written by social scientists on the various dimensions of Devraj Urs' regime that succeeded the Lingayats in 1972. In these works, his rule is described as one characterised by a number of reformist policies for the welfare of the weaker sections, which even gave him the title as the 'champion of the backward classes'. The rule by Urs came to have a number of social and political implications to the on-going process of caste-based mobilisation in Karnataka.

Urs assumed office as the chief minister of Karnataka when the state was in a condition of socio-political disequilibrium. Politically there was large-scale instability, perhaps, a reflection of the changes which occurred at the national level politics. In the social sphere, the system of reservations, though in its diluted form which lacked any consistent approach to it by the earlier governments since independence was successful in the formation of a class of 'liberated' and socio-politically awakened men and women who came to represent the upper-middle castes. To this group were added a few similar leaders from the SC and ST categories. Having reached the level of leadership and awakening primarily by relying upon the policy of protective discrimination, these urban elite, belonging to the backward classes, realised well the advantages of such a policy. This was complimented by an atmosphere at the national level with central government's sympathetic concern towards the upliftment of the downtrodden, particularly the SCs and the STs.

It is necessary to remind ourselves here that the policy of reservations to the SCs and STs was constitutionally resolved and settled, rather amicably, much earlier to independence and the policy of reservation to them at 15 per cent and 3 per cent respectively was continued after independence. But the situation as regards the OBCs was a source of much controversy, conflict and political instability throughout the years. The fundamental reason for this is that the OBCs in any state are invariably constituted by the dominant castes of the region, apart from the other middle and lower caste groups. The socio-political dominance exercised by a section of the dominant castes in each state has rendered any political decision or policy, either against them or excluding them, highly risky.

The matter is further aggravated by the fact that the dominant castes are a heterogeneous group with a number of subcastes which are unequal in their economic stature. Further, they are invariably the majority landowners in the rural areas and also control much of the administrative system in the urban areas. However, all members of the dominant castes cannot be generalised as owners of land or as economically resourceful. Poor people are common among them as among any other caste.

These inequalities within the OBC group in general and the dominant castes in particular have rendered any classification of the BCs difficult. The very category of the OBCs may be treated as constituting the crux of the whole problem of caste mobilisation, as it is this group that fills substantially the ranks of castes aspiring to politico-economic power through such means as reservations. The chief stages of caste mobilisation like the formation of caste associations and the establishment of private educational trusts by them relate largely to the OBCs' attempts to mobilise. Further, even the atmosphere of conflict and the prevalence of tensions and clashes between the different castes apply directly to the OBC category.

It is against this background that an analysis of Urs' emergence into the socio-political scenario in Karnataka is to be attempted. The imposition of President's rule in 1971, the mobilisational drive launched by a few upper-middle caste leaders during the same period, Urs' own mobility through the political channel and the general atmosphere wherein any Congress ministry was required to pay attention to the "welfare of the weaker sections" for its own survival – all these may be considered while exploring the reasons for the changes which occurred in Karnataka during 1972 and later.

In the mobilisation of public opinion that preceded the appointment of the KBCC, the initiative taken and the ground work of its Chairman late Sri L.G. Havanur is commendable. He has been described as not an individual, but an institution. When the Kaka Kalelkar Commission Report's recommendations were not accepted by the government, it directed the states to conduct socio-economic surveys to cover the deficiencies of the Report arising chiefly out of its use of caste as the principle of determining the economic backwardness (Aziz : 1980). It had not been attempted by any other state till then, and government of Karnataka took up the challenging task under his chairmanship.

The Havanur Report

Karnataka is credited as being the only state where a comprehensive survey of the various castes and tribes was conducted by a BCC. As soon as the ministry was formed in the state in 1972, with Sri Devraj Urs as the chief minister, the momentum for the demand for the appointment of a BCC further increased. As a prelude to his future actions, Urs had inaugurated a conference of denotified tribes at Hubli in 1971 itself. In this conference, and after Urs assumed office as the head of the ministry, Havanur and others (including the backward classes cell of the KPCC®) submitted memoranda stressing the need for a BCC in the state.

With the appointment of successive BCCs in the state, the Havanur Commission and its report have become part of history. The recommendations of the Havanur Report were submitted in the year 1975 and implemented in 1977, in the midst of both applause and opposition. Its suggestion to reserve 32 per cent of the seats in colleges and jobs in government for the OBCs were altered and the list of OBCs was expanded reserving 40 per cent of posts to them. Such a concession enabled some sections of the Lingayats and even the Brahmins, who were classified as 'forward' by the Commission to claim reservation benefits under the category of the 'Special Group'.

The forward castes (the Brahmins and Lingayats) were unhappy that the Commission had grossly underestimated their population by restricting the survey to only cities and towns. The Commission was also alleged to have neglected large sections of poor Lingayats living in rural areas, the converts to Veerasaivism from lower Hindu strata like Madivaalas, Ganigas and others.

The Lingayats' are against the Havanur Commission (and against Havanur also) is tracable to the denial of a backward class berth to them while, offering it to their rivals, the Vokkaligas. The justification by the Havanur Commission that the latter were socio-educationally backward than the Lingayats was never acceptable to the Veerasaiva Mahasabha which carried out a crusade against the Havanur Report under the guidance of its President, late Sri J.B. Mallaradhya.

As a numerically large caste group, the Lingayats were and are important determinants of political authority in the state. They have enjoyed political privileges, but also important in their representation in bureaucracy, judiciary and education where their number is quite high.

Having been so, the Commission's declassification of the community from the backward classe's list was not the only factor that affected them but was caused by a number of other political decisions and welfare programmes of the Urs government. Predominant among them were the land reform legislation and the abolition of bonded labour.[3] These and other actions of the Urs government were perceived as being anti-Lingayat by the Mahasabha and it threatened the government of grave political consequences. These gained momentum especially after 1978, a year after the passing of the Government Order on reservations recommended by Havanur. The grievances were squarely represented through caste associations and expressed not only through campaigning against the Devraj Urs ministry but through various other forms. In the historic Lok Sabha by-election in 1978, Mrs.Gandhi was supported by Urs, who offered her to contest from the Chikmagalur Constituency in Southern Karnataka. The Lingayats fielded Sri Veerendra Patil, the ex-chief minister, as the opposition candidate from the Janata Party. Their efforts did not yield the expected results.

Mass media, like the newspapers, were also used by the affected forward castes' spokesmen to express their displeasure about the Commission's recommendations. Apart from a spate of letters to the readers' columns, an article questioning the methodology and conclusions arrived at by the Commission was written to a local daily in Bangalore by a Toranto based Indian sociologist, and a Lingayat, Dr. K. Eswaran (1979:3). Further, during the elections in 1980, which is significant as it marked the rift between Urs and Mrs.Gandhi, the Mahasabha threatened that the support of the Lingayats to Congress (U) party founded by Urs would be withdrawn if the Havanur Report was not scrapped (Mallaradhya J.B., Mysore : 1981). This time Veerendra Patil contested elections and won.

Karnataka was not alone in carrying out agitations and tensions against the issue of classification of the backward classes. "The BCM being a sectional movement has tremendous potential for creating social tensions. This fact is ... observed in a great measure, in north Indian states, particularly in Uttar Pradesh and Bihar" (Aziz : 1980: 60). Galanter has also made references to this in his analysis of the backward classes (Galanter 1978: 1821).

Writing about "Backward Classes Commissions and State Practice", Paramananda Singh recognises rightly, that the "policy of compensatory discrimination has become the tool of aggrandisement in the hands of politically dominant castes and communities who are fighting hard to retain the privileges of being classified as backward class at the expense of the really needy and deserving.... The Lingayats and the Vokkaligas of Karnataka the Ezhavas and Nayars of Kerala, the Reddis and the Kammas of Andhra, the Nadars and the Vaniyars in Tamil Nadu, the Kurmis, the Ahirs and the Koiries in Uttar Pradesh and Bihar have always exerted pressure for their continuous recognition as backward classes." "The dominant castes are able to strike a political bargain with those in power for being classified as backward classes" (Singh : 1982: 154).

For example, in Bihar, the policy of reservations in jobs was introduced in 1978 by the government led by Sri Karpoori Thakur. Accordingly, 128 castes and communities coinciding with the lists of both Mugeri Lal Commission and the Kaka Kalelkar Commission, constituting about 47 per cent of the total population of the states were classified as backward. The list significantly included the Ahirs, the Kurmis and the Koiries, who constituted three-fifths of the total population of 128 castes. This led to massive violence and political intervention by the centre and ultimately these advanced-backward groups had to be excluded from the list. However, a separate provision was made for them in the form of Annexure-II.[4] (Singh : 1982).

Similarly, in the states of Andhra Pradesh, Kerala, Jammu and Kashmir and Uttar Pradesh communal politics affected the policy of reservations. In Kerala, the recommendations of the Nettur Commission were implemented by the Achuta Menon government. The Commission had followed the directives of the Supreme Court in the *Chitralekha case.*

But, both the forward and the backward communities launched a tirade against the Menon government.[5] The Vasudevan Nair Ministry that succeeded it "under political pressures exerted by the caste and communal leaders", announced its decision to reject the proposal and constitute a new committee to go into the whole question afresh. It is thus obvious that Kerala witnessed once again what it had been witnessing for nearly quarter of a century and what the northern states like Bihar witnessed (Namboodiripad : 1979b: 336).

Three factors could be delineated from the above discussion. One, the locally dominant castes have been an important segment of the backward classes everywhere; second, the policy of protective discrimination is used by politicians to seek own political benefits by conferring backward status on those who support them and; third, the policy has generated inter-caste war in many states and in others, it has found expression in court-battles.

Compared to most of the states discussed above, Karnataka stands apart as far as its resistance to the implementation of backward classes benefits goes. While similar exclusion of some of the forward communities in the list of the backward classes has been violently protested from the respective groups, the forward groups of Karnataka seem to have registered their opposition to their status conferred by Havanur Commission rather mildly.

This is not to deny the incidents of protest from the Lingayats and the Brahmins who, in Havanur's words "found full support in a major section of the press, which deliberately distorted my public speeches, demanded my resignation both inside and outside the Legislature". The opposition was not only against the Report but was more upon its author, the Chairman of the Commission. He was accused, in strong words, of having yielded to the power politics of Urs, by adding the latter's caste of Arasus to the list of the backwards, which was not in the original list.

The classification of the backward classes is generally influenced by such factors like:

(a) Social structure of Karnataka,
(b) History of reservation policy in the state, and
(c) The political charisma of political leaders like Sri Devraj Urs.

(a) Social Structure in Karnataka

The social structure in Karnataka is comprised of a caste hierarchy that is diametrically opposed to each other. The nature of inter-caste relationships is not tense, but not very cordial too. Further, north Karnataka exhibits a different regional, communal and linguistic picture as compared to its southern part. Brahmins are a minority in both regions. While traditionally the Lingayats alone were the dominant caste in the north, the south has the Vokkaligas also along with them. As agricultural communities in their traditional occupation, both enjoyed a dominant jajmani status over the professional and service communities. Dependency caused by this landowner-landless-worker situation between most of the lower castes *vis-à-vis* the Lingayats is more glaring in rural areas. The complexity is further stamped by certain sectarian features like the spread of the doctrine of Veerasaivism by Basava, the 12th century social reformer. The impact of this preaching of social equality against the external threat by the Marathas in the BK and the Muslims in the HK areas could be seen as the factors determining comparatively less hostile inter-caste relations in the north of the state.

Likewise, in the south, the minority status of Brahmins is a common factor. The inter-caste alliances between the dominant

Vokkaligas and the others need to be understood in the light of the BCM that is discussed as under:

(b) Historical Background of Reservation Policy in Karnataka

Compared to the other states, Karnataka was introduced to the system of reservations quite early i.e., in 1874 itself. The familiarity of the people with the policy is to be noted here. The movement for gaining equality with Brahmins carried out during the Princely regime was characterised by the participation of all the castes except the Brahmins since it was diverted against them. The Miller Committee recommended in 1918 that all except the Brahmins were eligible to claim benefits as backward castes/communities.

Thus, when the Havanur classified the Lingayats as forward, they should not have entirely opposed the system of reservations. They (and their caste associations) are apparently against the criterion of 'caste' and stress the need to classify the backward classes on economic criteria. To quote Professor Abdul Aziz, "At times even the much affected sections of the society like, for instance, the Brahmins have been graceful in their reaction to job and seat reservation. A sense of reconciliation to the claims of the backward classes appears to be visible where; on the contrary, a feeling of animosity and vindictiveness is expected" (Aziz : 1980 : 60).

(c) Role of Leaders like Devraj Urs

The Devraj Urs regime is one of the factors which should be taken note of while making an analysis of the nature and dimensions of caste mobilisation in the state. Urs was one of the rare politicians who had understood the social structure of Karnataka rather well. He not only knew but had even predicted a combination of caste-class nexus that the process of mobilisation was leading to in the state (Urs' Presidential address to mark the birthday of Dr. Ambedkar, 1982). He designed and implemented policies with care and discretion. In short, Urs knew his trump cards and played the game with ease and determination. These qualities raised him to the status of being named as the champion of the backward classes in the state. As he himself has asserted in an interview with James Manor, he was skilled in diplomatic politics which many of his contemporaries lacked. For example, he felt that one such leader in Bihar, Sri Karpoori Thakur "entered the ring before he could know how to box" (Manor : 1980).

Urs regime introduced a new era of caste mobilisation in the state. The systematic classification of the castes and communities into backward and forward by the Havanur Commission and the implementation of reservation benefits to them had, in course of time, literally led to a caste war in Karnataka. The protests by the forward groups made little dent on Urs' hold over state politics. His electoral loss in 1980 is at least partially attributable to the denial of backward status to the Lingayats.

The implementation of the Havanur Report, despite protest, has not resulted in any violent upsurge. But it has evidently signalled a series of mobilisational processes by all the castes and tribes who claimed backward status and continuation of and even a shift to more backward status. However, new dimensions to the achievement of greater political and economic power and other forms of mobility are found during this period. An important indicator being the rise in the number and diversity of caste based associations and private professional trusts after 1972.

The Gundu Rao Regime

The post-1980 era is characterised by the introduction of certain new vistas of the process of caste mobilisation in the state. The striking feature of this period has been the mounting dissatisfaction about the constitutional status which is conferred on each caste and tribe and accompanying such dissatisfaction is found, efforts to seek a 'greater backward' status. Backwardness has become a vested interest and even those caste groups who had been claiming upper caste status, through Sanskritisation and other modes of upward mobility have begun to demand their identification as backward castes in order to qualify as the beneficiaries of compensatory discrimination (Singh : 1980 : 154). This is evident from the demands of caste groups like the Madivalas (the washerman) and the barbers to be classified as SCs.

These developments in the sphere of caste based mobilisation were not entirely new or peculiar to Gundu Rao period. The foundation for them was laid during the Urs period itself. But their further enhancement was perhaps curtailed by the fact that they were not encouraged by the government then for deep-lying reasons of political insecurity. In other words, Urs knew the limits of his own policies and the effect they may have in future. It is here that one cannot refrain from commenting upon the much said and written slogans that describe him to be "the champion of backward classes". Urs was shrewd enough not to ignore the importance of the two dominant castes in the political map of the state and most of his policies have not affected them drastically.

Thus, encouraged by the situation, most of the middle castes and a few socio-politically awakened tribal groups have found a convenient setting to express their mobilisational spirits once the Gundu Rao ministry came to power. Its succession over Urs' government presented many-a-challenging situations to itself. Being a chief lieutenant of Urs, earlier, Rao was a witness to most of the former's pragmatic policies and programmes. He had also observed how the sectarian movement had influenced castes to organise themselves and intensify their movement for a tag of greater backwardness, on the eve of the implementation of the Havanur Report. The years 1979-1983 were remarkable for the sectarian activities that they focused upon. Gundu Rao only strengthened and supported them further.

A common feeling of frustration and disapproval about their constitutional position is inherent in the mobilisational activities of any community. Innumerable number of caste conferences is being organised and demands placed before government even now. Intra-caste competition is glaring besides inter-caste one. Caste-based tensions and conflicts have been more evident and conspicuous now than before.

The Issue of Capitation Fees and the Common Entrance Test

An important dimension of all this process of mobilisation for upward mobility is the system of capitation fees or paying of huge sums of money as donation in return for a seat in the professional course. The state has been witnessing a social crisis emanating from the frustrations of a section of the population which was theoretically against such a practice.

The matter took a stronger shape than ever before during the Gundu Rao's regime and further in the successive governments, particularly the Hegde Government, whose efforts to either resolve or find temporary solutions have been superficial. Some of the developments in this realm are as follows:

One of the glaring characteristics of the Gundu Rao government that came to power in the year 1980 was its liberal policy towards granting of professional colleges to private educational organisations in Karnataka. The assurance that he gave about granting professional colleges to caste-based associations and to individual trusts or "to whoever and whichever community comes and asks" (*Deccan Herald* :

December 4, 1980) led to the latter to make hay when he lasted. A number of medical and engineering colleges were started during his tenure holding the government above the Universities and the Medical and Technical Education Council of India. Rao's enthusiasm for expanding higher education in the state did not stop there. He even promised a separate university for the SCs and STs 'if he stayed long enough as chief minister'.

By the time Rao's actions came to encounter considerable opposition from the people, the state had started 13 new engineering and 10 medical colleges (6 private and 4 government colleges). Besides opposition from the Indian Medical Council, there was severe opposition from the state, centre and the committees[6] formed to look into the so-called capitation fee muddle that became a serious issue during his regime (*Deccan Herald* : November 15 , 1980).

The grant of permission to start few more medical colleges in Bangalore sparked off severe repercussions and sharp debates. Instead of serving the concerned communities, these new institutions were leading to proliferation and consequent fall in standard. The state had a dubious distinction of having the largest number of such professional colleges in the country. This was received by the leaders of the backward castes and religious minorities as coming from the forward castes with a view to perpetuate the backwardness of the former.

The issue triggered off a number of protests. One such was by the junior doctors who went on a long agitation in December 1980 criticising the issue from the point of view of large scale unemployment that any proliferation of medical colleges would eventually lead to. This led to a counter agitation by another batch of medical students from the OBC/SC background demanding an increase in professional colleges as they would facilitate the poor students to seek higher education (*Kannada Prabha* : December 1980). A high power committee with the chief secretary Narasimha Rau, Abdul Samad health minister, Veerappa Moily and the health secretary was formed to look into the issue with an open mind. A solution was worked out, with "capitation fee not being scrapped and the colleges not nationalised' (*Deccan Herald* : January 9, 1981), but was not effective in convincing the agitators. Those who were upset belonged to the aspirants to start new colleges who branded the committee's decision as enabling the existing colleges owned by upper castes to "block new ones so that they can collect capitation fee unabated" (*ibid.* : February 3, 1981).

The situation led to a complex battle with the management of some of the oldest colleges boycotting the practice of collecting capitation fees (like the Academy of General Education, Manipal). The report of an inquiry committee headed by the Director of Health and Family Welfare Services was accepted by the Academic Council of the Bangalore University. It has denied permission to new applications on grounds of lacking in proper[7] infrastructure. Two of the four colleges ultimately obtained permission but they belonged to a leading association of the Vokkaligas and the other was by the SCs, which are the sought after ones today, thriving with prosperity and good results. By-passing all norms, the government issued an ordinance on February 24, 1981 amending (for the second time within a week) section 53 of the Karnataka State Universities Act, 1976 that dealt with the affiliation of colleges empowering the government to grant affiliation to a college directly. Thus, the colleges could apply directly to the government thereby reducing the university to something of an irrelevance.

These actions of the state received a bolt from the blue when the Prime Minister categorically opposed the system of capitation fees and called it an unhealthy practice and a scourge of the south (*Deccan Herald* : Feb 26 and May 29, 1981). Even the state of Andhra Pradesh was also directed by the centre to look into the matter of scrapping the capitation fees. The then Chief Minister of the state, Sri T. Anjaiah defended that only one medical college was started in private sector before he assumed office (*Deccan Herald :* May 11, 1981). It was announced by the then Social Welfare Minister at the Centre, Sri S.B. Chavan that suitable steps are being taken by the Centre to undo the system of donations and a Bill was proposed to be passed to make the practice an offense. By 1981, Karnataka and Andhra Pradesh had started 25 and 10 such colleges, respectively.

The whole episode took a drastic turn with the agitation being called off by the striking students in March 1981, due to assurances by the chief minister to look into the matter while two more medical colleges (Vokkaliga and SC trusts) were given permission by his education minister. Seats in engineering and B.Ed colleges came to be refixed; a cabinet sub-committee was formed to study the situation; a central legislation was on the anvil to put an end to the unhealthy practice of capitation fee and the mushroom growth of private professional colleges (*Deccan Herald* : June 4, 1981).

Such assurances continued for many years but new batches of medical and engineering students were allowed to be admitted, with the state government maintaining a sphinx like posture. The education minister expressed helplessness and his hands being tied[8] due to the fact that among the applicants for new colleges there were many Muslim educational Trust. The Communist Party of India (Marxist) in its three-day meeting urged for opening of more colleges but to abolish the system of capitation fees.

This delay on the part of government's inaction to abolish capitation fees legally was to be seen in the political reference and the relationship between itself and the private management. Political bargains have been defining government's action in both encouraging sectarian interests to establish private colleges and to delay legislative or other measure for its eradication is clear.

The summary of this historical note is that the government was under tremendous pressure not to reduce the intake or affect the changes in the capitation fee system. The situation stood at 8,446 for 37 engineering colleges in the state for 1980-81 without any alteration. It was reported that seats were sold for anything between Rs. 15,000 and Rs. 80,000 in some of the prestigious colleges.[9]

What is notable is that at any point of time, the inaction of the government is due to its falling a prey to the communal caucus. "Every round everyday saw the government confused at best and colluding at the worst. At one point of time, the government even declared that capitation fee would be eradicated in phases and a period of five years to old colleges (medical); three for new ones it would be 7 years; it gave 10 per cent of seats to the managements in both cases. The old colleges were allowed to grant 65 per cent free seats in 1981-82 and for the next 4 years, it would go on increasing by 10 per cent till it reached 90 per cent (1984-85). Similarly for the new colleges in 1981-82, free seats would be 25 per cent and in the next six years, it would reach 90 per cent (1987-88)" (*Indian Express :* August 26, 1981).

In engineering colleges merit seats were likewise increased in terms of: 20 in 1981-82; 40 in 1982-83; 60 in 1983-84, 80 in 1984-85 and 90 in 1985-86. At a time when most colleges had completed admissions and left only left free seats unfilled, the High Court granted a stay on all writ petitions by managements of such colleges. Only Kempe Gowda College agreed to absorb the selected students from the lists announced by the government, but both Ambedkar and M. S. Ramaiah colleges closed their doors in the face of these students. Manipal College turned out 62 students. While some of these had a court cover, the Ambedkar College ignored the order as it was under the chief minister's patronage. Manipal College declared total independence from the government.

Whatever is the reaction of college management, the High Court stay really came as a face-cover for the Gundu Rao government which announced on September 22 that "until the cases were decided, status quo ante would continue." Ironically, even here it was an empty claim as the older colleges had restricted the government control to a mere 65 per cent compared to the earlier 90 per cent hold. Then came the centre's advice in November 1981 that the government should continue its policy on capitation fee for one more year. This was in view of the objection raised by managements of some private colleges selection procedure was over, before the government order was issued.

Conclusions

The above note clearly states that the political system in Karnataka has developed an intricate relationship with the caste network. Government's policies for the welfare of the backward and weaker sections have virtually started a process of caste mobilisation and also a caste battle in the state. These have come to affect and determine key political processes.

Any political control system would worsen if the people holding political offices themselves support the cause of caste mobilisation. In the case of Karnataka, the government during Gundu Rao's regime, for example, could not curb the evil practice of capitation fees since two such colleges were in fact sponsored by his own Ministerial colleagues (H.D. Deve Gowda and C.M. Armugam). While the practice of capitation fees dates back to the sixties, when S. Nijalingappa was the Chief Minister, the issue of foregoing the university in the matter was started during the Urs' time. For example, when the M.S. Ramaiah

College came into existence neither the university nor the Indian Medical Association was consulted. Whatever was created by Nijalingappa and Urs came to be perpetuated by their successors. However, commercialisation of education came in for severe criticism by people. For example, the managements which had sponsored these colleges were criticised by their own caste-folk for corrupt practices.[10] Although no college, irrespective of which caste it represented, has lived up to its own slogans and claims to work for the downtrodden and poor within its caste, the Ambedkar Medical College was singled out for such open criticism. That it came from not non-SCs but from own caste people add further dimensions to the issue. It was the Dalit Action Committee which demanded the resignation of Sri Armugam as the Chairman of the Ananda Educational Trust. A detailed account of the corrupt activities and wealth in his hometown KGF started to appear in local dailies of Bangalore. These accusations were supported by other dalit organisations as well like the Karnataka Dalit Youth Federation. 50 per cent of seats were demanded for poor students in the college. As this did not materialise, Armugam came to be branded as anti-dalit.

As most other comments on the college came from non-SCs like A.K. Subbaiah, Armugam took this as a matter of atrocity on him as a dalit, while the other caste organisations that had started colleges in greater numbers had been left out.

But, there were other controversies in the case of other colleges. For example, the government was charged for its alleged interference in offering subjects. The BIT started two new courses that came for severe criticism. The Vice-Chancellor and the Registrar claimed to have sought the permission of the syndicate, senate and the academic council. But later it was turned out to be untrue. The verification process made H.D. Deve Gowda a senior Vokkaliga leader to condemn government's action and the role of certain vested interests who have tried to bring dishonour to the 80 year old caste association of the Vokkaligas.

Thus, despite governmental efforts to tackle or solve the problem, private educational institutions have come to become institutionalised, not because of people adopting them, but because of the political leaders breeding such pernicious practices obviously to succeed in certain political bargains with the dominant and politically useful caste groups like the minorities or SCs/STs.

The Janatha Rule

Beginning with 1983, Karnataka's political situation has witnessed a major transformation when instead of a single party's rule (Congress) it came to have an alternative political party system and then on to coalition politics. It was in this year that it came to be governed by a non-Congress government. When Ramakrishna Hegde took over as the Chief Minister, he had the challenge of settling the capitation fee issue muddle and the increasing number of applications from sectarian organisations demanding sanction of professional colleges. His contemporary in Andhra Pradesh, Sri N.T. Rama Rao stuck to his election promise and promulgated an Ordinance through his Governor banning collection of capitation fee in all educational institutions, except minority institutions in the state with immediate effect (*Times of Deccan* : January 31, 1983). Thus he was hailed as setting an example to the other states "plagued with the same problem".

But the government led by Sri Hegde was not devoid of a caste caucus that surrounded it influencing its decisions. The dominant castes continued to have their sway over state's politics irrespective of the party in power. Having been at the core of the state's political power structure for long, the Lingayats and Vokkaligas had left a dent on it which was not easy to be altered.

Thus even after the non-Dominant groups made their entry, the situation was not any different than before.

A variety of means and actions were introduced by subsequent governments to deal with the issue of private professional education and capitation fees. The High Court stay on this issue was vacated through the Advocate General's office and a Comprehensive Education Bill to do away all the ills dogging the system, was promised. Many colleges announced reforms in admission rules like some percentage of seats reserved for diploma holders or cut in fee etc. On April 6, 1983, the High Court passed the judgment quashing the GO on capitation fees in the states' 39 engineering colleges, in view of any law prohibiting the collection of capitation fees. It upheld only that part of the GO which restricted the intake of students in those colleges. Justice Sri Chandrakantharaje Urs stated that 'silence is tantamount to consent'. "Ever since the government order on the abolition of capitation fees was brought out, it has not been supported by the parents or guardians of the students that the practice was extortion and that it had not voluntarily been paid by them." "Therefore, those who pay capitation fee are those who can afford to do so. Having secured a seat, they are not likely to question the raison d'etre of the capitation fee system." Since those who afforded to pay were the parents from upper classes of most castes, no protest came apparently from them.

A few months after this judgment chief minister Hegde stated that the government intends to ban capitation fee system for Karnataka students seeking admissions to medical courses on merit basis and restored the intake to the original quantum fixed by the IMC. It also hinted that by abolishing the government's discretionary quota of 10 seats from each of the seven private medical colleges of the state, the government has abolished in one stroke the 149 seats which were allowed to be admitted by Gundu Rao government.

But the Janata government evolved a different three point formula comprising of separate quota as government students from Karnataka, those from other states and foreign students. The government quota rested on merit basis and on reservation rules. It did not demand any capitation fees for the 261 seats it offers. The second category offered 70 seats (10 seats from each college) and demanded a refundable deposit of Rs.50,000 to be returned after ten years. In the third category, the seats allotted rose to 395 with the government fixing the quota to each college. Those from outside the state had to pay a donation of Rs. 1.5 lakh while for the foreign students the amount was fixed at Rs.2 lakhs. Apart from this, the government also fixed the fees at Rs. 5,000 against the existing Rs.3, 000. The press dubbed this as legislation of capitation fees and the refundable deposit of Rs.50,000 without interest after ten years was considered as a modified form of capitation fees.

A look at the distribution of seats under the various categories mentioned above to the 7 private medical colleges clarifies that caste politics held its sway over the government. 4 older medical colleges at Belgaum, Davanagere, Mangalore and Gulbarga had to admit a larger share of government quota – 52, 52, 60 and 52 seats respectively) their quota of foreign students was reduced to a minimum (with a ceiling of 38, 38, 55 and 38 seats respectively). The three new colleges – Ambedkar, Kempe Gowda and M. S. Ramaiah—were sanctioned the least government quota (of 15 seats each) and a maximum of foreign seats (of 75 seats each).

The government maintained a pristine silence about the admission in private engineering colleges stating that the matter was pending before the Supreme Court. The action of the previous government passing an Order regulating the taking of capitation fees had been struck down by the high court. It had upheld that the government had no power to fix the intake or make restrictions in regard to capitation fee as it violated Article 19 of the Constitution. The government referred the matter to Supreme Court.

The above comparative analysis of two governments during the periods when the issue of private professional education was encouraged by the state is only to show that the practice is deep-rooted, many-a-times nurtured by the government itself. If only the Congress-I governments that governed the state were to be blamed for encouraging such practices there should not have been any difficulty for the latter non-Congress governments to root it out. The system has its roots deep into the social structure upon which the government rests. Whatever a certain party argued against the system from the opposition benches came to prove that it was not free from the impact of power politics when it came to power. The debates on the issue did pull on for sometime, only to fade into oblivion subsequently. During this period, allegations and counter-allegations were made by the ruling and opposition parties, blaming each other. A comprehensive Education Bill was also passed empowering the successive governments to abolish the system or evolve an alternative.

What is interesting is to note that the government while finding out solutions or remedies to the "evil" did not touch upon the subject of private educational institutions that breed the practice. Only half hearted measures have been taken to curb the practice in the existing institutions, which created a range of problems to the government itself. No drastic move could be taken by it obviously because a number of political leaders, both inside and outside the government, are themselves either founder-presidents or patrons of such private educational trusts. This is evident in the contrasting stand taken by the then government in the case of sanctioning of new engineering and medical colleges. For example, the then Health Minister Mr. P.G.R. Sindhia assured that no new colleges would be permitted to be started in response to such a request by the JSS Educational Trust in Mysore. Paradoxically after a year of such a claim by the Minister, two medical colleges came to be started –one by the JSS Trust and the other by the Al Ameen Charitable Fund Trust of Bangalore. This decision was taken at a time when the Rajya Sabha was discussing the UGC Amendment Bill empowering the UGC to derecognise capitation fee based colleges in the country. The two new colleges were permitted by the State Cabinet to collect such fees under the prohibition of capitation fee Bill to which the President had also given his assent. The blame was squarely put on the Gundu Rao Government that it had done all ground-work and the ruling Janatha government had no option but to sanction them. Not just that, late Dr. Jeevraj Alva, a Minister also announced that a few more such colleges may be sanctioned in the near future.

This assurance and receptivity of the government kindled the aspirations of sectarian organisations/caste associations which came forward with requisitions for starting of professional colleges. Notable is the fact that the demand came, this time, more from the caste groups like the Kurubas, the Ganigas, the Marathas, the Devangas and the Raju Kshatriyas[11] who form the middle levels of the social hierarchy unlike in the past when such demands came from the dominant castes alone. This is an indication of the widening dimension of caste mobilisation in Karnataka. Just as in the past, such demands were put forth before the government during caste conferences organised by the respective caste associations. In most cases, such conferences also marked the first-ever conference of the concerned caste groups.

All this is sufficient proof of the fact that "the impunity and light-heartedness with which the state government is tackling these issues can only leave one dumb-founded. If the Gundu Rao government did such things brazenly, the Janatha regime accomplished the same with greater fitness." The successive governments have witnessed more complex changes in this link between politics and caste based mobilisation in Karnataka.

References

1. Twenty eight per cent for the backward classes, 22 per cent for the more backward classes and 18 per cent for the SCs and the STs.
2. Such as Messers N. Rachaiah, L.G. Havanur, K.H. Ranganath, M.H. Jayaprakash Narayan, K.P. Sachendranath, Kalle Shivothama Rao, A.B. Mariappa, S. Hanumanthaiah and S. Siddappa. Many of them, like Rachaiah, Havanur, Ranganath etc., became ministers later in the Urs ministry.
3. Manor (1980) has interpreted this as having helped the Sadar Lingayats.
4. The Bihar government subsequently fixed an income ceiling of Rs. 12,000 per annum per family to qualify to obtain reserved jobs. Out of the 26 per cent of jobs so reserved, 60 per cent went to those listed in Annexure I; and 40 per cent to those listed under Annexure II. Also see Ramashray Roy's: it argues that the proportion of middle castes in Bihar Pradesh Congress Committee increased after 1948, rose from 29 per cent in 1948 to 32 per cent in 1954.
5. The Backward Classes Reservation Commission was set up in Kerala under the Chairmanship of Sri P. D. Nettur, which gave its Report in 1970. The tests applied by the Commission were: educational attainment, economic position, appropriation in appointment to government service and social backwardness due to historical reasons. It recommended that the backward classes should be drawn from all communities, irrespective of caste or religion. It had also noted that more than two-thirds of the gazetted jobs were monopolised by the forward communities. Even the Ezhavas had a fairly good representation in non-gazetted and 'low-grade' services (KBCRC Report : 1970).
6. Like the Dr. K.N. Raj Committee.
7. The four colleges were: (a) the Islamiah Medical College, (b) the Kempe Gowda Institute of Medical Sciences, (c) the Dayanandasagar Medical and Dental College, and (d) the Ambedkar Medical College.
8. For example, Samad suggested a radical formula: total abolition of capitation fees in all colleges including new ones from 1982-83. Excluded from this were the Ambedkar and Kempegowda Colleges for one year while he allowed the M. S. Ramaiah College to sell 60 per cent of its seats. For the four old colleges, he suggested the formula of 65:25:10

(i.e., 65 per cent of seats were meant to be free seats, which did not come under the capitation fee system, 25 per cent of seats were meant to be allotted by charging capitation fees and 10 per cent of them were left to the discretion of the management). Any deviants from this were demanded to be nationalised.

But as a counter to Samad's proposal, the chief minister made the health secretary (who was at loggerheads with the minister) to present a note which pooh-poohed the minister's formula. (Sachidananda-Murthy, 1982) Capitation Fee Muddle, *Indian Express* : June 21, 1982).

9. The highest bid for a seat was Rs. 35,000 for locals and Rs.50,000 for outsiders (*The Hindu :* May 16, 1981).
10. Like M. Nanjappa, Vice President, Karnataka Dalit Youth Federation, Bangalore, he has criticised C. M. Armugam as being anti-Harijan and as attempting to cheat the Harijans by starting educational institutions in the name of Dr. B.R. Ambedkar (*Prajavani* : February 14, 1982).

    Apart from the mess that they created in relation to the issue of capitation fees, the new colleges also presented other problems. Chief among them was the controversy over the sites where the buildings for the Dayananda Sagar College and M. S. Ramaiah College came up.
11. While inaugurating the All India Raju Kshatriya Conference at Bangalore, the chief minister agreed to grant permission to the Raju Kshatriya community to establish an engineering college, stressing that the college should be started in a backward area like Kolar district (*Deccan Herald :* November 18, 1984).

7 Sectarian Mobilisation and the Emerging Social Conflict

Introduction

The preceding sections have made a detailed analysis of the nature and dimensions of social mobilisation with reference to its caste structure. The fundamental factors which have influenced the social fabric resulting in a process of social transformation have been identified. An argument referring to the extent of interference of "class" interests in caste-based activities has also been raised. Nevertheless, it would be relevant and useful that to emphasise the concept of "mobilisation" should be understood as a combination of economic and political factors, though it is commonly referred to as being social in nature.

These two assumptions, viz., that mobilisation includes the pursuit of economic interests under the mask of social goals and that it assumes structural importance in a stratified as well as segmented society, hold the key to an understanding of the nature and characteristics of caste mobilisation in Indian society today. A notable feature of this trend is the prevalence of "conflicts" between the different segments that constitute the social system.

In other words, the analysis of the emergence and working of caste associations, the rise and constitution of leadership pattern in them and the nature of demands charted out by each caste association indicates not only the social importance of the process of mobilisation, but contain certain underlying economic and political motives.

In a mass society, the different groups participating in the mobilisational process for the pursuit of certain broader and common goals tend to come into conflict with each other. "A structural feature facilitating mobilisation into protest movement is obtained when the society is not only highly stratified but segmented" (Oberschall : 1973:119).

As a social process, conflict is understood as "a struggle over values or claims to status, power and scarce resources, in which the aims of the conflict groups are not only to gain the desired values, but also to neutralise, injure or eliminate rivals" (Coser : 1957: 232). This definition of social conflict seems to broadly fit into the process of caste mobilisation that is on-going in India.

Social conflict is not new to Indian society but has been a feature of the social system as an essential component of the process of social movement. "Change and conflict are intimately linked. It is the rising and declining groups and classes formed and transformed during periods of change that usually constitute the core of social movements and organised groups who seek to reform and revolutionise existing institutions or, on the contrary, defend the social order under attack" (Moore : 1965: 84).

"Once a hallmark of western European and northern American society, social change has become a world-wide phenomenon in the 20th century" (Oberschall : 1973: 34). "Considered as a process of creative destruction, capitalism was also held as an appropriate characterisation of world-wide changes" (Schumpeter : 1951). It is widely believed that colonial rule in India no doubt influenced the existing traditional social structure, investing it with certain traits of modernity. This impact of the British rule on Indian society sounds rather exaggerated, but one cannot deny its role in introducing some forms of social change in the sub-continent.[1] Marx also thought that British rule would alter the caste system (Marx : 1853).

Despite being common to Indian society, like any other, "not all communities and societies experience the same degree of conflict, nor does a single society experience the same degree of conflict over time. The forms that conflict assumes, non-violent and violent, institutionalised or otherwise, vary in time and social space." "A theory of social conflict has to address itself to the complexity and variability of conflict" (Oberschall : 1973: 34).

Therefore, it is difficult to obtain studies on all aspects of social conflicts in India. The Havanur Report also remarks that "No systematic and comprehensive study seems to have been made on Karnataka as a whole" (KBCC Report Vol.I, Part I, 1975 : 1). The fact that caste mobilisation generates conflict has been indicated in the words of Constitutional Reforms, the Backward Classes Movement and related issues in South India. Studies by Eugene P. Irshick (1969) and Gail Omvedt (1976) have portrayed the socio-cultural upheaval which occurred in the Province of Madras and the Maharashtra region as a result of "movement for equality by non-Brahmins in the two areas. Similar is the work of Lelah S. Dushkin (1974) and to some extent by James Manor (1977) which deals with the non-Brahmin movement in Princely Mysore. Hettne and Tamm (1974) is an exclusive study of the process of mobilisation in Karnataka. In these as well as in many other works, references are made to the existence of conflict in the social and cultural fields of life in Karnataka.

The main thrust of these studies which have confined themselves to the analysis of the social and political aspects of the changing role of caste in India is, no doubt, upon the process of mobilisation. In their exposition of the traces of social conflict, most of them have tried to portray the process of caste mobilisation in the years before independence. Although the concept "social conflict does not appeal to be explicitly used as an index of mobilisation by the above studies, the very prevalence of a movement for equality (known popularly the Backward Classes Movement) is taken to be an indication of the existence of conflict."

Regardless of its presence in the periods earlier, the BCM not only of Karnataka, but wherever it occurred, set in motion a fight between the different caste groups. In its appearance and ideology, the movement, as its name suggests, was a struggle between the two broader sections of caste, viz., the Brahmins and the non-Brahmins.

However, it should be made clear in this context that regardless of its presence in the periods earlier, the BCM, not only in Karnataka, but also wherever it occurred, set in motion a fight between the different caste groups. It gave an appearance because of its nomenclature that it was the fight between two broad categories of caste groups, into Brahmins and non-Brahmins. However, it would be a misnomer to identify the Brahmins and the non-Brahmins as two unified caste groups. While the latter was a blanket term indicating, by definition, a combination of all castes and tribal groups except the Brahmins, the Brahmins were referred to as one single caste. The non-Brahmins also attempted to unify, however temporarily, all groups under their respective categories.

Both the divisions are not homogeneous but present a number of subcaste and class distinctions. They were only blanket terms used to denote a number of castes, but also presented a number of class divisions, which ran across caste distinctions. In the process of their crusade against the so-called Brahmin oligarchy, the non-Brahmins showed excellent 'class' characteristics. This is evident from the fact that the participants in the movement consisted of those who hailed from the upper strata of the two dominant castes, viz., Lingayats and Vokkaligas.

These features of caste distinctions were a natural corollary of the unequal, segmented and stratified social system of which they were a part. The goals to achieve equality with the Brahmins had given an indication of unity and cohesion to the process. But the same economic and political interests led in course of time to tensions and conflicts in the movement in the past and even now. The process of caste mobilisation initiated during this era did not just end with the appointment of a BCC in Princely Mysore, but continued later too. Its recommendations providing seats to members of non-Brahmin communities in educational institutions and government services that labelled them as backward classes intensified the caste struggle. Thus, the post-independence period, both in Karnataka and other states, is witnessing an unabated fight for economic and political privileges by all communities alike. It has not been exclusive to the Hindus but has included the Muslims and the Christians in its fold.

The basing of the reservation system or the policy of protective discrimination on the caste factor could be regarded as one of the chief determinants of the increase in the role of caste in socio-political life. Karnataka being one of the premier states for having implemented the policy, the simmering feelings of animosity and competition have acquired definite shape in the recent years. They have assumed quite alarming proportions even disturbing the social equilibrium at times.

What is true at the national level is found reflected at the state levels also. This is glaring in Karnataka because it is one of the few states in India where the reservation policy has been effectively implemented by the government, especially by the Devraj Urs government.

The simmering caste feelings or animosities and competition have acquired a definite shape in the recent decades and have sometimes assumed quite alarming proportions, even disturbing the social equilibrium at times. A critical evaluation of the incidents of social conflict in Karnataka in the light of its caste mobilisation is attempted below, with a view to understanding the social framework and the politico-economic compulsions which have followed the process.

Before embarking upon the subject of social conflict in relation to caste mobilisation in Karnataka, conceptual clarity is desirable about some notions and usages. The introductory chapter in the thesis has also stressed this point. By social conflict is meant, in the present context, those cases of rivalry, competition, frustration and extreme socio-cultural actions and programmes by certain caste groups whose interests are affected, directly or indirectly, positively or negatively by the process of caste mobilisation. More crucial to its understanding is that social conflict may occur without generally recognised traits like violence, turmoil or revolutions.

Perhaps, one may find answers to these peculiarities of social conflict in the very substance of social change or mobility from where it generates. Being characterised and termed as an evolutionary process, social change would lead automatically to comparatively slow and latent conflicts and tensions. It is therefore not possible to expect always the same degree of protest or in the same form. Tensions arising out of caste conflicts and competition assume different forms depending upon the socio-cultural circumstances operating at that time. The form these tensions adopt to express themselves may be legislative, economic, political or religious in nature. It is also necessary to consider all these forms as complementary to each other and not being contradictory in nature.

Nature and Classification of Caste Conflict in Karnataka

In the above context, the following layers of caste conflict are evident in the state in the recent decades:

- There is a longstanding rift between all the caste-Hindus against the SCs which is deep-rooted and arises out of the traditional distinctions based on purity and pollution that institutionalised the practice of untouchability.

- Secondly, there is an attack on the Brahmins as the progenitors of caste system by all others in the hierarchy resulting in the occurrence of series of non-Brahmin movements, referred to earlier.
- Thirdly, there is noticed in recent years, the existence of a rift between the "backward" and the "forward" caste groups that is solely attributable to the policy of reservation.
- Likewise, the classification of the various backward groups by the BCCs has led to a growing tendency of mutual antagonism and competition aimed towards the securing of a greater share of the Constitutional Guarantees reserved for them.

The above are in the nature of inter-caste rivalries. Besides these, there are certain intra-caste tensions too, an extension of the fact that caste is not homogeneous but consists of many subcastes and sub subcastes. Each one of them is necessarily endogamous.

- Being not an exception to the heterogeneous nature of caste, the Brahmins are also characterised by considerable factions amongst themselves. Intra-caste rivalries within the community are a feature of not only the present day process of mobilisation, but date back to the period earlier to the setting up of the Miller Committee.
- Secondly, the various caste categories within the BCs, SCs, STs and BTs present a picture of intra-group factions and rivalries.
- There is also evidence of the prevalence of intra-group conflict between the SCs and STs.

Mobilisation and Caste Conflict in Princely Mysore: A Note

One can argue that compared to the situation before independence, caste rivalry and competition in the years earlier to it were less, both in degree and tempo. This is true of both intra and inter-caste conflicts. The BCM taking place in Princely Mysore is credited to have inaugurated a continuous chain of caste struggle in the state. This movement for equality was fundamentally a fight for certain economic gains for the so-called non-Brahmins who launched a state wide agitation. This ultimately resulted in the setting up of a Committee to decide the criteria for assessing backwardness. It no doubt generated inter and intra-caste frictions among both the groups — Brahmins and the non-Brahmins.

Even as the non-Brahmins were preparing themselves for a movement seeking reservations in government service, during the first decade of the twentieth century, local Brahmins were fighting for a similar cause. As a counterpart to the conflict between the Brahmins and the non-Brahmins, the Mysore Brahmins went against the "import" of Brahmin Dewans from the Madras Presidency (Hettne and Tamm : 1974). The process commenced from the "import" of the first Dewan Sri Rangacharlu and stopped before Sir M. Visvesvaraya who was a Mysorean. The contention of the Mysore Brahmins was that with such a practice, "their own prospects would be affected adversely" (Natraj : 1979:3). The appointment of Dewans hailing from Madras was alleged to have adversely affected the selection of local Brahmins to Mysore Civil Service because their counterparts in Madras were generally preferred for such posts. This was vehemently opposed by a group of highly educated and sophisticated young Brahmins of Mysore. The Mysore press, which had just developed, also supported the cause of the Mysore

Brahmins through its writings[2]. Such a tendency is found to have continued till 1910 when the Brahmin-non-Brahmin controversy loomed large on the social scene. However, furious debates in the Representative Assembly and more so in the Legislative Council "continued" even in the twenties and the thirties on this issue.

Thus the BCM in Karnataka was not monolithic in character. It tried, instead, to place on the platform, the needs and aspirations of the minority - consisting of the elite from the upper castes among the non-Brahmins - under the mask of a popular movement by all the non-Brahmins as a class. Leadership and power vested, however, in the hands of a few upper caste/ class non-Brahmins who consisted of young, rural-based, English educated Vokkaliga and Lingayat men. The movement in Madras Presidency provided both inspiration and moral and ideological strength to the movement in Princely Mysore. Its impact on the latter in Mysore is marked not only by purpose and ideological emulation, but it was characterised by mobilisation of certain cultural traits and arranging for marital alliances with homogeneous background.

Secondly, it should be emphasised that conflict or rift between different castes and communities, which is on the rise of late, is dealt with in the present analysis as a consequence of the process of caste mobilisation.

The seemingly unified character of the movement did not sustain for long. The divisive forces, which were already at work when the movement was active, culminated in action once the Miller Committee gave its report in the year 1918, recommending certain privileges to the backward classes. The Committee classified all castes, except the Brahmins, as "backward". As could be imagined, the beneficiaries were largely from the two dominant castes with a small percentage of upper middle groups staking their claims in a feeble way.

One essential conclusion the above discussion leads to, though indirectly, is that the policy of reservations has gone a long way in initiating a fight for spoils amongst the various castes through the process of mobilisation. In other words, the efforts of the non-Brahmins of Mysore to fight for equal status with the Brahmins resulted in certain governmental provisions to the BCs. This further kindled the hopes and aspirations of those castes which were immediately below the Lingayats and the Vokkaligas in the hierarchy. Thus we observe the growth of awareness about mobilisation among the caste groups (occupying social positions below the Vokkaligas) like the Kurubas, the Kunchitigas and the Devangas, in the twenties and thirties.

An interesting aspect of these developments is that the impact of caste mobilisation in Karnataka was not restricted only to the Hindu castes and tribes. It has affected the life of even the non-Hindus, predominantly the Muslims and to some extent even the Christians. The Muslims were treated on par with the non-Brahmins as a backward community by the Miller Committee, "but this did little to keep the alliance together : (Natraj : 1979:4). It did not take long for the differences to surface. The highly communal politico-social situation in the country during the twenties and thirties at the macro-level may be said to have added more fuel to the already tense feelings between the Hindus and the Muslims at different micro-levels (Dushkin : 1966). Princely Mysore also witnessed certain communal clashes during that period. "By the thirties the Mohammedans wanted to be excluded from the non-Brahmin group and treated as a special entity. The Kunchitigas wanted to be truncated from the Vokkaliga category. The depressed classes who had had no representation in the Miller Committee argued for special treatment. The fight for spoils was on" (Natraj : 1979: 4).

The Miller Committee and its report also led to tension between the Brahmins and the non-Brahmins. While the years earlier to the appointment of the Committee witnessed agitation by the latter for certain privileges on par with the Brahmins, in the post-Miller Committee days, the Brahmins joined the fray in criticising the non-Brahmins and their movement. Arguing on the point of efficiency, the Brahmins disapproved of discrimination against any caste or community. But their argument could not sustain itself strongly in the light of their (Brahmins') own fight against their Madras counterparts. The non-Brahmin leaders argued that when the Mysore Brahmins "themselves had sought a measure of protection by seeking the restriction of the Civil Service examination only to Mysoreans", thereby "could not later deny it to others".[3] (Natraj : 1979: 4).

The widespread prevalence of caste tensions emerging especially out of the differences of opinion on the issue of reservations may be explained as constituting a fundamental aspect of social conflict in Princely Mysore. The fact that reservation of seats in government services led to socio-political changes is evident from the reports in the press. For example, commenting on the elections held in February 1927 for the Representative Assembly and the Legislative Council in Mysore, in which most of the "Brahmana candidates" suffered defeat, the press alleged that, "those who have succeeded have managed to do so, in a majority of cases, by rousing and riding upon the forces of rabid communalism .... The presence of a majority of the former (non-Brahmins) in any public body should only be viewed as a matter of course and as no cause of surprise or disappointment. What we are now concerned with is not the statistics of victory, but the spirit that stands behind the victory". The argument then turned more sharp "......Narrow caste mentality is by no means unknown among them (the Brahmins) and the NBM could not but produce its reaction on them making their sectarianism all the more eager and pointed. But with all that, can it be said that those who have now replaced them are better? ...... or is it only 'some' narrowness is replaced by 'more' narrowness; and 'some' competency by 'less' competency?" (The Karnataka and the Indian Review of Reviews, Vol.XII, February 1927, Editorial).

It is obvious from the above reports in the press, that the effects of the NBM created anxiety and insecurity, apart from hatred and enmity in the minds of the Brahmins. The above note taken from the Karnataka and the *Indian Review of Reviews*, a journal edited by a renowned journalist of that time, Sri Thirumale Thathacharya Sharma, should only be considered as a reflection of the sour feelings of the Brahmin elite towards the 'attempted' political supremacy of the non-Brahmins due to the reservation policy. There is no doubt that whatever tensions arose and conflicts generated, are attributable to the politico-economic loss suffered by the Brahmin elite with the non-Brahmins occupying positions of power in the political system. To this may also be added the feelings of contempt and prejudice that may have lived in the hearts of these Brahmin leaders, obviously due to the influence of the traditional caste rules and norms, which it is feared, might have led them to suspect the capacity of the non-Brahmins to carry on their new responsibilities (as political leaders) efficiently and effectively. This is evident from the following press reports: insecurity and uncertainty about the "fairness" in the policies of the non-Brahmin rulers was writ large in the writings of the Brahmin leaders. They wrote: "Though frankly disappointed", (by the success of the non-Brahmin candidates), "it is hopefully and prayerfully" looked forward for "the day when what is now a matter for disappointment may turn out a matter for congratulations, in consequence of the tolerant sobriety and broad-hearted sympathy of those who have now captured places of power. A policy of vengeance after success is hardly becoming. The melancholy story of the Panagal Ministry in Madras must serve as a warning to those who would use power wantonly and in disregard of fairness and justice to the public at large. There is some power inherent in righteousness which irresistibly moves and wins the hearts of the common people; and when considerations of righteousness are violated, it is certain to produce a reaction in the unsophisticated mass-mind and bring the violators to their doom. If the non-Brahmin leaders in Mysore will bear in mind this common but grave truth, and shape their policies accordingly, they will save themselves from ignominy and the country from distress" (Karnataka and the Indian Review of Reviews, Vol. XII : 1927).

That the non-Brahmin movement did threaten the existing administrative structure generally dominated by Brahmins is clear when the press acknowledged that the non-Brahmins "deserve the success they have won from one important point of view at any rate - they organised well. They were earnest and took trouble to woo their constituencies. If they will now show friendliness and consideration for those who fear them, they will have deserved their power even better. In fact, their present success is such as should render their communalism useless and meaningless hereafter. Now that their ascendancy is assured, it would be patriotic of them if they will hereafter grow into something finer and larger. It is good to acquire the strength of a giant, but not to use it in a giant's way. Our specific suggestion to the non-Brahmin party in Mysore is that henceforward it should eschew all controversy about the distribution of government jobs and all other communalistic topics in the Assembly and the Council and should address itself to the larger questions of state-wide public policy and nation-building" (*ibid.*).

The question of merit and efficiency versus group and proportional equality, which constitutes the fundamental characteristic of the debates on 'reservation policy', has been discussed under various headings in the present book. Just as it has instigated a battle between the supporters of both schools of thought, the "principle of merit" is seen to have formed the basis upon which the 'anti-reservation' arguments were made in the post-Miller Committee days. It also culminated in the resignation of the office of Dewanship by Sri M Visvesvaraya.

However, the resignation of Sir M.V. also ended, temporarily though, the long rule by Brahmin Dewans in Princely Mysore. Sardar M. Kanthraje Urs, under whose regime the Brahmin non-Brahmin cleavages are understood to have sharpened, replaced him. These cleavages reached their zenith during the Dewanship of Amin-Ul-Mulq Sir Mirza M. Ismail Sahab, who was third in succession after Sir M.V. To the existing cleavages, between the dominant groups of Lingayats and Vokkaligas was added another new conflict - that between the non-Brahmin leaders and Muslims, which gained momentum especially after the Bangalore communal riots of 1928 (Hettne and Tamm : 1974: 151). It was also rumoured that the Brahmins fanned the riots.

Nevertheless, the Brahmin press wrote that "If Mr. Mirza M. Ismail who spoke in his first address to the Representative Assembly of restoring 'the ancient vision of a united national life' is still being haunted - as we fully hope he is - by that noble and inspiring vision, he must see a golden opportunity for its realisation in the present triumph of the non-Brahmin party". Unlike "an administrator of the common variety", Mr. Mirza has kept a more exalted mission before himself, and he therefore will be expected to deal with the powerful party in a different way, so that it may be of help of him in the fulfillment of his mission".[4] (*ibid.*).

These and many other reports in the press in old Mysore, especially those published from the capital city of Bangalore, go a long way in reflecting the attitude of the so-called forward group - the Brahmins - against the system of reservations and its beneficiaries - the non-Brahmins. Though not explicitly expressed, the policy of granting reservations to members of the backward classes was no doubt looked upon with resentment and hostility beneath which lay deep-rooted fears of economic and political insecurity by those who were denied such facilities.

Viewed from this perspective, the seeds of caste tensions were sown in the pre-independence era itself, the BCM and the Miller Committee being the starting point of a caste movement in Karnataka. What we observe today in the post-independence decades could be described as a continuation of the same process but under new and varied socio-political circumstances. In other words, any close observation of social conflict in relation to caste not only in Karnataka, but in the country as a whole, exhibits certain basic structural identities and similarities both in the years prior to and after independence.

However, the above instances of the three layers of conflict traced in relation to the existence of inter and intra-caste frictions, viz., (a) that existing between the Brahmins and the non–Brahmins; (b) between the different subcastes among the Brahmins, and (c) within the non-Brahmins as a heterogeneous category—continued with additional dimensions and proportions in the fifties and the sixties.

The nature of caste conflict in Princely Mysore shared most of the characteristics of its post-independence counterpart. However, in the case of the former, whatever enmities and animosities that prevailed over the issue of reservations, were generally latent in character. The incidents of physical violence and material loss caused due to caste tensions and even open exclusive discussions about caste and its manifold impact appear to have been comparatively limited in Princely Mysore. It should be emphasised that the above statement keeps communal (Hindu-Muslim) tensions out of its purview. It would be better to explain that after independence, a number of social, political and demographic factors which operated at the level of the implementation of the reservation policy by the government, both State and Central, and its continued implementation, have caused much flutter and resentment coupled with a feeling of prejudice among the forward caste groups. This has also resulted, not infrequently, in cases of expression of anguish and frustration through violence as well as non-violent means.

Mobilisation and Caste Conflict in the Post-Independence Era

One of the chief tasks that the Indian government undertook in the post-independence period was attending to the welfare of the weaker sections of the country. A major dimension of the measures chalked out in this regard has been the policy of protective discrimination. Despite the utilisation aspects of this policy, the fact that some sections of the population were excluded from the reserved category has created a slow but steady growth of inter and intra-caste conflicts. Such tensions though they originated at a time when the Miller Committee recommended reservations to the backward classes in Princely Mysore,, have increased, both in their degree and intensity, in the years after independence.

Tensions between Caste Hindus and the SCs

Compared to the situation after independence, caste rivalries and competitions in the years earlier to it were less, both in their degree and tempo. This observation refers to the prevalence of inter as well as intra-caste conflict in the state. However, the BCM which took place during the early decades of this century in Princely Mysore is credited with having inaugurated, in its own way, a continuous chain of caste struggles in the State.

Further, the above explanation does not rule out the prevalence of widespread and longstanding rift between the two social groups. In fact, such a conflict is a natural corollary of the economic and political cleavages which exist between them. However, these tendencies of antagonism have largely been in the nature of indirect expression of actual social relations.

Though the constitutional guarantees are extended to some of the upper castes including the middle and lower groups in the hierarchy, the SCs and the STs constitute the crux of such welfare policies. In their case, the benefits are also greater in their quantum, which are granted with the hope of improving their low socio-economic status. It may even be said that the creation of the 'other backward classes' category during the time of the reforms in 1919, was a result of the non-Brahmin movement in various states. Moreover, the idea of "reservation in government service was first mooted in Princely Mysore" (probably for the first time in the country),"for the purposes of removing inequalities of representation of certain communities in the state services (KBCC Report : 1975) as early as during the Commission's days in 1874 and 1895" (Galanter : 1978).

What is emphasised here is that since its beginning, the system of reservation has been more ideologically and politically committed to the amelioration of the SCs and the STs. This also included the wide range of social reformers and political protagonists of Harijan welfare belonging, generally as they did, to upper Hindu castes. It is not intended to suggest that their intentions were completely selfish or self-centred and their attempt for the emancipation of the Harijans was superficial. However, there is evidence in history to the effect that the Harijan issue was no doubt utilised by some of the upper caste leaders for purposes of achieving, or at least in support of their fight for personal gains for their own group. For example, the leaders of the depressed classes apprehended that the Government Order following the Miller Committee Report lacked any special provisions for them. But their major fear was that their inclusion along with the caste-Hindus for purposes of granting Constitutional guarantees would facilitate the latter (the Caste-Hindus) to grant all the opportunities.

Thus, it appears that under the banner of equal representation, the battle was for the reallocation of certain basic economic and political resources and not for fundamental, 'structural' changes in the societal framework. The fact that the movement preferred to rest itself upon the same traditional foundation of 'caste' or 'sectarianism' for 'secular' grants did not result in altering the existing socio-ritual relationships between the participating castes. Instead, it may be commented that the whole effort was based on stabilising the existing system with certain functional modifications. This is where the system of reservations is referred to, by its critics, as having further institutionalised the caste set up.

The result was more drastic than what caste system would have been if anything like reservations were not to exist. The compartmentalisation of caste groups, including the ex-untouchables, into 'backward', 'forward' and 'most backward' by the government has placed them at extreme heights of conflict—both manifest and latent.

What is derived from the above discussion is that the ex-untouchables are facing more challenging situations than the other caste groups due to the Constitutional Reforms directed towards them. The entire category of the SCs[5] are being looked upon as "privileged"[6], enjoying certain benefits at the cost of the caste-Hindus[7] among whom also there may be found poorer sections.

It would be necessary to clarify at this juncture that the category of caste-Hindus covers within its fold all the castes and subcastes which are traditionally above the Harijans. Notwithstanding the existence of inter-caste rivalry and tension, all of them came to muster a common, though not a clear, attack on the facilities enjoyed by the Harijans.

While there could be noticed a common front of antagonism by all the caste-Hindu groups against the SCs as a class, the nature and the means by which conflict is expressed are varied. In other words, their feelings of anguish and jealousy are reflected in a number of different, dissimilar social actions by the caste-Hindu groups.

Mobilisation and Caste Conflict in the Post-Independence Period

The Forward Communities and the Scheduled Castes

At least till recently, and even now, perhaps, the terms 'forward caste and the Brahmins' have come to be identified as being one and the same. The fact that the Brahmins stand traditionally at the apex of the caste ladder and are the upper-most caste enjoying, by its virtue, a higher socio-ritual status, had denied them the facilities of protective discrimination. What is more, their 'monopoly over the fields of education and government service had also been lost, in course of time, because of the BCM in Princely Mysore which introduced the system of reservation to the non-Brahmins.

This precarious situation in which the forward castes (Brahmins) were placed due to the implementation of successive BCCs' recommendations led to an economic crisis as well as a psychological one. A new phase of interaction characterised by frustration of loosing the age-old privileges and virtual monopoly over the two sectors is what is observed in recent years.

The Brahmins who constitute the important forward group were alleged to have monopolised the field of education and government service in Princely Mysore, by the leaders of the non-Brahmin movement. After the implementation of the Miller Committee Report, we find the Lingayats gaining access to these two positions in course of time. They were categorised as 'forward' by the Havanur Commission in 1975. Coupled with this denial of their long-cherished backward status, the

Urs government introduced certain stringent measures of social reform like the abolition of the practice of Bonded Labour and the introduction of Land Reforms.

These three developments in Karnataka, brought forth since 1972 (not underestimating the various other changes) have affected the 'forward' groups, squarely. It is attempted here only to explain the resultant situation in terms of the confrontation it had brought between the SCs and the forward groups.

Being largely urban based in their occupation, the Brahmins are generally found living in towns and cities. However, they also own agricultural lands despite the fact that tradition barred them from tilling it themselves. Thus, much of their land was converted into tenancy holdings. The Brahmins complain that their lands were taken over by the Government in one clean sweep when the Land Reforms Legislation was strengthened and enacted in 1972 by the then Chief Minister, late D.Devraj Urs.

Though the constitutional guarantees have been extended to some of the middle and the lower groups in the hierarchy, the Scheduled Castes and the Scheduled Tribes constitute the crux of such welfare policies. In their case, the benefits are also greater in their quantum, granted with the hope of improving their socio-economic status. The creation of the "Other Backward Classes" category during the time of the Reforms in 1919, was a result of the non-Brahmin movement in various states. Moreover, the idea of "reservation in government service" was first mooted in Princely Mysore (probably for the first time in the whole of India), "for the purpose of removing inequalities of representation of certain communities" in the state services (KBCC Report, Vol. I Part I : 1975 : 57) as early as during the Commission days in 1879 and 1895.

But there is a difference between contempt being felt and contempt being expressed in action. It may be considered broadly that the Brahmins are today left with fewer channels where their feelings against the SCs and STs can find an outlet. The incident where the socio-political set-up facilitated such a situation appears to be less in the case of the Brahmins than, it is, for example, in the case of the Lingayats and the Vokkaligas. That is to say, the fact that the SCs are generally rural based brought them into close economic links (or dependency) upon the Lingayats and the Vokkaligas, who are the dominant landed castes of Karnataka. Even to this day, a large majority of untouchables in the state are rural dwellers, working as landless agricultural labourers. Thus, they may be considered as being easily accessible for their masters for exploitation. Their rural settlement is also amenable for a number of other disadvantages.

Their extreme backwardness, lack of education, political awareness and power has added to their miseries. A major factor in the generation of conflict between them and the forward/ dominant castes is that legislative reforms have not resulted in any far-reaching changes in the socio-economic position of these much envied communities, especially among the poorer classes among them. Thus, we find that on the one hand, the dependence of the SCs and STs upon upper castes for social and economic living, particularly in rural areas has continued to leave them at the mercy of the latter groups. On the other hand, is noticed, the heightened assault and threats to their lives and property (by the upper castes in the wake of the feelings of jealousy and contempt that the system of reservation has wrought on them.

As a result, with all its name for the absence of substantial manifest caste tensions of a Caste-Hindu Vs. ex-untouchable nature, Karnataka does present a picture of such conflict. These cases of assault are on the rise and seem to occur in certain intervals.

The urban areas present a different picture. Antagonism is no less prevalent against the ex-untouchables or the SCs, in most cases, it is found to be not expressed directly. Simmering tensions have always prevailed between the forward and SC groups.[8]

There is an important reason to this phenomenon of anti-SC rift. To begin with, the facilities granted to the SCs and the STs are being looked upon with resentment by all the caste-Hindus. This is strange in the light of the fact that a major section of the caste-Hindus constituted by the OBCs also enjoys the benefits of reservation. The resentful attitude of the OBCs and other non-SCs is not spelt out openly but is generally expressed under the mask of some or the other social events. Resentment against them seems to be mainly due to the SCs and the STs getting large share of benefits from the state. Sympathy and concern towards the dalits has become a 'political' issue among the upper Hindu groups. Support is also expressed in public platforms and in the policies and programmes of a number of voluntary organisations. But beneath such pseudo-sympathy may be found highly tense feelings of anti-reservations. Generated greatly out of social and economic cleavages, such tensions also reflect the frustration surfacing them.

The OBCs and the SCs

The OBCs, as a constitutional category, include a number of caste groups ranging from upper-middle, middle to lower levels of the traditional social hierarchy. A commonality between them is that they all depended on agriculture for survival, both as owners of land and as labourers. Only a minority of them are landowners while even among them, as among the SCs, there are hundreds of wage workers.

These economic pursuits present a situation where confrontation between the OBCs and the SCs is unavoidable in a rural set-up.[9] Traditionally, the two categories were guarded in their interactions and social relations by a system of socio-ritual hierarchy. But the changed circumstances introduced by the policy of reservations which emphasises equality between the ex-untouchables and the caste-Hindus and liberation from age-old practices of discrimination coupled with occupational mobility have, in course of time, generated resentment and hostility against them by the caste-Hindus. The enactment of land reform legislation, the abolition of the practice of bonded labour and many other policies have further disturbed the traditional socio-economic set-up.

To these were added the various welfare measures introduced from time to time by the government, all of which have created awareness among the ex-untouchables about the need to get rid of exploitation and discrimination at the hands of the caste-Hindus. The Vokkaligas, and the Lingayats, have been threatened by the growth of this awareness among the dalits.

Cases of anti-dalit tensions and assaults led by the members of the OBC groups tend to occur at places where the two groups and their mobilisational drives come into clash with one another. An important area of mobilisation is education which is looked upon as crucial to gain economic status. Establishing private educational trusts and using them to start professional colleges had gained momentum as a consequence of the emphasis on professional education. It is interesting to note that when the Gundu Rao government in 1980 sanctioned private medical and engineering colleges, to a few caste and religious groups, there was competition between the leaders of the Vokkaligara Sangha and a few SC elite to avail of the opportunity.

Cleavages between the Vokkaligas and the SCs/dalits are found being more intensely felt in those spheres where the latter compete with the Vokkaligas (specially in the sphere of education and government employment). The problems and the challenges are greater for the SCs once they join the fray with the other caste members. This is true where the system of roaster and the reservation facility in promotion to higher jobs have been in operation thereby creating greater contempt among the OBCs.

These factors may be supported by taking into consideration a few incidents of student unrest in several places in the state's universities over the past few years. Mysore University, for e.g., covered under its jurisdiction the districts of Mandya, Mysore, Hassan and Chikmagalur, among others, which are the strongholds of Vokkaliga population. Frequent disturbances involving the two groups, the Vokkaliga and the SCs, are common in the campus which reach their zenith and assume a concrete shape during certain competitive events like admissions to the student councils, matters like admissions, examinations results and even the appointment of higher officials and teachers of the University.

One chief characteristic of such clashes was that they have started showing themselves outwardly. This trend of organising and unifying is found to have led to a counter process of mobilisation among the SCs.

The hypothesis that the fundamental threat to SCs is provided by the dominant castes should be answered by the above explanation which represents the Vokkaliga caste in Southern Karnataka. Similarly, in North Karnataka, the Lingayats are hostile to the SCs. As a sect of many contradictions, (like for example, while Veerasaivism preached the tradition of equality of all castes, untouchability and its allied practices, like 'Jeetha' (bonded labour) are found to have been sheltered under it) the Lingayats appear to be no different from their dominant counterparts, the Vokkaligas, in exhibiting anti-SC tendencies. Direct economic and political relations, including the Lingayats and the SCs and their disruption by the scheme of compensatory legislation appear to have triggered of a series of conflicts between them. These tendencies of conflict have further increased with the reservation where upper castes have to compete with the SCs.

More than the Vokkaligas in southern Karnataka, the

Lingayats with their sectarian autonomy (in the form of mutts and monasteries) and dominant position, have established themselves politically, economically and culturally at a different level in the northern districts where they are numerously found. After the state's reorganisation in 1956, there was a change in the nature of political leadership with successive Lingayat Chief Ministers coming to power (from 1956-1972).

Once in power, they had given prime importance to caste mobilisation. Various administrative and political seats of power came to be occupied by them. For example, in the case of the Karnataka University, its origin and growth travels in line with the formation and ideals of the Lingayats' attempts to mobilise themselves. Ever since its establishment in the year 1950 till today, generally Lingayats have been its vice-chancellors.[10] In fields such as judiciary, education and administrative service they came to occupy positions next only to the Brahmins. This was besides the field of education where they started many private colleges especially professional ones supported by both their mutts and caste based associations.

Tensions between the OBCs and the SCs may not be, by any estimation, new to Karnataka. But the process appears to have grown more manifestly in recent years. The implementation of the Havanur Commission's Report and various other welfare measures oriented towards the upliftment of the SCs undertaken by the Devraj Urs ministry led to the generation of higher level of tensions. It was in this ministry that many SC and other backward class ministers could mobilise themselves for the achievement of higher political positions. It is also true that their number has increased since 1970. We also find many SC and BC political leaders occupying berths in the subsequent ministries in Karnataka. The process of political mobilisation and the gaining of power by them may be explained as a natural corollary of the reservation system itself and secondly, that their political ambitions were accommodated by the Devraj Urs government. This could be attributed to the changed political conditions as the central government given to Dalit welfare by the Congress (I) ministry led by Mrs. Indira Gandhi.

But a beginning was probably made for the Dalit movement in Karnataka during the early 1970s. It came at a time when caste cleavages between caste-Hindus and the Harijans became sharp, perhaps, owing to certain politico-social changes introduced by the Urs' government. The hidden anti-SC feelings may be termed as having found an outlet in the famous "Bhoosa episode" which occurred in September 1973. Enraged by the remarks of a SC Minister, Sri B Basavalingappa, in the Urs' cabinet, who allegedly compared Kannada literature to "Bhoosa" (cattle feed), a section of the population, particularly comprising the dominant castes, organised a protest demanding the resignation of the said minister. It is remarkable to note here the controversies that the issue raised in its due course. The Vokkaligas took a leading part in the agitation. Statements condemning the Minister's remarks were given by many, notably by the national poet, Dr. K. V. Puttappa (popularly known as Kuvempu). The episode provided the Vokkaliga leaders an opportunity to mobilise their anti-SC attitudes. Clarifications were sought and the whole episode ended with the resignation of the minister. This also illustrated the somewhat fragile nature of Urs' backward classes' formula.

While the Vokkaligas constitute one but a major component of the OBC category, the remaining section of the same group is made up of a number of middle and lower castes and sub-castes. These castes did not lag behind the former in their own attempts at mobilisation by also following similar strategies of starting caste associations and opening private professional colleges. The system of protective discrimination came as a boon to them.

Irrespective of the quantum of reservations granted to them

in the various spheres, there appears to be a feeling of dissatisfaction amongst these groups. This has resulted in many intra-backward class conflicts. There have been unanimous negative reactions by them towards reservations granted to the SCs and the STs. Most of these are latently expressed assuming different dimensions.

To begin with, organised, direct protests against the facilities given to the SCs and the STs have not been reported. But it does not amount to their absence. In the rural areas, where one or the other middle caste is the land-owning, dominant caste, land and other forms of political relations enable much exploitation involving them and the landless SC labourers. Urban areas are not lagging behind in their own contributions to this phenomenon. In all these types of conflicts, caste alone is not the deciding factor, since class cuts across caste in many matters of such interactions. One of its characteristics is that it has a caste-Hindu attitude reflecting the same views against the downtrodden. Caste mobilisation among them has adopted two ways: one is the process where they have been emulating what their own upper castes have been adopting as the strategy for social mobility. This includes formation of caste associations and the starting of private educational trusts and through them, educational institutions that return capitation fees. But what is important is their second effort that refers to their demand to be classified as SCs/STs obviously lured by the economic benefits that such reservation would offer them. The lower castes like the Barbers and Washermen have been making claims to a lower social status of their caste than what it actually is and to be included in the list of backwards. These service communities have been equating their own low and degraded status with that of the ex-untouchables. They have been arguing as being no less in discrimination as compared to that of the SCs and the STs. They have been basing their arguments on the fact that being service communities, they are equally looked down upon by the upper castes. The social stigma attached to their professions is no less in importance than those pursued by the ex-untouchables. An interesting practice that they have taken to in recent years refers to the production of false caste certificates claiming an inferior social status than what they enjoyed, for purposes of obtaining reservation facilities. A number of such cases of fake SC/ST caste certificates produced by candidates not really belonging to those groups, in order to seek seats in educational institutions and jobs in government institutions have been reported in the press since the past few years. Many such cases were identified and the concerned culprits were handed over to the state vigilance commission.

The Mysore government made a provision, for the backward classes as early as in 1874 and in 1895. Appointments were made in the Police department for Brahmans, Musalmans and other Hindus castes. Through circular no. 218-98 dated 19th/21st January 1895, the government of Mysore issued a further circular reserving posts to BCs. In 1914, posts of Assistant Commissioners were reserved for them (Singh : 1982).

However, the so-called monopoly came to be conquered by the economically and numerically dominant caste of the Lingayats, who have been consistently classified as the backward caste by successive BCCs (except by the Havanur report which was soon corrected and the Lingayats, continued with their backward status). Some of the policies of the Urs government came to affect them directly, like the abolition of the practice of bonded labour and the introduction of land reforms. The Brahmins also suffered the brunt of the policy of land reforms since they owned agricultural lands, despite tradition barring them from tilling it themselves. Therefore, much of their lands were converted into tenancy holdings. The Brahmins were the worst affected when their lands were taken over by the government in one clean sweep when the land reforms legislation was strengthened and enacted in 1974 by the then chief minister Sri D. Devraj Urs.

The above explanation does not rule out the prevalence of widespread and long-standing rift between the upper caste groups. In fact, such a conflict is a natural corollary of the economic and political cleavages which exist between them.

While Lingayats also came under the same legislation, their position was different. In the case of the Brahmins their dependence upon government service (in the absence of land or agricultural work), made them to compete with the rest of the caste groups, all of whom enjoyed the benefit of reservations at one point of time or another.

The SCs working largely as landless agricultural labourers, are easily accessible for upper caste dominance and exploitation. In addition, the government's favourable programmes for their development have led to much envy and contempt against them. Thus, cases of assault are on the rise and seem to occur at certain defined intervals.

The anti-SC/ST rift is supported by the resentment against the facilities that these two groups enjoy as reserved categories. This is strange in the light of the fact that a large section of caste-Hindus also enjoy similar benefits as OBCs. The resentment of these communities is not expressed openly but is expressed under the mask of some or the other pretext. Resentment is mainly caused by the fact of the SCs getting a larger share of benefits. But put together the share of the OBC is much larger. Sympathy and support to the SCs has become a political drama rather than a willful act. The issues of merit and efficiency are stressed instead of the heinous practice of untouchability that was imposed since centuries on these communities.

Thus, it appears that under the banner of equal representation, the battle was for the reallocation of certain basic economic and political resources and not for fundamental, "structural" changes in the social framework. The fact that the movement preferred to rest itself upon the same traditional foundation of 'caste or sectarianism' for securing grants, did not result in altering the existing socio-ritual relationship between the participating castes. Instead, it may be commented that the whole effort was based on stabilising the existing system with certain "functional modifications". This is where the system of reserva-tions is referred to, by its critics, as having further institutionalised the caste set-up.

Beneath such pseudo sympathy is found tense feelings of anti-reservation, generated greatly out of social and economic cleavages. Such tensions also reflect the frustration that surfaces it. Despite this common factor, the so-called forward groups also differ in their attitude towards reservation policy.

The result is stated by the above critics of the reservation policy as being perhaps more drastic than what the caste system would have been if anything like reservations were not to exist. The compartmentalisation of caste groups into "backward", "most backward" and "forward" by the political machinery has placed them at extreme heights of conflicts, both manifest and latent.

What is derived from the above discussion is that the dalits today are facing more challenging situations than the other caste groups due to the Constitutional Reforms directed towards them. The entire category of the SCs in particular are being looked upon as privileged, enjoying certain benefits at the cost of the caste-Hindus among whom there may be found poorer sections. The category of caste-Hindus covers within its fold all the castes and subcastes which are traditionally above the SCs. Not-withstanding the existence of inter-caste rivalries and tensions amongst the various caste-Hindu groups themselves, we observe all of them mustering a common, though not a clear, attack on the facilities enjoyed by the SCs.

While there could be noticed a common front of antagonism by all the caste-Hindu groups against the SCs as a class, the nature and the means by which conflict is expressed are varied. In other words, their feelings of anguish and jealousy are reflected in a number of different, dissimilar social actions.

What is presented above as a picture of social conflict between caste-Hindus and the dalits (or SCs in particular) is an All-India phenomenon. While there is a common atmosphere of strained social relations between the two groups in almost any social situation, they are found as being manifest to greater degree only in some States than in others. Further, the way in which caste antagonisms are made explicit varies from state to state in its content and intensity.

Thus a situation exists where confrontation between the two groups is unavoidable particularly in a rural set-up. While tradition had guarded the interactions between the two categories, the policy of reservations introduced a change emphasising upon equality between the ex-untouchables and the rest of the society. It promoted liberation from age-old practices of discrimination coupled with occupational mobility generating a lot of hostility against them by the caste-Hindus. The enactment of land reform legislation and the abolition of the practice of bonded labour further disturbed their complete control over the SCs. Besides these, the various welfare measures introduced from time to time by the Government created awareness about their degraded position and exploitation meted out by the caste-Hindus. The upper castes felt threatened by this growing awareness among the ex-untouchables. However, much of this was not made explicit by any violent outburst against them but found expression in various social situations.

In other words, anti-untouchable conflicts led by members of the OBC groups are higher in such situations where the two groups and their mobilisation activities come in close proximity with one another. An important area of mobilisation is education where there is latent conflict between these categories. Establishing of private educational institutions by caste based trusts gained momentum after 1970s. As noted in Chapter V and VI, the Gundu Rao government for example sanctioned a number of such colleges in engineering and medicine to the upper castes as well as to few trusts founded by prominent dalit leaders. There was a keen fight at that time to avail of this opportunity, particularly by the two categories.

While the above was one area where the dalits had to face competition with the Vokkaligas and the Lingayats, there are other such areas of conflict when the system of reservations gave way for roaster method when dalits and tribals were given facilities of reservation seats in promotions. This created greater contempt among the OBCs against the SCs and the STs.

It has been noted earlier that though not the only one, reservations have intensified the struggle for spoils. Logically, caste tensions are found to be deeper and more extensive in those states where the policy of protective discrimination has been more effective in its implementation. One such is the state of Karnataka. Since it is observed that the tendency for mobilisation on caste grounds has become more evident specially after the Havanur Commission gave its Report, it is proposed here to base the discussion of conflict on the categories provided in the Havanur Report, i.e., into the forward and the backward groups. This classification was adopted by the Nagan Gowda Committee also, the only difference being in the number and type of castes included in or excluded from the above categories. The backward section included the backward caste-Hindu groups which are known by the Constitutional term the "Other Backward Classes", including castes from upper-middle, middle and lower levels of the social hierarchy.

With this classification in mind, an analysis of the rift that exists between the above categories and the dalits/SCs is attempted below. The nature of antagonism differs from group to group in accordance with their relative position in the socio-legal order and the type of confrontation they are expected to make with the SCs to derive the Constitutional benefits.

The Forward Castes versus the Scheduled Castes

In north Karnataka, similar threat to SCs came from the dominant caste of Lingayats. As a sect of many contradictions the Lingayats also have direct economic relations with the dalits particularly in the rural areas. Already they were upset with the reservation benefits given to the latter and innumerable government programmes evolved for their development. Added to these, when in 1975, under the Urs' government when they were declared as forward by the Havanur Commission, the existing rift widened and triggered off series of conflicts against the SCs. The presence of a wide network of religious mutts in the northern districts, especially, gave them added strength besides the economic, numerical and political support they had already gathered by virtue of being a dominant caste. This had resulted in the state being ruled by a series of chief ministers hailing from this caste (1956-1972).

Under the circumstances, the precarious situation in which the upper castes, are placed and the problem and complexities it had led to may be explained from the angles of (a) The economic crisis that the policy of reservations is alleged to have led the forward groups, and (b) The psychological tensions of a new phase of social interactions characterised by the frustration of loosing the age-old privileges.

Tensions between the OBCs and the SCs are not new to Karnataka but the process has grown manifestly in the recent years. The post-1970s has in particular led to an increase in the self-assertion by the SCs. It was Urs' ministry which accommodated their political ambitions encouraged by the support from the Congress-led Mrs. Gandhi's rule at the centre. It had for the first time given many ministerial berths to this as well as the backward classes. But the decade also gave rise to the emergence of the dalit movement with added rigour. It came at a time when most of the conflicts between the caste-Hindus and the Harijans became sharp perhaps owing to certain politico-social changes introduced by the Urs government. The hidden anti-SC feelings found an outlet in the famous 'Bhoosa' episode which occurred in September 1973. Enraged by the remarks of an SC Minister, Sri B. Basavalingappa, in the Urs' Cabinet, who was alleged to have compared Kannada literature to cattle fodder (Bhoosa), a section of the population comprising the dominant castes, organised a protest demanding the resignation of the said minister. It is remarkable to note here the controversies that the issue raised in its due course. Debates and newspaper articles subjected the issue to severe criticism (Parvathamma : 1973). The Vokkaligas took a leading part in the agitation. Statements condemning the Minister's remarks were given by many, notably by the national poet Dr. K. V. Puttappa (hailing from this caste). The episode provided the Vokkaliga leaders an opportunity to mobilise their anti-SC attitudes. Clarifications were later sought and the whole episode ended with the resignation of the Minister. Sooner another such instance followed where another SC Minister in the same Cabinet, Sri R. D. Kittur, was made to resign following allegation of sexually misbehaving with a woman called Sumitra Desai, a Lingayat. All these illustrated how the simmering feelings of hatred and jealousy against the dalits by the upper castes came out openly when the occasion arose. It also showed how fragile was Urs' backward classes formula. The above two episodes should be analysed being complementary to each other.

Conflict between the Forward and the Backward Groups

The tussle for backward status not only in Karnataka but all over India has led to increasing divisions between the backwards as a category and the forwards as their opponents. This is an important dimension of caste conflict in Karnataka where reservations were introduced quite long ago in 1874.

It is only natural that the special treatment given to a few people to the exclusion of the others leads to conflicts. The whole issue of reservations has been consistently opposed by the members of the forward groups ever since it was introduced during the times of Princely government itself way back in the 19th century. This point has been brought out elaborately in various parts of this work. It has been discussed there that the opposition to reservations to the backward classes was so strong that Dewan Sri M. Visvesvaraya relinquished his office in support of his argument that merit should be the sole criterion for any governmental provisions to the needy sections of the population. Although one may not agree with Sir M. V. it would perhaps be fair to add that he was at least not against giving the backward classes educational facilities (Narayana Rao : 1973).

During the thirties and the forties, the freedom movement dominated all other movements in the country. Princely Mysore was no exception to this. Even after independence, till the reorganisation of the state, in 1956, there was little manifestation in the sphere of caste conflict. This does not rule out the fact that there was dormant or imperceptible violence. Further, the principle of "merit" within each community was also stressed. In other words, whatever protest existed regarding the reservation system, it does not appear to have exceeded certain levels. Secondly, though there was no apparent conflict up to 1956, a lot of "casteism" was practiced. Mobilisation of public opinion against reservations and any open action to condemn it — like organising conferences or meetings - seems to have been absent among the Brahmins, during the years earlier to the fifties. In fact, the Akila Karnataka Brahmana Mahasabha, the caste association of the Brahmins and their chief spokesman in the state, came into existence only in the year 1970.

The policy of reservations which introduced the division into the "forward" and the "backward" groups, has led to a series of protests and opposition against the government led by the members and leaders of the forward groups. This process has assumed the form of a continuous process of socio-legal battle against the system of reservations in its various dimensions. The details of the legal confrontation between the forwards and the government, in the form of court cases, have been covered earlier.

A member of the Constituent Assembly and later a Minister in Nehru's Cabinet, Mr. T. T. Krishnamachari, "echoed the doubt that Article 16 (4) would be a Paradise for lawyers". Similarly, after the judgment in *Balaji case,* tirades have been carried on in almost all the High Courts against reservation to BCs on the ground that the Supreme Court in *Balaji Case* invalidated reservation on communal grounds (*ibid.*).

Once in power, the Lingayats seem to have given primary importance to caste mobilisation basing upon communalism. This has evidently left the various positions of political and administrative power occupied by the kith and kin of the Lingayats. This is particularly true of the field of education. In the case of the Karnataka University, its origin and growth travels in line with the formation and ideals of the Lingayats' attempts towards mobilisation. Ever since its establishment in the year 1950, till today, generally Lingayats have been its vice-chancellors. Similarly, regarding their representation in the field of judiciary and administrative services also, Lingayats may be roughly found next only to the Brahmins. Thus, the two decades — 1950-60 and 1960-70 — witnessed protests and expression of resentment against the policy of reservations which were in the form of legal battles. But the communities affected by the policy in terms of denial of backwardness were not many in number i.e., till the 1970s the Brahmins were the only community to be declared so. Although the Nagan Gowda and the Havanur reports declared the Lingayats as forward, the decision did not sustain for long. Being a dominant community, its power made the respective state governments to yield to pressure by legislators and leaders of the community that resulted in their inclusion as backwards.

However, after the 1980s not only the demand for backwardness but also other material gains from the state government came to characterise the mobilisational attempts by a number of other communities. The seriousness with which the successive governments went on implementing the reservation policies both for the SCs and STs and the OBCs stirred off a continuous battle for backwardness and more backwardness.

For example, the Brahmins, who were hitherto engaged in court battles about the injustice meted out to their ability to compete through merit by reserving a major portion of seats under reservations, began to similarly demand quota for themselves, like the rest of the communities. The practice of forming caste associations and the starting of caste based educational institutions that was in vogue among the OBCs and SCs, came to be emulated by them also. This was an important aspect of their protest against the BCs expressed as a challenge. It was also somewhat an indication of their growing sense of insecurity about the dominant public life by the two communities, now joined by many others.

The new wave of mobilisation among the Brahmin emphasised upon organisational efforts. It is difficult to account for the delayed establishment of one single caste association (The

Akila Karnataka Brahmana Mahasabha) of the Brahmins in the year 1970 with any other satisfactory reason. There have been separate associations of the three major castes among them viz., the Smarthas, the Madhwas and the Sreevaisnavas. It marked the coming together of the different Brahmin associations under one platform. As endogamous groups, the various Brahmin subcastes had established separate associations earlier in history. The first such was the representative of the Srivaisnavas viz., Sree Hebbar Srivaisnava Sabha established way back in 1910 at Bangalore.

While the Vokkaligas constitute one but a major component of the OBC category, the remaining section of the same group is made up of a number of middle and lower castes and subcastes. A detailed account of the associations these castes have formulated in the recent decades and the efforts to secure the sanction of private professional colleges by a few more resourceful castes among them, all indicate their attempts to mobilisation on the line of the upper caste attempts.

The new association chalked out a number of programmes for the benefit of the community, now united irrespective of subcaste differences. Expansion of educational activities, economic support to poor Brahmin families and representation in political circles were its chief goals. Thus, the Brahmins as a forward group expressed their need for social justice through the legal battle where a majority of affected cases filing writ petitions in the court were from this caste. The second process refers to the growth of a counter process of mobilisation running parallel to the one that existed among the BCs. Their caste association came to be the platform from where the demands of the community are represented to the government. Beginning with such personalities like late Sri P. H. Krishna Rao ex-census commissioner, GoM in 1941 who was its founder president in the year 1970, there have been eminent people leading the association in its activities notwithstanding factions between the different subcastes within the Brahmin community to occupy that seat.

A notable difference between the demands of Brahmins and the rest of the communities in their mobilisational activities is that the former has never claimed that they have to be categorised as a backward caste or community. In fact their leaders have attributed certain stigma to the very concept of backwardness (Conferences of the Mahasabha). Their argument is that caste should not be the criterion of backwardness. Instead, "reservations may be given on economic considerations". The arguments of the leaders of the Mahasabha that the ex-untouchables and the tribals, and to some extent the other lower sections of the Hindu society should be supported and encouraged by the government convey indirectly their negative attitudes towards granting any such facilities to the OBCs. In other words, they seem to hold the OBC category, which includes the dominant caste(s) as a threat to themselves.

There is no doubt about the well-known unanimity among all the middle and lower castes in their criticisms against the government's programmes for the welfare of the downtrodden. However, this dissatisfaction is expressed by them directly but has begun to assume different dimensions.

Conflict between the forward and the backward groups is also having its political implications. In fact, the very basis of the policy of reservations rests upon the political machinery which implements it. The frustration that is supposed to be present amongst the Brahmins may also be attributed to the fact that as a minority group, their hold over resources in the state has been meager through the decades. This situation was further aggravated by the non-Brahmin movement that deprived them of monopoly over administrative set up to loose land to land reforms.

One aspect of whatever resentment exists against the SCs and STs, by the members of the middle and lower castes is, that it has, in most cases, assumed the form of a total caste-Hindu attitude. In other words, it tends to reflect the same attitude of caste-Hindus in general against the SCs and STs.

After independence and the re-organisation of the state, the representation of Brahmins in the political system also came to be substantially reduced. When the rule by the two dominant castes together for 25 years ended there came a change in the caste structure of political leadership in the state. But even this never benefited the Brahmins as the assumption of power by Urs, though a member of a non-dominant caste, "brought to them more direct and unjustifiable troubles" (resolutions of the Mahasabha 1980). The emphasis laid by Urs and his government, as a continuation of the Indira wave, at the national level, upon the welfare of the weaker sections of the society and the consequent measures undertaken like the land reform legislation and the appointment of the KBCC and the other schemes gave a hard blow to the Brahmin caste. "Due to the policies of the government like retrograde land reforms, land for the tiller and so on he has lost his traditional occupation and has been deprived of land....". Further, the Brahmins allege that the policy of encouraging the BCs has affected the employment potentials for the Brahmins as village school-masters. "The Brahmin has been treated like the step-child and his representations for justice have proved a cry in the wilderness" (Rao : 1979: 11).

But, it is further interesting to note that the middle and lower castes seem to favour the caste-Hindus or the SCs and the STs depending upon the circumstances. Caste mobilisation among them seems to adopt two interesting channels. The first method is the process by which upper caste culture is emulated by them, which included the formation of caste association and the establishment of private education trusts. The second dimension to their mobilisational attempts lied in their efforts to identify themselves with the SCs and the STs for economic benefits. This is particularly true of the lower and the lowest sections of the middle caste category. Such an identification is with reference to the poor economic living conditions and even socio-ritual (degraded) status that are claimed by the middle and lower groups to be similar compared to that of the SCs and STs.

As is evident from the above, though anti-backward group feelings were lingering in the activities of the Brahmins as a forward group, they became more manifest and active after the successive verdicts on the BCs.

The leaders of the Barber, Washermen and other service communities have also begun to assert the backwardness of their respective caste-folk in a novel way by equating it with the backwardness encountered by the untouchables. They based their arguments on the fact that as service communities, they are "equally looked down upon by upper castes". The social stigma attached to the professions of the Barbers and the Washerman is claimed, by the president and members of their caste associations as being less in importance than those followed by the untouchables. Further the category of the SCs, being a blanket term, also included a few non-untouchable groups like the Lamanis, and the Bhovis (the stone cutters). Likewise, the two service communities noted above also desire to be categorised as non-untouchable SCs.

As could be expected, the various BCC reports and its chairmen came up for severe criticism by the groups which were denied berths in the list of BCs. For e.g., Havanur's decision to combine the Brahmins and the Lingayats in the same position of forwardness, had a different impact. While the Brahmins had already been accustomed to their denial of a constitutional status, to the Lingayats it came as a rude shock. The recommendations of the Havanur report were branded as biased and unscientific which was suspected to be the revenge that Urs has taken on the community. The political and economic implications of the recommendations of the Havanur report led to an intense fight to scrap them. Led by the forward castes, who in fact wanted them to be also included in one way or another, this constituted an integral part of the social conflict in Karnataka and the essence of social tensions that arose between the so-called forwards and the backwards. The net influence of the resentment of the forwards over the pattern of backward class classification was displayed subsequently in many ways.

Middle and Lower Castes Versus Scheduled Castes

Among the middle and low caste category are found a number of small and marginal groups, whose categorisation is complex. They are the result of the process of fission in the caste system occurring since many decades. Smaller castes and subcastes have always stood as problems for any attempt to classify caste groups by the Census officials and by the Backward Classes Commissions. These groups are also those which exist as border lines between the lower castes and the untouchables. In other words, they almost shared the traits of the untouchables, but for the stigma of untouchability. However, these marginal groups have always tried to identify themselves with their superior castes rather than their inferiors. An interesting change in this attitude is noticed in recent years wherein they have taken to producing false caste certificates claiming an inferior social status, than what they enjoyed for purposes of obtaining reservation facilities. A number of such cases of "fake SC/ST caste certificates" produced by candidates not really belonging to those groups, in order to seek seats in educational institutions (specially in professional colleges) and jobs in the government institutions have been reported in the press since the past few years. It is also observed that such incidents were more in number during the years following 1980. Such cases were unearthed and handed over to the State Vigilance Commission by the said government itself.

Conflict between the 'Forward' and the 'Backward' Groups

What has preceded is a detailed analysis of the traces of conflict, which the process of compensatory discrimination generated between caste-Hindus against the SCs. Increased caste mobilisation in recent years in the state has only intensified the above caste conflict.

One way was to fight through the legal channel where a number of Writ Petitions have been filed challenging the validity of the GO on reservations. Between the years 1977-79, the war against it led by the Lingayats reached its zenith.

The second way was a latent layer of conflict expressed by these two groups over the BCs in general. Though the definition of the term includes even the SCs and STs, there is a feeling of sympathy towards them and they are found excluded from the ire of the forward castes against the system of reservations.

While the Brahmins and the other castes declared as forward by the Havanur Report share that as a similarity, it was limited by the many differences that the two groups presented. First of all, they are dissimilar because while the Brahmins have been declared a forward group ever since the history of reservations for the Lingayats it was a new experience introduced by the Havanur Commission. Secondly, the year 1972 also indicated their political downfall after the rule for nearly 16 years continuously. Further, the nature and type of resources that characterised motivational attempts by the two groups also tended to differ owing to the different structural position they occupied in the society in Karnataka.

Because of the above and other differences, the nature of conflict that each one of them has risen against the backwards needs to be dealt with on separate lines.

As noted earlier, the organisational drive launched by the upper class of the Brahmin elite, in the form of stabilising their caste associations and the like, itself is a challenge that that community has taken up as an expression of its reaction to reservations. The Mahasabha which represented the united Brahmin caste associations came into existence in 1970 as a state body. After 1973, its chief concern became fighting against the injustice done to the Brahmins. The Mahasabha held meetings in Bangalore and opposed the very system of basing reservations on the criterion of caste. The protest from the Brahmins was feeble compared to that of their counterparts—the Lingayats, who carried it on a very big scale.

The protest movement organised by the Brahmins gained momentum once the Havanur report's recommendations were implemented. This is evident from the frequency with which the Mahasabha met during and after 1979. Annual conferences have been regular since then at least till the end of 1990s. The 1982 conference was held on a grand scale with the presence of heads of mutts from all parts of the state. Inaugurated by late Sri R. Gundu Rao, the then chief minister, it gave importance to the condemning of the verdict in the Havanur report.

The significant aspect of such conferences was the unifying work it did by bringing together all the subcastes of Brahmins under a common pedestal. This signalled one dimension of their mobilisation. It gave encouragement to strengthen the community's base, numerically and ideologically. This is expected by the leaders of the Mahasabha to facilitate the caste to present a united front to face the problems and challenges posed by the issue of backward classes' classification. The fallacies of the report were written down and distributed to members of the community during conferences. These activities reached their zenith during 1980s when the state was ruled by a ministry headed by a Brahmin, for the first time in the political history of the state. Caste conferences also assumed a serious form during this time when Gundu Rao was the chief minister. More than being communal in its origin, this was a consequence of Urs' own policies. The liberal promises made by Rao encouraged the leaders of the Mahasabha to set out to make demands to the new political set-up.

But it was the Lingayats more than the Brahmins, who protested against the Havanur verdict. These began with a caste conference in 1973. The president of the Veerasaiva Mahasabha, late Sri J. B. Mallaradhya was (like Sri P H Krishna Rao) a retired civil servant and the census commissioner in 1951. As the chief spokesman of the Mahasabha, he led the battle against the report till his death in June 1982.

The first set of protest against the report was registered in the form of a memorandum submitted to the government after the Veerasaiva conference held in Bangalore in December in1973. It highlighted the weaknesses of the report and described it as a "fraud on the Constitution, the Government and the people" (Mallaradhya). The main attack on the report was that it has violated the Supreme Court's decision on the *Balaji case.* It was charged with committing a fraud on the Constitution "by including in the lists of backwards, castes that are demonstrably advanced". It was also criticised for "excluding from the lists, on its own admission, as many as 396 castes that have stronger claims for the 'Backward' label than many of the castes that have now been surreptitiously smuggled in".

Another complaint that the Mahasabha made against the report was that its conclusions were unscientific. The Commission was alleged to have underestimated the numerical strength of the community drastically. This was due to the professional Lingayat groups registering themselves with only the name of their profession, like the Madivalas, Barbers, Ganigas, Kumbaras etc. without adding the suffix 'Lingayat' to each one of their names (*ibid.* : 18). "Such a wrong entry had resulted in categorising all these groups and their populations under similar non-Lingayat professional castes".

The Mahasabha did not conclude its fight with the more submission of a memorandum. A number of caste conferences and meetings were organised subsequently by it. Apart from subjecting the Report and its Chairman to severe criticism, these conferences also reportedly worked towards building up political resistance to Urs' rule. The leaders of the Mahasabha attempted to mobilise public opinion among its community folk to try to oust the government. "They threatened the Devraj Urs government that they would not vote for the Congress (U) party in the forthcoming general elections to be held in January 1980, if the recommendations of the Commission regarding their community were accepted" (Aziz :1980: 58). Further in 1979, Professor K Ishwaran, a Toronto based Sociologist and a Lingayat by caste "wrote a detailed article questioning the methodology of investigation and approach followed and the conclusions arrived at by the Commission" (Aziz 1980:58). "This drew strong rejoinders from scholars who were working in the areas of sociology, economics and jurisprudence, some of which appeared in the letters to the editor columns of the daily that had published the said article. Later a booklet containing these rejoinders also appeared (*ibid.*).

The next and further mode of protest by Lingayats against the injustice by the Havanur Report was by way of filing writ petitions in the Karnataka High Court challenging the validity of the recommendations of the Report. Upon the court upholding the recommendations, the matter was later taken to the Supreme Court. The High Court gave a judgment making marginal modifications in the G.O.

Further, the Mahasabha under the leadership of Mallaradhya made a futile attempt to enlist the Lingayats as constituting a separate religious group in the Census of 1981 (*Deccan Herald* : December 18, 1980). An intensive drive was launched by the Sabha under his leadership to create awareness among the people of the community especially those living in rural areas. Meetings and conferences were held stressing the need for this new identity to the community. The district units of the Mahashabha were strengthened and their heads and other office bearers were appointed with care. However, this call failed to evoke response from the community.

The last question that this section on social conflict between the forwards and the backwards seek to address is whether the whole category of OBCs and the SCs has become the object of hatred by the forward or does this have any class character? The study of social conflict is made difficult as it does not always project itself in strict sectarian terms but tends to be coloured by the class factor. Secondly, it is indirect and not quantifiable. Conflict is often present in a subtle form and is highly qualitative.

Lingayats and Vokkaligas

The conflict between the two dominant castes is attributable to their differences despite being called as dominant groups. The two groups exhibit considerable cultural differences despite being dominant castes. These include differences in food habits, religious practices and even economic and educational levels. In all these, the Lingayats have claimed superiority over the others, though this is neither heeded to by the Vokkaligas nor has it stood as any hindrance to their mobilisational activities.

However, the fact that both are dominant has rendered them as conflicting groups. These further deepened with the Havanur Report treating them on unequal grounds. The Commission did so, it was alleged, despite knowing the economic backwardness of at least some sections of the Lingayats. They have alleged that while the report has "conceded certain sections of them as backward, the Constitution has failed to identify those sections ..... Actually, the supposedly Lingayat backward castes are really non-Lingayat castes, the corresponding Lingayat castes sinking their identity under the name Lingayats or Veerasaivas". "If the agricultural communities are backward as conceded by the Commission", then, "the Lingayats also should be treated as backward". "The fact is too often overlooked that though the Lingayat literacy percentage may be slightly above the state average, the total number of illiterates belonging to this community is almost equal to the entire Vokkaliga population, including literate. If the overall literacy is higher than the state average, it is because of heavy urban contributions. So far as the rural areas are concerned, the Lingayats sail in the same boat as Vokkaligas and in districts like Mysore, they almost share the bracket with the Scheduled Castes (vide chapter on literacy in Mysore Census Report for 1951, Volume I). At least the rural Veerasaivas are entitled to be treated as backward, on par with the Vokkaligas".

The simmering conflict between the two communities in the form of a caste and class war has increased since the late 1970s. The Lingayats have been upset that they lost hold over state's political power which ended after Urs came to power. They are also upset that the Vokkaligas have been "utilising their backward status, rather discretely". Truly the community has been making a concerted effort to mobilise on both caste and class lines. This is evident in the efforts it made to strengthen the religious base of the community (Sree Adichunchangiri Peetha) and the starting of private professional colleges. Governmental support was also contributive to their demands.

An important dimension of the caste conflict situation in this regard is the resentment by the Brahmins against the system of capitation fees that has been encouraged by the mushroom growth of the private colleges. Categorised as a forward group, only merit would fetch them seats in educational institutions. Such facilities are also offered at the government and aided institutions. But as the government institutions alone cannot cater to the ever-increasing demand, especially in the sphere of technical and medical education, "the Brahmins are forced to look for seats in private colleges which is difficult owing to the exorbitant rates of capitation fees" (Lakshminarayana, representative of the Brahmana Mahasabha : February, 1982).

During the regime of Gundu Rao, there was an unprecedented battle against the issue of capitation fees in Karnataka. The system affected the middle and lower income groups from all castes. Even when students from the same caste that has started the college applied for admission, they were from the upper classes of the castes that were able to pay the required capitation fees. Merit is the outcome of not only intellectual factors but also subject to cultural factors. With the handicap of intellectual deprivation among their students these sections constituted one major part of the frustrated conflicting groups. Reservation system was of limited help to them, as within the reserved quota, merit was given preference. All the applicants to the course did not get automatically enrolled. With the professional courses being the first choice of many students, it was difficult for an 'average' student to seek admission.

The Brahmins claimed to be the worst hit. This was supported by the argument that the remaining forward groups who were economically well off could afford the cost of higher education. Despite the Lingayats owning the highest number of professional colleges in the state, it does not mean that the community's poor students could seek admission into them. Class factor had gathered more momentum than caste considerations. It appeared that the Brahmins were more frustrated over the issue of capitation fees and reservations. In the absence of any other traditional occupations and hitherto monopoly over the merit pool they found these as hindrances to their own advancement. But it is also true that in recent years, they face competition even in the merit pool with more and more children of the non-Brahmins obtaining higher education and the access they are able to have to good quality schooling.

There is no guarantee that the members of the BCs and their community claim seats in colleges only by virtue of belonging to that community. But the non-BCs always look upon them as the beneficiaries belonging to the same caste. Often, they are also ridiculed and made fun of as not being qualified enough to study these courses. All these are outbursts of the resentment against them as privileged ones. It is not surprising to find the case of a rail accident or an unsuccessful medical operation or even the collapsing of a bridge being linked with the policy of reservations "which selects workers on the basis of caste and not merit".

The anti-reservation attitude by the forward castes assumed some concrete form when the disappointed students from this and other non-backward communities launched a statewide agitation in Bangalore, Gulbarga, Bellary and Hubli to protest against the indiscriminate sanction of colleges. The agitation was against corruption, poor quality of colleges (medical) etc. It led to a lot of tension, violence and disrupted academic and social life.

What is relevant to this chapter is to see how the starting of new medical colleges by caste based educational trusts evoked resentment among others. For example, the sanctioning of such colleges to the Vokkaligara Sangha and Ananda Educational Trust of the (SCs) was not liked by both Brahmins and Lingayats. But the former has allies who have differed substantially from the views of others. The Brahmana Mahasabha also responded to the occasion by asking the Chief Minister to grant such colleges to them. It even expected a fair response by virtue of the fact that the chief minister belonged to their caste.

The Lingayats on the other hand, took it as a blow to their monopoly over the field of private professional education. That the rival Vokkaligas obtained them added more fuel to the fire. This was evident from the colleges from where students participated in the state wide agitation against capitation fees. They were drawn from colleges founded by Lingayats in Lingayat dominant places like Hubli, Davanagere, Belgaum, Bellary, Gulbarga etc. Their resentment was also supported by evidence. While the starting of professional colleges during 1979-80 came to be opposed by the above agitation, the continuation of the process during the following years, did not receive their support. This was due to the obvious reason that these colleges were initiated by Lingayat educational trusts.

Thus, the rift between the forward and backward groups showed itself through many channels, issue of capitation fee being just one of them. Efforts to abolish caste disparities by encouraging them to come up with own efforts and by providing them reservation benefits have resulted in intensifying the differences between castes.

The caste tensions are greater in intensity between closely positioned castes than between those which are widely spread out on the social hierarchy. Between the forwards and the backwards, the closely set groups are more conflicting in nature than those with poor mutual social, political and economic relations.

The next type of caste conflict is between the Brahmins and Lingayats as the two upper castes and the Vokkaligas as a dominant caste. This is true of southern Karnataka where the latter caste group is found. The interplay of such caste/class factors has hindered progress on various counts. For example, the issue of increase in the number of private colleges was not tackled effectively by the government due to the interplay of caste in these matters. A majority of these institutions owned by dominant castes make news every now and then. Since they were sponsored by leading politicians (like Sri H.D. Deve Gowda applying for the medical college in 1980-81) a drastic move in this direction was expected to lead to a caste war in Karnataka.

Any major decision to be taken by the government in the fields of appointments, transfers, or promotions or the formation of any reformative measures for the public - all is affected by the interplay of caste and class. This has even shaped the political structuring of successive governments. Providing equal representation to the members of these groups and the SCs, STs, Minorities has been the main task of any government in power or any party that aspires to achieve political power. While distributing portfolios to Ministers, care is taken to avoid any possible caste-based deprivations. The role of caste in elections is too common to be discussed at length.

The same thing is echoed at lower levels too. These have been occurring at typical contexts. The universities have become chief centres where the broader politico-caste structure is portrayed in their working. Selections to different positions are caste based and are increasingly politicised. Elections to student organisations, to the senate and the syndicate have turned out to be a battle ground where caste and class tensions dominate the scene.

Another area influenced by caste is in the eruption of social movements in the recent times. Farmers' movement is a classic example. The state witnessed an agitation by them in the eighties demanding revision in the policies of the government towards them, like revision of procurement prices, decrease in levy on agricultural produce, etc. Originating in the year 1980, the farmers' movement gained momentum to become a political party (Karnataka Rajya Raitha Sangha) in course of time. Although except the Brahmins all other castes are agricultural in their occupations, traditionally, the movement did not reflect the needs of all of them. The demands put forth by its leaders are such that only the rich and big landowners were kept in its view while framing them and any positive action by the government would ultimately benefit only them. Thus the movement became highly debatable and controversial. It also enlarged the scope for the widening of caste cleavages between the Lingayats and the Vokkaligas. Both being agriculturally strong communities and dominant groups, they competed for the gains of the movement. The movement lacked a unified approach to it by the above two caste groups. Each time the movement became active during 1980-1988, a particular region in the state took interest in participating in it. The first agitation was launched in Navalgund, in Dharwar district, and spread to the rest of the state. In 1983, it chose the south as its encore and participation by farmers from north Karnataka was almost negligible (*The Hindu* : December 8, 1983). In other words, the movement showed ample tendencies to lean towards one particular caste-force each time, either towards the Lingayats or Vokkaligas.

Intra-Caste Conflict

Another significant dimension of social conflict in Karnataka is that existing between the various castes and tribal groups classified under one category. The categories like backward communities, backward castes, backward tribes, Scheduled Castes and Scheduled Tribes are heterogeneous ones and exhibit conflicting tendencies against each other. They contain castes and tribes that are endogamous. The categories in which they are grouped like OBCs, SCs etc. are blanket ones representing uneven socio-economic groups but brought under one common banner for constitutional guarantees. They tend to share certain common socio-cultural traits (KBCC Report : 1975).

The forward castes are made up of Brahmins and a few others which are different culturally. But the most problematic is the OBC category which has castes ranging from dominant castes of Vokkaligas to service groups like the Barbers. The category is further divided into A, B, C categories bringing together backward and more backward communities. Again these are highly heterogeneous. The SCs again are highly heterogeneous in their cultural and economic profiles. Basically they include the touchable and the ex-untouchables.

The system of reservation under which all these various castes came together has turned them down into conflicting groups. This appears at the exterior as caste based, but intrinsically has class interests. To brand them as just caste tensions would be a misnomer as they are fighting keeping certain class interests.

The backward classes in Karnataka include two major divisions into the other backward classes (OBCs) and the SCs and STs. The Havanur Commission classified the OBCs into backward communities, backward castes and backward tribes.

"The question of who are the OBCs is not simple" and "over the years there has been an ongoing debate on the question of an acceptable criterion for determining social and educational backwardness. Despite the Report of the Central Backward Classes Commission or the Kaka Kalelkar Commission, the reports of the state backward classes committees, court rulings and policy declarations, the age-old issue of job reservation continued to be the cause of social tensions and political conflicts" (Singh : 1982 : 146). For example, when way back in 1977, the Uttar Pradesh and Bihar governments expanded the policy of reservation to the OBCs, after the Janatha Party's victory in 1977, it "led to widespread agitations necessitating the intervention of central leadership". As a result, the government appointed a BCC under Art. 340, under the Chairmanship of late B. P. Mandal whose task, unlike his predecessors, was to prepare lists of BCs by defining their backwardness.

As remarked by Galanter, "the question of who were the SCs was debated and roughly settled before independence within the executive and without the participation of the courts. But who are the BCs is a post-independence question which the constitutional recognition of the category made one of all-India scope" (Galenter : 1978).

These quotations only prove the complexity of the OBC category. What is inherent in them is not difficulty or in defining or setting boundaries to the OBC category, which is in a way, the reflection of the complexities involved in the system of caste itself.

In Karnataka which is incidentally one of the eight states where a policy of reservation in services are in practice since long, the OBCs resent a picture of disharmony and mutual resentment. The fundamental source of disorganisation and conflicts within this broad group is the very basis upon which the OBCs are drawn. They contain many castes/tribes that are different from each other, in terms of numerical strength, economic and educational level, ritual standing and politico-cultural control. All these variables are interrelated and form the index by which caste groups are placed as high and low. The BCCs have unified them under certain categories for granting of constitutional benefits. But in reality the three or four such major categories under the OBC category are marked by layers of conflict.

The backward castes included under the BCM in the Havanur report contained many numerically small and lower castes as compared to the Vokkaligas who were included along with them. The latter are numerically (11.82 per cent) and socially, economically and politically a dominant caste of the state. These service communities are again diverse in their own status. Traditionally, the Devangas claim a higher status than the Barbers or Washermen and the latter claim superiority over the Edigas for example. Then there is the Satanis who are treated as inferior among Brahmins. Even they claim backward status that is paradoxical. On the one hand, they claim ritual superiority while on the other, they demand for backward status on grounds of economic backwardness. There service groups worked as landless labourers or lived by marginal farming combined with some of their caste occupations like pottery, oil pressing, leather work etc. Thus, they were economically dependent upon the dominant groups, along with whom they came to be grouped under the OBC category. Constitutional grouping together of these diffuse unequal groups together to share the same quota of benefits has triggered off caste rivalries and conflicts due to competition for availing reservation benefits. This phenomenon is felt in recent decades gaining momentum with the increasing importance laid on reservation to the BCs.

But the grouping together of these diverse groups for economic gains in itself led to series of conflicts indirectly instigated by the reservation policy itself, awakened by the political, economic and social benefits that are due to them, making them more alert to the process of mobilisation. Thus, the smaller groups have developed a hatred towards their inclusion in the same category as the bigger castes. Their fears revolve around the fact that the latter would enjoy greater share of the quota for backward classes than themselves. It is further noticed that the anti-Vokkaliga resentment is glaring in the case of those castes in whose case the process of mobilisation is comparatively more active, than in the case of those who are rather weak in their resources for mobilisation. Thus, the upper among the backwards other than the Vokkaligas, like the Kurubas, Devangas, the Ganigas and the Edigas have shown greater propensity to improve their caste associations and organise caste conferences and fight for state sponsored resources than the others. Some of them have even started religious trusts and founded mutts headed by Swamijis, on the lines of the Adichunchanagiri mutt of the Vokkaligas. Increased mobilisational activities are noticed among these communities since the years 1979-83, when the Gundu Rao government encouraged them by promising professional colleges. The president of the Ganigara Sangha was nominated to the Rajya Sabha during Rao's tenure as Chief Minister.

The Vokkaligas and the Lingayats too have been perturbed by the inclusion of certain other communities as more backward than themselves, since the latter cut into their own share of the spoils. Intra backward caste relationships are more strained in the urban areas in such contexts like competing for seats in educational institutions, in government offices for promotions and in political circles for representation. In all these, superficial cordiality is observed. But beneath them are found tense caste feelings. Since most relations are guided by class factors, with caste acting only as an underlying force, most of these rifts are not glaring to the outside world. But the reservation policy has definitely made inroads into the rural traditional infrastructure leading to considerable mobility attempts. Efforts to avail of the constitutional benefits and their utilisation in daily life coupled with the implementation of other policies like land reforms, etc., have led to a caste war in rural areas, which is manifested in various direct and indirect forms.

The castes coming under the other category of backward castes is also no less heterogeneous. Comprising the middle and lower castes of traditional caste hierarchy, like the Kurubas, Thigalas, Kumbaras, Upparas, Agasas, etc., it represents communities, which are economically minor and less resourceful. They were those who were not even able to organise themselves till the Havanur Commission encouraged them to do so, indirectly. Most of their caste associations have been formed during the years when the Commission was active (1972-75). Most of their conferences were inaugurated by Sri Devraj Urs. They reached a stage where they demanded reservation facility only after the Commission held sittings with their leaders.

The grouping together of these socio-economically unequal groups into one single category since they shared similar low caste status, has not been smooth. The ritually upper castes among them are resented by the others as the sole benefactors of the policy as they are in a better socially and economically better position to utilise the benefits, with well established caste associations and other such support. The comparatively improved and better socio-economic status of some against the others, has made the former to forge themselves ahead of others in pushing candidates to claim seats in educational institutions and in government service, to the utter denial of the same to the people from weaker BCs.

The intensity of the above problem of intra category denial has reached such stages that in the recent past there is a strong case made by some of the latter deprived groups for seeking a SC status despite the stigma attached to it. For example, the Agasas (washerman) and the Nayindas (Barber) who are categorised as backward castes are claiming a SC or even a ST status through their caste associations by issuing statements and passing resolutions. They argue that their ritual status as polluting castes is no higher than the ex-untouchables. Hence, they argue that in all fairness the same constitutional position should be given to them also (Proceedings of the III Akila Karnataka Madivalara Sangha, Chikmagalur : April 17 & 18, 1981).

The backward tribes form the third component of this list of backward groups which similarly have developed antagonistic tendencies against the groups categorised along with them in a common category. Information on this trend is however lacking as most of these tribal groups are so backward as not to have even an association on their own to put forth their grievances in an organised manner. Although they exist in the case of a few, they are not fund to be articulate enough to put forth their views or demands. Examples of such communities are Bedas, Lamanis, Gollas, Valmikis, Parivara Nayakas, Koracha, Korama, Koraga, Bunde Besthas, Gondalas, Haranshikaris, Hugars, Helawas, Yerakula, Bovi, Waddar etc. The Havanur Commission has listed 63 such backward tribes under Art : 15 (4) and 61 under Art. 16 (4) (KBCC Report : 363-365). But most of them are so backward that they cannot even claim the benefits of reservation guaranteed to them.

But these very backward groups among the backward tribes are in contrast to the improved ones like the Valmikis or Bedas, Gollas and others who are planning to claim a ST status instead of BT, well recognising that the ST status offers greater share of benefits.

Thus the backward tribes are on the one hand, trying to de-sanskritise themselves by claiming a downward status. On the other, some of the backward castes are attempting to claim a BT status. For example, the Kurubas are claiming the status of a tribe as some sections of the community are found living in forest and hilly areas pursuing tribal activities (*Deccan Herald* June 16, 1981). Likewise, the Gangakula (Fishermen) community is also a BC, but their counterparts Bestars are a BT. This has led to conflicts between them.

Sometimes back, the Banjaras or Lamanis are classified as both a BT and a SC. These complexities in caste classification and categorisation arise from the very nature of the Hindu social stratification which is a collection of heterogeneous caste groups. The process of fission over the last few decades has invariably led to a substantial increase in their number. The granting of benefits on caste basis has further intensified this process of splitting of one caste into many small but more or less similar units. These diversities within the same caste group like its occupation, place of residence or any other cultural trait may be held as chiefly responsible for the overlapping of the same castes and subcastes in more than one backward category.

A significant development that has come about as a result of this perplexing system of classification of castes and tribes for backward status is the misuse of these titles of backwardness by people who are classified outside these categories. Non-BTs and non-SCs/STs claiming such statuses are generally observed, among others, in the spheres of admission to professional courses or higher government services. Such misdeeds have been on the increase during and after the years 1979-82 at a time when caste mobilisation as a process was very active in the state.

Intra SC /ST Conflict

The SCs and the STs are not spared of social strata among them. The SCs are comprised of a number of castes that are unequal in their social and economic activities. Further, the ex-untouchables among them are comprised of large castes and subcastes. They are hierarchically arranged within the broader category of the SCs. Harold Isaacs wrote that the "official list of the scheduled castes, first published by the government in early 1930s and reissued by the Government of India in 1957, shows that there are about 1,100 of those castes" ... But in their greater mass, these remain separate and distinct groups, each with its own name, its own particular slice of the tradition of pollution, its own local set of ritually impure tasks to perform, its own local set of rules to observe, its own different local master caste not to contaminate (Isaacs : 1964:29).

To this already heterogeneous nature of the ex-untouchable castes, is added more complexity with a few non-Untouchable castes also being included in the list of the SCs. The Bhovis or the Voddas have been grouped as SCs in Karnataka as they were found to be more or less experiencing the same ritual backwardness as the ex-untouchables.

The major component of the ex-untouchable category is the Holeyas and the Madigas who are also identified by the names of the Right Hand and the Left Hand groups. The Holeyas form the numerous one with 1.32 per cent followed by Chamars 0.87 per cent and the Madigas with 0.76 per cent of the state's population. They are also known as the Adi Karnataka and Adi Dravida. The latter are more popular and hold to connote fewer stigmas and are less derogatory than the terms like Holeya and Madiga. However, today not even these are used, but all are identified by the egalitarian term SC, in official and daily usage and any use of former terms is considered bad and an offence.

These variations in the usage of nomenclature may be treated as indicators of the growing awareness among the ex-untouchables about their discriminated status in the hierarchy. That old concepts have given way for new ones is clear when we look at the differences in the percentage of population each of these categories have recorded during the Havanur Commission's survey. The Adi Karnataka is shown as representing 5.37per cent on the state's total population while the Holeyas are only 1.32 per cent. Similarly, the Adi Dravidas who are equivalent to the Madigas show a percentage of 1.5 per cent. The latter are 0.76 per cent of the total population. Apart from these, the Chamars (who are known by a number of synonymous names like Samagara and so on) constitute 0.87 per cent of the state's population (KBCC Report : 1975)

Of the various ex-untouchable communities, the Adi Karnataka or the Holeyas or right hand ex-untouchable caste are not only numerically dominant, but are found to be even economically and politically more resourceful than their left hand counterparts, viz., the Adi Dravidas or the Madigas. This disparity has stemmed from their traditional position in the jajmani system. The Holeyas are generally found pursuing economically and ritually better or even superior occupations like agricultural labour and related jobs than the Adi-Dravidas who are engaged in Scavenging, Tanning and Chappal Making and even the now abolished job of night-soil carrying. Being highly polluting these jobs pursued by the Madigas has been responsible for the most-degraded and inferior status accorded to them in the hierarchy even by the other SCs. Removing the dead animal, skinning and tanning are not only considered highly polluting not only by the caste Hindus, but also by the upper strata of the ex-untouchables themselves.

The discrimination meted out to the Madigas by all the castes above them (including the other ex-untouchable groups) has resulted in the practice of untouchability within the ex-untouchable communities. It is common to find the two groups living in separate residential quarters with strict endogamous practices and bound by ritual discrimination. This practice, though a regular feature of all villages, is found even in towns and cosmopolitan cities. While the Holeyas' plight itself is very deplorable, the Madigas can be seen living under still more precarious conditions. The inequality that exists between them has no doubt proved to be a stumbling block in their progress. The gravity of the situation was upheld by the campaigns for equality within the ex-untouchable community by a number of dalit organisations.

The barriers between intra-SC and intra-ex-Untouchable categories have (in course of time and with increasing competition for economic gains) led to tensions and clashes between the various segments of the broader SC category.

The term 'SC' like the term 'OBC' is a constitutional jargon used as a blanket name for a set of broadly similar caste groups. Beyond this meaning, the concepts should not be intended to denote any intra-caste unity.

The simmering caste-antagonism and competition that existed even earlier than the introduction of legislative reforms, have been strengthened by the government's policy of protective discrimination which has put all these otherwise culturally diffuse groups, under one roof. As is the case with any other category like the BCM, BC, and BT even the SCs are no exception to the existence of intra-group conflicts.

Conflict within the SC groups is understood to have stemmed mainly from two factors, which relate to the very composition of the SC category. The first source of tension revolves around the fact that the grouping "SC" is made up of both touchable and untouchable castes. The former group which includes the castes of the Bhovis and the Lamanis can be rated as being economically and culturally superior to the ex-untouchables. By virtue of their slightly higher socio-ritual status, these touchable SCs are found to be in a better position to avail the constitutional guarantees reserved for them. Economically also, they may be found to be more resourceful, as ritual superiority often goes together with a higher politico-economic standing in a traditional caste hierarchy. However, no evidence is available to prove the last observation.

Similarly among the ex-untouchable SCs, only some segments like the AK or the Holeyas are in a better position to respond to the governmental help to them than many other castes and subcastes inferior to themselves in the social scale.[14]

Thus, the numerical preponderance and socio-economic advantages enjoyed by the touchable SCs and certain upper castes among the ex-untouchables have led to the extreme situation wherein, majority of the governmental provisions reserved for the entire category are being used by these minority castes. It may even be proper to explain this as a class problem since even among the touchable and upper ex-untouchable groups, the upper "strata" or "class" is the main beneficiary of most of the benefits.

While these misgivings of the reservation policy came to be criticised by the affected groups themselves a few years ago, they are now being openly attacked in the form of press statements and protests. Such an interactional change also testifies the rise of awareness among the lower ex-untouchable groups—perhaps another aspect of the advantages of the reservation policy.

The caste associations of the ex-untouchable castes are not only opposing the policy of government as unfair, but also are demanding a reclassification of the SCs wherein they should be given an independent constitutional status. Representations are being submitted to the government and to the subsequent BCCs by the leaders of the organisations to this effect. In fact, a dalit organisation of the so-called left hand ex-untouchables of Bangalore carried out a protest morcha during 1983 under the leadership of a prominent ex-minister late Sri N. Rachaiah, belonging to the left hand Untouchable group, aiming at the separation of the touchable from the SCs' list.[15]

These fundamental layers of caste conflict which are observed in the recent years in Karnataka are an important aspect of the mobilisation process that is in vogue in the state. While many of them are still in their formative years, they are also qualitative in their appearance and impact. These qualities have even rendered any deeper analysis of the subject of caste tensions in whatever form they may exist, a difficult and formidable task.

Further, the entire range of such caste tensions are required to be treated as being interrelated. They generally tend to emerge out of the interplay of a number of social, political and economic variables, set in motion by the social environment where they prevail. The policy of protective discrimination is one such basic and primary criterion of this dimension of social change in India.

References

1. For example, it is stated that "Ideas of social and economic equality, individual freedom and human dignity were not known to Indians until the British rule was established (KBCC Report, Vol I, Part I, Chapter I : 1, 1975). This is somewhat of an exaggeration; British rule is seen by many as the beginning of non-Brahmin ascendancy. Andre Beteille's (1983:83-84) comments on Manu in his 1980 Ambedkar Memorial Lecture are pertinent to be noted in this context.
2. The press at that time comprised mostly of members from the Brahmin community.
3. Also, see the KBCC report Vol I, Part I, 1975 for details on this point in Chapter I on 'Movement for Equality in Karnataka'. It has reference to K. T. Seshaiya's speech in the Representative Assembly, who said that " I do not ask for a living for the Brahmins... My only point is, we must have efficiency in the Public Services. Public Service is not a representative institution to which recruitment should be made on a communal basis" (KBCC Report : 3, 1975).
4. Brahmins expressed their fear over the possible favourable attitude by the Dewan, who was a Muslim, towards non-Brahmins and wrote in a way that warned Mirza about any such act of favouritism.
5. The brunt of the problem of social conflict in the form of upper caste hostility characterised by feelings of jealousy is found to be inflicted more upon the SCs than on the STs. This may be attributed to the fact among others that the former constitute numerically a larger group and therefore, have access to a greater share in the reservation quota than the STs. It may be also because the STs have generally enjoyed a better socio-ritual status than the ex-untouchables even in rural areas. It is common to find 'Lambani' or a 'Soliga' being treated with less ritual norms of purity /impurity than a 'Handijogi' or 'Sudugadu Sidda' who constitute the Harijan group. Such a disparity in social relations may be because of various reasons. The fact that tribals are considered non-Hindus and therefore, do not come under the four-fold Varna system may be one reason. Secondly, their general settlements in hilly and forest areas and not in villages in the midst of caste Hindus has facilitated an

entirely different socio-cultural attitude towards them. But the more fundamental reason appears to be the fact that their numerically and otherwise less dominant status, and also their comparatively low tendency for competence to claim the constitutional guarantees seems to be the driving force behind a less hostile attitude by the caste-Hindus towards the STs than towards the SCs.

6. The SCs used to be addressed ironically as 'Sarakari (government) Brahmanaru' by the caste Hindus.
7. The twice-born or the dwijas.
8. A look at the incidents of intercaste tensions in the state in recent years bears evidence to this. These started to show up especially in the years following the implementation of reservation policy rather rigorously by the Urs government. For example, in April 1981 Narayanapur in Bidar district initiated a series of similar tensions in the district that it was 'teetering on the brink of a civil war' (*Deccan Herald* : April 30, 1981). Small incidents stirred such tension that assumed a gigantic proportion following police firing and imposition of curfew. Religious matters were the cause of such tensions. On the day when Ambedkar Jayanthi was being celebrated the Lingayats were celebrating the Barsi festival. Verbal duel between the two groups as to who should take their procession through a particular road in the town led to tension. The police opening fire led to death and injuries to many, but the latter being caste-Hindus and the Sub Inspector of Police being a SC led to the incident assuming a communal character. They were the cause of further trouble in other towns of the district like Bhalki where a few caste-Hindu youths were stabbed by the SC, and a prominent leader of the SCs was burnt alive by the Lingayats. The dalit youth taking the cue from the dalit panthers across the border in Maharashtra are unlike their counterparts in other districts in the state, volatile, aggressive and assertive in securing their rights. They are, therefore, naturally on a collision course with their caste Hindu big brothers. Largely impoverished, unemployment is rampant among them that have infuriated them against the system as such. "How can a Harijan, the lowest, live on an elevated plot of land? Why should SC students alone enjoy the various hostel and scholarship facilities? These and the other questions seem to be worrying the caste Hindus" (*ibid.*).
9. With the exception of Prof. M. Jayalakshmammanni, who hailed from the Urs community.
10. Following the starting of Janatha rule in the state on January 11, 1983, violence broke out at Devarasanahalli, a village in Nanjangud taluk of Mysore district, following clashes between Vokkaligas and the dalits, in

which four persons were killed and several injured. The clash was a sequel to the alleged assault on a dalit two days before, resulting in his death. This sparked off clashes resulting in the murder of members of both communities including the president of the village Panchayat. These incidents "only precipitated a flare-up that was brewing for quite sometime, but had gone unnoticed or neglected by all leaders". The reason was the rivalry between local SCs and Vokkaligas that had been brewing over a year came to ahead during the assembly elections 1983, when a member from SC community, Mallanna, contested as an independent candidate against a Vokkaliga. The village is SC dominated (about 1,500 SC residents as against 750 Vokkaligas) (*Times of India* : January 31, 1983). Similarly, in Kolar district's Chillapanahalli, barely 12 kms from the district HQ, saw clashes between the SCs and the Vokkaligas. On Vijayadashami day in 1982, for the first time in the history of the village, the SCs took police protection to enter the Maramma temple, which is in the upper caste locality. After this, the caste-Hindus stopped going to that temple and it was locked. The event of forceful entry made by the ex-Untouchables under the leadership of the government officials led to a lot of problems to them. They were ex-communicated and socially ostracised by the caste-Hindus, no food and water were given and they were thrown out of their employment also. Even the neighbouring villagers also withdrew all contacts and facilities (like flour mill, hotel etc.) with the SCs of this village. It is these hidden and longstanding quarrels that led to the clashes of 1983.

11. Secretary of the Karnataka State Savitha Samaj, the caste association of the Barbers and the president of the Karnataka Madivalara Sangha have admitted this. The matter was stressed in the caste conference of 1984 and even later.
12. The Mysore government made a provision for the backward classes as early as in the year 1874 and in 1895 wherein "appointments in Police Departments were made by reserving posts in proportion in favour of the Brahmins, the Musalmans and the other Hindu castes. Despite the scheme of communal reservation from 1874, the representation of other communities in the government Department continued. In January 1895, the Mysore Government issued further circular reserving posts in favour of the backward classes" (Circular No. 218-98 dated 19th/21st January 1895 (Singh : 1982: 8-81). In 1914, a system of recruitment by nominations was introduced by which the posts of assistant commissioners were filled by members of the backward classes.
13. The famous 'Hunsasikote' murder case (1977) involving the conflict between Vokkaligas and the Agasas (a backward caste) serves as an

example here. Seshagiriyappa a member of the Agasa (washerman) caste was murdered in Hunasikote in Kolar district owing to longstanding enmity between the two castes. The case was taken up by the Dalit Sangharsh Samithi (against much opposition from dalit leaders that the case is not to be taken up by the DSS since it does not involve a dalit but a washerman) was fought for 3 years. The main suspect was the president of the taluk development board of Malur, the taluk where the village was situated and a Vokkaliga leader.

14. Like the Handijogis, Killekyathas, Sudugadu Siddas and innumerable other castes who are even less than 0.01 per cent of the state's population (the KBCC Report : 1975).
15. Called the 'All India Scheduled Caste Federation' founded by N. Rachaiah led this demand. The touchable-untouchable controversy formed an important part of certain other untouchable caste conferences held since the past two-three decades.

8 Conclusions

Mobilisation occupies a place of importance in the process of development and it acts as a catalyst in regard to a whole range of socio-political processes. It occurs as a response to emerging changes in the social, economic and political spheres. The threat of exclusion from the gains of change and development is a major force behind this process. It is obvious that mobilisation processes are influenced by several factors such as the social structure, the economic framework and the political system. It is this recognition of the multi-faceted nature of mobilisation that has now led to it being treated as something more complex than a mere political or religious or cultural phenomenon. Also, mobilisation exerts a powerful influence upon all social processes.

In the introduction, it is suggested that mobilisation, change and development acquire intensity or momentum and even the degree (extent) of their impact, from the social fabric of the society in which these processes occur. Thus, social movements are bound inevitably to inherit the characteristics of the social segment which has initiated the movement. In other words, no social movement can be completely free, or isolate itself from, the influence of the socio-cultural factors which characterise that particular set of people for whom the movement is meant to result in the desired changes.

The present study has probed into the implications of sectarian mobilisation for the development process. In our frame of reference, sectarian mobilisation is seen as representing caste and/or class interests. One of the principal manifestations of such a process in the context of this book is the fight for reservations from the backward classes and the response to this from the state. The latter has taken several forms such as fixing criteria for determination of backwardness and setting places in educational institutions and in service under the state to the groups so classified. Another, and equally important, manifestation of sectarian mobilisation has been the formation of caste associations, sometimes, although not always, followed by the establishment of educational institutions. There are instances of the latter existing without the former and vice versa.

It has to be emphasised that the very nature of the subject precludes any quantifiable conclusions. It is not possible to offer more than what may be called explanatory generalisations regarding the crucial nexus between development and mobilisation.

One crucial question which the study attempted to find answers to was whether the articulation of caste/community interests is really an articulation of the interests of whole castes/communities or whether it contains within itself a large element of class interests. The interesting phenomenon that stands out in the melting pot and which deserves careful scrutiny is the important question of why there is a clamour for reservations and more essential, who benefits from them? An important derivative point of the whole analysis of mobilisation in the state of Karnataka is that it cannot be understood or studied from the standpoint only of caste. Class interests along with caste in all the dimensions of mobilisation, whether in the pre-independence period or later.

The importance of class has been highlighted in the present study. It is intended to point out that it is certainly the upper strata of the upper castes and tribal groups coming under the backward section which benefit from policies such as reservations. To a great extent, the basic substratum of economically poor people seems to have remained largely where it was with the benefits reaching the more vocal, articulate upper and middle classes within each backward class.

The above situation has, added more complexity to the whole system of traditional stratification. In other words, instead of abolishing castes or a hierarchical order based on strata that consists of castes and tribes, these developments have, over a period of time, added more hierarchies to the existing ones. New hierarchical orders have emerged replacing older ones, retaining, nonetheless, traits of both tradition and modernity.

This leads to examine the effects of the present efforts at mobilisation by various caste/community/tribal groups. It would seem that the process of fission among that amorphous group called the Other Backward Classes which took birth in Karnataka almost simultaneously with the backward classes' movement, has now acquired a more distinctive character. In other words, the OBCs now reveal quite vividly several layers. We find that those groups which in the pre-independence era were not active participants and appeared quite content with a dormant status have now begun to assert themselves. The policy of reservations and also the climate of the times particularly after 1972, have contributed to this. Hence, the increase in the number of caste associations belonging to the minorities and/or a spurt in their activities like the Kuruba, Devanga, Kumbara, Korama, Viswakarma, Madivala, Raju Kshatriya, Yadava, Beda, Ganiga and, in a lower key the Nayanaja Kshatriya.

Another important point which comes out of this work is that there is today a fairly vocal resentment at the Lingayats and Vokkaligas skimming off a major portion of the benefits accruing to the OBCs – due to their numerical and relative economic superiority.

We find too that this process of fission has permeated to even lower levels. As an example, we may cite the case of the Devangas. They are weavers by tradition specialising in silk weaving. While relative to the Vokkaligas and Kurubas, the Devangas keep a low profile, among the weaving community which in addition to the Devangas includes the Padmashalis, Swakula Salis, Thogataveeras, Bhavasara Kshatriyas, Pattegars and Neygis, there is resentment at what is perceived to be the dominance of the Devangas. The problem is complicated by the fact that all these are endogamous groups.

The Kurubas have begun to emerge as a well organised and articulate group among the OBCs. They also enjoy the advantage of being well represented in all the districts. Even though they have not made much of a mark in the sphere of private educational institutions they are prolifically well represented.

What has been said above is symptomatic of the conflict among the OBCs – sometimes latent, sometimes overt, but conflict all the same. When we move down the caste hierarchy we find that the service communities in particular are now seeking the SC or ST tag. It may be mentioned that some of these communities follow traditional professions which are stigmatised – such are the barbers and the washermen. Even the Kurubas who are an intermediate caste have demanded the ST tag.

These demands indicate a certain consciousness, a drive towards mobilisation and the ability to articulate and organise, traits that were missing in the past. Yet, we see that these minorities do not cohere and frequently tend to cut across each other's interests. The alliance of backward classes and minorities is rather more fragile than what appears on the surface.

Looking at the forward groups we find a different picture. The Lingayats are resentful of sharing their backward status and political power with the other dominant caste and have been making untiring efforts to regain both. The Akila Bharatha Veerasaiva Mahasabha has attempted to bring together all those originally converted to Veerasaivas, which group includes several service and artisan castes (Ganigas etc.) under the nomenclature of Lingayat. However, while the ABVMS has attempted to initiate a process of fusion neither the five main sub-divisions of Lingayats nor the intended target group have shown much enthusiasm for this fusion. Loyalties to caste have taken diverse routes and have gained complexity, besides being unpredictable. This is proved by a number of recent trends in accessing political power and during elections.

The Brahmins, for long silent in terms of mobilisation, have also started working towards a unification of different endogamous subcastes. The reasons for the long Brahmin silence have been discussed in several places in the book. Suffice it to say that the Brahmins are now demanding what they demanded in the early years of this century although only by implication then, that is, reservation on purely economic criterion.

The Bunts who for a short while were tempted to align themselves with the Vokkaligas have now parted company with the latter. This is not surprising considering the overt Bunt fear that the Vokkaligas with their numerical dominance could practically obliterate the former. Also, the latter have a better organisational base and so it is more than likely that they do not now deserve an alliance with the Bunts.

Viewed against this backdrop we should not be surprised that the post-Havanur forward castes alliance – Brahmins, Bunts and Lingayats – was short-lived.

What is most interesting is the conflict between the Vokkaligas and the Lingayats. Both are aspirants for power and there is an understandable feeling of being left out in the cold on the part of the Lingayats after 1975. Since 1989, they are back to power with few successive chief ministers hailing from their caste. But they frequently act in tandem to prevent the emergence of SC dominance. We thus find the Vokkaligas and the Lingayats acting alternately together and separately in order to exercise influence over state politics.

At what may be considered the lowest level, we find two processes at work. One is the difference between touchable and the so-called untouchable SCs and the other is the difference between the different ex-untouchable groups – for example, between the Adi-Karnatakas and the Holeyas (right hand) and the Madigas (left hand). Both these are proving to be intractable problems particularly for organisations like Dalit Sangarsh Samithi which have been working for unity among all Dalits.

On the whole, we find that the mobilisational activities initiated by the upper castes have permeated down the ladder and have been imitated by others with varying degrees of success.

It should be mentioned that the process of sectarian mobilisation which has a long history in Karnataka has had, and indeed continues to have, significant implications for development. To some extent, the consciousness of rights and the ability to assert on the part of numerically and economically weak groups is a positive sign. It contributes in no small measure to general awareness. However, given the caste-class dimensions, this consciousness has not yet percolated fully down the various class strata within these caste groups. It is for this reason that class divisions among castes are likely to become more sharply focused in the years to come. If this is met by a radical movement within each caste group which aims at attacking vested interests which emerge inside the group then the issue would perhaps be capable of resolution through a process of polarisation which will ultimately take the form of a class struggle. But what militates against this is the not very speedy tempo of economic development and interventions like structural adjustment policies, globalisation and declining livelihood bases of the poor which have rendered the already backward, more backward and vulnerable. The lack of speedy economic development means that there will be keener fight for constant spoils. In such a situation radical alternatives in this society would be difficult to implement. We have adduced evidence of this difficulty while discussing the activities of the DSS in Chapter - 4. The difficulty is by no means unique to them. In any society, where planning has yet to result in a more egalitarian structure, the field is wide open for caste and class divisions to be manipulated with ease. Ultimately the difference should come only from increasing radicalisation within each community/caste by which we mean a growing awareness that exploitation from within is no different from exploitation from outside. The recent reforms in governance with decentralisation of planning and governance as the new 'mantra' is expected to lead to far-reaching changes in this scenario. There is need for further research in this area to understand the impact it has made on sectarian mobilisation in Karnataka, which is hailed, in fact, to be a progressive state as far as decentralised governance is concerned.

BIBLIOGRAPHY

I. Government Reports and Documents

Government of India (1918-19). *Report of the Committee Appointed by the Secretary of State for India to Enquire into Questions Connected with Franchise and Other Matters Relating to Constitutional Reforms* – Chairman: Lord Southborough.

——,(——). *Report of the Backward Classes Commission* – Chairman Kaka Saheb Kalelkar, 3 Vols. Delhi: Manager of Publications, Government of India Press, Delhi.

——, (1969). *Report of the Committee on Untouchability, Economic and Educational Development of the SCs and Connected Documents* – Chairman L Elayaperumal, Delhi: Department of Social Welfare.

——, (1971). *Census of India, District Census Hand Books for Karnataka.*

——, (1980a). *Report of the Backward Classes Commission*— Chairman, B P Mandal, 2 Parts, Vols. I –VII, New Delhi: Controller of Publications.

——, (1980b). *The Constitution of India*, New Delhi: Ministry of Law, Justice and Company Affairs.

Government of Mysore (1919). *Report of the Committee Appointed to Consider Steps Necessary for the Adequate Representation of Communities in Public Service.* Chairman Leslie C Miller, Bangalore: Government of Mysore.

——, (1939). *Report of the Committee on Constitutional Reforms of Mysore.* Bangalore: Government of Mysore.

——, (1961). *Final Report of the Mysore Backward Classes Committee*, Chairman Dr. R Nagan Gowda, Bangalore: Government Press.

Government of Karnataka (1975). *Report of the Karnataka Backward Classes Commission* – Chairman L G Havanur, 4 Vols. In 5 Parts, Bangalore: Government Press.

——, (1986). *Report of the Venkataswamy Commission*, Bangalore: Government of Karnataka.

——, (1989). *Report of the Justice Chinnappa Reddy Commission*, Bangalore: Government of Karnataka.

Parvathamma, C. (1976). *Report of the Socio-Economic Survey of the SCs and the STs in Karnataka*, Mysore: Department of Sociology, Manasagangotri, Mysore University.

Debates of the Constituent Assembly, 1948-52.

Proceedings of the Mysore Representative Assembly, 1881-1947.

Resolutions Passed in the Caste Associations' Meetings.

Memoranda Submitted to the GoK by Various Caste Aassociations.

II. Books

Abbasayulu, V R (1979). *Scheduled Caste Elite*, Hyderabad

——, (1953): *Hindu Manners, Customs and Ceremonies.* Translated by Henry K Beauchamp. Oxford: Clarendon Press.

Abraham, M F (1968). Social Contours of a South India Village. *Interdiscipline*, III(3): 135-49.

Adelman, Irma and Cynthis Taft Morris (1967). *Society, Politics and Economic Development*, Baltimore: Hopkins.

——,(1973). *Economic Growth and Social Equity in Developing Countries.* Stanford, Calif: Stanford University Press.

Agarwal, L B (1934). *The Harijans in Rebellion.* Bombay: Taraporewala & Sons.

Aggarwal, Pratap C and Mohammed Siddiq Ashraf (1976). *Equality Through Privilege: A Study of Special Privileges of Scheduled Castes in Haryana*, New Delhi: Shri Ram Centre for Industrial Relations and Human Resources.

Aiyappan, A. (1944). *Iravas and Culture Change*, Madras: Superintendent, Government Press.

——, (1965). *Social Revolution in a Kerala Village*, New York: Asia Publishing House.

Aiyappan, A. and Balaratnam (1956). *Society in India*, Madras: S. S. A. Publishers.

Alexander, K C (1968a). *Social Mobility in Kerala*, Poona: Deccan College.

——, (1968 b). Changing Status of Pulaya Harijans of Kerala, *Economic and Political Weekly*, 101-04.

——, (1968c). Changing Religious Beliefs and Practices of the Pulayas of Kerala. *Social Action*, 390-97.

Alse, A. J. (ed.) (1979). *Adventure of Ideas: Story of T. M. A. Pai, The Academy of General Education*, Manipal.

Ambedkar, Bhimrao Ramji (1925). *What Congress and Gandhi have done to the Untouchables*. Bombay: Thacker & Co.

——, (1930). *Address to the All India Depressed Classes Congress*.

——, (1943a). *Gandhi, Ranade and Jinnah*. Bombay: Thacker & Co.

——, (1943b). *Mr. Gandhi and the Emancipation of the Untouchables*, Bombay.

——, (1945). *Annihilation of Caste*. Bombay: The Bhusan Press.

——, (1946). *Who Were the Sudras?* Bombay: Thacker & Co.

——, (1947). *States and Minorities*. Bombay: Thacker & Co.

——, (1948). *The Untouchables: Who Are They and Why They Became Untouchables*. Delhi: Amrit Book Co.

——, (1951). *Manifesto, Scheduled Caste Federation*

——, (1963 & 1969). *Thus Spoke Ambedkar, Selected Speeches compiled by Bhagawan Das*, Vol.I (1963). Vol. II (1969), Jullundar: Bheem Patrika Publication.

——, (1957). *Buddha and His Dharma*.

Anand, Sudhir (1973). *Poverty and Inequality in Malaysia*. Oxford.

Anant, Santokh Singh (1972). *The Changing Concept of Caste in India*, Delhi: Vikas Publications.

Anderson, Arnold C. (1961). *A Skeptical Note on Education and Mobility*. In Hasley *et al*, (ed.), *Education and Society*.

Apter, D. (1965). *The Politics of Modernisation*, Chicago

Arnold, David and James Manor (1976). Caste Associations in South India : A Comparative Analysis. *The Indian Economic and Social History Review*, 8(3).

Aron, Raymond (1968). *Progress and Disillusion*. Pall Mall Press.

Atal, Yogesh (1968). *The Changing Frontiers of Caste*. New Delhi: National Publishing House.

——, (1972). *Changing Pattern of Caste*. Indian Sociological Society.

Atkinson, Dick (1971). *Orthodox Consensus and Racial Alternative*, London.

——, (1976). *The Economic Inequality*, London: Oxford University Press.

Aurora, G. S. (1968). Caste and the Backward Classes. *Man in India*. 48:297-306.

Azariah, V. S. (1932). The Caste Movement in South India, *International Review of Missions*. 21: 457-87.

Aziz, Abdul (1980). The Backward Classes Movement in Karnataka 1918-1979. *Journal of Historical Studies*. 16

Aziz, Abdul & B. David Arnold (ed.) (1996). *Decentralised Governance in Asian Countries*. New Delhi: Sage Publications.

Babb, L A (1970). The Political Involvement of a Religious Movement: The Satnamis. In J.M. Manor (ed.) The Untouchables in Contemporary India, The University of Arizona Press, Tuscon.

Bailey, F. G. (1957). *Caste and the Economic Frontier*, Manchester: Manchester University Press.

——, (1960). Tribe, Caste and Nation , Bombay: Oxford University Press.

——, (1963). *Politics and Social Change: Orissa in 1959*, Berkeley and Los Angeles: University of California Press.

Baker, C. J, and D. A. Washbrook (1975). *South India: Political Institutions and Political Change 1880-1940*. Delhi: The Macmillan Company of India.

Banks, J. A. L. (1970). *Marxist Sociology in Action*. London.

Baron, Paul (1957). *The Political Economy of Growth*. New York: Monthly Review Press.

Barber, Bernard (1957). *Social Stratification*, New York.

Barnabas, AP (1961). Sanskritisation. *Economic Weekly*, XIII (15) : 613-18.

——, and Subhash C. Mehta (1965). *Caste in Changing India*, New Delhi: Indian Institute of Public Administration.

Bendix, Reinhard and S M Lipset (1957). *Class, Status and Power: A Reader in Social Stratification*. Glencoe, Illinois, USA: The Free Press.

Berreman, Gerald D. (1965). Stratification, Pluralism and Interaction: A Comparative Analysis of Caste. In Anthony de Reuck and Julie Knight (eds.), *Caste and Race*, London.

——,(1981). *Comparative and Development Approaches*. Academic Press.

Beteille, Andre (1961). Politics of Caste. *Indian Express*.

——,(1964). A Note on the Reference of Caste. *European Journal of Sociology*, V.

——, (1965). The Future of the Backward Classes – The Competing Demands of Status and Power, Perspectives, Supplement to the *Indian Journal of Public Administration*, II.

——, (1967). Elites, Status Groups and Caste in Modern India. In Philip Mason (ed.), *India and Ceylon: Unity and Diversity*, Oxford University Press.

——, (1969a). Ideas and Interests: Some Conceptual Problems in the Study of Social Stratification in Rural India. *International Social Science Journal*. 21(2).

——, (1969b). *Castes: Old and New, Essays in Social Structure and Social Stratification*. Bombay: Asia Publishing House.

——, (1969c). *Social Inequality, Selected Readings*. Harmondsworth: Penguin.

——, (1971a). *Caste, Class and Power: Changing Patterns of Stratification in a Tanjore Village*. Berkeley: University of California Press.

——, (1971b). *Harmonic and Disharmonic Social Systems*. Sydney: University Press.

——, (1977). *Inequality Among Men*, Basil Blackwell: Oxford University Press.

——,(1978). *Inequality and Social Change*. Delhi: Oxford University Press.

——, (1981). *The Backward Classes and the New Social Order*. Delhi: Oxford University Press.

——,(1983). *The Idea of Natural Equality and Other Essays*. Delhi: Oxford University Press.

Bhat, G. S. (1945). The Chamars of Lucknow, *The Eastern Anthropologist*. III(I): 24-41.

——, (1961). Trends and Measures of Status Mobility among the Chamars of Dehradun, *The Eastern Anthropologist*. XIV(3): 229-41.

Bhatt, Anil (1971). Politics and Social Mobility in India, *Contributions to Indian Sociology*, New Series, 5.

——,(1975). *Caste, Class and Politics: An Empirical Profile of Social Stratification in Modern India*. Manohar, India.

Blunt, E. A. H. (1931). *The Caste System of Northern India*, Oxford.

Bose, N. K. (1948). Some Aspects of Caste in Bengal, *American Journal of Folklore*, LXXXI.

——,(1951). Caste in India, *Man in India*, 31: 107-23.

——, (1954). Who are the Backward Classes?, *Man in India*, 34.

——, (1967). *Culture and Society in India.* Bombay: Asian Publishing House.

——, (1975). *Structure of Indian Society,* New Delhi: Orient Longman.

Bottomore, T B (1964). *Elites and Society,* New York.

——,(1966). *Classes in Modern Society,* London.,

Bougle, C. (1958). The Essence and Reality of Caste System, *Contributions to Indian Sociology.*

Brass, Paul (1965). *Factional Politics in an Indian State: The Congress Party in Uttar Pradesh,* Berkeley, California: University of California Press.

Buchanan, F. (1807). *A Journey Through the Countries of Mysore, Canara and Malabar,* London.

Buckley, William (1959). 'Social Stratification and the Functional Theory of Social Differentiation', *American Sociological Review,* 23 (3).

Chauhan, Brij Raj (1967). 'Special Problems of Education of the Scheduled Castes'. In M. S. Gore & I. P. Desai (eds.) *Papers in Sociology of Education in India.* New Delhi: NCERT.

——,(1969). 'Scheduled Castes and Scheduled Tribes'. *Economic and Political Weekly,* 257-63.

Chennabasappa, K. (1979): *Havanur Report: Its Fallacy,* Bangalore: Sri Aravinda Prakashana.

Chenery, Hollis and Syrquin Moises (1974): *Redistribution with Growth,* London: OUP.

——,(1975). Patterns of Development, 1950-1970. London: Oxford University Press.

Chitnis, Suma (1981). *A Long Way To Go.* Delhi: Allied Publishers.

Cohn, Bernard S (1955): The Changing Status of a Depressed Caste. In McKim Marriott (ed) Village India: Studies in the Little Community. Chicago.

——, (1959a). Changing Traditions of a Low Caste. In Milton

Singer (ed.) *Traditional India: Structure and Change*, Philadelphia: American Folklore Society.

——, (1959b). Madhopur Revisited. *The Economic Weekly*, XI (28,29,30): 966.

Cole, G. D. H. (1955). *Studies in Class Structure*. London: Routledge and Kegan Paul.

Coser, Lewis A (1957). Social Conflict and Social Change. *British Journal of Sociology*, VII (3).

Dahl, Robert (1961). *Who Governs: Democracy and Power in an American City*. New Haven: Yale University Press.

Dahrendorf, Ralf (1959). *Class and Class Conflict in Industrial Society*. Stanford.

Damle, Y. B. (1968). Reference Group Theory and Mobility in the Caste System. In James Silverberg (ed.) *Social Mobility in the Caste System in India*, The Hague: Mouton & Co..

Das Veena (1977). *Structure and Cognition, Aspects of Hindu Caste and Ritual*. Bombay: Oxford University Press.

Davis, Kingsley and Wilbert E Moore (1951): Some Principles of Stratification. *American Sociological Review*.

Dennis , Daliton (1967). The Gandhian View of Caste and Caste After Gandhi. In Philip Mason, (ed.) *India and Ceylon: Unity and Diversity*. Bombay: Oxford University Press.

Desai, A R (1966). Social Background of Indian Nationalism. Bombay: Popular Book Depot.

Deutsch, Karl W. (1961). Social Mobilisation and Political Development, *American Political Science Review*, LV(3).

Deveerappa, H. (1980). *Mysuru Basavayyanavaru*, Gadag: Verasaiva Adyayana Samsthe (in Kannada).

D'Souza, Victor (1962). Changing Values of Scheduled Castes. *The Economic Weekly of India*, XVI(48).

——,(1967). Caste and Class: A Reinterpretation. *Journal of Asian and African Studies*. 2: 192-211.

Dube, S.C. (1955). *Indian Village*. Ithaca, New York: Cornell University Press.

——,(1958). *India's Changing Villages.* London: Routeledge and Kegan Paul.

Dubois, Abbe, J.A. (1906): *Description on the Character, Manners and Customs of the People of India and of Their Institutions, Religious and Civil Society for the Resuscitation of Indian Literature.*

Dumont, Louis (1961). Caste, Racism and Stratification: Reflections of a Social Anthropologist. *Contributions to Indian Sociology,* 5.

——, (1966). *Homo Hierarchicus, The Caste System and its Implications* (Nature of Human Society Series).

Durkheim, Emile (1964). *The Division of Labour in Society,* Glencoe.

Dushkin, Lelah (1961). The Backward Classes. *The Economic Weekly.* 13(43, 45 & 46): 1665-83, 1695-06 & 1729-38.

——,(1972). The Scheduled Caste Politics. In Michael Mahar (ed) *The Untouchables in Contemporary India,* Tuscon: University of Arizona Press.

——, (1974). *The Non-Brahmin Movement in Princely Mysore.* Unpublished Ph.D Thesis, Philadelphia: University of Pennsylvania.

——, (1978). Backward Classes Benefits and Social Class in India, 1920-1970. A Paper presented at the *Annual Meeting of the Association for Asia Studies,* April, Chicago.

——, (1980). Caste Associations in Bangalore. *Economic and Political Weekly.* XV(37).

Dutt, N. K. (1930). *The Origin and Growth of Caste in India.* V. I Calcutta: The Book Company.

Enthoven, R. E. (1920-1922). *The Tribes and Castes of Bombay.* 3 Vols. Bombay.

Epstein, Scarlett (1962). *Economic Development and Social Change in South India,* Manchester: Manchester University Press.

——, (1973). *South India: Yesterday, Today and Tomorrow, Mysore Villages Revisited.* London: Macmillan.

Etzioni, A. (1968a). Mobilisation as a Macro-Sociological Conception. *The British Journal of Sociology.*

Fernandes, Walter (1981). Caste and Conversion Movements in India. *Indian Social Institute Monograph Series,* New Delhi: Indian Social Institute.

Fox, Richard G. (1967). Resiliency and Change in the Caste System, *Journal of Asian Studies.* 26

Galanter, Marc (1969). Untouchability and the Law. *Economic and Political Weekly,* Annual Number.

——, (1978). Who are the Other Backward Classes? An Introduction to a Constitutional Puzzle. *Economic and Political Weekly.* XIII (43/44): 1812-28.

——,(1984). *Competing Inequalities: Law and the Backward Classes in India.* New Delhi: Oxford University Press.

Galtung, J (1976): *The Politics of Self-Reliance,* Oslo, (Mimeo), Quoted in the Political Economy of Indirect Rule: Mysore 1881-1947, Bjorn Hettne, Ambika Publications, New Delhi, 1978.

Gerth, H. H. and C. W. Mills (eds.) (1947). *From Max Weber: Essays in Sociology.* London: Routledge and Kegan Paul.

Ghurye, G.S. (1924). 'The Theory of Caste'. In *Man in India,* IV.

——,(1961). *Caste, Class and Occupation.* Bombay: Popular Book Depot.

Ghurye, G. S. (1932). *Caste and Race in India.* London: Kegal Paul.

Gough, Kathleen (1952). The Social Structure of a Tanjore Village. *Economic Weekly,* 4.

——,(1957). *Caste and Class in India.* Bombay: Popular Book Depot.

——,(1961). *Caste, Class and Occupation.* Bombay: Popular Book Depot.

——, (1963). *The Scheduled Tribes.* Bombay: Popular Book Depot.

Gould, Harold A (1960). Castes, Outcastes and the Sociology of Stratification. *International Journal of Comparative Sociology*, I(2).

Government of Mysore (1968). *Ameliorative Measures for Backward Classes in Mysore State*. Bangalore: Department of Social Welfare, Department of Information and Tourism.

Griffin, Keith B and John L Enos (1970). Planning Development. London: Addison-Wesley.

Gundappa, D. V. (1971). *Mysurina Dewaanarugalu, Swathanthra Poorvada Aaru Dashakagalu*. Mysore: Kavyalaya (in Kannada).

Gupta, Dipankar (2000) *Interrogating Caste : Understanding Hierarchy and Difference in India Society*. New Delhi : Penguin Books.

——, (ed) (2004) *Caste in Emostion : Identity* or *Hierarchy Qiestopm* New Delhi : Sage.

Hardgrave, Jr. Robert L. (1965). *The Dravidian Movement*. Bombay: Popular Prakashan.

——, (1968). 'Caste, Fission and Fusion'. *Economic and Political Weekly*, Special Number.

——, (1969). *The Nadars of Tamil Nad : The Political Culture of Community in Change*. Berkley and Los Angeles: University of California Press.

Harper, Edward B (1968). Social Consequences of an Unsuccessful Low Caste Movement. In James Silverberg (ed.) *Social Mobility in the Caste System in India*, The Hague: Mouton and Company.

Havanur, L. G. (1963). Backward Classes. *Mysore Law Journal*, (2): 15-19.

Heggade, O.D. (2003). *Halumatha Kuruba Janangadha Abhivrudhdi Samasyegalu*. Mysore: Human Development Study Centre (In Kannada).

Hettne, Bjorn and Gordon Tamm (1974). *Mobilisation and*

Development in India: A Case of Mysore State. Stockholm: Swedish International Authority.

Hoselitz, Bert P. and Wilbert E. Moore (1975). *Sociological Aspects of Economic Growth*. Delhi: Amerind Publishers.

Hutton, J.H. (1946). *Caste in India: Its Nature, Function and Origins*. Oxford University Press.

Irschick, E.F. (1969). *Politics and Social Conflict in South India: The Non-Brahmin Movement and Tamil Separatism (1916-1929)*. Berkeley: University of California.

Ishwaran K. (1966). *Tradition and Economy in Village India*. Bombay: Allied Publishers.

Issacs, Harold (1964). *India's Ex-Untouchables*. New York.

Jacob T.G. and P. Bandhu (2009) *Reflections on the Cast Question : The Dalit Situation in South India*. Oolacamund : Odyssey.

Kananaikil, Jose (1983): *Christians of SC Origin*. New Delhi: Indian Social Institute.

——,(1993). The Emerging Dalit Identity in India. *Social Action*, 43.

Kane, P. V. (1974). *History of Dharmasastra*. Poona: Bhandarkar Oriental Research Institute.

Karve, Irawathi (1958). 'What is Caste?'. *Economic Weekly*, X (4-6).

——, (1961). *Hindu Society: An Interpretation*. Poona: Sangram Press.

Kotani H. (ed.) (1999) Caste System Untouchability on other Depressed, New Kelhi : Manhor Publications.

Kothari, Rajni (ed.) (1970). *Caste in Indian Politics*. New Delhi: Orient Longmans.

——, (1976). *Democratic Polity and Social Change in India: Crisis and Opportunities*.Bombay: Allied Publishers.

Krishnappa, Chandramani N (1982). 'Sree Adichunchanagiri Sidda Simhasana', *Souvenir of the Vokkaligara Sangha*, Bangalore.

Kroeber, A. L. (1930). 'Caste'. *Encyclopaedia of Social Sciences*, III (254b-57a).

Lakshmisagar, G (nd). Reservation for Social Justice, Formation of a New Society.

Leach, E.R. (1960). Introduction: What Should We Mean by Caste?, *In Aspects of Caste in South India, Ceylong and North-West Pakistan*. Cambridge : Cambridge University Press.

Leiten, George Kristoffel (1979). Caste in Class Politics. *Economic and Political Weekly*, Annual Number, February.

Lenin (n.d.). Selected Works, II.

Lenski, Gerhard E. (1966). *Power and Privilege: A New Theory of Stratification*. McGraw Hill.

Leys, C. (1977). 'Underdevelopment and Dependenycy: Critical Notes'. *Journal of Contemporary Asia*,7(1).

Lynch, Owen (1969). *The Politics of Untouchability: Social Mobility and Social Change in a City of India*. New York: Columbia University Press.

Mahar, J.M. (1972). *Untouchables in Contemporary India*. Tuscon: The University of Arizona Press.

Mallappa, T. N. (1973). Basava Poorva Veerasaiva Shivadwaitha Darshana. *Souvenir of the 19th Conference of the Akhila Bharatha Veerasaiva Mahasabha*. Bangalore.

Mallaradhya, J.B. (1977). Veerasaivas to be classified as Backward Class. *All India Veerasaiva Mahasabha*. Bangalore.

——, (1977). *Havanur Report: A Fraud on the Constitution, the Government and the People*. Bangalore: All India Veerasabha Mahasabha.

Mandel, Ernest (1968). *The Marxist Economic Theory*. London.

Manor, James (1972). *Political Change in an Indian State, Mysore 1917-1955*. New Delhi: Manohar.

——, (1977). 'The Evolution of Political Arenas and Units of Social Organisation: The Lingayats and Vokkaligas of Mysore'. In M.N. Srinivas, *et. al.* (ed.) *Dimensions of Social Change in India*. Bombay: Allied Publishers.

——, (1980). Pragmatic Progressives in Regional Politics, the Case of Devraj Urs. *Economic and Political Weekly*. Annual Number.

Marriott, McKim (ed.) (1955). *Village India: Studies in the Little Community*. Chicago: The University of Chicago Press.

——, (1959). 'Interactional and Attributional Theories of Caste Ranking'. *Man in India*, 39 (2).

Marx, Karl (1853). 'The First East India Company – Its History and Results and the Future Results of the British Rule in India'. Reprinted in D Fernbach (ed.) (1973), *Karl Marx, Surveys from Exile, Political Writings*, Vol.2, Penguin.

Mathew, George (ed) (1984). *Shift in Indian Politics*. New Delhi: Concept Publishers.

Mayer, Adrian C. (1960). *Caste and Kinship in Central India*. London: Routledge and Kegan Paul.

Mazumdar, D.N.(1958).*Caste and Communities in an Indian Village*. Calcutta: Asia Publishing House.

Mencher, Joan (1972). Continuity and Change in An Ex-Untouchable Community of South India. In J.M.Mahar (ed.) *Untouchables in Contemporary India*. Tuscon: The Arizona Press.

Merton, Robert K. (1957). *Social Theory and Social Structure*. Glencoe.

Moore, Wilbert E. (1965). *Social Change*. New Delhi: Prentice Hall.

Muddulinganna (n.d). *Kunchitigara Sankshipta Charithre*. Bangalore.

Murthy, Chidananda (1973). 'Lingayatha Padada Nishpatthi', *Souvenir of the 19th Conference of the Akhila Bharatha Veerasaiva Mahasabha*, Bangalore.

——,(1979). The Religious Practices of the Kuruba Community. *Souvenir of the Conference of the Kurubara Sangha*, Bangalore.

Myrdal, Gunnar (1957). *Eonomic Theory and Underdeveloped Regions*. London: Duckworth.

——, (1968). *Asian Drama, An Enquiry into the Poverty of Nations*. Vols. I-III. New York: Pantheon.

Mysore Legislative Secretariat (1969). *Proceedings of the Meeting of the Committee on the Welfare of SCs and STs*. Bangalore.

Naganna, M. L. (n.d). *Veerasaiva Samajada Duravasthe Matthu Adara Sudharane*. Mysore: Aatma Vikasa Mandira.

Namboodiripad, E M S (1979). Caste Conflicts Vs, Growing Unity of Popular Democratic Forces. *Economic and Political Weekly*.

——, (1979). Caste Conflicts Vs, Growing Unity of Popular Democratic Forces. *Economic and Political Weekly*.

Nanjundayya, H. V. and L. K. Anathakrishna Iyer (1930). *Mysore Tribes and Caste*. (4 Vols. + Appendix, 1930-36). Mysore: Mysore University Press.

Natraj, Lalitha & V.K. Natraj (1982). Limits of Populism: Devraj Urs and Karnataka Politics. *Economic and Political Weekly*. XVII (37).

Natraj, Lalitha (1983). *Dalits and the Non-Brahmin Movement in Karnataka*. Mysore: Institute of Development Studies, Mysore University.

Natraj, V.K. (1979). *The Havanur Report: An Approach*. Unpublished Paper, IDS, Mysore: Mysore University.

———— and K.G. Gayathridevi (1981). *The Harijan Issue as Caste and Class*. An Unpublished Paper, IDS, Mysore: Mysore University.

Natarajan S.P. (1959). *A Century of Social Reform in India*. Bombay: Asia Publishing House .

Nesfield, J C (1885). *Brief Review of the Caste System of the North-West Province and Oudh*. Allahabad.

Nettl, J.P. (1967). *Political Mobilisation, A Sociological Analysis of Methods and Concepts*. London.

Oberschall, Anthoy (1973). *Social Conflict and Social Movements*. Englewood Cliffs, New Jersey: Prentice Hall, Inc.

O'Malley, L.S.S (1932). *The Indian Caste Customs*. Cambridge: Cambridge University Press.

Omvedt, Gail (1976). *Cultural Revolt in a Colonial Society: The Non-Brahmin Movement in Western India, 1873 to 1930*. Bombay: Scientific Socialistic Education Trust.

——, (1979). 'Caste Struggle or Caste War?'. *In Frontier*. September 30.

Oommen, T.K. (1976). Scheduled Castes and Scheduled Tribes. In S.C.Dube (ed) *India Since Independence*. Delhi: Vikas Publishing House.

Ossowski, Stanislaw (1963). *Class Structure in the Social Consciousness*. London.

Pandit, Nalini (1979). 'Caste and Class in Maharasthra'. *Economic and Political Weekly*, Special Number, XIV (7 & 8):

Parkin, Frank (1971). *Class, Inequality and Political Order*. London: Tivistock Publications.

Parsons, Talcott (1940). An Analytical Approach to the Theory of Social Stratification. *American Journal of Sociology*.

Parsons, Talcott (1953). 'A Revised Analytical Approach to the Theory of Social Stratification'. In R.Bendix and S M Lipset (eds.) *Class, Status and Power, A Reader in Social Stratification*. Glencoe, III.

Parvathamma, C. and R. T. Jangam (1969). India's Scheduled Caste MPs: A Socio-Economic Profile. *Journal of the Karnatak University*. V( ):1-14.

——, (1971). *Politics and Religion: A Study of Historical Interaction between Socio-Political Relationships in a Mysore Village*. New Delhi: Sterling Publishers.

——, (1972). *Sociological Essays in Veerasaivism*. Bombay: Popular Prakashan.

Patankar, Bharat and Gail Omvedt (1979). 'Dalit Liberation Movement in Colonial Period'. *Economic and Political Weekly*. XIV (7 & 8).

Patil, Sharad (1979). 'Dialectics of Caste and Class Conflicts',

Class and Caste in India'. *Economic and Political Weekly*, Annual Number, XIV(7 & 8).

——, (1982). *Dasa, Sudra and Slavery*. Delhi: Allied Publishers.

Patwardhan, Sunanda (1968). 'Social Mobility and Conversion of the Mahars'. *Sociological Bulletin*. XVII (2).

——, (1973). *Change among India's Harijans – Maharashtra: A Case Study*. New Delhi: Orient Longmans.

Puttaiah (n.d): *Kunchitigara Charithre*. Mysore.

Radhakrishnan S. (1948). *Religion and Society*. London: Allen and Unwin.

——, (1967). *Religion in a Changing World*. London: Allen and Unwin.

Rajagopalachari, C. (1946). *Ambedkar Refuted*.

Rajashekar, V. T. (1979). *Class-Caste Struggle, Emerging of a Third Force*, Bangalore.

Ramaswamy, Uma (1974). Scheduled Castes in Andhra: Some Aspects of Social Change. *Economic and Political Weekly*, 9 (29): 1153-8.

Ranadive, B.T. (1978): Caste, Class and Property Relations, in Caste and Class in India –Dialectical Relationships. *Economic and Political Weekly*, Special Number, XIV (7 & 8).

Rao, P.H. Krishna (1978). Havanur Report and the GO thereon Examined. *Pamphlet*. Bangalore: Akila Karnataka Brahmana Maha Sabha (AKBMS).

——, (1979). Castes and Communities in Karnataka: With Special Reference to the Brahmins, (AKBMS), Bangalore.

Rao, M.S.A (1957): Social Change in Malabar.

——,(1958). 'Political Elite and Caste Associations'. *Economic and Political Weekly*. III

——, (1970): *Urbanisation and Social Change*. New Delhi: Orient Longmans.

——, (ed): (1978). *Social Movements and Social Transformation*, 2-Vols. New Delhi.

Rao, V.S. Narayana (1973). *Mokshagundam Visvesvaraya: His Life and Work*. Mysore: Geetha Book House.

Reddi, N S (1950). 'Community-Conflict among the Depressed Classes of Andhra'. *Man in India*, XXX(4): 1-12.

Rice, B.L. (1897). *Mysore, A Gazetteer.* London.

Risley, H.H. (1915). *'The People of India', Tribes and Castes of Bengal – 1891.*

Rosen, George (1966). *Democracy and Economic Change in India.* Bombay: Vora and Co.

Roy, Ajit (1979). Caste and Class: An Interlinked View. *Economic and Political Weekly*. Annual Number, XIV(7 & 8).

Roy, Burman B.K. (1970): *Social Mobility Movements among Scheduled Castes and Scheduled Tribes of India.* New Delhi: Registrar General of India, Ministry of Home Affairs.

Rudebeck, L (1970). Political Mobilisation for Development in Guinea-Bissau: A Case Study of the Conditions and Mechanisms of Mobilisation, Chapter I, quoted in Hettne and Tamm.

Rudolph, Lloyd I and Susanne Hoeber Rudolph (1967). *The Modernity of Tradition: Political Development in India.* Chicago: The University of Chicago Press.

Runciman, W.G. (1969). The Three Dimensions of Social Inequality. In Andre Beteille (ed.) *Social Inequality*. London: Penguin Books.

Saberwal, Satish (1979). Sociologists and Inequality in India : The Historical Context. *Economic and Political Weekly*, XIV (7 & 8).

Schumpeter, Joseph (1951). *Imperialism and Social Classes.* Oxford: Basil Blackwell.

Seers, Dudley (ed) (1972). *Crisis in Planning, Vols I & II.* London: Chatto and Windus.

Shah, G. (1977): Caste Associations and Political Process, Popular Prakashan, Bombay.

——, (ed) (2001). Dalit Identity & Politics. New Delhi : Sage.

——, (2002). *Caste and Democratic Politics* in India. New Delhi : Permanent Black Publishers.

——, *et al* (2006). *Untouchability in Rural India.* New Delhi : Sage.

Shrikant, L.N. (1968). Scheduled Castes and Their Welfare. In M.S. Gore (ed.) *Encyclopaedia of Social Work in India.* Delhi: Government of India. II :168-80.

Silverberg, James (ed.) (1968). *Social Mobility in the Caste System in India: An Interdisciplinary Symposium.* The Hague: Mouton Company.

Singer, Milton and Bernard S. Cohn (1968). *Structure and Change in Indian Society.* Chicago: Aldine Publishing Company.

Singh, Paramanand (1982). *Equality, Reservation and Discrimination in India, A Constitutional Study of Scheduled Castes, Scheduled Tribes and Other Backward Classes.* New Delhi: Deep and Deep Publications.

Singh, T R (1969). *The Madiga: A Study of Social Structure and Change.* Lucknow: Ethnographic and Folklore Society.

Singh, Yogendra (1977). *Social Stratification and Change in India.* New Delhi: Manohar.

Siversteen, D (1963). *When Caste Barriers Fall: A Study of Social and Economic Change in a South Indian Village*, London: Alen and Unwin.

Smelser, Neil J. and Seymour Martin Lipset (eds.) (1966). *Social Structure and Mobility in Economic Development.* London: Routeledge and Kegan Paul.

Srinivas, M. N. (1955). The Social System of a Mysore Village. In Mckim Marriott (ed.), *Village India: Studies in The Little Community.* Chicago: Chicago Univesity Press.

——,(1952). *Religion and Society among the Coorgs of South India.* Oxford: Oxford University Press.

——, (1956a). 'Some Hierarchical Aspects of Caste'. *South Western Journal of Anthropology.*

——,(1956b). 'A note on Sanskritisation and Westernisation'. *Far Eastern Quarterly*, XV(4).

——, (1959). 'The Dominant Caste in Rampura'. *American Anthropologist*, I.

——, (1960). *India's Villages*. Bombay: Asia Publishing House.

——, (1961). 'There is a vested interest in backwardness', *The Statesman*. October 9 & 10.

——, (1962). 'Pursuit of Equality'. *Times Survey of India*, January 26.

——, (1964). *Caste in Modern India and Other Essays*. Bombay: Asia Publishing House.

——, (1966). *Social Change in Modern India*. Berkely and Los Angeles: University of California Press.

——,(1968). 'Mobility in the Caste System'. In Milton Singer and Bernard S. Colin *Structure and Change in Indian Society*, Chicago: Aldine Publishing Company.

——, and Andre' Beteille (1969). 'Harijans in India'. In Beteille (ed.) *Castes: Old and New*.Bombay: Asia Publishing House.

——, (ed.) (1977). *Dimensions of Social Change in India*. Bombay: Allied Publishers.

——, (1979). Future of Indian Caste. *Economic and Political Weekly*, Annual Number, XIV(7 & 8).

——, (1980). *India: Social Structure*. Delhi: Hindustan Publishing Company.

——, and M.N. Panini (1984). 'Politics and Society in Karnataka'. *Economic and Political Weekly*. XIX(2).

——, (1993). *On Living in a Revolution: Caste in its Twentieth Century Avatar*. New Delhi: OUP.

Stanton, Gregory H. (1979). *Three Concepts of Equality: Compensatory Discrimination in Indian and American Constitutional Law*. An Abstract.

Stinchcombe, A. L. (1963). Some Empirical Consequences of David-Moore Theory of Stratification. *American Journal of Sociological Review*.

Streeton, Paul (1972). *Frontiers of Development Studies.* Macmillan.

Subramaniam, V. (1969). 'Emergence and Eclipse of Tamil Brahmins: Some Guidelines to Research. *Economic and Political Weekly.*

Subramanian, N. A. (1969). *Case Law on the Indian Constitution.* Madras: Vimala Publications.

Sweezy, Paul M. (1972). *Modern Capitalism and Other Essays.* New York: Monthly Review Press.

Tara Chand (1967). *History of the Freedom Movement in India.* Delhi: Publications Division, 1961-1972. Vols.I-IV

Tawney, R. H. (1929). *Religion and the Rise of Capitalism: Historical Study* (Holland Memorial Lectures 1922). London: John Murray.

——, (1964). *Equality.* Unwin Books

——, (1967). Inequality and Social Structure. In Melvin M Tumin (ed) *Social Stratification: The Forms and Functions of Inequality.* Englewood Cliffs, New Jersey: Prentice-Hall.

Thimmaiah, G. (1993): *Power Politics and Social Justice : Backward Castes in Karnataka.* New Delhi : Sage Publications.

Thurston, Edgar (1907). *Ethnographic Notes in Southern India,* Madras.

Tinker and Bramsen (1976):

Titmuss, Richard M. (1962). *Income Distribution and Social Change.* London: George Allen and Unwin.

Trivedi, Harshad R. (1977). *Scheduled Caste Women: Studies in Exploitation with Reference to Superstition, Ignorance and Poverty.* Delhi: Concept.

Todaro, Michael P. (1977): *Economic Development in the Third World, An Introduction to Problems and Policies in a Global Perspective.* London: Longman Group Limited.

Toye, John (1980). Does Developmnt Studies have a Corea.

Institute of Development Studies, *Sussex Bulletin*. III (3) July.

Tumin, Melvin M (1953). 'Some Principles of Stratification: A Critical Analysis. *American Sociological Review*, 18(4).

——, (1963). 'On Inequality'. *The American Sociological Review*.

——, (1967). *'Social Stratification: The Forms and Functions of Inequality*. Englewood Cliffs, New Jersey: Prentice Hall.

Washbrook, D. A. and C. J. Baker (1975). *South India: Political Institutions and Political Change, 1880-1940*. Delhi: The Macmillan Company of India, Ltd.

Weber, Max (1952). *Essays in Sociology*. Routeledge and Kegan Paul Limited.

——, (1958). *Religion of India*, Translated and edited by Gerth H.H. and Don Martindale.

Weiner, Myron (1962). The Struggle for Equality in India. *Foreign Affairs*, July pp 1-9.

Wesolowski, W. (1969). *Class, Strata and Power*. London: Routledge and Kegan Paul.

Yadav, S. Manohar (1998). The Career of Dalit Movement in Karnataka. *Journal of Social and Economic Development*

Zelliot, Eleanor (1966). 'Buddhism and Politics in Maharashtra'. In D.E. Smith (ed.) *Religion and Politics in South Asia*. Princeton, New Jersey: Princeton University Press.

——, (1970). 'Learning the use of Political Means: The Mahars of Maharashtra'. In Rajni Kothari (ed.) *Caste in Indian Politics*. Delhi: Orient Longmans.

——, (1972). 'Gandhi and Ambedkar: A Study of Leadership'. In J.M. Mahar (ed.) *The Untouchables in Contemporary India*. Tuscon: University of Arizona Press.

Index